A Symposium for Pianists and Teachers

A Symposium for Pianists and Teachers:

Strategies to Develop the Mind and Body for Optimal Performance

Contributors:
Gail Berenson, Jacqueline Csurgai-Schmitt
William DeVan, Dr. Mitchell Elkiss
Seymour Fink, Phyllis Alpert Lehrer
Barbara Lister-Sink, Robert Mayerovitch
Dr. Norman Rosen, Dylan Savage

Edited by Kris Kropff

HERITAGE MUSIC PRESS
A DIVISION OF THE LORENZ CORPORATION
Box 802 / Dayton, OH 45401-0802
www.lorenz.com

Typesetter: Gregg Sewell
Illustrator: Carolyn S. Kubiak
Cover Design: Janine Marker

Heritage Music Press
A division of The Lorenz Corporation
P.O. Box 802
Dayton, OH 45401-0802
www.lorenz.com

Printed in the United States of America

ISBN: 0-8932-154-9

Foreword

Luiz de Moura Castro

Nobody denies that knowledge about pianists' occupational injuries and their prevention is necessary. Thanks to the new mentality of the second half of the 20th century, problems are acknowledged and the search for solution is intensified. Thus, musicians' injuries came out from the shadow, where they were carefully kept, disguised as changes in career orientation, etc.

My early training under Jóseph Gát in Budapest made me aware of these issues, since I witnessed the considerable number of pianists, celebrated or not, that came to him for retraining. Even if I never actually experienced any pains or injuries, his instructions brought me greater efficiency in my personal technique and, even more important, they paved the way for a pedagogical approach that included prevention of misuses of the playing apparatus.

When I met the Committee on Technique, Movement and Wellness at one of the World Piano Pedagogy Conferences for the first time I learned about their project of a comprehensive, practical book on technical aspects of piano playing, including medical and psychological support – with the emphasis on functionality and injury prevention. My reaction was at the same time enthusiasm but also a little skepticism about achieving the final result due to the complications and difficulties of the task. Alleluia! Here it is!

In its finished form we have a refreshing complement to single-author's books, limited by necessity to an individual's experiences, however invaluable, and publications coming from congresses and conferences that lack a structural continuity. I compliment the authors for preserving their personal points of view and at the same time achieving precision and coherence allowing for an interesting reading and clarity of purpose. I particularly appreciated the inclusion of chapters on musicality, audiation and advanced techniques because we must never forget that all of these concerns should result in better serving music and its interpretation.

This book fulfils a gap in the piano pedagogy literature, addressing important issues in a useful way for a diversified public: all kinds of piano teachers and pianists (at all levels) and serious students, professional or amateur.

I want to applaud the authors for the elegant and persuasive way they accomplished their difficult mission – the result is a very worthy contribution to the general knowledge of some of the most troublesome aspects of the art of the piano.

Authors' Preface

We acknowledged some years ago the need for a comprehensive volume that dealt with the specifics of healthy piano technique and movement. Realizing that our individual expertise was, by temperament, limited to particular areas, we came together as a committee of pianists and doctors, all recognized experts in our own fields. From the beginning, the purpose of The Pianist's Committee on Technique, Movement and Wellness was to produce a volume that would make accessible to pianists and teachers the best thinking of twentieth and twenty-first-century piano pedagogy. This was never meant to be an historical review of pedagogical thought; rather, a practical 'how-to' book that could help all those pianists confused over the vast complexity of material now available.

As the involved pianists began to meet on weekends to discuss and share individual views on piano playing, it quickly became apparent that there were areas of piano technique on which we could not agree. Here were eight pianists – trained in various traditions and at various stages of their careers – who could not completely accept one another's approach to the keyboard. As we argued and contemplated our impasse, our thoughts ran thus: Was our project doomed to failure from the very first? If we could not agree, did that mean that there was no such a thing as one perfect way to play the piano?

At the end of our first long weekend together, it finally (and surprisingly) dawned on us that we agreed about many more things than we disagreed. Major points, such as whether to begin piano playing with arm movements or with finger movements, were not in question; it was the exact application of the arm and hand to the keyboard that created certain disparities. As we looked at issue after issue, we found that, for the most part, we agreed. Where there was disagreement, we agreed to disagree. In doing that, we stumbled upon what could be this volume's greatest strength: a diversity of opinions and approaches that speaks to the multi-faceted needs of pianists, who, as individuals, likely have different needs at the instrument.

You will find in this work statements that do not completely agree from author to author, chapter to chapter. As eight separate pianistic minds, we have each uncovered successful solutions to some of piano playing's most difficult conundrums. We now wish to share our collective experience with future generations of students and teachers in order to spare them the blind alleys, wasted time and unnecessary mental and physical trauma with which we have all had experience.

Despite above-average training and careful work, most of us, at one point or another, have worked incorrectly or reached our physical, psychical, or emotional limitations. We have all successfully weathered varying degrees of this debilitating crisis of confidence. Some have even faced the long, frustrating process of retraining and know now that this painful experience is not necessary. Together, we stress the overriding importance of developing good physical and mental habits from the very beginning, habits upon which an efficient, coordinated, and consistent techniques can be systematically built for a lifetime of enjoyment and success at the piano.

Being aware of the many pianists who are already suffering from pain and dysfunction at the piano, we asked two well-known medical experts to contribute to this volume. These chapters are a great addition to the literature, helping to raise awareness of the physical disabilities pianists face while offering real strategies to both solve existing problems and to avoid them in the future. As there has been much confusion among pianists in regard to the medical options available to them, we trust these articles will give some hope and guidance to those of our colleagues who are in need of these resources.

We realize that, in such a rich and complicated aesthetic venture as piano playing, there is no one truth, nor is there only one way to do things. While pianists and students learn in a variety of ways, we believe you will find a consistency of thought and approach in this work that can help you answer some of the age-old questions keyboard players have asked since the time of Couperin, Rameau and Bach. Perhaps this underscores the fact that even with the nature of music and its performance, the nature of the piano and its mechanics, and the nature of the human mind and body, the possibilities are still limited.

Editor's Preface

Kris Kropff

A Symposium for Pianists and Teachers is not unlike a collection of short stories grouped by genre but with the independent voices of its multiple authors unconstrained. The process was individual, the style personal, and the content limited only by the broad umbrella of piano pedagogy and the collective agreement that each of the ten co-authors would write on the aspect(s) of piano pedagogy about which they felt most knowledgeable. The result: a collection of chapters diverse in personality and philosophy that together form a significant offering in the field of piano pedagogy.

The operative word in that sentence, from an editor's perspective: together. Initially, the ramifications of that word did not quite register. When they did, my excited pursuit of the project diminished somewhat. It soon became apparent, though, that the strength of the material would make my job easier, and the interaction with each of the authors would make it enjoyable.

My primary goal was to stand back and let insights of ten preeminent figures in piano pedagogy shine through. To this end, I hope the abstracts included in the contents are additive. I also hope that the overall organization is, for lack of a better word, friendly. I feared that if readers were met with the same challenge I was, it could detract from what is a wonderful source of invaluable information. That challenge – tackling an overwhelming collection of writings on so many varied topics, each with its own subtleties, and all under one cover – was daunting throughout. Hopefully the larger, sectional organizations are a practical guide and serve to make the reader comfortable with the initial overview. After that, I have no doubt that the knowledge and information presented here will hold any interested reader's attention.

I would like to thank each of the contributors for their patience and flexibility. The Lorenz team was also pivotal in bringing this project to fruition and they have my thanks, particularly Gregg Sewell for his creative and exceptional work as the typesetter and Larry Pugh for mentoring me through this project. To my family and friends, your lifelong support and encouragement cannot be thanked in words. And to Dr. Charles Larkowski, thank you for helping to shape my mind and my sense of self, and for guiding my future along a path of musicianship and professionalism.

Introduction

What follows is a unique volume built on the selected areas of interest and expertise of ten different authors. More a compendium of thoughts dealing with the playing of the piano most easily, efficiently and without physical injury, than a 'this is the only way' approach. Concise and accessible, readers can glean something concrete and usable, some practical, 'down-to-earth' advice, from each chapter.

This includes interpretations of and insights into some of the twentieth-century's foremost piano pedagogy texts, including *The Physiological Mechanics of Piano Technique* by Otto Ortmann, Arnold Schultz' *The Riddle of the Pianist's Finger*, and *The Visible and Invisible in Pianoforte Technique* by Tobias Matthay. Out-of-print and, at times, a challenge to approach, it is hoped that the descriptions contained will aid those pianists who are not able to study these works for themselves and support them in their search for understanding of the biomechanics of movement at the keyboard.

Wellness methodologies, medical problems of and treatments for pianists, and overall musicianship also feature prominently. Five sections – *The Mechanical, The Technical, The Musical, The Healthful (Mind and Body)* and *The Pedagogical* – organize the material and easily lead the reader through a process of discovery. While there is a natural sequence to the chapters, it is not necessary to read them in the order in which they are presented. Some chapters refer the reader to others for a more in-depth discussion of a certain topic, and these are footnoted for easy reference. A description of each chapter is also included in the contents, making it possible to move around the book as personal interest dictates.

Contents

MIND

BODY

THE PEDAGOGICAL

The Mechanical

Mechanics of the Piano

Seymour Fink

To tap the piano's expressive potential, pianists must fully understand the mechanical workings of the instrument.

The piano is a large, percussive, keyboard instrument, homogenous throughout in timbre, with an exceptionally wide range of pitches (larger even than a symphony orchestra) and dynamics. An extremely expressive instrument, it projects easily in large spaces. It is one of the few instruments where the fingers simultaneously control both pitch and dynamics, and where a player is freed from concerns of intonation. Pianists can also play many tones simultaneously and, at the same time, control the dynamics of individual pitches. The pedal mechanism is truly unique in that its use greatly enriches the overall warmth of the sound and presents unparalleled possibilities for the accumulation and mingling of sounds that no other instrument or group of instruments can imitate.

To tap this expressive potential, pianists must fully understand the mechanical workings of the instrument. Only then can they discover and craft an efficient physical approach to the instrument that best integrates with its unique technology and capacities.

HOW IS SOUND PRODUCED?

Piano sound is generated percussively. As a key is depressed it catapults a freely traveling felt hammer that strikes the string (or strings) of a given pitch. The hammer recoils at impact, ending all contact with the string. Simultaneously, an associated felt damper is raised, allowing the sound of the vibrating string to decay over time. Players lose all ability to affect a particular hammer stroke slightly before a key reaches its bottom, at the keybed. At this point, control of the vibrating string is limited to sustaining the ebbing sound (by holding the key down) or terminating it (by releasing the key). Nothing else is possible.

It follows then, that once a tone has sounded, any weight or pressure at the bottom of the key, beyond the minimum necessary to keep the key depressed, is wasteful. This all-too-common mistake, referred to as keybedding, squanders energy and interferes with the arm's ability to shift quickly to subsequent positions. Students can, through proper timing and angling of the stroke, develop ways of playing that discourage or eliminate keybedding, and at the same time permit effective control of the lengths and intensities of the tones being produced.

HOW ARE DYNAMICS CONTROLLED?

Pianists control the dynamics of a particular sound by varying the speed of a key's descent. Depressing individual keys quickly produces bold sounds, while a correspondingly slower pressure results in softer sounds. This fundamental concept should be one of the first points addressed in piano study; unfortunately, it has escaped the conscious knowledge of many reasonably advanced piano students. Consequently, in an attempt for a big sound, students will too often tighten and constrict muscles and joints or apply useless pressure too late in the keystroke. Both are counterproductive, for they interfere with the very freedom of joint movement, the speed of which they need to generate louder sounds. Rather, what is needed for greater resonance are sharper, well-timed, loose motions downward that deescalate upon approaching the keybed. Although teachers must focus their students' listening on the qualities of the sound they make, including length, loudness, and evenness, it is imperative that students are made consciously aware of how to manipulate the instrument to control a wide variety of tones.

This includes selectively breaking the rules for musical considerations, be they speed, legato, or the like. In these cases there will be times where varying pressure is maintained at the bottom of the key between tones. In quick finger passages for instance, the hand or arm is too large a unit to release and reset between tones. As a result, hands and arms are lightly fixed close-by, providing a support base for the fingers and causing a slight even pressure at the bottom of the keys. In slow-moving melodic passages, a slight pressure might be added just before playing a subsequent note to enhance the feeling of legato connection. Pianists continually make these kinds of subtle kinesthetic adjustments for both technical and expressive reasons, and are able to do so wisely only after becoming thoroughly aware of the mechanics of the instrument.

HOW IS SOUND SUSTAINED? TERMINATED?

The duration of a single unpedaled sound is controlled by gauging the length of time the key is held down, and eventually releasing it. Mechanically, releasing the key will lower the felt damper that was raised in conjunction with the original hammer stroke. Functionally, these two mechanisms are unrelated. Underlying the development of an advanced piano technique is this realization: the activation of sound and the sustaining of sound are separate and distinct activities on the piano. This contrasts sharply with what is experienced by wind and string players, who sustain sound by continuing the same activating breath or bow; as a result they are able to control and alter the quality of its duration. Relatively helpless, pianists cannot change the color or dynamic of a held tone; they can only let it decay at its fixed rate or terminate it.

The activation of sound and the sustaining of sound are separate and distinct activities on the piano.

Pianists must create a technique that responds to this reality, one that minimizes keybedding, is loose enough to sense and respond to the weight and depth of the keys, and is able to control dynamics and velocity – all in a manner that promotes musical fluency. Although it may happen slowly, students will come to accept the somewhat counterintuitive fact that it takes no more pressure at the bottom of a key to sustain a loud sound than a soft one. Further degrees of comfort and control at the instrument come as pianists discover, internalize, and respond to two inherent values of any instrument: the depth of the keystroke and the weight of the key. Because sound is generated percussively and sustained with limited control, students must also develop the expert ability to switch instantly from striking a key, to holding it, to releasing it. Success in this is an important measure of technical efficiency and finesse.

Wise use of the arms can go a long way towards helping students master these complex technical issues, creating conditions that encourage finger looseness and fluency, and are necessary for reducing keybedding. Players should avoid vertical key entry; they should instead depress the keys obliquely or diagonally as part of a pulsating cycle. The arm cycles might move in either a pushing or pulling direction from the shoulder girdle joint, with fingertips tending to slide either forward or backward. Keybed pressure is quickly and naturally released as the arm follows through beyond the point of deepest contact. (In the pulling stroke, the wrist must recoil to allow the arm cycle to continue smoothly.) The glancing keystroke releases pressure instantly without the need to change arm direction, sparing players the tiring, stop-start changes of direction that vertical key descents make necessary. Longer sounds are achieved by using the wrist as a control gear allowing the fingers to stay at the bottom of the key as long as one wishes while the arms continue to cycle above the held finger without losing their momentum.

In addition to the circular stroke described above, there is another generic arm stroke – the washboard stroke. This is a non-circular, straight-line, back and forth movement, largely in the elbow, but some in the shoulder. Tracing forward diagonal paths to the keyboard, these strokes are quicker than upper arms and circling wrists can manage. They can even reach vibratory speed. The straight-line stroke must be carefully timed to end at the keybed, much as a drill-press operator sets his or her machine not to drill too deeply. Students can lessen the danger of keybedding by maximizing the gravity free-fall aspect of the stroke. They can also incorporate a ballistic throw quality to the stroke that causes it to rebound instantly upon hitting bottom. It is necessary to minimally set or firm all joints on either side of the swinging joint, while at the same time relaxing the active one.

HOW DOES THE DAMPER PEDAL ACHIEVE ITS EFFECT?

Arguably the most unique mechanism of the piano is its damper pedal. When it is engaged, the entire bank of felt dampers is raised, overriding any individual control of single dampers and allowing players to hold, connect, and blend pitches well beyond what their fingers alone can do. Tonal quality and resonance is greatly increased, not only by the accumulation of activated pitches, but also with the added richness provided by the sympathetic vibrations of open strings. In addition, the pedal often masks a good deal of the percussive nature of tone production, allowing the instrument to sing in its own unique way. The musical 'losses' in the transcriptions of the idiomatic piano works of Chopin or Debussy exemplify just how special pedaled sonorities are to the quality of piano sound.

Students must come to grips with these mechanical issues, viewing them in an objective manner, as an engineer might, and use them to develop a knowing, consistent, efficient, and effective piano technique. For it is only when one begins to exploit the piano's infinite subtleties of voicing and pedaling that the true wealth of creative possibilities is opened, providing real grist for the musical imagination and serving the most inspired flights of inner hearing.

The History, Evolution and Application of Biomechanics and Physiology in Piano Playing

Dylan Savage

Pianists have long been thinking about the how body actually functions (physiology) and how to best use the body to play the piano well (biomechanics).

The modern concert grand piano has not evolved much since the 1880s. Consequently, there have been some 120 years to develop theories and teaching methods on the technique of playing the piano without the interruption of a major design modification that would have required pianists to change the way they approach the instrument. During this century-plus time span, hundreds of books on how to play the piano have been produced, many of which delve into the physical manner of how to play. Today, the terms most commonly used to encompass the myriad of issues regarding the physical movement of piano playing are *biomechanics* or *physiology*.

While it may be tempting to think that these concepts are relatively new to piano pedagogy, this is not actually the case. Although the two terms have only been recently incorporated in the vernacular, pianists have long been thinking about how the body actually functions – *physiology* – and how to best use the body to play the piano well – *biomechanics*. In fact, the integration of the concept that the whole body plays a vital role in keyboard playing and is subject to the same laws of physics as other moving bodies (such as levers) are, mirrored the evolution of the piano into its latest form.

DEPPE AND BREITHAUPT

Some of the first explorations into the interaction of body with mechanical object came in the early part of the eighteenth century, as the pianoforte was being developed. During this time, the harpsichord was still the most popular keyboard instrument, and it remained this way until the latter half of the eighteenth century. As more music was written for the pianoforte and it gained prominence as a concert instrument, keyboard players began using this new instrument with more regularity. However, keyboard players were playing the pianoforte with an isolated finger technique much more suited to the harpsichord than to the new pianoforte. It took some time for teachers to realize that this isolated finger technique was not ideal for playing the new pianoforte, with its new capabilities for producing large-range, gradated dynamics and requiring a wide variety of attacks and forces.

In 1885, German piano teacher Ludwig Deppe, in his book, *Arm Ailments of the Pianist,* notably challenged the isolated approach. His observation that tone must be created by the "coordinated action of all parts of the arm"[1] demonstrated a biomechanical understanding that was ahead of his time. This is particularly true with his inclusion of "coordinated" because, as we know now, *all* parts of the arm, indeed the whole body, share a critical role in being able to perform efficiently at the piano.

Deppe also wrote that each finger should, when possible, form a straight line with the key. There is a wealth of physiological understanding behind that statement: fingers by design have limited ability to deviate from the neutral position (move side to side), and are best guided with help from the upper arm instead of reaching sideways for a note with the finger. If a finger is deviated to the left or right, it is subject to the negative aspects of antagonistic muscle contraction. For example, a finger at the far reaches of side motion will have restricted vertical movement because the tensed, laterally-pulling muscles (the abductors and adductors) produce a resistance which must then be overcome by the muscles that move the finger up and down (the flexors and extensors). He knew that a finger in its middle range of motion is freest to move up and down; also, that load-bearing capabilities are diminished in a deviated finger because the finger can no longer depend on the natural ability of the skeletal structure, when in alignment, to diminish muscle loads during a key strike.

Another important and extensive contribution to this new school of thought was the multi-volume set *Die Natürliche Klaviertechnik,* written by Rudolph Breithaupt in 1906. He espoused the doctrine of the loose and heavy arm, a technique that incorporated weight playing and relaxation. His basic understanding of physiological principles is evident in that he understood that it is far easier and efficient to generate a series of *legato,* full-toned notes utilizing the weight of the upper arm than from the finger alone. And like authors of other piano method books of the time, he included pictures and explanations of human anatomy, especially of the arm, hand, and wrist.[2]

George Kochevitsky, in his *The Art of Piano Playing: A Scientific Approach,* examines the historical importance of Deppe and Breithaupt, and the new school of physiological and anatomical thought they began:

> Representatives of the new school believed that perception and conscious training of correct movement would substitute for mechanical exercise. To solve complicated technical problems almost instantly one need only understand which limbs, muscles are involved, what they do, and how they do it.[3]

Kochevitsky also expressed his belief that the work of Deppe and Breithaupt held "an absolute faith in the objectivity and accuracy of science,"[4] and would continue to gain in popularity among researchers and pedagogues. It is important to note here that the study of pure biomechanics alone was not (and is not) seen as the only means for improved piano study and performance. Early on Ignaz Mos-

---

[1]Ludwig Deppe, *Arm Ailments of the Pianist (n.p.,* 1885).

[2]Rudolph Breithaupht, *Die Natürliche Klaviertechnik* (Leipzig: Kahnt, 1906).

[3]George Kochevitsky, *The Art of Piano Playing: A Scientific Approach* (Evanston: Summy-Birchard, Co., 1967).

[4]Ibid., 10.

cheles and Anton Rubinstein recognized and taught that the mind should practice more than the fingers.

ORTMANN

As the first quarter of the twentieth century drew to a close, published work on physiological and biomechanical approaches to piano playing was steadily growing. As Arnold Schultz wrote in his preface to Otto Ortmann's book, *The Physiological Mechanics of Piano Technique,* general beliefs about building strength started to be replaced with a focus on the nature and functioning of movement at the piano. There was, however, a great deal of contradiction among the various early proponents to this new school of thought. Schultz communicates this clearly in his preface:

> Viewed as a whole, the literature represented not nearly so much a partnership in seeking truth as a competition in proclaiming it, with none of the proclaimers being especially interested in the proclamations of others.[5]

Schultz also felt that in the various camps of thought, the theorists reinforced their conclusions with only the physiological facts that best supported their case and that they did not give enough thought to the differences evident in their preconceptions.

This changed with Otto Ortmann's revolutionary book, *The Physiological Mechanics of Piano Technique,* which did not give any theories on how the piano ought to be played. Rather, he was the first to offer substantiated technical proof regarding the most efficient and physiologically correct positions of the piano-playing mechanism, setting forth, with extreme and meticulous care:

> ...how, given the laws of mechanics and the facts of physiology, the piano must be played if it is to be played well; and second, how, when measured by laboratory instruments, the piano is played by artists of great skill.[6]

In a specially designed laboratory, Ortmann tested hundreds of examples of various arm, hand, and finger motions through experiments in order to find the ideal position and range of motion for each digit and appendage. Every possible motion that pianists use at the keyboard was tested, including angles of muscle pull, types of levers, wrist and finger flexion, passive and active muscle contraction, types of finger and arm strokes, wrist jerk and key impact, arm mass, volar flexor contraction in full arm drop, hand motions, passing under of the thumb, arm rotation, and variation in finger abduction to name a few.

Schultz praised Ortmann's scientific approach to answering the many problems, concerns, and misconceptions regarding piano technique. He also remarked on the fact that, just as today, many musicians cringe when their art is faced with such controlled scientific scrutiny, believing that their playing should not have to be subjected to detailed scientific analysis. Ortmann and others were met with resistance and skepticism from teachers and players when they examined the playing process with a scientific eye. Ortmann's goal was simple and well intentioned.

---

[5]Arnold Schultz, preface to *The Physiological Mechanics of Piano Technique,* by Otto Ortmann (New York: E.P. Dutton and Co., Inc., 1929) xvi.

[6]Ibid., xvii.

He wanted to apply irrefutable scientific truths as the basis for understanding and then, after examination and testing, to set forth the exact ways in which the piano-playing mechanism worked.

Piano playing is done through a series of complex arm, hand, and finger motions, and it is upon these elements that Ortmann placed his main focus:

> The fact remains that the units of the body with which we play the piano are essentially levers of the third class and obey laws pertaining to their structure and their attachments to the skeletal parts; and the interaction of the bodily movements with the resistance of the piano keys proceeds according to strict mechanical laws.[7]

Although Ortmann's experiments substantiated a number of pedagogical practices, it could be argued that in disproving a number of practices and beliefs, which, until then, were widely held and could not be explicitly disproved, he made his greatest contribution. One such common notion was the myth of being relaxed while playing. Ortmann demonstrated that for a muscle to work, it must employ varying levels of contraction and tension, depending upon the dynamic wished for. More emphatically put, muscles cannot function in a truly relaxed state. The great value of this insight is appreciated as strongly today as when it was made when helping students understand the concept of relaxation in piano playing. For it is thanks to Ortmann's work that we speak of reduced muscle contraction or minimal muscle contraction, rather than complete relaxation, when playing.

WHITESIDE

One of the two most prominent contemporaries of Ortmann is Abby Whiteside. Like her predecessors, she grappled with developing new ways in which to teach students techniques that would help free their playing mechanism as much as possible. In the course of discovery, she came to have greater insights into biomechanical applications at the keyboard. One such insight is as follows:

> Acquiring technique easily means gaining control with as little interference as possible from the muscles not in involved in the action. An important factor in this connection is the differentiation between the actions of placement and production...The slightest confusion in the controlling factors must out of necessity affect the entire mechanism.[8]

In her 1929 book *The Pianist's Mechanism,* Whiteside recalled what led her to discover and embrace the physiological and biomechanical approach in her piano teachings. She asked herself how outstanding pianists could play with such ease and lack of effort; immediately, she recalled, the answer came to her – it lay in physical motor patterns. But it took her years to work out a simple method of teaching that would produce that simplicity in her students' playing. She goes on to mention the frustration that she and many other teachers have had in trying to impart exactly what transpires in the playing mechanism that enables the great pianists to play the way they do. This frustration is compounded by the fact that those very pianists, gifted with enormous natural talent, are often not able to

---

[7]Ibid., xviii.

[8]Abby Whiteside, *The Pianist's Mechanism* (New York: G. Schirmer, Inc., 1929) 27-28.

clearly articulate how they play as they do.

Whiteside mentions another frustration when trying to glean information from watching great pianists perform: the eye cannot follow accurately the rapid movements of hands and fingers in fast passages. She goes on to say that there is little to be learned from the practice of slowing the movements, because they employ different motions all together.

SCHULTZ

The second pedagogue to follow closely in Ortmann's footsteps is Arnold Schultz, who, in 1936, published *The Riddle of the Pianist's Finger,* a book that supported a great deal of what Ortmann had written. Schultz, like Ortmann, felt physiology was very important to the study of the piano, stating, "I earnestly recommend that schools of music inaugurate courses in physiological mechanics."[9] Beyond that, Schultz advocated teaching piano students different types of movement that have proven to be the most efficient, instead of having students choose and create their own, maintaining that this should constitute a large part of their technical education.

Aware of the resistance that many musicians would have to any other analytical processes as they relate to their art, he tried to counter their arguments by conveying the extraordinary potential results, saying:

> ...that intellectual analysis has worked in so many fields outside piano playing, has yielded, in fact, such extraordinary results, that it is more reasonable to doubt the method itself.
>
> ...Since learning the movements of technique consist principally in coming to identify them in order to choose among them judiciously, we might expect this process also to be hastened by conscious analysis.[10]

Schultz also turned his attention to the perplexing problem of developing velocity at the keyboard, which was often misunderstood in the early years of piano pedagogy. Prior to Schultz, methods used to develop velocity were often designed solely to develop downward fingertip speed without taking into account other critical factors. Although important, the speed of the finger descent is only part of the equation, as Schultz addressed very specifically:

> By velocity in piano playing we do not mean, in a given succession of tones, the speed of each key descent, but the speed with which the key descents follow upon one another; or, translated into terms of the physical organism, not the speed with which the playing parts move into each key, but that with which they recover their original positions after each descent in order to affect another.[11]

In other words, it is coordination between the descent *and* the release or accent that creates velocity in playing. One should think of this down/up finger movement as one entity instead of two. This means that in fast playing there is often a small element of positive antagonistic muscle action at work, caused by the

---

[9]Arnold Schultz, *The Riddle of the Pianist's Finger* (Boston: Carl Fischer, 1936) xii.

[10]Ibid., 11-12.

[11]Ibid., 8.

flexor muscles overcoming a small amount of contraction produced by the extensor muscles. When the balance between the two contracting muscles groups is well in the favor of the flexors, tension is not created, hence the *positive* antagonistic muscle action. Fast playing results when the extensor muscles, with their minimal amount of *ongoing* contraction, act like springs to instantly lift the finger after the flexor muscles have released.

Another point that had been argued over for decades which Schultz addressed was over the value of strength in piano playing, and whether or not greater strength was more desirable:

> Technical books have been published by the scores with this as their underlying thesis; the greater the finger strength, the greater the finger velocity. Yet strength has, as a matter of fact, very little direct bearing on velocity. We have seen that the highest velocity for a given arm-unit is reached when its movement does not involve the reactionary movement of the larger arm units, and that movement of these larger units is prevented by limiting the degree of contraction on the part of the muscles operating the smaller unit. This means that the strength of these latter muscles cannot be a determinant of velocity, for when velocity is greatest they contract to a degree which is less than the maximum of which they are capable.[12]

MATTHAY

At the forefront of the next generation's pedagogues, Tobias Matthay was one of the strongest proponent yet of teaching precise muscular coordinations, writing:

> We can learn which section of the playing limb should be exerted and which should be left lax; and by thus willing the desirable limb stresses into action and by inhibiting the undesirable ones, the concerned complex muscular coordination will indirectly but surely be called into responsive action. This basic principle underlies all my technical teaching.[13]

In spite of this insistence, Matthay (like Anton Rubinstein and others) did not believe that biomechanical principles alone were an end unto themselves, merely that they must ultimately serve musical expression:

> Technique means the power of expressing oneself musically. To acquire the necessary muscular discrimination for playing, implies the acquisition mentally of the power muscularly, so to direct your limbs in their work, that your musical purpose shall accurately be fulfilled.[14]

GÁT

As more and more books on piano playing embraced physiological thinking and the inclusion of science and technology, one in particular stands out: *The*

---

[12]Ibid., 22.

[13]Myra Hess, preface to *The Visible and the Invisible in Pianoforte Technique,* by Tobias Matthay (New York: Oxford University Press, 1947) x.

[14]Tobias Matthay, *The Visible and the Invisible in Pianoforte Technique* (New York: Oxford University Press, 1947) 3.

Technique of Piano Playing, by József Gát. This 1965 book integrated the latest applications of biomechanical and physiological thinking with piano playing. In addition, he added some advanced applications of his own, many involving technology. One such application was the use of the oscilloscope to identify overtones the piano creates when hammers strike with varying degrees of speed, and to measure the rate of decay in dynamics.

Gát also employed technology to help determine exactly what motions were being used for specific passages. One specific example was his use of a camera with fast shutter capability to capture clearly the motion of the hands and fingers of highly skilled pianists during performance. To this end he wrote:

> It is not a new, more modern method of piano playing we need, but good piano playing. The structure of the human organism has not undergone any changes since Beethoven's time – in its essentials – the mechanism of the piano has also remained the same. Thus we have to find the common factors in the relation of the great artists to their instruments.[15]

He goes on to express his belief that only information derived from physics and anatomy, verified by physiology and then combined with experiences from teaching and performance, should be acceptable sources from which to draw conclusions on correct methods of piano playing.

Gát fully supported the now-popular belief that the whole body should participate in the act of piano playing. He wrote that the entire body should function as an elastic mechanism of support and that problems occur when the whole body does not "fully participate in apportioning the resistance."[16] He felt that it was every bit as natural to involve the whole body in kinds of activities where accuracy and subtlety were paramount (such as piano playing) as in instances where great energy was expended (such as in athletics). The power and importance of these statements is reinforced by the introduction of the Feldenkrais and Alexander methods. Both methods were based on the idea that "to view the problems of performing artists in isolation is to lose sight of the fact that these programs are only elements in the whole behavior complex."[17]

The use of physiological nomenclature, and the growing knowledge of basic laws of physics by piano pedagogues, had become fairly widespread by the middle of the twentieth century. Gát was no exception, writing about piano playing using words or phrases including movement patterns, arc rotations, planes of motion, and trajectories. Without knowing those words came from a piano pedagogy book, one could easily believe that they instead came from a treatise on advanced diving. This reveals an important point – all human bodies must conform to certain laws of physics in order to extract the highest levels of performance, regardless of the activity.

Gát had an ally in pianist and teacher Paul Pichier. In his book, *The Pianist's Touch,* Pichier expressed his conviction that there was a direct connection "between the mechanics of making a tone and musical expression."[18] Pichier was aware of the substantial task he would be undertaking when trying to convince

[15]József Gát, *The Technique of Piano Playing* (London: Collet's, 1965) 9.

[16]Ibid.

[17]A. Murray, "The Alexander Technique," *Medical Problems of Performing Artists* 1 (1991): 131.

pianists to recognize this fact and apply it to their playing; this is reflected when he recognized the enormous amounts of energy that ordinary people waste on simple day-to-day tasks such as writing or speaking and yet this same wasteful, inefficient biomechanical approach is found in the daily practice routines of many serious pianists. He goes on to say that many pianists acquire a minimal level of coordination by chance and never become aware of just how wasteful their motions are at the piano. He believes that pianists should "aim unerringly"[19] at the kind of coordination at the piano that will allow them the freest, most efficient movements and thus the greatest amount of musical expression. This unerring aim may well take the pianist through a great deal of reading, self-examination, experimentation, study, and, ultimately, change. Hopefully pianists will see a pursuit of this nature as a worthwhile and exciting endeavor.

Due to the increasing amounts of credible evidence, more and more pedagogues began to accept these realities and embrace the importance of physiology in piano playing. As the twentieth century progressed, pianists became more open to the thinking of diverse fields, if they felt that the resulting applications to piano practice and performance were valid. One such field that showed a great deal of potential for helping musicians was athletics.

MUSIC MEDICINE AND WELLNESS

Research in the newly emerging field of music medicine began in the early 1980s, using the latest medical and physiological resources available. Not unlike the training teams that surround athletes, this specialty brought a new comprehensive approach to the many problems and conditions that affect the human body of the performing musician with the evolution of multi-specialty teams. Necessary to treat injuries found in the performing arts field today, these teams consist of individuals with training in many different fields and specializations, such as music, medicine, physical therapy, kinesiology, and sports psychology. Some of these persons have dual backgrounds, such as physician with significant music performance experience.

Working together, these teams are able to more thoroughly address the wide range of questions brought about by the considerable mental and physical demands of performing, including:

- How do I, coming back from an injury, practice without re-injuring myself?
- How can I better refine my motions at the keyboard to play more efficiently?
- How does diet affect my playing?
- Given my body type, how should I sit at the keyboard?
- How might a physical fitness regimen affect my musical performance?
- What can I do to develop a more secure memory, deal with stage fright, and build confidence?
- What can I do to make my muscles more responsive?

---

[18]Paul Pichier, *The Pianist's Touch* (Marshall, California: Perelen Publishers, 1972) 12.
[19]Ibid.

From a physical standpoint, anyone with a normally sound body has the musculature to play the piano. If anyone doubts that non-pianists have less finger mobility and speed than those of trained pianists, then a study by Oscar Raif may be of interest. Raif found that persons who had never played the piano could make as many as seven finger movements (taps) per second while some trained pianists could only manage five per second.[20] The answer to this apparent contradiction lies in the ability of the mind, through practice, to process the many various and complicated movements at the keyboard into seamless sequences through 'chunking'. Through this process, many motions are linked together and the mind thinks of them as a single unit.

By the 1990s, these multi-specialty teams became a greater part of the mainstream, and greater numbers of musicians came to accept and incorporate their advice. Articles began to appear with greater regularity in keyboard magazines and music journals, espousing ideas that reflect the new, multi-disciplined approach:

> ...that just as a physician should check your vital organs at regular intervals so should a trained physiotherapist or body tuner check your biomechanical systems for active, passive, or intrajoint motion."[21]

That author, Shmuel Tatz, also recommends regularly getting up from the keyboard to move about physically. An increasingly mainstream idea, it was generated by multi-specialist teams, who believe that taking purposeful breaks significantly benefits practice efficiency.

In order for students to realize the full benefit of this new and challenging body of knowledge, piano teachers must be willing to spend some time reading, researching, and learning in this area and then encourage their students to do the same. The same can be said for the wealth of information to be gleaned from sports-training techniques.

PARALLELS TO SPORTS TRAINING TECHNIQUES

CROSS TRAINING

Today, many sports training techniques routinely used by athletes as part of their daily regimens also have the ability to help pianists, when the basic concept is applied. One such technique is cross training. The concept is simple – employ a type of exercise that is not directly related to the specialty event, but which will benefit the athlete in competition. For example, competitive swimmers do not just swim to get into racing form; their training routines now include, among other things, extensive weight training to help their performance in the pool. Similarly, cross country skiers may ride bicycles or use in-line skates to develop complementary leg muscles that will help their performance on skis. For pianists, examples of cross training would include stretching or aerobic exercise.

Although it was not called cross training at the time, François Couperin seemed to recognize this basic premise when he wrote these words in his *L'art toucher le Clavecin:*

> People who begin late, or who have been badly taught must be careful; for as sinews may have become hardened, or they may

---

[20]Kochevitsky, *The Art of Piano Playing*, 12.

[21]Shmuel Tatz, *The Piano Quarterly* 152 (1990-91): 62.

> have got into bad habits, they should make their fingers flexible, or get someone else to do it for them, before sitting down to the harpsichord; that is to say they should pull, or get someone else to pull their fingers in all directions; that, moreover, will stir up their minds, and they will have a feeling of greater freedom.[22]

Certainly the above advice has some questionable practices and would benefit from more clarity and greater specificity, but it is clear that Couperin was aware of the importance of pre-practice stretching and warm-up routines, and advocated doing so. This, arguably one of the first examples of cross training, also illustrates that the notion of employing a specific routine to help the performance of the keyboardist *before* actually touching the keys has been around some two-hundred-plus years.

And Couperin was not alone. Later, in 1864, E. W. Jacson, from Great Britain, published a book called, *Finger and Wrist Gymnastics.* This book of specific hand movement and stretches caught the attention of Franz Liszt, who began suggesting some of them to his pupils, writing:

> In this way we will give striking proof of the supremacy of this new method, because I am convinced that less-developed pupils, taught by this method, will soon surpass even the best pupils having been taught according to the old one.[23]

Much later, William S. Newman mentions the virtues of exercise for the pianist, writing in his 1984 book, *The Pianist's Problems:*

> Good physical condition is a kind of antitoxin for nervousness. The pianist who is free of colds, unusual pains, outside worries, and fatigue is in a much better position to meet stage fright than one who is not.[24]

In addition he suggests doing "a few easy calisthenics and body stretching exercises before going on stage."[25] Although Newman does not go into much detail, he clearly recognizes that exercise and good health will be of great benefit to pianists, mirroring his many contemporaries who now believe strongly in the benefits of whole-body fitness.

INTERVAL TRAINING

Another sports training technique that pianists can adopt as their own is interval training. Its basic premise, as applied to pianists, is to alternate the intensities of the practice session by changing the demand-levels of repertoire to counter mental and physical fatigue. More specifically, the best results come when pianists *experiment* with and take note of varying intensities of technical demands, duration of rehearsal sessions, and lengths of rest periods, both mental and physical.

This idea is not altogether new, as Frank Merrick, a British pianist and teacher from the Royal Manchester College of Music, recognized the importance of taking breaks in the 1970s, saying:

---

[22]François Couperin, *L'art toucher le Clavecin* (Wiesbaden: Breitkopf and Hartel, 1961).
[23]Gát, *Technique of Piano Playing,* 249.
[24]William S. Newman, *The Pianist's Problems* (New York: Da Capo Press, 1984) 162.
[25]Ibid., 164.

> ...it seemed that occasional spasmodic bouts of work are more useful and, surprisingly enough, of more permanent value than the hour or (even) half hour of technical exercising which is usually so piously advocated for daily fare, year in, year out.[26]

(Merrick also points out the relevance of another 'sports' principle – limiting excess body motion. "From the technical point of view the elimination of superfluous body movements can vastly reduce the physical complexities and the sum total exertion in difficult passages."[27])

What separates true interval training from simply taking randomly interspersed breaks lies with the fact that in the former, every decision regarding the juxtaposition of varying intensities of mental and technical demands and rest periods are all carefully calibrated for the single purpose of learning efficiency. Tailoring interval training to best work for you is developed through thoughtful experimentation and using a journal to record various results. In time, every pianist will begin to know what works most effectively for them: whether a break every 40 minutes is more effective than one every 60 or 90 minutes, or whether alternating demanding repertoire with that of less demanding repertoire a few times an hour is more beneficial than once an hour. Interval training practice should never remain in a fixed pattern, constantly re-evaluate. As concentration abilities increase, so may the length of practice times and the way repertoire is rotated throughout a rehearsal.

PEDAGOGY AND TECHNOLOGY

In addition to appropriating the innovations of medical and sports research, pianists have long looked to technology for ideas to improve performance. The same can be said of the pedagogues discussed earlier. All were the pioneering figure of their respective generations, and, as one would expect, each looked to the technology of the day to see if it could offer any insight on the mechanisms of piano playing. In Ortmann's case, one of the more compelling innovations in his book was the use of still photography to aid in the tracking of various hand, arm, and finger motions.

In high-speed ballistic motion, the human eye is not able to clearly follow the intricate movement of various parts of a pianist's playing mechanism. This inability was (and still is) a major reason for the number of misconceptions regarding many aspects of piano playing. However, by incorporating the use of photography, Ortmann was able to substantiate pieces of evidence when proving a point about certain characteristics in the motions of high-level pianists.

One of these substantiations came through his photographic procedure. He attached a tiny light to the third finger of his test subjects' hands, and then had each of them play two different passages: one was a quick octave leap back and forth many times, the other was ascending a fifth, descending a third, ascending a fifth, and so on, up the keyboard. Pictures were taken with the camera in time-lapse mode, and the resulting series of photographs revealed that the light created symmetrically arched lines in the photographs of the more skilled pianists. The same cannot be said for the photographs of the less-skilled pianists, which had highly irregular lines. Ortmann's experiment confirmed what many pianists had theretofore thought: a feature of playing well is highly coordinated and regulated movement.

---

[26]Frank Merrick, *Practicing the Piano* (New York: Denman and Farrell, 1953) 100.

[27]Ibid., 96.

A few decades later, József Gát used the latest developments in still-camera technology to "find the common factor"[28] in the playing of great pianists. Gát's insistence on the importance of using the camera to solve vexing questions regarding piano technique helped him realize the degree to which even the smallest mismanagement of motion at the keyboard could create a technical problem. He wrote that shifting the hand a mere fraction can make considerable differences in the outcome of a passage and that, in light of this, pianists should take special care in order "to have the most favorable body position"[29] in front of the piano.

Certainly the writings of both Ortmann and Gát reinforce the notion that it is important to find a way to slow down, or even stop, the hand movements of fine pianists, in order to scrutinizing precisely what they do, on a note-by-note basis, in the hopes of obtaining new insight on being able to play difficult repertoire with ease. Whiteside agrees, stating that the eye cannot follow accurately the rapid movements of hands and fingers in fast passages. She also reveals an inherent problem in slowing down fast passage work for the purposes of examining the movement – in slow playing the movements employed are altogether different, and therefore offer no insight into fast playing. Therefore, she summarizes, little is to be learned from this practice.

It took almost a half a century before piano pedagogues again synthesized the wealth of information, both in and out of their fields, and presented some new insights, particularly the use of a video camera as a pedagogical tool. Two major concepts that lead to the modernization are as follows:

In sports, biomechanics and kinesiology are the sciences applied to athletes in order to increase their performance potential. In the study of motion it is important, for clarity and understanding, to dissect a motion into small, understandable parts. Paul Pichier understood this, and spoke of the great importance of both "preparatory and after motion movement"[30] during piano playing, especially in the playing of difficult and fast passages. Said another way, the manner in which your fingers, hand, and arm coordinate the approach to a difficult section will have a great deal to do with the outcome of that section. For example, if an ascending octave passage is immediately followed by a descending arpeggio, the hand position for the start of the arpeggio passage must be anticipated and partially or wholly assumed micro moments before the actual start of it.

Claire Le Guerrier's revelation that a mirror, when placed near the piano, enabled him to observe himself playing and was of enormous help, also served as incentive. "As this bad habit of mine could not be corrected, someone decided to put a huge mirror next to me so that I could behold my own physiological changes at the piano. 'Twas the instant cure."[31] Published in 1987, this text was another reminder of the benefits of self-observation, however using it as a means to improve motion remained an area largely unexplored, despite the fact that video technology was readily available at the time.

Le Guerrier's comments, along with Whiteside's insight that the eye cannot accurately follow fast passages, form a powerful reason for the use of today's new technology – the video camera. Affordable, this technology allows the researcher and pedagogue to examine, in minute and comprehensive detail, every kind of

---

[28]Gát, *Technique of Piano Playing.*

[29]Ibid.

[30]Pichier, *The Pianist's Touch,* 77.

[31]Claire Le Guerrier, *The Physical Aspects of Piano Playing* (New York: Vantage Press, 1987) 69.

pianistic motion, no matter how complex or fast. It eliminates the difficulties that come with observing the playing mechanism at real (actual) speed. First used in sports to observe physical motion in great detail, slow-motion video analysis is the natural next step in the evolution of piano pedagogy. Useful as both a teaching as diagnostic tool, specific applications are discussed in "Video Camera Applications for Enhancing Practice and Performance."

Exploring the history of piano pedagogy provides a worthwhile lesson in discovery and innovation and serves not only to remind us where we came from, but also to spark in us the desire to evolve.

A Fundamental of Movement: The Action of Third-class Levers

Jacqueline Csurgai-Schmitt

Considering the vast array of literature already written about the subject of piano technique, one must ask why there still exists so much confusion among pianists and teachers as to the most efficient way of using the body at the keyboard? The laws of mechanics do not change from pianist to pianist, yet there appears to be many, seemingly different theories of the best way to play the piano.

To be sure, the physical differences between individuals' bodies, minds, and nervous systems will create a wide and diverse range of sound and color, strength and sensitivity, virtuosity and musicianship, helping to sustain the idea that there exists no 'one way' to play the piano and tending to negate the concept of an underlying, fundamental mechanics of movement. This wealth of diversity among pianists tends to obscure the fact that there exists an underlying, fundamental mechanics of movement that does not change from person to person. This will be examined, along with some apparent contradictions in various approaches to playing.

Otto Ortmann wrote, "Piano playing is movement, not position."[1] Regardless of what part of the body is making the movement and which muscles are incorporated to make that movement, we know that it is movement which creates the sound at the piano. In piano playing, each body part involved in sound production moves off some kind of base, be it the finger off the hand, the hand off the arm, or the arm off the torso. For this reason, any discussion about piano technique must ultimately consider this relationship of a moving part to its stationary base. The seemingly different methods proposed by the various schools of piano playing – Breithaupt's weight and relaxation, Tobias Matthay's invisible rotation, Arnold Schultz' contra-fixation, József Gát's synthesizing movements, the French 'finger' school, the German school, the Russian school, to name a few – are attempts to deal with the mechanical issue of stabilization of the base of movement.

To understand what is required to stabilize any base, we must delve into a

[1]Otto Ortmann, *The Physiological Mechanics of Piano Technique* (New York: E.P. Dutton & Co., Inc., 1962) 33.

vocabulary unfamiliar to most pianists. The concept is not difficult to understand, only perhaps the words that one must use to describe it. Once the basic principle is understood, it can be readily apply in many ways and forms to one's own and one's student's playing.

According to Ortmann, all of the parts the body uses to play the piano are levers.[2] The lever is an easy concept to understand because we use levers throughout the course of our daily activity. For instance, we use crowbar-type levers to lift heavy objects, pry things apart, and open cans of soda. These are levers of the first class, and have an advantage of power over speed of movement.[3] In other words, the working end of the lever, the part in contact with the object being leveraged, moves very slowly, but is able to exert great force.

The class to which a lever belongs is defined by the position of its fulcrum, the resistance to its movement, and its power source. In the case of our fingers, which are third-class levers, the fulcrums are the hand's knuckles, often called the 'bridge' or *metacarpal phalangeal* joints. The base off which the finger levers work is the hand, and by continuation, the arm.[4] Supplying power are muscles which originate in the base (the hand or the arm), cross the fulcrum (hand knuckles), and insert into the finger levers, causing movement in the joints and placing the fingers into a new position in relation to the hand. Due to the position of the muscle's insertion close to the fulcrum, all third-class levers have an advantage of speed over power, as the far end of the lever moves very quickly (the tip of the finger, for instance). Because of this insertion point, these levers do not work with great force.[5] They work very efficiently when moving quickly through the air. If they meet resistance that does not slow momentum considerably, these levers will begin to slow down only at the end of their range of movement, such as occurs when swinging a baseball bat or golf club.

On the other hand, if a small muscle moving a finger meets a larger resistance, like the piano key, the forward momentum of the finger will be slowed considerably. When pianists were taught to raise their fingers high (the 'finger school' of piano playing) it was in order to develop sufficient momentum to swing through the resistance of the piano key. This was a legitimate use of the finger at this time, as the resistance of the keys was minimal on eighteenth and nineteenth-century pianos. However, as the instrument developed in size and power, and as key resistance increased in the twentieth century, pianists often resorted to the use of the long finger flexors for key descent. While one may increase the force of finger movement by adding these muscles which originate in the arm, it is done at the expense of speed and endurance.[6]

Although the fingers, powered by the small, intrinsic muscles (the *lumbricales* and *interossei)* of the hands, do not have much strength for moving against the resistance of the keys, the good news is that virtuosic speeds are virtually guaranteed by simply using these muscles instead of the larger, more powerful – and slower – finger flexors. Since the small, intrinsic muscles reside in the hand itself and do not cross the wrist, they are much more efficient at moving the finger quickly than the longer finger flexors which originate in the arm and are more

---

[2]Ibid., 7.

[3]Ibid., 6.

[4]Ibid., 6.

[5]Ibid., 7,12.

[6]Ibid., 6.

appropriately used for chords and octaves, and for *forte* playing.[7] Also, in using these muscles over the long flexors, the wrist and forearm can remain more relaxed. Speed of the fingers is already 'built-in' to the body. A layman's finger can move as fast as that of a trained pianist.[8] The specialized training of pianists only becomes a factor in speed when individual fingers are called on to function one after another in various sequences, and to have the endurance to play long passages.

You can demonstrate this speed by fluttering your fingers in the air. Virtuosic speed is inherent in the small finger muscles. Finger flexion at the hand knuckle is performed by these muscles, which are responsible for the most rapid movements of the finger used in piano playing.

It should come as a relief to pianists to know that such speed is innate to all of us. However, this potential finger velocity is slowed as it contacts the piano key's resistance, and it is here that problems begin to develop. The reason is simple: at this point, one has several choices about how the base will be stabilized by the muscles, and some of these choices are less advantageous than others.

SUPPLYING A BASE FOR MOVEMENT

A playing unit is defined not only by the part that is moving, but also by the part that is not – the base. Consequently, the playing unit can be a finger, hand, forearm, upper arm, torso, or any combination thereof. For example:

- The finger may be the sole playing unit.
- The finger may be used as a moving lever in conjunction with a larger moving lever.
- The finger may be used solely in a supportive, non-moving role, such as when the arm is the playing unit.

One of the central issues of piano technique, around which much confusion has arisen, concerns the question of how to stabilize the base of finger movement at the keyboard.

When the hand or arm is performing the stroke, and the finger is used in a supporting capacity, muscles (i.e., the small finger muscles, the finger flexors and/or wrist flexors) must contract in order to keep the hand-knuckle joint and wrist joint from 'breaking-in' at the moment of key resistance. If this muscular activity does not take place, the force from the arm cannot be transmitted to the key and no sound will result. "It does not matter if there is no *actual* feeling of tension in these muscles. If key depression has taken place, these muscles have contracted."[9]

Usually, piano playing occurs through a complex combination of two or more levers and two or more joints working in synergy with one another. Indeed, it is well documented that isolation of movement is, virtually, an impossibility.[10] For purposes of description and understanding, though, it can be helpful to consider a single playing unit in its simplest movement.

---

[7]See the chapter, "A Pianist's Physiology," for a more detailed description of the muscles of the hand.

[8]George Kochevitsky, *The Art of Piano Playing,* 12. In the experiments of Oscar Raif, a pianist and teacher, it is noted that, "trained pianists by no means had greater mobility of the individual fingers than did people who were not pianists. The requirements of an individual finger in piano playing are usually much less than its natural ability. The normal mobility of a single finger is fully used only in performing a trill."

[9]Ortmann, *The Physiological Mechanics of Piano Playing,* 125.

[10]Ibid., 47.

Using the finger lever as an example, the base (hand and arm) must remain in position for the finger lever to work against the resistance of the key. One of Ortmann's most important achievements was his observation that this resistance of the key to finger movement will cause an upward movement, away from the keyboard, in the nearest, relaxed joints.[11] If the player allows this displacement, the full force of the finger cannot be delivered to the key, and key descent cannot be controlled.

It is important to note that this refers only to the mechanical laws governing action and reaction to resistance, where the arm may move away from the work needing to be done because the base has not been stabilized. It is quite possible to deliberately move the arm either into or away from the keys while the finger is moving into a key. As long as the arm does not move away from the keys in *upward reaction* to the finger movement and maintains a leveraged relationship to the moving finger, it can still be thought of as supplying a stable base for the finger movement

This is easily demonstrated at the keyboard by relaxing the hand knuckle and wrist joint and moving just one finger into the key, with the arm weight supported at the shoulder. If the joints of the bridge and the wrist remain relaxed (and if you do not add the weight of the arm to counteract the upward movement) the base (in this case, the hand and the arm) will move upward, away from the keys.

Since it is impossible to play either rapidly or musically with the hand and arm moving away from the key with each finger movement, it becomes necessary to find a way of keeping the hand and arm stable to provide a relatively unmoving base for finger movement. To get a feel for the necessity of supplying a non-moving base for leveraged activity, stand in your socks and try pushing a chair away from you with both your arms. Without 'fixing' the base (contracting muscles to keep the torso from moving), the torso will be pushed backwards and the work (moving the chair) will not get done.

Tobias Matthay describes this action and reaction thus:

> When you exert your finger-tip against the key *downwards*, there is an equal *reaction*...at the other end of that finger-lever, *upwards* therefore at the knuckle. This *invisible* reaction upwards at the knuckle must again be *countered* at the knuckle by supplying a sufficiently stable *Basis* (or foundation) there for the desired action of the finger. In short, the exerted finger needs a Basis at the knuckle-joint, equal to the force to be exerted against the Key.[12]

Here begins one of the great debates of twentieth-century piano technique: How should the base of finger movement be stabilized? We have found that it is a mechanical necessity to stabilize the base with muscular contractions. Ortmann has assured us that it is impossible to accomplish any task, much less the task of key depression, without such necessary fixations:

> Such a condition, since it is necessary in some degree at all joints in order for any movement to occur, involves no undue or unnatural strain upon the organism or any of its parts. If the...hand were

[11]Ibid., 83.

[12]Tobias Matthay, *The Visible and Invisible in Pianoforte Technique* (New York: Oxford University Press, 1968) 20.

> not held fixed (by appropriate fixation of the wrist), as the finger tip strikes the piano key the hand knuckle would be pushed up. In order to permit maximum functioning of the finger tip, the knuckle must remain fixed during the movement.[13]

Ortmann is careful to state that this rigidity is not *felt* as stiffness, because it is necessary for the proper execution of the movement and aids, instead of interferes with, the coordination. If, however, the rigidity reaches an unnecessary degree, it can then be called stiffness, and if it exceeds the tension necessary to perform the movement, it is wasted effort and becomes an incoordination.[14]

In Ortmann's chapter on the States and Properties of Muscles, he proves once and for all that complete relaxation is not desirable in piano playing, as the slack in the muscle must be first taken up before movement can take place. He states that the feeling of relaxation, rather than the actuality, is useful, and suggests that a more appropriate term would be coordinated. During his many experiments with trained pianists, it became apparent that the pianists were incapable of judging what was actually occurring muscularly from their subjective sensations alone.

Unfortunately, these very appropriate contractions of involved muscles have received such bad press from the weight and relaxation schools of piano playing that it is controversial even to mention the term muscular fixations in reference to these completely coordinated, muscular events. Regardless of how unpalatable it may sound, Otto Ortmann and Carl Schultz have indisputably, and for all time, proved that muscular contractions do take place, and are absolutely necessary to fix the base of any coordinated movement of the body, including pianistic movement at the keyboard.[15] We can no longer allow the term fixation of joints to interfere with our understanding of the process.

Proponents of the weight and relaxation school of piano playing believed that the base of finger movement should be supplied by the weight of the arm. In considering this theory, we must accept that:

1. Only a small percentage of the weight of the arm can actually rest on the keys, as the shoulder is, by necessity, supporting much of this weight through its connection to the arm.

2. Whatever weight is leftover for key descent can only rest in the keys if *every joint,* from the shoulder to the fingertip, is contracted enough to support this weight.[16]

Ortmann states:

> The shoulder...is the only fully relaxed joint...All other joints are fixed...up to the resistance point necessary to support the arm-weight. Since the aim of the movement is just this support of the arm, the movement is fully coordinated. Here, then, coordination and relaxation are actually opposed.[17]

---

[13]Ortmann, *The Physiological Mechanics of Piano Playing,* 58.

[14]See Ortmann's chapter on Coordination and Incoordiation, *The Physiological Mechanics of Piano Playing.*

[15]Arnold Schultz, *The Riddle of the Pianist's Finger* (New York: Carl Fischer, 1936) 62. (The entire book is a discussion of the necessary fixation of the joints involved in piano playing.)

[16]Ortmann, *The Physiological Mechanics of Piano Playing,* 101.

Thus, the concept of weight playing and relaxation, as it is normally used, is a mechanical oxymoron.

Weight playing, the release of arm weight into the keys for key depression, requires a fixation of the joints of the arm in excess of that required when the arm is supported by the shoulder, and the intervening joints are fixed to withstand key depression by the playing unit. Ortmann's and Schulz' chapters on weight transfer inform us that a complete transfer of weight is not possible except at the very slowest tempi. The idea that weight is transferred completely or rolled from fingertip to fingertip, *Rollbewegung*, is a psychological conception rather than a mechanical fact. The truth is, for key depression to take place by pure weight transfer, the first finger must remain on the keybed until the second key has sounded, in order to take up the job of weight bearing.[18] This not only slows considerably the process of movement from key to key, it tends to drive the finger into the keybed, forcing great fixation of the supporting joints. Therefore, it can be concluded that weight playing causes the greatest fixation of the joints and is the mechanical antithesis of relaxation.

Weight playing causes the greatest fixation of the joints and is the mechanical antithesis of relaxation.

In addition, Ortmann reminds us that the size of an inert mass determines the force necessary to move it or change its direction, and the time necessary to accomplish either. "Assuming now that the weight of the arm is resting on the keys, any change from this position will require a greater force or will consume more time than if the arm is poised by contraction of the appropriate shoulder muscles."[19]

In most cases, the weight must be and is – subconsciously and in a most coordinated manner – recovered at the shoulder before the next key depression. In addition to requiring a considerable amount of time, using the weight of the arm to hold a key down when only a few ounces are necessary is a waste of effort, and is considered an incoordination. A naturally coordinated response will automatically remove the excess weight (more than 95 percent) from the key.[20] Therefore, much of the weight, supposedly transferred from finger to finger, is unconsciously recovered by the shoulder between finger movements, thus reducing the amount of fixation necessary to support that weight at the joints and allowing the pianist to have more control over key descent. Since beauty of tone at the piano is the result of control over key descent, performing controlled arm strokes with muscular fixation is the most effective way of producing a premeditated, controlled tone.[21] A minimal amount of weight may be released unconsciously and may occur in response to key resistance. The arm, however, still *feels* as if it is being supported by the shoulder. To force the fingers to support the weight of the arm as speeds increase will overwork the flexors and extensors, because the small finger muscles in the hand that produce the greatest finger speed are incapable of supporting arm weight.

There are more detrimental factors involved with weight playing than just an ugly sound and great fixation of joints. If the fingers are obliged to carry the weight of the arm, thus activating the long finger flexors, they will be forced to move more slowly in succession. The long finger flexors are ideal for power and

---

[17]Ibid.

[18]Schultz, *The Riddle of the Pianist's Finger,* 36.

[19]Ibid., 146.

[20]Ibid., 180.

[21]Ibid., 71.

strength and will act in support of the fingers when playing chords or octaves, or in response to a downward movement from the arm.[22] However, they are *not* the muscles one wants to use when velocity and the highest speeds are required. Using only the long finger muscles for the rapid notes of a Chopin etude will inevitably produce pain in the forearm, a complaint of many pianists. In addition, overuse of these finger muscles can cause ganglias to form, which can ultimately interfere with the movement of the involved fingers. Learning to use, instead, the small finger muscles for the fastest speeds opens the door of virtuosity to one and all.

THEORIES OF STABILIZING THE BASE OF MOVEMENT

In order to learn how to use the finger, hand, and forearm levers to best advantage, it is absolutely necessary that one learn *how* to stabilize the base of their movement. While Ortmann specifically speaks of this "stabilization of the base,"[23] ("contra-fixation"[24] in Schultz' terms) many other pianists have referred to and attempted to explain this necessary and coordinated movement of the body through other subjective terms and descriptions, possibly hoping to avoid the dreaded word fixation.

Jószef Gát uses the term "synchronizing movements"[25] to describe the positioning of the forearm necessary to support the fastest possible finger movements. Unfortunately, his description, provided below, can be misleading because of the misuse of mechanical terms. I would suggest making several substitutions: instead of rebound, substitute resistance, and instead of elastic resistance, substitute fixation or muscular contraction. These are also inserted in brackets in the following:

> The rebound [resistance of the keys] will displace the active swinging unit unless this rebound is counterbalanced...unless we increase the elastic resistance [fixation] of the support simultaneously with the increase in the force of the stroke. In finger playing, the arm and...the whole body will serve to absorb the rebound of the keys, *so that the hand does not move from the position required by the active function of the fingers.* [emphasis mine] The arm resistance must be increased in proportion not only to the force of the stroke but also to any increase in the tempo...
>
> ...This requires a gradual increasing of muscle work. When playing in slow tempo only a small amount of muscle work is required for the purpose of resistance; the player practically "holds" his arms. In quick tempo the resistance must be increased and the player has the impression of being forced to press his arm to the keys.[26]

A serious problem with Gát's description is that an object offering resistance is not rebounding. Gát never mentions the resistance of the key to a downward movement of the arm. Only if the key has been 'thrown' at the keybed by a finger and then not retained on the bed by the finger can it truly be said to be rebounding. It appears that Gát is speaking here of Schultz' "trans-fixations movements,"[27]

---

[22]For more information, see the chapter, "A Pianist's Physiology," page 45.

[23]Ortmann, *The Physiological Mechanics of Piano Playing,* 83.

[24]Schultz, *The Riddle of Pianist's Finger,* 62.

[25]József Gát, *The Technique of Piano Playing* (London: Collet's, 1965) 31.

[26]Ibid., 26.

where the finger is causing a rebound *in the base* (or arm), *after* hitting the keybed. Obviously, when Gát speaks of "holding" the arm, he means supporting the arm at the shoulder. And, he is correct is saying that, as speed increases, the upward reaction from the resistance of the keys increases and appropriate adjustments (stabilizing muscular contractions) to the arm are necessary. Double notes, thirds or sixths, for instance, will also produce a need for greater muscular contractions in the base as there is twice the resistance of single notes, thus, twice the force moving against the base in an upward direction. However, in every case, he is speaking of trans-fixation movements caused by the finger hitting the keybed, and not contra-fixation movements, which use less muscular energy to maintain a stable base.

Having confused the issue by referring to the upward-moving hand as a "key-rebound," and the fixation required to offset it as a series of rebounds or "elastic resistance," Gát further adds to the confusion by stating:

> The constant regulation of the resistance requires that the whole body functions as an elastic support…
>
> …As the player has the sensation that this occurs with the aid of the weight of the arm or the body... it is called "weight-effect" or "weight-complement."[28]

The state of elastic resistance in the body being referred to is a series of coordinated muscular contractions, not weight, so why use the terminology at all? After making this remarkably misleading statement, Gát attempts to clarify himself with the following:

> The term "weight-effect" is incorrect from the physical point of view, because there is no question of an actual weight-effect, but only of regulating the resistance of the elastic support. From a psychological point of view, however, the term "weight-effect" seems to be more serviceable than the word "resistance." To use the latter word may induce a strained, even cramped state of the body...while the word "weight-effect" brings about a state of relaxation.[29]

This is the precise opposite of what actually takes place physiologically, which Gát finally acknowledges when he writes:

> The expression "while letting the arm loose at the shoulder, support it with the fingers" is of course erroneous, but sometimes it helps the pianist to find the right way for the arm to function…
>
> ...hence it is absolutely wrong to bring any real weight – be it arm, shoulder or body – to bear and to apply pressure to the keys.[30]

Is it any wonder that the statements of great pedagogues, like the one above, have confused pianists and teachers throughout the twentieth century?

Tobias Matthay had similar difficulties in describing the subjective sensations of good piano playing and the biomechanical issues involved. Beginning with his

---

[27]Schultz, *The Riddle of the Pianist's Finger,* 93.
[28]Gát, *The Technique of Piano Playing,* 27.
[29]Ibid.
[30]Ibid.

book, *Act of Touch in All Its Diversity*, published in 1903, and ending with the final revision of *The Visible and Invisible in Pianoforte Technique*, in 1947, Matthay tried to analyze and describe this elusive, but essential, aspect of piano technique.

A supposed proponent of the weight and relaxation school of piano playing, Matthay was actually of the impression that "passing" or "rolling" weight from key to key "will render every passage, thus misplayed, thoroughly dull and uninteresting musically, since such solidly-resting weight precludes that nice *choice* of the tone-colour for each note, so imperatively needed if the result is to be Music-making."[31] Indeed, his first two Components of the "Playing Apparatus" consist of fingers alone and hand alone against an immovable arm supported at the shoulder (contra-fixation movements).[32] He states "no part of its (arm) weight or force rests upon the keyboard *when the arm is **fully** poised — or completely balanced by its own muscles.* When fully (or nearly fully) poised, its inertia, alone, suffices as a basis for the exertion of the hand-and-finger in light, rapid passages, etc."[33]

While Third and Fourth Components consist of forearm and Upper-arm arm weight upon the keys, for "cantando and cantabile-tone," Matthay says:

> The inevitable drawback in the use of "Weight-transfer" touch lies in the fact that it very materially interferes with *your ability to choose the tone* for each note *individually* – both with regard to loudness and duration. In short, with "Passing-on" (or Weight-transfer) touch, we can practically only have "Mass-production" effects – swirls of *crescendo* and *diminuendo,* produced by the respective gradual increase or decreases of this passed-on Weight-basis. Therefore, strictly avoid "Weight-transfer" touch for all passages which need every note to be *musically individualized* – that is, for all *melodic* passages; since melodic passages always require meticulous *selectivity* of tone and duration for every note.[34]

In actuality, Matthay misuses the term inertia, for it is not inertia that supplies the immovable base of the "fully poised" arm, but both the mass of the arm and the fixation of necessary muscles. The fact that the fixation is so slight as to be unnoticeable to the pianist's mind does not change the reality of the muscular involvement. If one studies this and other statements of Matthay's closely, it becomes apparent that weight plays little or no role in supplying an immovable base from which the fingers can work. In fact, what he describes is a contra-fixation movement. Therefore, he is in full agreement with Ortmann, Schultz, and Gát.

Matthay's mention of the role of rotation is interesting, and he describes two distinct forms. The first is an actual movement of the arm propelling the finger into the keys. This, he states, is minimally useful. The second, he calls "rotary-adjustments"[35] or "muscular exertions,"[36] which he says are necessary for every note in every kind of touch, even though there might not be the slightest *movement,* rotarily, to give a visual clue to the process. Since rotary movements are often suggested as a means of supplying a base for finger movements, let us examine what Matthay actually says about them.

[31]Matthay, *Visible and Invisible in Piano Playing,* 34.

[32]Ibid., 22.

[33]Ibid., 27.

[34]Ibid., 30.

Matthay states that the central position of the hand in relation to the arm (the position occurring without any contraction of the rotator muscles) is vertical to the keyboard with the thumb upward. (He is describing the position of the hand that occurs when the arm is hanging by the side of the body. If one then contracts the forearm in a 90-degree angle, the hand assumes the position described above.) Therefore, in order to place the hand in a horizontal playing position, it becomes necessary to contract the pronators in the forearm, and if these muscles relax, the forearm will again rotate outward so that the thumb faces upward.

Subsequently, he observes that for the forearm to supply a base for movement of the fingers, the pronator muscles, the supinator muscles, or a combination of both will be in a constant state of contraction, no matter how unaware of this condition the pianist is. As each individual finger is called upon to play, a slight adjustment of these muscles takes place to properly support the finger movement. As this adjustment is a "muscular exertion," rather than an observable movement, the support of these muscles in the forearm is "invisible." Matthay states:

> Let us be quite clear then... that my discoveries on this point do *not* refer merely to the actual rotatory *movements* before-mentioned, but, on the contrary, deal particularly with those *invisible* changes of state rotationally...which, although *unseen*, are needed for every note we play, whether we know of them or not, and ever have been needed, and ever will be – so long as keyboards are used.[37]

This is a far cry from those who would advocate an *actual* rotary movement for every key descent. While one understands the reason for suggesting the movement at slow tempi – to free the arm and fingers of tension, and to supply a base which does not require weight released from the shoulder – this touch, in its visible form, is limited to the speed with which the arm can move into and out of a key, certainly not anywhere near as fast as a sequence played by the fingers and supported by invisible contractions of the rotary muscles.[38]

Ortmann accepted the mechanical fact that piano playing required contraction of muscles to stabilize the base of movement. He was far more interested in whether this contraction was a coordinated or an incoordinated event. Insufficient fixation or an excess of fixation are both classified as incoordinated movements because, from the standpoint of interaction, a coordinated movement is one in which action and reaction are equal and opposite. His records show that with key resistance, there is a reaction at other joints. By starting *pianissimo* and proceeding to *forte*, muscular spread will naturally take place in the hands and arms from minimal contractions to maximal contractions. As he states, "to demand of a pupil a tone-production of even moderate loudness with the finger, while the other joints of the hand and arm are fully relaxed, is to demand the impossible. No one ever has played that way, and no one ever will."[39]

Arnold Schultz comes closer than any writer in understanding the mechanical truth behind beautiful and virtuosic piano playing. In using the term "contra-fixation" to describe the underlying mechanical principles of movement, however, he probably did himself a huge disservice. As the word fixation is simply unaccept-

---

[35]Ibid., 50.
[36]Ibid., 51.
[37]Ibid., 50.
[38]Ibid., 64.

able to most pianists, his book *The Riddle of the Pianist's Finger,* first printed in 1936, has been relegated to the dustbin of piano pedagogy.

Schultz states that a "contra-fixation" movement must fulfill three conditions:

1. The joint in which the playing unit swings must show little or no movement. (To have absolutely no movement would be impossible. Schultz is speaking here of a reactionary movement upward which takes place in the joint when the playing unit encounters resistance.)
2. The playing unit must not support the base (i.e., releasing weight from the shoulder).
3. The muscles which contract to stabilize the base must not contract in excess of what is necessary to withstand the resistance of the key. If they do, an incoordinated movement has transpired and endurance is decreased.[40]

In summary, both Ortmann and Schultz state that a coordinated movement is one in which muscular contraction in the base perfectly balances the work being done by the playing unit. Any contraction of muscles in excess of this constitutes an incoordination.

THE PEDAGOGY OF STABILIZING THE BASE

It is important to remember, in speaking of supplying an immovable base for finger movement, that we do not mean that the arm must remain immobile. The arm may be moving in any direction, either toward or away from key descent, while the finger moves into the key simultaneously. It is the *reaction* to the resistance of the keys that is at issue here. The pianist usually attempts, unconsciously, to counteract the upward pressure in one of the following two ways:

1. By tightening the finger flexors and extensors which cross the hand's knuckles and the wrist.
2. By releasing weight into the fingers, which also tightens the flexors.

As these are the muscles that support arm movement when playing octaves and chords or when playing *forte,* their contraction creates a tension in the joints of the knuckles and wrist. This has the unfortunate effect of slowing down the speed of finger movement. If the pianist then tries to make the fingers move faster against the muscular resistance of a tight bridge and wrist, speed and endurance decline even more.

As speed increases, though, arm movements must become ever smaller until, at the fastest speeds, even the smallest movement of the arm – up, down or rotationally – will negatively impact the ability of the fingers to reach the keybed in the time allotted. The fingers will be flexing and lifting in approximately one-fifth of a second, in rapid sequence, and if the hand and arm have not positioned the fingers accurately, they will either not sound the note, or they will run into the keybed.[41] And, if the arm is not aligned behind the fingers that are playing – horizontally, vertically, and rotationally – the small finger muscles will not have the support of

[39]Ortmann, *The Physiological Mechanics of Piano Playing,* 87.

[40]Schultz, *The Riddle of the Pianist's Finger,* 135.

the base to move through the key resistance. The inability of many pianists to play at the fastest speeds lies in their lack of awareness of the necessity of positioning the base properly.

The small finger muscles (the *lumbricales* and *interossei)* are the muscles that move the finger at its fastest speeds.[42] Because the hand knuckles and the wrist are as relaxed as possible when these muscles are used, a movement using these muscles will, at first, force the arm up and away from the keyboard until a base has been established for this most agile kind of finger movement.

To establish a base for the use of the small finger muscles against the resistance of the key, place the left hand under the palm of the right hand and press down with the right arm. Do not press the fingers into the keybed. The left hand and arm must keep any weight or pressure from being released into the key by the right arm. Move individual fingers into the keys, feeling the heaviness of the key resistance against these small muscles. Gradually recover the weight of the right hand and arm back into the shoulder until there is no pressure on the left hand and the finger is moving against key resistance, perfectly balanced with its base, without the slightest sensation that the hand and arm are being forced upward. With this, a perfectly coordinated base has been established to support the work of the small finger muscles.[43]

Using the small finger muscles for key depression requires the least effort on the part of the hands, arms, and body. Since these small muscles will be doing most of the work, the key will feel very heavy, and the pianist will have the sensation that finger movement is completely detached from the hand and arm. When the fingers are finally released from the bondage of the long flexors and extensors, they will move at top speeds through any passage. The faster the tempo, the closer to the keys the fingertips must be. Since the muscles, at this point, are probably not developed, a sensation of heaviness of the key will remain for a period. If the key feels easy to push down, at this point, the pianist is probably using the long flexors and extensors for finger movement. However, the pianist can incorporate the use of the small muscles of the finger at any speed, and students should be learning their use, at least, by the time they attempt their first fast sixteenth-note passages. (Once the feeling of this finger coordination is established, mental control of the fingers, instead of physical control, will take precedence.[44])

This finger movement works well when merged into larger movements of the arms:

> Move the arm in a downward direction, without releasing weight from the shoulder, at precisely the moment the small finger muscles move a finger into the key. The downward movement of the arm will easily counteract the upward force of key resistance being exerted on the hand knuckle and wrist since the entire mass of the arm is acting against the resistance of the key. Since the flexors and extensors now have no need to tighten to stabilize the base, the pianist should experience looseness and freedom in the bridge and the wrist with the finger moving easily in the joint.

---

[41]Kochevitsky, *The Art of Piano Playing,* 12.

[42]See the chapter, "The Pianist's Physiology," page 45.

[43]See the sections on the pedagogy of arm and finger movement in the chapter, "A Child's First Lessons."

[44]For further exploration of this concept, please see William DeVan's chapter, "Technique for Advanced Playing."

It is important to note that this downward movement is not the release of weight from the shoulder, for if weight is released the flexors and extensors must contract in order to support this weight. In order for the small finger muscles to work against the keys, the shoulder must continue to support the weight of the arm while simply moving the arm in a downward direction at the moment of key descent. The pianist experiences a feeling of sinking or relaxing on both sides of the hand knuckles instead of a feeling of the hand being pushed or leveraged upward during key descent. This feeling of gently balancing on each side of the fulcrum is a critical sensation for the pianist to discover, as it is the only coordination that allows the maximum release of tension in the bridge.

The pianist should continue with a single finger until the coordination is comfortable. Using the same finger, move the arm in a scale pattern up and down the keyboard. It is important to keep one's awareness on both sides of the fulcrum. If the pianist thinks only of the finger, the base will start to experience upward pressure. And if the pianist thinks only of the arm, the finger will stop moving, fusing itself into an arm stroke. Because consecutive finger movements are one of the most complicated examples of muscular coordination a pianist must perform, it takes time to experience this sensation with each finger individually before attempting to move from one finger to another. This will allow the pianist to adjust to the subtle sideways shifting that is required when the arm is placed behind each individual finger to function as a stable base.

After each finger has been exposed to, and is comfortable with, this coordination, the next step is to move from one finger to another. I suggest a non-*legato* approach at first. The tendency to *not* move the arm sideways to support the next finger descent, and the *non-release* of tension in the first finger to play, are difficult habits to break. By totally releasing the finger flexion after the first movement downward, the pianist can then experience more easily the degree to which the arm must move sideways to support the next finger. At this point, it is wise to keep using a separate down motion of the arm for each finger movement. When the feeling of a perfectly balanced finger movement and arm movement is comfortable, the pianist can then make a *legato* between the fingers, still using the down-up movement of the arm for the time being.

The remarkable thing here is that this coordination – moving the arm up and down for each finger movement – is the natural coordination a child chooses when left to his or her own devices. Unfortunately, many teachers try to stop the arm from moving in this way in an attempt to produce a beautiful *legato* line. However, by stopping the arm movement prematurely – before the student has learned to support an arm movement first with minimal finger tension – the student will be forced into overusing the flexors and extensors, causing his or her finger movement to be filled with extraneous tension *from the very beginning.*

After the pianist has experienced the freedom and looseness of the bridge and wrist for every finger movement, including the thumb, he or she may gradually make smaller and smaller movements with the arm until no down motion is visible, with the exception of the first note of a passage. (Again, this does not mean that the arm cannot move up, down, and around that keyboard as we play. The attempt here is only to experience the use of the small finger muscles with the lease amount of tension in the knuckles, the wrist, and the forearm.) If tension creeps back into the hand knuckles and wrist, it can be easily released by going back to the down-up movement of the arm. When all visible arm movement has ceased, there will be a slight, unnoticeable contraction of the rotary muscles of the arm in response to finger movement by the small muscles. The pianist will have attained Matthay's poised arm with invisible muscular exertions – the coordination necessary for the fastest speeds and most virtuoso passages.

IN CONCLUSION

In an attempt to clarify the information presented in this chapter, it seems appropriate to highlight the central points:

1. The use of arm weight released into the keys as a base for finger movement is hardly ever used in fine piano playing because of the pianist's inability to then control key descent.

2. Arm weight released into the keyboard causes muscles to contract to support this weight. The more weight released into the keys, the more that must be carried by the finger flexors, and the slower the individual fingers will be able to move.

3. Arm movement and arm weight are two different things. The whole arm may be moving either in the same or the opposite direction from which a finger lever is working. It is quite possible to move an arm in a downward direction to supply a base for finger movement *without* releasing arm weight into the keys.

4. For most of piano playing, including the very fastest speeds, the whole weight of the arm is supported at the shoulder and provides a base upon which the finger levers, the hand lever, and the forearm lever may move.

5. This base must remain immovable only in relation to the work of the finger lever. Any arm movement towards or away from the finger movement becomes a problem only when the movement is a reaction to key resistance and interferes with the effectivness of the finger and control of key descent.

6. Actual downward arm movement to supply a base can become, with practice, a non-movement of invisible (and for the most part, unconscious) muscular contractions in the arm that perfectly balance the finger, propelled by the small finger muscles. The biomechanical term for this coordination is fixation.

It is time for pianists to acknowledge the scientific work done by the great minds of the twentieth century by adding the biomechanical term fixation – a necessary component of movement at the keyboard – to their vocabulary. We should stop being afraid of the word; it is an impossibility to move around in our world without muscles contracting to supply a base for our movement. And it is only in accepting that some muscles will be working to play the piano that we can seek to find the most efficient coordination possible in ourselves. The great pianists found this coordination in order to play at virtuoso speeds. This chapter is offered to you in the hope that you too will be able to experience this most remarkable sensation.

Biomechanics of Healthy Pianistic Movement

Seymour Fink

Nothing happens until we move; nothing worthwhile happens until we move with musical purpose.

Piano technique may be best defined as any purposeful movement for musical ends – large or small, fast or slow, recurring or infrequent – *any* movement that enhances the end result. Although purposeful, wiping one's brow is not technique, because the movement is directed at comfort, not music. But sliding the left foot out to counterbalance body weight while both hands are playing far right is technique, for the added equilibrium helps control what the hands are doing. Purposeful movement is the key to expressiveness; musical expression and movement are so tied that the very nature of a gesture is itself part of the message. In effect, we become dancers at the keyboard, creating musical meaning through the movement of our bodies.

AUDIATION

Nothing happens until we move; nothing *worthwhile* happens until we move with musical purpose. This subtly defines and embodies piano technique. Toward this end, good technical training stresses efficiency, consistency, and adaptability as we develop and refine a myriad of potentially useful coordinations aimed at increasing the variety and emotional range of our playing. And despite the many physical differences among players and the complexities of movement required in creating a variegated musical fabric, there are clear principles and necessary skills of healthy movement that can be articulated.

Establishing the habit of audiation – the conceiving of music inside our head *before* performing – is the primary skill of piano technique. The specific musical idea that one mentally projects into the silent recesses of the imagination becomes the trigger for all playing movement. The habit of audiation is as critical for playing rudimentary exercises as it is for performing difficult works of the literature. Attempting any technical movements without this prior musical intention leads to the senseless, numbing training that separates body and mind and, at worst, removes the musical constraints that protect us from debilitating overuse syndromes.

If our being is involved, if our body becomes the primary instrument of musical organization, if we conceive persuasive musical shapes, sing inside, and feel rhythm internally then transmitting this to the piano will have meaning well beyond the display of purely physical skill. Although in practice the goal is to accomplish both the conception of a musical work and the physical expertise, neither will be achieved if musical intention is not established at the outset. It is only when we securely link technical movement to musical purpose that we impart integrity and conviction to our playing both on and away from the concert stage.

COORDINATED MOVEMENT

A coordinated movement is one that meets the intended musical requirements with the least amount of muscular effort. This efficiency is gained through the proper positioning, sequencing, timing, tension, and movement trajectory. While most of this happens subconsciously, a coordinated movement implies and demands certain realities of biomechanics:

- One should take maximal mechanical advantage of the skeletal structures so that the tensile strength of bones, rather than energy-consuming muscle power, carries the brunt of the load.
- Muscles and joints work best in their midranges. Consequently, the workload should be comfortably spread to adjoining units of the playing structure, rather than allowing extreme contractions of any one muscle or muscle group, or extreme extension of the range in any one joint.
- Smaller muscles, adept at speed and repetition, must be protected from overexertion in terms of force, and larger muscles, capable of mass and power, must be protected from overexertion in terms of speed.
- Muscle contractions intended for fast movements of large units should be sudden and greater at the beginning to overcome inertia, and less once momentum has been established. This describes a twitching or throwing type of ballistic activity.
- Agonist and antagonist muscles should be well integrated so that proper degrees of tension or relaxation are operative all along the mechanical line. The moving joint(s) should be as relaxed and 'oiled' as practical. The fixed joint(s) should be tensed no more than necessary to withstand the pressure of the counter forces.
- Pianists control only biomechanical intention, not individual muscles or muscle groups. Said another way, they are only able to command a certain type of finger or arm movement, and must rely on the muscles and joints to respond. After careful practice, pianists project their musical ideas and the body responds to the goal-oriented request, but it takes supreme awareness to monitor this complicated system, and to make the continual, integrative adjustments necessary for optimal functioning.

It is important to remember that because these movements are always carried out with the musical ends in mind, there will be times, when expressing struggle for example, when a certain amount of studied inefficiency is called for.

In a coordinated pianist, movement flows smoothly from the center of the body outward. This center-outward orientation is clearly illustrated by the swimmer who kicks from the hips, not the toes. For pianists, the shoulder girdle complex is the hips of their playing. It is a flexible, yoke-like structure made up of collarbones (clavicles) and shoulder blades (scapulae). Connected to the breastbone in front and designed to float freely over the rib cage in a sea of muscles, the mobility of the shoulder girdle promotes the wonderful range and dexterity of upper arm movement. The first link in the piano-playing chain, it initiates, supports, and controls most of the aiming and playing gestures of the arms. From here, movement radiates outward to the fingertips. Arms thus shape and lead the overall rhythmical flow of the music, as they anticipate and support the intricate and changing needs of the fingers.

It is an all-too-common mistake to isolate and exaggerate finger movement, to lift them unnecessarily high, or to stretch them laterally. When overactive fingers lead, they often confront reluctant arms encased in frozen shoulders. The result is strain, inferior alignments, and weakened playing. In a well-coordinated technique, fingers take their place as the last link in the chain, moving only after the upper arms are pre-positioned and primed to support them. Muscles and joints work cooperatively all along the line. Joints on either side of the one primarily responsible for key descent need to be minimally fixed. Those on the body side provide a stabilizing third-class lever base for the moving joint; those on the keyboard side transmit undiluted force to the keyboard.

INERTIA

The law of inertia, introduced by physicist Sir Isaac Newton, is the tendency of matter to remain at rest, or continue in a fixed direction, unless acted on by an external force. This fundamental law of motion should serve to enlighten pianist that continually moving arm cycles are the ideal. Whereas sudden stops and starts and changes of direction consume energy and tend to disrupt the musical flow, uninterrupted motion lends fluidity and momentum to music making.

Coordinated pianists use curvilinear actions to outline changes in melodic direction and apply pulsating arm cycles to undergird repeated action. Cyclical arm action involves the integrated functioning of loose shoulders, elbows, and wrists, all of which support the hands' and fingers' ability to trace pulsating ellipses at the keyboard. The circles move forward or backward. Straightened fingers slide along and diagonally into the keys on their pads at glancing, oblique angles, releasing without a change of arm direction. One stroke's follow-through imperceptibly becomes the next stroke's preparation. Up to moderate speeds, cyclical arm action is the coordination of choice for sustaining playing activity. It creates fluidity and grace and, where necessary, easy power with admirable control of sonority and pacing.

TWO ARM COORDINATIONS, THREE PLANES OF MOTION

Two primary arm coordinations fill the three-dimensional space between pianists and their instrument:

- The first coordination, described earlier, is a whole-arm, cyclical pattern. It is the archetype for an enormous variety of pulsating gestures of various speeds, elliptical shapes, and directions.

- The second is the washboard stroke, a single-plane, back-and-forth movement, which also varies in size, speed and direction.

These movements take place laterally in a horizontal plane, vertically in the sagittal plane,[1] and forward and backward in the frontal plane.

The two types of arm motion represent opposite extremes of a continuum, each of which shifts imperceptibly towards the other. Visualize making a slow, large, pulling or pushing circle of the entire arm with elbows close to the body and in the frontal plane. If we flatten the top and bottom of the circle and decrease its size as we increase speed, the resulting tiny, pulsating ellipses reach ever closer to straight-line movement. Next, imagine a fast arm-vibrato coordination, like the one used to play fast octaves. Gradually slowing these permits a pianist at some point to merge into cyclical action, thus taking advantage of the upper arm mass and its continuity of motion.

The whole-arm cycle coordination calls for a balanced integration of the entire mechanism, and can circle in either a pulling or pushing direction. The *pulling* whole-arm circle feels like petting a cat. The wrist, elbow, and shoulder joints contribute as upper arms pull, generating pulsating, elliptical passes at the keyboard. Fingers slide diagonally backward to play with falling wrists, which instantly recoil upward to start the forward turn of the arc. This is a relaxed, powerful coordination that generates a wave-like momentum that meshes admirably with the wave-like rhythmic flow of most music. Circle size varies to pace the rhythm and to allow for faster repetitions. Their pulsation speed at the point of key depression is varied to control dynamics. The *pushing* whole-arm cycle coordination turns this same basic motion in the opposite direction. Upper arms slide prepared straightened fingers forward and downward. After a note sounds, the wrists rise to start the turning action and the upper arms relax backward towards the body, pulling the fingers with them. The energy-saving principle of inertia is well served by these continuously moving pulsations.

At the opposite extreme of the continuum is the washboard coordination, which moves forward and back in a straight line. Extending forearms and pushing upper arms propel mostly prepared fingers along a forward diagonal. Arms prepare for a subsequent stroke by withdrawing along the same path. At faster speeds, the straight-line stroke incorporates a thrown, bouncing character, which lessens the energy loss inherent in the sudden changes of direction. Very fast tempos are attained, at least for short periods, by vibrating the forearm in a reduced range, which requires a controlled tightening of the upper arms. At quicker speeds, one should take care that upper arms push forward (a movement related to throwing a punch) not backwards (a movement related to the pulling whole arm circle) during the stroke. The latter is a slower, more cumbersome stroke that often leads to tightening in the shoulders and can be avoided by taking care not to begin a stroke directly above the keyboard, which necessarily causes the upper arms to fall backwards.

Straight lines are rare in nature. Likewise, in piano playing they are unnatural and complex, calling for the synchronized movement of at least two separate

[1]The sagittal plane is parallel to the central plane of the immovable, fibrous joint between the bones of the skull.

joints. For example, the washboard stroke requires both forward movement in the shoulder and downward movement in the elbow before the hands and fingers can traverse a straight path. Further, the law of inertia militates against using sharp changes of direction. A much more natural movement of the playing apparatus is in curvilinear patterns. When arms travel laterally over large distances, they seek to avoid both sharp edges and wasted motion, and curvilinear paths provide for only two spherical vectors between takeoff and landing keys. On the lateral plane, say of a three-octave jump, the hand arches upward before descending. On the frontal plane, the hand moves slightly inward towards the body before returning to the keyboard to find its note. Often, in virtuoso playing, the difference between almost and right on boils down to the paths and planes of motions a player discovers and uses. In any situation, these choices should be consciously made after thoroughly understanding the variables that apply.

Speed demands largely determine the choice of which arm coordination to use. Cycling requires that the upper arms move forward and backward with each stroke, but their mass allows this to happen at only moderate speeds. Taxing shoulder cycles beyond their limit, whether the cycles contain a single note or chord, or multiple linear notes, becomes awkward and burdensome. What had contributed to fluidity and comfort at slower tempi turns to wasteful motion at high speeds. In these instances, the straight-line washboard stroke becomes necessary. Although quicker than a cyclical stroke, it is important to be aware of the increased likelihood of keybedding, the wasteful pressing at the bottom of the key after a tone has sounded, which is a danger unless there is exact timing.[2]

ALIGNMENT

Imagine trying to prevent an intruder from forcibly opening a door. Intuitively, we straighten our arm before pushing back. In so doing, we maximize the skeletal efficiency of the arm by exploiting the tensile strength of its aligned bones set directly against the door. Compare this with attempting to hold the door back with elbow half bent, or with a straightened arm at an oblique angle. Enormous effort would be required to equal the relative steeliness of the straightened arm aimed directly at the opposing force.

The same biomechanical principle follows in piano playing. Take posture as an example. Proper alignment connotes that the skeletal parts of the playing apparatus are so arranged, in relation to themselves and to the keyboard, that they execute pianistic tasks with the least amount of muscular exertion. When we sit with exemplary posture, that is, positioned with an elongated and aligned trunk, neck, and head, we establish a balanced, vertebra-on-vertebra stability for the torso that can be sustained with a minimum degree of muscular contraction of the trunk. Believe it or not, slumping takes more energy than sitting up straight.

This principle can be applied to the finger as well, which, in ideal circumstances, should be positioned as follows to serve as a landing support for a forearm drop:

1. The finger is straightened so that its three bones are firmly in line to take the blow. Small muscles (those in the palm of the hand) hold the extended finger at an approximate right angle to the hand.

---

[2]Please see "Mechanics of the Piano," page 3, for more information on minimizing keybedding.

2. The wrist angle is adjusted vertically, so that the finger points along the trajectory of the descending arm, and lands centered on its tip in the frontal plane. The counterforce directly confronts the tensile strength of the aligned finger bones; the arm lends skeletal support as well.

3. The lateral verticality of the finger is adjusted by rotating the forearm (pronating or supinating), to insure that the finger strikes without tilting to one side or the other. Again the counterforce is directly confronted.

4. The wrist is laterally adjusted (inward towards the thumb or outward towards the fifth fingers) so that the forearm is centered behind the finger in use. Thus the wrist is set further out to support the fourth and fifth fingers. This also serves to align the fingers with the keys they are playing, which is itself an important consideration.

Finger and arm are now positioned to take maximum advantage of the aligned bones moving through an optimal plane of motion. Minimum energy is required to hold it all together. Were the finger more curved, greater muscle contraction would be required to stabilize it. Were the finger not aligned to land centered on its tip in both the vertical and horizontal plane, some of the force would be dissipated, producing a weaker sound. Were the angle of approach faulty, this too would detract from the result.

As faulty positioning and aiming wreaks consistency, weakens the entire playing mechanism, and wastes precious energy, improving alignment is the quickest way to gain strength, speed, and control at the piano. In real life, though, composers rarely give pianists the simple note patterns or the time necessary to set the perfect alignments described above. So while tradeoffs and compromises abound, pianists should be aware of these ideal relationships, deviate from them only when necessary, and return as quickly as possible.

TIMING

Timing can be thought of in two ways. In musical terms it relates to the temporal placing of the notes, and involves such things as tempo, r*ubato, accelerando,* phrase shaping and the like; all critically important for the presentation of musical ideas. In mechanical terms, good timing relates to the optimum sequencing of muscle contractions between the various aligned parts of the mechanism as it approaches the keyboard. Our concern here is the latter.

The grasping touch is a clear example of timing. This combination touch requires the synchronization of descending arms and snapping fingers. Fingertips scoop sharply under just as the forearms enter the keys. If the fingers snap too soon, their only effect is to be out of position for the landing. If they snap too late, they merely scratch the key bottom and have no effect on the sound. When executed successfully, the grasping touch gives the tone more body by increasing the key depression speed. It also provides a quicker release for the arms, allowing them earlier freedom to move on. The coordination depends on a balanced alignment and precise synchronization between the parts.

Timing refers as well to the physical variables relating to a keystroke – its musical time, acceleration, speed, and depth – which are the essence of control. If our key acceleration is late, the energy is not applied to the hammer throw, but wasted at the keybed. If we do not push far or fast enough, the tone is weak and ineffectual. In general, keystrokes should be aimed at the escapement level, where the hammer begins its free flight, which allows for some deceleration before actually reaching the keybed. For instance, in loud playing, pianists make short, quick, vigorous movements at just the right time, and of just the right depth. The piano hammer responds only to the precise time and speed generated just prior to the escapement point.

Although this mechanical truth tells us how to effectively manipulate the instrument, it has little to do with surrounding subjective issues, such as a player's musical conception, his or her choice of coordination, the distance from the key that the stroke began, or the tension in muscles both near and far, before, during, or after the stroke. These are important factors for technique and musicianship, but none answer the question "What does the piano respond to?" and thus are not integral to this discussion. Calculating the precise speed and timing of a key depression, and aligning and coordinating the mechanism with itself and with the keyboard, eventually become unconsciously wired to pianists' inner and outer hearing. Ultimately, the ear and the body become the master controllers, determining the effectiveness and efficiency of output at the instrument.

SPEED

There are both mental and physical components to the ability to play fast. And though spoken about separately, they in fact cannot be separated; for the mental preparation for speed is every bit as important as preparation on the physical side. Mentally, pianists learn to incorporate larger numbers of notes into a single thought unit. The physical training parallels this in striving to incorporate a greater numbers of notes within a single physical impulse. A reasonable metaphor of the process can be found in the gearbox of an automobile. Thinking in slow tempo with small units is like driving in low gear – the motor revs noisily with each slow turn of the wheels, but there is great potential for power. In high gear, the motor purrs along with relative quiet; the wheels go much faster, but there is little potential for power.

Mentally changing gears is, at times, all pianists need to accomplish greater speeds. Consider for a moment the common experience of increasing speed simply by shifting ones thinking from $\frac{4}{4}$ to $\frac{2}{2}$ time, or counting a fast $\frac{3}{4}$ scherzo in one, rather than three. Not only do these faster tempos become possible, it feels as if the music is imposing them upon us. Fewer wider-spaced beats in a given musical space make faster tempos possible. Closely spaced beats, akin to driving in low gear, make slower tempos inevitable.

The primary physical adjustment the body makes for speed is to eliminate excess motion, drastically reducing movement range in all the joints affecting key depression. Fingertips stay close to the keys with almost no movement through the air. Alignments must be optimal, for there is little room for error. Loudness, as a relative term, has special meaning in fast playing. The playing is contrasted and shaped, but it takes place at a reduced tonal level at the quieter end of the dynamic scale. There is an apparent contradiction when thinking about speed and dynamics which may become a source of confusion: in fast playing the keys go down in quicker succession one to another, but each separate key depression is itself slower and therefore softer.

TENSION

In coordinated joint movement, the opposing muscle groups of a joint cooperate automatically, with one releasing as the other contracts. Tension arises when the opposing groups contract simultaneously. Provided this tension is consciously controlled, it is not a bad thing. For example, an optimal amount of tension is necessary for stabilizing joints on either side of a primary working joint and a great deal is needed for speedy repetitions. But often pianists use tension in the wrong places, to the wrong degree, and at the wrong times. Only the smallest amount of tension should be applied to any moving joint, and none at all in far away places that have nothing to do with the playing mechanism, like the neck, shoulders and mouth. To avoid the many problems that excess and misdirected tension can create, pianists need to develop an awareness meter that gauges the amount and location of joint tension. This will give students a baseline for calculating just how much tension is needed to accomplish a given task and allow for the myriad of subtle adjustments required for beautiful piano playing.

Fortunately, this awareness meter, and the accompanying knowledge, can be consciously learned. Begin by sensing how a relaxed muscle feels, which is sometimes made easier by tensing as much as possible before letting it go. Once limpness is attained, a student might experience the amount of tension it takes to make the softest sounds at the instrument. Playing a slow, contrary chromatic scale centered on middle D works well in gaining this familiarity.[3] In general, students overtighten their shoulders and fingers, interfering with free movement in the active joints and reducing sensitivity to the weight and arrangement of the keys. These exercises will be particularly beneficial for those students who are oblivious to the fact that they are habitually in a state of excessive tension.

Once students have learned to recognize tension, they must learn how and where to apply it. For example, pianists set both their upper and lower arms to support an efficient articulation in the wrist in the woodpecker hand-bounce coordination. Knuckles and finger joints below the wrist are also tightened, assuring that the hands' power is transmitted to the keyboard. A slow, loose, waving action allows for alternating contractions in the forearm. When the hands play louder or faster, increased stabilizing tension is needed to counteract the heightened counter-forces. Ideally, all joints are minimally stabilized to meet the changing requirements of the moment except for the moving wrist, which is responsible for key activation. To further insure a freely swinging wrist, the fingers must be stabilized with the small muscles in the hand. Otherwise, the tendons moving through the wrist that connect them to their longer muscles in the forearm will tense and interfere with free wrist movement.

Increased tension in a stabilizing limb also supports an increase in the repetition speed of the joint just below it. Tightening the forearm allows the hand to repeat faster, moving towards a vibrating hand. In vibrating action, the flexing muscles are used intermittently while the extending muscles remain tight and the hand springs back whenever it stops flexing. We no longer have an alternating coordination, but rather a staccato springing action. Additional forearm tightening allows speedier repetitions and a reduced range of motion. At maximum speed, the hand trembles and finally stops.

Occasionally agonist muscles are forced to fight the pull of antagonist mus-

---

[3]"Orienting to the Keyboard: Middle D" explains more fully the pedagogy of centering on middle D.

cles, causing stiffening in a joint when the opposite is called for and inadvertently opposing what another part is trying to accomplish. Called isometrics in bodybuilding, this is a legitimate way to build muscles. But if the immediate goal is the efficient movement of a joint in one direction or another, in order to locate, lower, or raise a key, then these muscle groups must cooperate and work alternatively. If not, there is serious loss of control and energy.

The application of tension is not universal. It varies from one joint to another, even when several participate in the same task, and when improperly placed, it affects tone quality and plays havoc with endurance. Players must eschew misplaced muscular contractions (a common one is tightening of the mouth when trying to play loud or fast) and avoid using correctly targeted contractions that are greater than needed. Pianists should monitor misplaced tension as assiduously as they check for wrong notes, wrong rhythms, or wrong dynamics. And with practice, one's ears will ultimately become centrally wired to tension awareness, and control its application.

LEGATO

The art of piano playing presupposes an unwritten contract, a theatrical convention so to speak, between the audience and the performer; one where listeners unconsciously supply that which they would like to hear and filter it through their musical understanding. Performers do much the same thing, but in the opposite direction. Listening becomes an active and selective process that tunes out irrelevant noises like creaking chairs or coughs, and provides that which is missing – the sustaining of long notes no longer sounding, crescendos on diminishing held notes, the illusion of smooth connection in slow melodic passages – all something quite beyond the mechanical capabilities of the instrument. Nowhere does a listener give a pianist a greater benefit of the doubt than in *legato* playing.

Much of the awkwardness of fingering, arm shifting, and disadvantageous alignments that have come down to us through our traditions can be traced to attempts to physically connect one finger to another, as though musical logic depended on uninterrupted touch. When in fact, each piano sound diminishes at a preset rate, and even physically connected pitches are not really *legato* in the same way that a violinist's bow or wind player's breath creates an unbroken sound source within which pitches change. In addition, the pedal is a truly unique wild card. It connects tones beyond the fingers' reach, supplies sympathetic resonance, and allows the indefinite accumulation of differing pitches.

That is not to say that the control of non-pedaled sonorities, from an overlapping *legato* to a highly articulated finger *staccato,* is not a useful and necessary skill. It is. Finger pedaling, the conscious overlapping of notes with held fingers, greatly enriches non-pedaled sound. A highly articulated *leggiero* communicates its own lightness of mood. All variety of touches and textures, along with tempo, create the possibility for wonderful contrasts within non-pedaled sound and, even more strikingly, between non-pedaled sonority and a multitude of pedaled sonorities. But here we are dealing more with quality of sound, that is, with the packaging of musical substance, not with musical coherence itself.

Technically speaking, it is better for pianists to approach their craft with a certain ease, grace, and detachment than to distort musical values in a futile attempt to physically connect keys. Keybedding, finger substitutions, awkward fingering, and contorted stretching in the service of *legato* are all likely to be counterproductive, resulting in stilted, jerky playing. Well placed articulations, that is, breaks in the continuity of sound, can help to define and enhance musical meaning, after all, the smooth *legato* ideal of much of the music of the Romantic period is accomplished largely with the aid of the pedal, and careful control of rhythm and voicing.

The illusion of *legato* is created in many ways. Listeners hear legato when the tones make musical sense, when they are rhythmically and tonally coherent, when phrases are carefully contoured, and when a player's discreet smaller gestures are subsumed within the smooth movement of a larger entity, like tasteful swaying. They hear melody when it is separated dynamically from carefully molded, softer, or differently textured accompanying patterns. Audiences respond as well to body language: if a pianist moves gracefully, the music is apt to be heard as being full of grace. Musical coherence and intelligibility, a flowing rhythm, sensible (and sensitive) note groupings, and well-shaped phrases also have more to do with an audience's perception of legato than the nature of the pianist's finger connections. Physically connected tones that do not make musical sense are simply not heard as legato. Musically realized expectancy is the true underpinning of the *legato* illusion.

Musically realized expectancy is the true underpinning of the legato illusion.

HABIT FORMATION

Practicing involves the conscious development of new habits. Unlike the flashy insights that our intellects can sometimes achieve, kinesthetic learning – learning within the body – is slow and plodding. There are no wondrous short cuts as mind and body toil together; the essence of the process is the sheer repetition of physical actions. Conscious habit formation requires thoughtful, disciplined application paced over an extended period. We are dealing with skill learning that changes the body, permanently. Like learning to walk or ride a bike, new neural patterns of balance and control are developed and internalized. We become fundamentally changed, with more subtle and effective mental control of a wider range of pianistic skills.

We begin the process of learning a new skill with slow, exaggerated movements. Then gradually, with inner awareness and carefully monitored feedback, the movements become smaller and quicker. The journey progresses from slow deliberate repetitions of new, self-conscious, carefully controlled actions to quicker, more goal-oriented, automatic actions. Ultimately, we can perform a new coordination or particular skill task with a minimum of mental effort. (The double-edged sword of this process is that if the body repeats a bad habit, it too will become automatic. Thoughtful monitoring is absolutely essential because breaking a bad habit is harder work than establishing the right one at the beginning.) During the process we *purposely* render the conscious unconscious and discard the unnecessary. This is the essence of habit formation.

We gain experience in learning the most productive ways to pace ourselves; we discover the optimum number of repetitions at slow speeds, when and how much to quicken the pace. In effect we learn how best to program our mental computer so we can finally push one button and a whole series of sure-footed, goal-oriented actions result. The repetitions create new neural pathways that become more firmly established, as though inscribing a deepening groove in our skulls – grooving, as students may come to designate this exciting developmental process that is at the very core of our growth as pianists.

PEDAL

The pedal, or more specifically the damper pedal – the only pedal that requires dexterity and subtlety, and the only one where proper technique is an issue – is often delineated in aesthetic or mechanical terms, but receives little attention in terms of the biomechanical principles that govern proper foot action. In an effort to resolve those omissions, an outline of the fundamental positions follows:

- The right foot is placed far enough forward on the damper pedal so that the ball of the foot, not the toes, takes the reverse pressure.
- The heel remains hinged to the floor.
- Engaging the quadriceps, the foot feels as though it is sliding forward as it depresses the pedal, an outward (extending) movement of the leg. Backward friction is to be avoided, as this brings the hamstring into play and interferes with freedom and speed.

And the fundamental coordination:

- The pedal stroke originates in the hips; it moves through the knee to the ankle, the last joint involved.
- It is useful to try this with the leg outstretched to the right of the pedal to experience leg freedom and the potential for a relaxed *vibrato* movement. Pianists need this speed and control of a tiny range of movement to master the subtleties of advanced pedaling.
- They should sit far enough forward on the bench so their leg action is not hindered.

The primary pedal coordination is the *legato* pedal, which seeks smooth clear connections of separate, distinct sonorities. Comprised of two strokes, the downward motion is a more relaxed phase of the cycle, while it is the rapid and precise upward release motion that produces the clean transition from one sonority to the next. This critical upward motion of the foot must coincide exactly with the downward movement of the fingers. A contrary activity, it sometimes proves difficult to master. Many students try to depress the pedal at the same time as they depress the fingers, causing a gap between sonorities or, just as often, muddied exchanges. The coordination between hand and foot should be practiced away from a musical context, until the contrary action is well established. In preparatory foot practice, the students should release the pedal so quickly and vigorously (lifting the foot high) that they hear the thud of the dropping dampers, a thud that will ultimately match the new downward movement of the finger. This tires the shin muscles, but it also alerts students to the need for sharp, precise, upward pedal motions.

Each piano's pedal has an engagement point that marks the exact spot when the dampers actually leave and return to the strings. When pedaling fast, there is no time to traverse the free play area on either side of the engagement point. The ear discovers this exact level. It constantly monitors what the foot does, checking that the exchanges are smooth and clean, or blurred to the extent intended, or clearly spaced, and all without mechanical noises such as the thud of the returning dampers or the noise of the foot on the pedal surface. With experience, this process becomes automatic and unconscious as the player's whole body responds directly to the inner musical thought.

The pedal is central to our whole concept of piano sonority, an absolutely unique attribute of the instrument. Understanding how machine and player can biomechanically integrate will open up all the artistic pedaling that ear and imagination can create.

TAKING THE INITIATIVE TO LOOK FURTHER

This chapter has dealt with how the pianist's body moves when it plays the piano efficiently; said more formally, the biomechanics of healthy piano playing. Descriptive in nature, it introduced important concepts, variables, and frames of reference that help to describe precisely the motions made by pianists. Concepts like audiation, alignment, and timing allow for a more sophisticated understanding of what really goes on when we play the piano and, more importantly, for an improved aural result.

What it is not is pedagogic. To truly realize the benefits of these ideas, concepts, and coordinations it is important to find concrete ways to systematically develop and apply them to our own playing and teaching. Several chapters in this text address these issues, as does the book and video *Mastering Piano Technique.*[4] As teacher or performer or both, seeking an in-depth understanding of all the physical elements that affect piano playing is beneficial for all involved parties; for the greater the number of tools you have, the better equipped you will be to communicate your musical message. And that is, after all, the golden ring we all pursue.

[4]Seymour Fink, *Mastering Piano Technique* (Portland, Oregon: Amadeus Press, 1994).

The Pianist's Physiology

Jacqueline Csurgai-Schmitt

A pianist does not need a health practicioner's knowledge of bones and muscles in order to play the piano. On the other hand, a total lack of biomechanical information, can allow many maladaptive movements to slip into our own or our student's playing that can cause problems later on. A middle ground can be found in learning rudimentary musculoskeletal information, valuable in understanding the basic mechanical principles of movement.

Since the muscles of the body involved in piano playing function in a complex combination of contractions and interact, for the most part, in a coordinated manner beyond our conscious control, there are only a few muscles which merit our individual attention.[1]

THE LONG AND SHORT FINGER FLEXORS, THE FINGER EXTENSORS, AND THE SMALL FINGER MUSCLES OF THE HAND

To understand the placement and function of these muscles, it is important to first become familiar with the bones and joints of the hand:

Bones of the hand

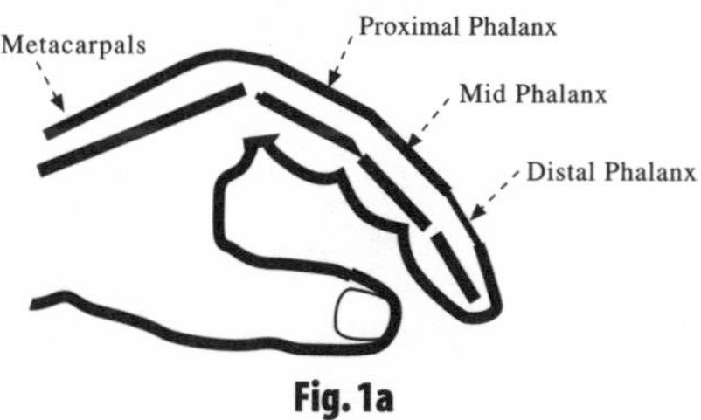

Fig. 1a

[1]Otto Ortmann, *The Physiological Mechanics of Piano Technique* (New York: E.P. Dutton & Co., Inc., 1962) 47.

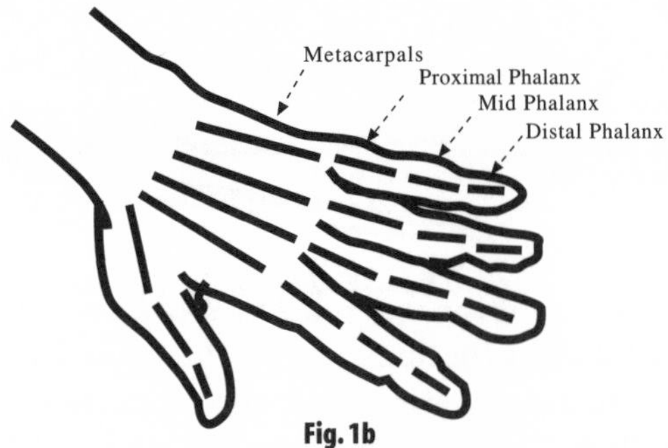

Fig. 1b

Joints of the hand

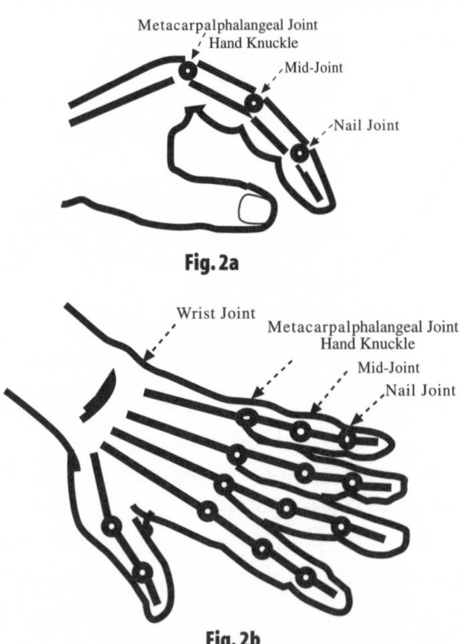

Fig. 2a

Fig. 2b

The long flexors originate in the forearm near the elbow, on the bottom *(ventral)* side of the arm. They cross the wrist joint, the hand knuckles *(metacarpalphalangeal* or MCP joints), the first *(proximal),* second (mid), and third (nail) joints of the fingers. These then insert into the furthest *(distal)* finger bone *(phalanx)* (fig. 3). The long flexor's function is to curve the tip of the finger in toward the palm.

Long flexors

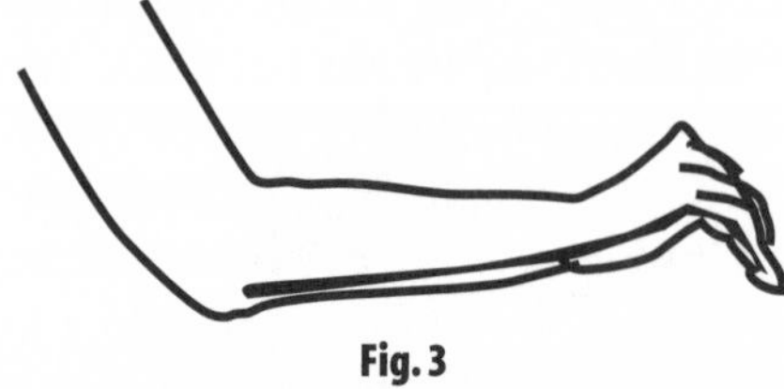

Fig. 3

The short flexors, originating in the back (*posterior*) of the upper arm (*humerus*), cross the elbow joint, the wrist joint, the MCP joint, the mid joint of the fingers, and insert into the mid phalanx (fig. 4). Causing flexion at the mid joint, they draw the middle bone of the finger back toward the hand. When the short flexor is used alone and the fingertip is placed against resistance, breaking-in of the nail joint will occur.

Short flexors

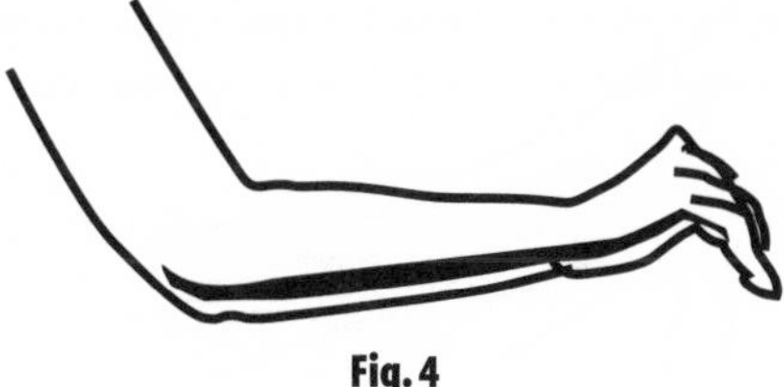

Fig. 4

These downward-moving (flexing) muscles are opposed on the upper (*dorsal*) side of the arm by the finger extensors, which also originate in the humerus of the upper arm near the elbow. They cross the elbow, the wrist, and the MCP joints and insert into a tendinous expansion in the fingers known as the *extensor hood* (fig. 5). Their action lifts and extends the fingers.

Finger extensors

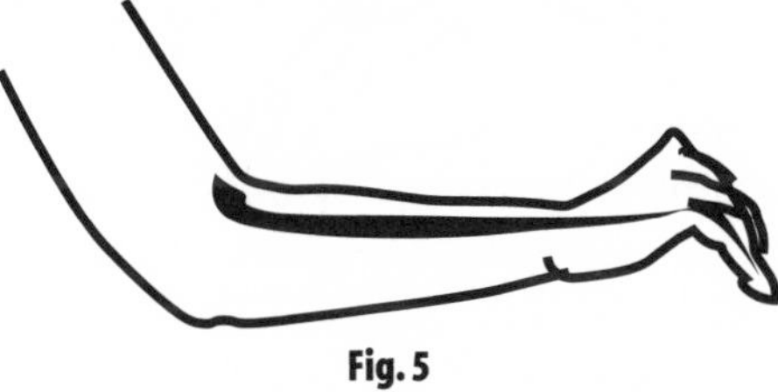

Fig. 5

The long finger flexors and extensors are powerful muscles and support all work requiring great strength. They have excellent endurance when holding a continuous contraction, such as gripping a heavy object with the hands. (We carry a suitcase, for example, by gripping the handle with our finger flexors.) At the piano, these muscles can easily sustain the continuous contractions required by chords and octaves, provided the contractions are not excessive and the finger movement is restricted to selecting the notes of the chord pattern or octave. They also act as supporting muscles for single-note melodies produced by arm movement, weight release, or muscular exertion. The degree of contraction of these muscles is partially under the control of the pianist, and, as with all muscles, excessive contraction will limit endurance.[2]

The small finger muscles, the *lumbricals* and *interossei*, originate in the base of the hand and insert not only in the proximal phalanx of the finger, but also in the extensor expansion (fig. 6). Thus, they cause flexion in the proximal phalanx, and extension in the mid and distal phalanges. Unlike the finger flexors and extensors, these muscles do not cross the wrist and are consequently most ideally suited for the rapid flexion of the finger required by fast tempi. While this shortness can produce the fastest speeds, this same quality limits their ability to produce a big sound. The greater the volume required, the more need there is to add long finger flexors to the movement. However, as these long muscles are added to the movement, the tempo must and will slow down. Attempting to play very fast while using these long muscles will eventually cause a build-up of tension, eventually decreasing the speed of movement.

---

[2]Ibid., 56.

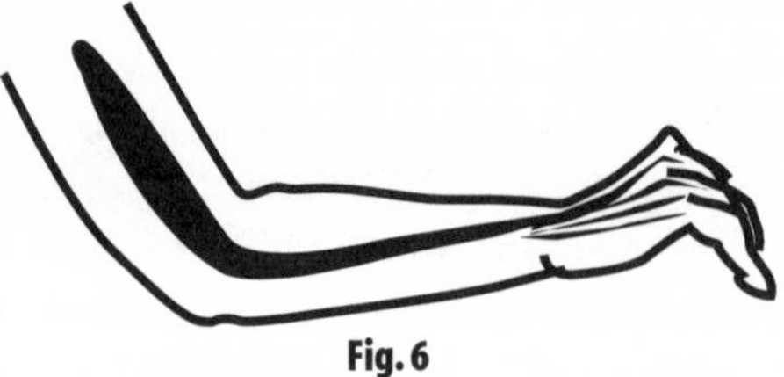

Fig. 6

MUSCLE ACTIVITY IN PIANO PLAYING

Movement is created in a joint when one muscle (the *agonist*) contracts and the opposing muscle (the *antagonist*) relaxes. If a finger flexor contracts to depress a key, the extensor muscles must relax in a controlled manner. To release the key, the extensor must contract while the flexor relaxes.

These opposing muscle contractions are made much more complicated by the need to play two consecutive notes, a necessary requirement of piano playing. As one finger is extending to lift a finger from the keybed, an adjacent finger is flexing to play the next note. This opposing muscular activity can cause a great deal of tension in the fingers and arms, due not only to the length of these long muscles that originates in the arm, but to the tendinous connections between them in the hand. The long finger flexors function more easily when allowed to contract simultaneously in strong, powerful movements rather than operating individually. Even though the second finger (the index finger) has its own sheath allowing for more freedom of individual movement, there remains a strong tendency to operate with the other fingers.

This can easily be demonstrated by pressing down against the hard surface of a table with the second finger. The action produces a tendency for simultaneous contraction in the remaining fingers; they want to move in the same direction. Contraction of the extensors is necessary to keep the other fingers from pressing also into the table.

You can see that the extensors must contract to keep non-active fingers from playing when using the long finger flexors for key depression. This explains why it seems so difficult to individualize the movement of the fingers. When using these muscles, it is advantageous to keep the fingers from lifting too high above the surface of the keys (a tendency of inexperienced players). As speed increases, the fingers must make smaller and smaller movements until the finger movement is limited to the depth of the key. The inclination to lift the fingers can be counteracted by practicing with the non-playing fingers touching the surface of the keys.[3]

These alternating contractions of flexors and extensors can produce a wide dynamic range and are excellent for controlling key descent. They are also ideal for carrying weight at slow to medium speeds. Because they are so powerful, children will intuitively use these muscles when they play. However, these muscles are not ideally suited for rapid up-and-down movement of the fingers. If one strives to continue these alternating contractions as tempos increase (especially if the finger is traveling through a wide arc) the contractions will begin to overlap as the alternating muscles are unable to release the preceding contractions quickly enough.[4] Eventually, the speed of finger repetition slows as the overloaded muscles contract more slowly, and pain, usually in the forearm, causes the pianist to cease the effort.

[3]For more information, see The Learning Process from the chapter, "A Child's First Lessons."

[4]Ortmann, *The Physiological Mechanics of Piano Technique*, 56.

Fatigue of the muscles occurs more quickly when one attempts to play both loud and fast for an extended length of time, an action that, although necessary in piano music, should be limited as much as possible, allowing the muscles time to recover.[5] Rather than overworking the long flexors, the pianist can often simulate loudness by playing only some of the notes in a passage with force.

When virtuoso speed becomes a necessity, we must shift to a coordination involving the smaller, weaker muscles of the hand: the lumbicales and interossei. Because they are muscles, they can and will develop with use, thus making their use in extended, fast passages indispensable. Unfortunately, though, it is here that problems can arise, for the need to change muscular coordinations is not always obvious, and the pianist does not necessarily stumble upon the proper coordination: flexion of the small muscles in conjunction with muscular support in the hand and arm (the base). For while the small muscles can move the finger through the air very rapidly, they need the support of the hand and arm when they encounter any resistance, such as the piano key.[6]

THE ALIGNMENT OF SKELETAL BONES

Borrowing from the field of mechanics, we learn that positioning the distal finger bone perpendicular to a piano key and then stacking the mid and proximal finger bones in a straight line above it is the strongest and most efficient skeletal alignment (fig. 7a).[7] Although we rarely use this position to play the piano, we know that the more vertical the bones are to the keyboard, the stronger the position for volume and endurance. As we bring the hand into a normal playing position by increasing the angle in the mid and MCP joints, we can preserve the inherent strengths of the vertical position by maintaining the distal bone's perpendicular relationship to the key (fig. 7b). When we slowly open the nail joint, resulting in a distal joint less-than-perpendicular to the key, we increase the need for support through muscular contraction of the long flexor (fig. 7c).

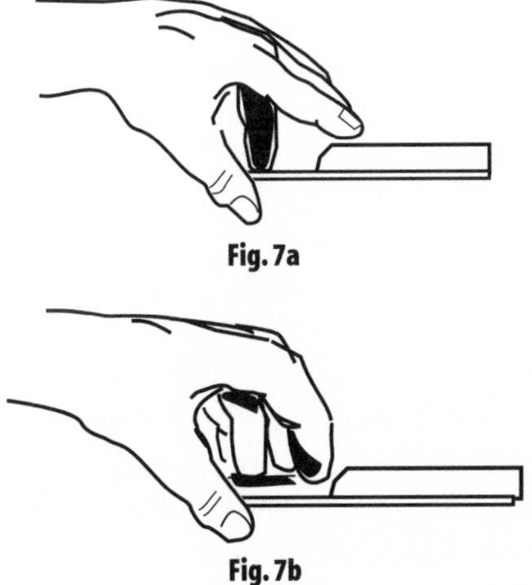

Perpendicular to key

Fig. 7a

Vertical nail joint

Fig. 7b

[5]Ibid., 57.

[6]This coordination and the pedagogy involved in using it are discussed at length in the chapter, "A Fundamental of Movement."

[7]Otto Ortmann, *The Physiological Mechanics of Piano Technique*, 217.

Angled

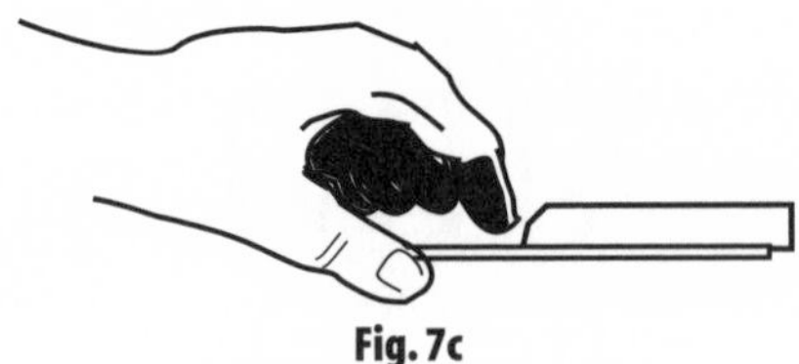

Fig. 7c

Ultimately, finger position should depend upon the musical context, the dynamics, and the articulation required by the music. It should be chosen not only for physical endurance and comfort, but also for pianistic color and expression.

By maintaining the same degree of curvature in each finger, which will place the longer fingers in toward the fallboard and the thumb and fifth fingers further out of the black keys, we help neutralize the difference in finger length and thus aid the small finger muscles in their work of key depression.

As with any simple machine, there is a trade-off here between force and speed. While the arrangement of perpendicular fingertip with a curved finger is strong structurally (because the end of the finger is close to the hand knuckle, which becomes the fulcrum), it cannot move with as much speed as the straight or 'flat' finger. The flat finger moves with less tension and the already mentioned speed, but it is comparatively weaker and therefore fatigues more easily.[8] Also, because of the skeletal structure of the joints, flat fingers spread more easily allowing more natural lateral movement around the keyboard. With this in mind, we see the two most critical limitations of an insistence on a curved hand position:

1. It decreases the lateral movement of the fingers.
2. Presetting the hand with curved fingers tends to create tension, even before any key depression has taken place.

From the above discussion, it would seem that there is no one, ideal hand position for all piano playing. Nevertheless, we can easily discover a reasonable working position from which to start:

> Allow the hand to hang by the side of the body. The fingers fall naturally in a semi-curved position – neither flat nor curved. Bring this position to the keyboard and notice how open and relaxed the fingers feel. Now curve the fingers. Notice the difference in feel.

Ultimately, finger position should depend upon the musical context, the dynamics, and the articulation required by the music. It should be chosen not only for physical endurance and comfort, but also for pianistic color and expression. Therefore, the pianist should be familiar with several positions of hand and fingers, and their respective effects on the color of the tone produced. By careful listening and awareness of the feeling associated with each position, the pianist adds to the diversity of his or her artistic expression.

LATERAL ALIGNMENT

Commonly accepted in piano pedagogy is the need to keep the hand in as straight a line as possible relative to the arm (fig. 8a), as opposed to turning the hand into *ulnar deviation* (a 45-degree angle to the line of the forearm) (fig. 8b).

[8]Ibid., 222.

Straight line with forearm

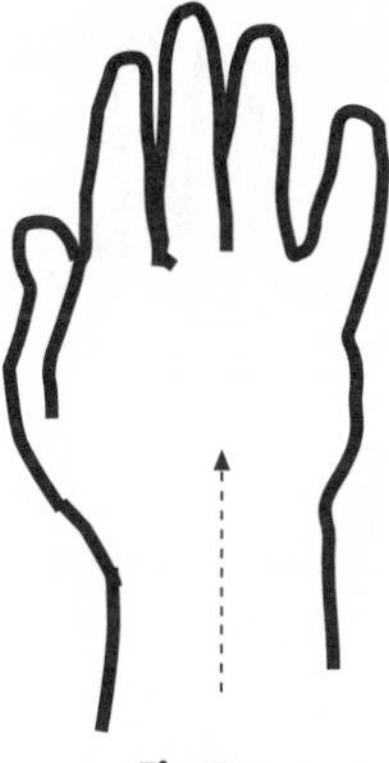

Fig. 8a

Ulnar deviation

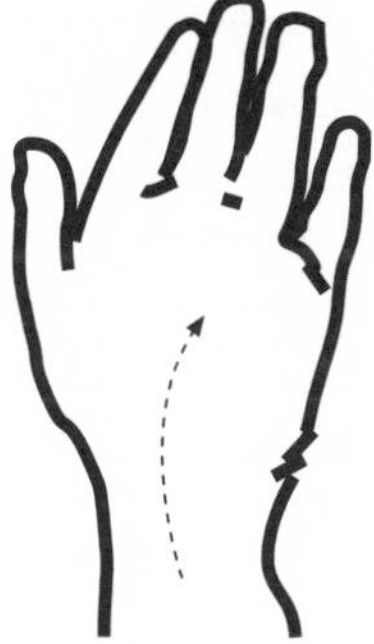

Fig. 8b

This is based primarily on physiological requirements, as a straight line of the skeleton allows the muscles and tendons to pull in a straight line, a more efficient movement that promotes endurance. However, because this straight-line position places the hand not in the center of its range of motion, but at one end of the range of motion it would seem to fly in the face of medical and pedagogical teaching from the mid-twentieth century that instructed you to use the hand in the middle range of its motion.[9] This injunction came about because the extreme ends of the range of motion can only be attained through muscular contractions that actually limit movement, making them less efficient. We are not considering these extreme ends here.

The mechanical fact of joints being stronger and muscles more efficient at one end of their range of motion is also applicable to other joints, such as the shoulder. While the shoulder is capable of moving far forward to increase the reach of the arms, its strongest and most stable position is with the shoulders back, near the end of their backward movement. (Again, this is not the *extreme* end reached through muscular contraction.)

The fingers are no exception to this rule. Placing the bones of the fingers in a straight line with their corresponding metacarpal bones (fig. 9a) allows the muscles to pull in a straight line as well, thus reducing the amount of work they must do for key depression. (Note that the fingers are now at one end of their lateral range of motion.)

---

[9]Ibid., 31.

Short flexors

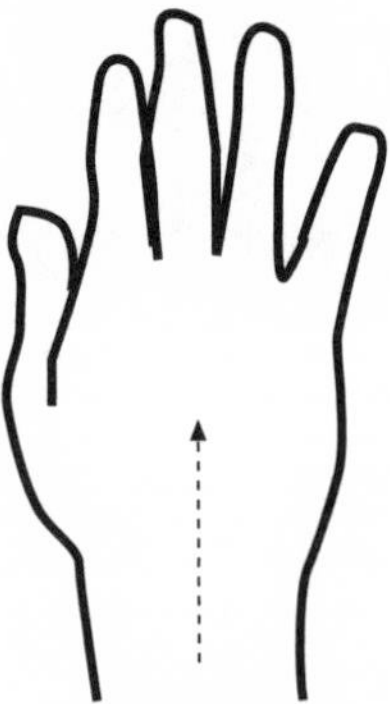

Fig. 9a

Fig. 9b

PROBLEMS RESULTING FROM INEFFICIENT ALIGNMENT

The ability of our fingers and thumbs to oppose each other and grasp objects is indispensable to daily life. And while we are all certainly happy to be able to pick up a pen, sandwich, or our most recent piano solo, the musculature that makes this possible can create many obstacles to our efficient functioning at the keyboard.

Anterior (palmar view) opponens digiti minimi

Fig. 10a

Anterior opponens pollicis

Fig. 10b

When the *opponens pollicis* in the thumb (fig. 10b) and the *opponens digiti minimi* in the fifth finger (fig. 10a) contract, they pull the fifth-finger hand knuckle (along with all of the fingers) toward the thumb. This rotation not only pulls the hand knuckles out of their ideal horizontal line in relation to the keyboard, it places the fingers (especially the fourth and fifth fingers) in an oblique position to the keys (fig. 11a). In this position, the finger does not flex off the hand knuckle easily. Consequently, key depression is accomplished by either increasing finger rotation (fig. 11b) or by contraction of the opponens digiti minimi muscle, which moves the entire MCP joint during key descent (rather than just the finger) (fig. 11c).

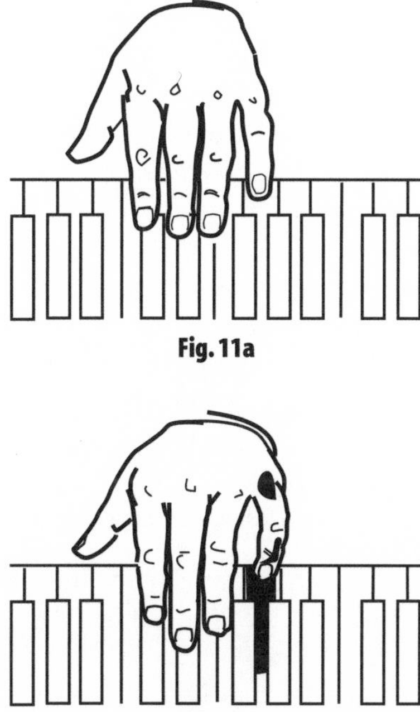

Fig. 11a

Fig. 11b

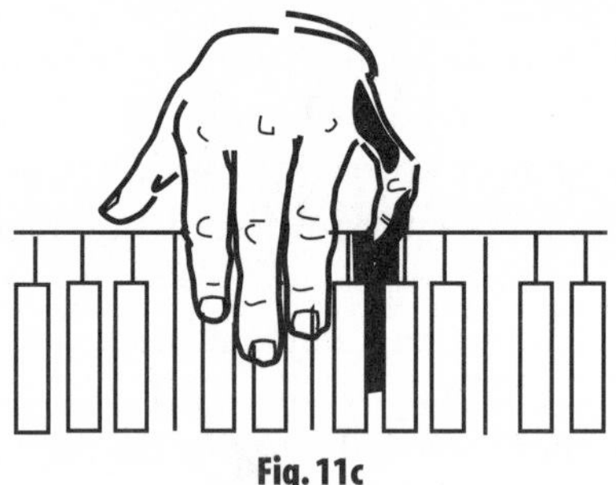

Fig. 11c

Much of the subjective feeling that the fifth finger is difficult to move is actually the result of moving the entire MCP joint during key depression. Needless to say, movement of the whole joint (as opposed to the finger off the joint) will slow down a rapid passage considerably. This contraction of the opponens pollicis also pulls the second joint of the thumb toward the palm, increasing the tension on that side of the hand. If the pianist tries to play octaves and chords with contractions of the opponens muscles collapsing the thumb and fifth-finger joints toward each other, injuries can easily result.

Another anatomically incorrect position that can result in injury is the tendency to move the fifth finger with the large muscles on the outside of the hand rather than locating the small-finger muscles that will flex the finger without moving the whole bridge. Young students, in particular, will find this movement easier, and may even feel that it will extend their reach. Ironically, rotation of the fifth finger actually decreases its lateral reach.

This mal-alignment of fourth and fifth fingers furthers the chances of muscle overload because it will not support the force of the arm. Since it is an inherently weaker position, any pressure from the arm can eventually bow the fingers outward. Strong skeletal support of the arm with bow-shaped fingers becomes impossible, and permanent physical damage to muscles, ligaments and tendons may result. Picture, if you will, walking on the side of your ankles for any length of time, and you can easily imagine the damage that can occur from lack of skeletal support. Playing the piano while allowing the hand knuckle and thumb mid-joint to be pulled in toward the palm can create serious physical dysfunction over the long haul.

For anatomically efficient movement, the bottom of the hand knuckles can be thought of as a bridge that should remain relatively horizontal to the keyboard. If the flexion of the finger off this bridge takes place by contraction of the small finger muscles, this movement will allow the joint to remain stable. The following exercise will help isolate these muscles, and illustrate their independence:

- Place the closed fingers of the left hand on the palm of the right hand behind the knuckles (not under them), in the natural crease.
- Use the left hand fingers to keep the joints of the right hand level.
- Move the fingers off the hand knuckles, noticing how easily they move when the joints are not allowed to move.
- Apply these finger movements to the keyboard, noticing how easily the fingers move the keys when the hand knuckles have been stabilized.

If a pianist has been playing a long time with the hand knuckle moving in conjunction with the fifth finger, he or she will feel the tendency on the outside of the hand for the joint to move down with the fifth finger. Do not allow this to happen. Relax the muscles causing the downward movement and hold the bridge with the left hand fingers until this tendency disappears. Do not bend the thumb at the nail-joint. Flexion to move the thumb under the hand may take place at the mid-joint, but the last two phalanges of the thumb will move more efficiently if they are in a straight line, not curved. By curving the thumb, the pianist shortens its length to no advantage. In addition, the curved thumb retains unnecessary tension.

When the fingers are used to support the larger playing unit of the arm, such as in octaves, there must be contractions in:

- The small finger muscles of the fifth finger to flex the finger in the hand knuckle
- The flexor pollicis brevis to flex only the mid joint of the thumb
- The long finger flexor of the fifth finger and the flexor pollicis longus of the thumb to support the movement of the arm into the keys

As the fingers reach the keys and flexion takes place in the MCP joint of the fifth finger and the mid-joint of the thumb, these joints will move upward and outward as the force is transmitted along the skeleton from the arm to the key.

In order to place the fingers in a position most likely to aid in vertical movement, we also need to examine the placement of the fingers on the keyboard by the forearm, whose position is controlled by the upper arm. Theories on placement of the forearm abound, with many pianists advocating a position that places the elbows next to the body. Practical experimentation will show you that, if the elbow is allowed to hang by the side of the body, even excessive pronation (inward rotation) of the forearm is incapable of allowing the fingers to flex in a straight line to the keys. In order for the forearm to place the fingers in even a somewhat vertical position, the upper arm must be abducted (moved away) from the body approximately 20 degrees. Far from causing unnecessary muscular contractions, this position is the most efficient and coordinated, as piano playing demands that the shoulder muscles support that weight of the arm as it moves around the keyboard.[10] (When the arm moves outward, take care that the shoulders remain down.[11])

Much of our everyday movement, such as opening doors and turning keys and screwdrivers, strengthens supination (outward rotation) of the fingers on their individual axes. Consequently, their normal muscle tone will still cause the bones of the finger to roll outward if they are relaxed upon the keys, even with slight abduction in the shoulder joint. However, as the arm moves into the keys and the small finger muscles contract to support the movement, the finger will straighten, because, when these muscles flex, they will pull the fingers into a straight line. This muscular action also causes the hand knuckle to move up and

[10]Ibid., 41.

[11]See also the chapter, "A Child's First Lessons," for more information on lifting the forearm to the keys.

the mid joint of the thumb to move outward, creating a strong skeletal position for transmitting force to the key in the most efficient, muscular way.[12]

Eventually, the development of muscle tone in the small finger muscles will hold the hand knuckles on a level plane (without external support), and the tendency for the fourth and fifth-finger joints to move up and down during piano playing will cease. Surprisingly, it takes only a few weeks for the fingers and hand muscles to learn this new coordination. If the piano teacher takes the time to teach this coordinated and efficient movement, the student's playing career should not be troubled by pain, dysfunction, and limited technical ability.

[12]See the section Rotation of the Fingers in, "A Child's First Lessons," for more information.

The Technical

Fingering: The Key to Arming

Seymour Fink

Pianists approach the keyboard (and the entire process of music making) in highly personal ways, in large part because their playing mechanisms differ vastly in size, shape, and in the playing coordinations they employ. Despite this, there are general principles of good fingering that can be articulated; principles that will enhance practice efficiency and promote authentic, consistent performances. All are judged by their ability to contribute to successful music making and to enhance both mental and physical ease and efficiency. Fingering that promotes musical effectiveness in performance is good fingering. Fingering that detracts from the musical possibilities is inferior fingering. More specifically, pianists should finger the expressive patterns of the music, not the black-white configuration of the keyboard.

FINGERING AND THE ARM

Pianists must be aware that the fingers are not isolated units, but rather, integrally connected parts of a larger playing mechanism that begins at least as far back as the shoulder girdle. The movement of the entire apparatus is so crucial a dynamic in projecting musically intelligent and technically competent performances its freedom becomes a top priority. And because the choice of fingering limits and controls the ways in which the arms can move to support the shaping of musical phrases, it is important to finger so that the arms can most naturally and consistently mould, in performance, the requisite musical shapes.

Take an obvious example: In the tune *Mary Had a Little Lamb* in C major, fingering the first seven notes in the right hand (beginning on E) with 3 2 1 2 3 3 3 allows the arm to move in a comfortable, distinctive pattern. Common sense tells us that when transposing the same motive to D-flat major, one would employ the same finger pattern so that the arm could move similarly. It would be a mistake to try to use D-flat major fingering, 1 3 2 3 1 1 1 on these seven notes, because of the difficulty of making both versions look and sound alike. This is a blatant example that few students would bungle; but in more subtle situations this kind of conceptual mistake happens all the time.

Because the meaningful units of musical comprehension are clusters of notes with recognizable harmonic or melodic contours that have little to do, per se, with the color of a piano key, it seems logical to use uniform arm choreography to negotiate the recurring musical shapes. Adherence to this consistency principle speeds the learning process, aids mental clarity and physical efficiency, and makes for open, more direct expression. It also reinforces memory, which can be compromised in performance by slips often traced to the practice of using two different fingerings for the same musical shape.

HAND-VOCABULARY THINKING

Hand-vocabulary thinking implies the use of a consistent, comfortably aligned, finger-interval equivalency, regardless of the black-white pattern of the keyboard. Much of the finger editing that we encounter grows out of a slavish devotion to the principles of scale fingering, which by definition prohibit the use of thumb and five on the black keys. In some ways, one can appreciate the superficial logic of this practice: black keys are farther away, and consequently more difficult for short fingers to reach. In addition, one assumes that we have already invested much time in mastering scale fingerings.

In truth, though, extended scale playing is a slight part of musical composition. Pianists should instead express and be attentive to the essence of musical meaning, which resides in the motivic groupings of notes that have characteristic intervals and direction. Embracing musical logic is a far more worthwhile determinate of intelligent fingering than choices based on keyboard design. By avoiding, for example, the use of thumbs on black keys, we end up fingering similar musical shapes with discrepant fingering and divergent arm patterns, a task much more debilitating than playing thumbs on black keys. This is especially true in fast tempos. In general, when we mindlessly avoid thumbs on black keys in fingerwork patterns, we undercut previously learned habit patterns already dedicated to a given musical shape. We also undercut our ability to implement consistent arm choreography, our most powerful expressive tool.

Take the familiar case of a melodic sequence occurring perhaps two, three, or more times. The distinctive shape of the primary motive should be fingered so that a characteristic arm pattern can physically bind the notes, allowing easy repetition on each of the sequence levels. The intervals and direction of the motives have little to do with their configuration on the keyboard. Furthermore, pianists should forego the 'perfect' fingering for any single utterance of a sequential motive in favor of a single fingering that works best for all repetitions. It is the arm and finger consistency that is important. To be sure, there are times where the attempts at consistent fingering lead to unacceptable awkwardness. Certainly there is room for exceptions, but now one makes the adjustment consciously, and it becomes one of the memory aids for the passage.

Two excellent examples are as follows:

J. S. Bach
Italian Concerto
First Movement
m. 105-111

J. S. Bach
French Suite
in C Minor
Couranté
m. 4-11

Consider also the case of a second theme in a Classical sonata. In this situation, the same music appears in two different keys, with certain differences in their black-white organization. The solution is to find the fingering that works best for both tonalities, and finger them identically, in both keys.

L. van Beethoven
Sonata in G Major
Op. 14, No. 2
First Movement
second theme
m. 26-33

L. van Beethoven
Sonata in G Major
Op. 14, No. 2
First Movement
second theme
(recapitulation)
m. 153-160

There are skills that must be mastered before we can take complete advantage of hand-vocabulary thinking. Pianists need to gain an ability and comfort in using the entire depth of the keyboard. They must learn to play their longer fingers on the narrow part of the white keys, and in general to negotiate the uneven, crowded terrain of the black key area. Chromatic transposition (playing almost entirely in the black key area) is the best method for obtaining these skills. Students should mould various intervals, chords, and melodic patterns, all consistently fingered, and move them systematically through the twelve half tones of the octave; height adjustments in time become automatic. Playing black-key scales with C-major fingering is another useful way to acquire this readiness. Soon we are disposed to finger all passages as though they were in diatonic C major.

We then focus on issues that concern the arms – changes of direction, skips, motivic activity, balance of hand positions, and on the rhythmic implications of a given fingering – and translate all of our newly developed skills to the bumpy real world near the fallboard. The resulting inconvenience is more than made up for by the simpler, more direct mental effort, and the expressive power of the arms that is unleashed.

A corollary of this consistent fingering principle is that we do not change fingers on repeated notes, except in those rare instances when the notes repeat faster than the arm or hand can manage. It is advantageous to repeat the same finger so as to allow the arm to remain in position for what follows; a one-time shift is, however, possible to prepare the next position. Performers can create a sense of line by moving the upper arm in or out as the finger, hand, or arm plays the repetition. This will cause the fingertip to strike the key in a slightly different place with each reiteration. Consider the following:

L. van Beethoven
Thirty-two Variations in C Minor
First Variation
m.1-4

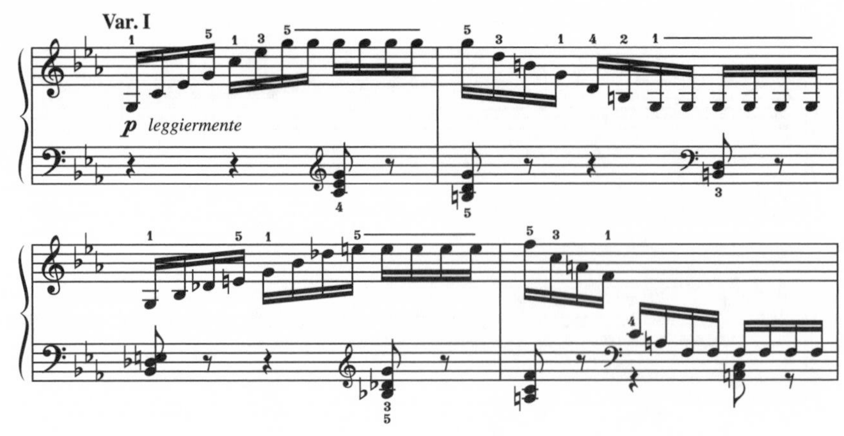

L. van Beethoven
Sonata in G Major
Op. 49, No. 2
First Movement
m.19-28

OTHER PRINCIPLES

When fingering extended patterns that are transposed through various octaves, pianists should use the same fingering in each octave:

W. A. Mozart
Fantasy in D Minor
K. 397
m. 34

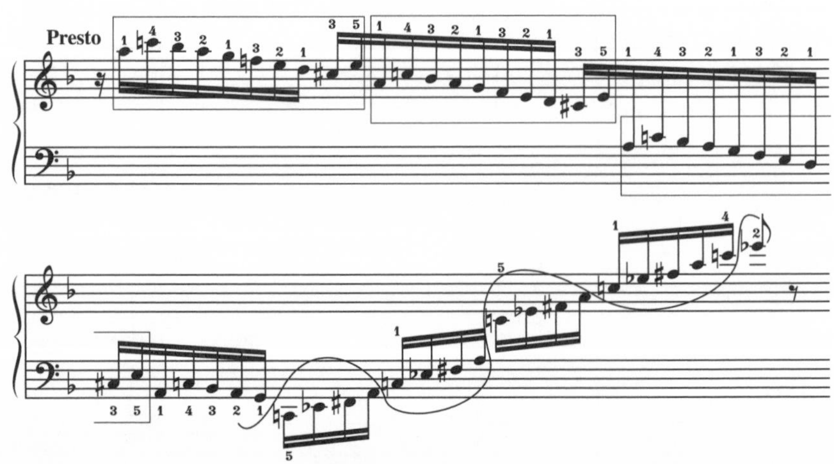

Pianists should shift their arms and fingering earlier than expected to insure accuracy and ease for a critical note, as indicated by the line below:

F. Chopin
Valse in B Minor
Op. 69, No. 2
m. 79-85

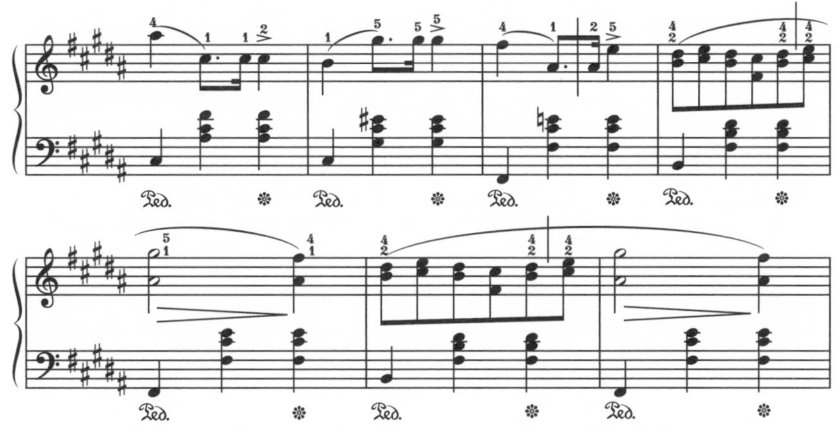

F. Chopin
Etude in
A-flat Major
Op. 25, No. 1
m. 10-12

Pianists should finger so that the arms can move in a smooth, circular arc when the notes change direction:

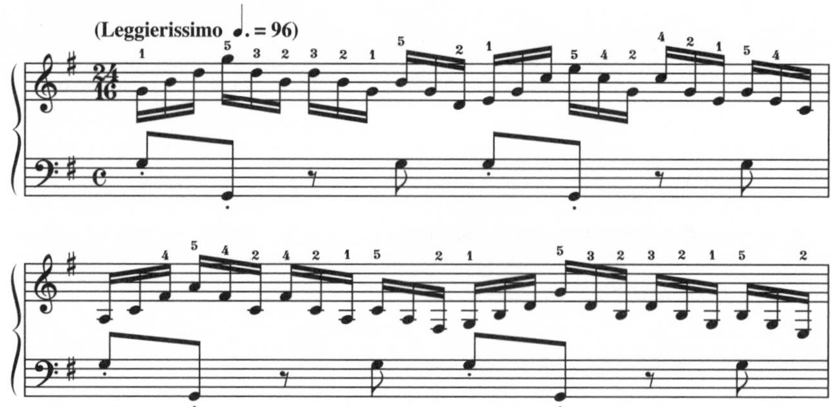

J. S. Bach
Prelude in G Major
***Well-Tempered* *Clavier* Book I**
m. 1-2

J. S. Bach
Prelude in F Major
***Well-Tempered* *Clavier* Book I**
m. 1-2

J. S. Bach
Prelude in A-flat Major
***Well-Tempered* *Clavier* Book I**
m. 12-17

Pianists should finger so that the rotary action of the arms (more specifically the forearms) can best support the playing of alternating patterns:

J. S. Bach
Fugue in E Minor
***Well-Tempered Clavier* Book I**
m. 1-3

W. A. Mozart
Sonata in A Minor
K. 310
First Movement
m. 104-106

Rather than contort the hand, it is preferable to move the arm sideways and repeat a finger:

J. Brahms
Capriccio in G Minor
Op. 116, No. 3
m. 8-11

Pianists should minimize hand shifts as much as possible when fingering long arpeggio patterns:

F. Liszt
Concerto No. 1 in E-flat Major
Second Movement
m. 13-16

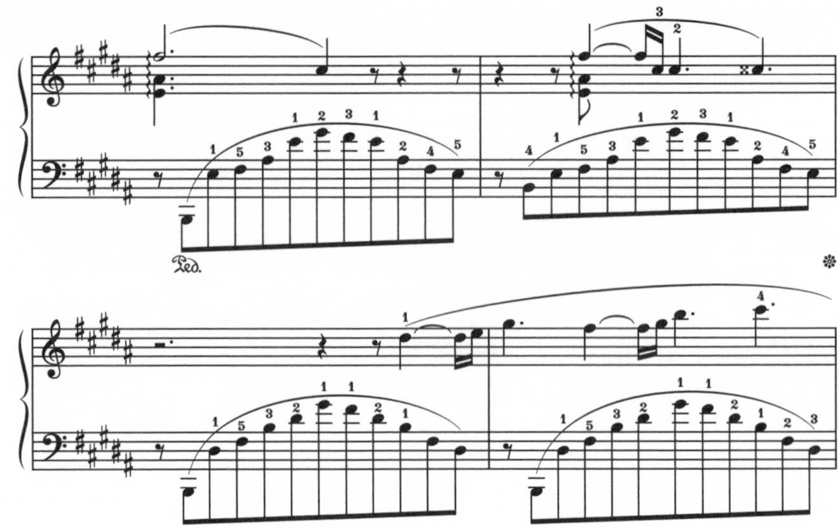

FINGERING CAN EVOLVE

Fingering is so central to the physical process of piano playing that it permeates all aspects of the art. It continues to evolve along with a deepening conception of a work. As ideas change about interpretation, so too must the fingering adjust to more effectively project the new musical vision.

So fingering is never set in stone, nor will it be the same for different individuals who use varying coordinations and have variously sized and shaped hands and arms. Fingering is truly personal. Respect what your body tells you as you search for a more profound, beautiful rendition of a work. If a new fingering slips into your practice, accept the greater wisdom of the body. But do not give up the principle of a consistent arm choreography, nor give up the unending search for the perfect fingering that might be just around the corner.

Developing a Technique for Advanced Piano Repertoire

William DeVan

As pianists study more advanced repertoire it becomes necessary to review their individual techniques and determine how to build further. A true virtuoso technique consists of intense listening coupled with a mindset that enables control of the entire playing unit. Besides good fingers, a pianist wishing to play this repertoire must develop and practice the proper mindset for such playing. This goes far beyond sheer willpower or courage. It means the development of an extremely fine kinesthetic sense and the ability to recall particular sensations when under great stress, hence the need for much routine. In order for students to develop these advanced techniques, the teacher will find that it is just as important to teach them how to think as how to play and that when speaking about either, it is important to be able to speak in concrete terms about what work needs to be done at the piano and in what order.

PREREQUISITES FOR BUILDING AN ADVANCED TECHNIQUE

Initially, it is important for the student to have covered several aspects of technique, including a thorough knowledge of all scales and arpeggios. It may well be the case that the pianist does not feel able to play scales and arpeggios at a very rapid tempo; nevertheless these finger patterns should be memorized at this time. Until the fingerings are memorized it will be difficult to achieve more velocity, since velocity depends, in part, upon the ability of the mind to think in groups of notes (as opposed to individual notes). This very fact is often one of the first insights into the interrelationship of the mind and the physiological playing mechanism for the developing pianist. Virtuoso playing depends not only upon what part of the mechanism is working, but also on what instructions the mind sends to the part of the body doing the work.

Correct alignment of the spine is of critical importance in all facets of piano playing. Students must be taught exactly where their spine ends (they generally believe it is at the bottom of their back instead of the coccyx bone), otherwise they tend to sit on the base of their spine. This pulls the whole playing mechanism away from the keyboard and robs them of the ability to play with a real *fortissimo.*

Sometimes instructing them to 'sit up over the keys' is sufficient, but the teacher needs to constantly check the posture of the students to assure that they are sitting in a way that allows for stabilization of the entire upper body, because in brilliant *fortissimo* work the whole body is used for power.

Once students have established a good posture and are lifting the playing unit in one piece (a rather complex skill covered in depth later in this chapter), they are ready to employ the shoulder. As it provides great power, the shoulder unit is indispensable in passages that require great strength and speed. When introducing this element of the playing mechanism, it is important that teachers not overuse the 'shoulders down' directive, especially when they may really want to correct the shrugging motion of the neck muscles often seen in students who are nervous. Downward pressure in the shoulder area can push the shoulder blade out of position, causing the bottom part of the blade to stick out instead of being flush with the rest of the back. This is known as 'winging', and is undesirable in piano playing because it causes the upper arm to press against the torso. This in turn creates problems that will be addressed in detail later in the chapter.

In addition to these tangible keyboard skills, there are several educational factors that must be addressed at this time. Students must build a comprehensive knowledge of structure and style along with an ongoing study of harmony and rhythm. This is a part of technique that cannot be overlooked because, without it, the mind is not able to send instructions to the playing mechanism regarding what kind of sound the mechanism should produce. The aural image of the sound must be present before the actual sound can be produced. Failure to work on this aspect of piano technique results in playing that is colorless and lacking in shape and direction. Once these aspects of piano playing have been addressed, revisited, or revised, it is time to investigate the 'nuts and bolts' issues of advanced playing.

THE IDEA OF A BASIC HAND POSITION

Hand position has long concerned pedagogues and all teachers are interested in developing a position for the hand that serves to accommodate the needs of the player while providing a good sound. To that end, a good hand position should:

- Not put any part of the mechanism, including muscles, bones, and tendons, at an extreme range of motion
- Allow the fingers (particularly the fourth and fifth) to play on the tip and not on the side
- Not require excessive fixation of the hand
- Allow for speed as well as intensity
- Enable fine control of *legato*, key descent, and key release
- Permit the fingers to negotiate passages that use non-adjacent keys
- Be effective over the entire range of the keyboard

This list serves to show that there are many characteristics to consider when establishing a 'basic' hand position. We can also see that it is much more than simply the position of the fingers: the basic hand position must consider the use of the hand in actual passagework, something that serves to remind us that piano technique does not involve a static position of the fingers, hand, arms, and torso.

CLOSE OR OPEN POSITION

Further explanation of a basic hand position must take into account another important issue: should the fingers be close to one another while playing, or spread apart? Close or open position, respectively.

Close position is the position most familiar to beginning and intermediate students because beginning piano repertoire concerns itself mainly with pieces that do not contain large intervals. Also, the fingers will likely curve naturally when they are in a classic five-finger position, which is another reason this is the position in which most young pianists begin playing. However, as repertoire begins to include passages where adjacent fingers must play intervals of a third, the pianist finds that it is difficult to maintain a closed position, because when the fingers are close (and therefore very curved and arched) it is not possible to spread them apart with ease. To illustrate this, close the hand and point the fingers down. In this position it is easy to move the fingers towards the palm. But any attempt to spread the fingers apart with this high arch is difficult, especially for small hands. Only when the fingers are spread apart from one another by flattening the fingers, out away from the palm, is it possible to span intervals larger than a third with adjacent fingers. This leads the student to an open hand position.

A good open position should exhibit the following characteristics:

- The fingers are not completely straightened out, but they are in a much longer curve than they exhibit in the close position. The first phalanx (the finger bone that attaches to the hand knuckle) assumes a more horizontal position and the fingers play further into the key (closer to the fallboard). They are also more spread apart and therefore capable of spanning intervals encountered in chords.
- The bridge of the hand is slightly flatter than in closed position.
- The wrist is in a neutral position, that is, neither very high nor very low (as either of these positions is more taxing for the flexor and extensor muscles that cross the wrist) and is level with the forearm, when viewed from the top of the forearm.
- The forearm is level with the top of the white piano keys.
- The arm must also be abducted (moved away) from the body to allow the fourth and fifth fingers to play on their tips instead of their sides.

When playing advanced literature it is this basic open position that is more typical and comfortable, mainly because of the demands that advanced repertoire makes on the hand, such as chords, octaves, and large intervals between adjacent fingers.

As one would expect, there are also important refinements of these basic characteristics that help accommodate these demands. A very important concept in mastering passagework is the idea of recovering the hand to as closed a position as possible during the playing of a passage. Instead of having a spread between all fingers, the main spread in the hand should be only between the two fingers currently involved in making a legato connection. Let us use as an example, the passage C, E-flat, G and then B-flat:

- The thumb plays the first note C.
- The second finger then plays E-flat and the thumb comes off the C and passes under the hand in a small motion that places it under the second finger. (The lateral movement up the keyboard made by the hand and arm will carry the thumb the remaining distance to its next note.)
- When the third finger plays G, the second finger comes up off its key and sidles up close to the third finger, which quickly eliminates the spread between the second and third fingers.
- Likewise, when the fourth finger plays the B-flat, the third finger should come off the G and move toward the fourth finger, thus eliminating the spread that existed between the third and fourth fingers as quickly as possible.

In this manner, the fingers are not constantly in a spread position, which is very fatiguing. All scales and arpeggios should be played in this manner, with the arm moving up and down the keyboard so that it can remain directly behind the finger that is currently playing. Such practice leads to even playing and also helps to eliminate a great deal of fatigue that comes from *reaching for* notes in a passage as opposed to *moving to* notes. It also develops in the fingers and the hand the tendency to keep the hand closed whenever possible, which aids the player's endurance in complex and extended passages.

When determining an ideal open hand position for a given student, it is important to consider his or her hand size. Pianists with small hands cannot expect to use the exact position that large-handed students use, in part because a pianist with a large hand can play with a higher bridge (and therefore a smaller degree of stretch) while playing large chords due only to the sheer size of the hand. Students with smaller hands must, by necessity, use flatter fingers to span the intervals of chords and navigate complex passagework since the spatial relationships of the keyboard are fixed.

THE QUIET HAND IN ADVANCED PLAYING

While most pianists have heard of the quiet hand at some point during their training, it can become only a hollow term without some knowledge of the mechanics behind the technique. There are certain basic principles of physics that form the mechanics of motion. Of these, one of the simplest is the lever; more specifically, for our application, the third-class lever. There are three important parts of this lever: the base, the power arm, and the fulcrum. While these levers adhere to many rules of motion, the most important one for students to understand is this: if the force of the power arm acting upon a resistance is greater than the resisting force of the base, the base will be displaced upward while the power arm moves downward.

This is important because, when playing the piano, the parts of the hand become a third-class lever. The hand is the base, the knuckles are the fulcrums, and the fingers are the power arms. The hand must become the balancing and stabilizing force that opposes the downward motion of the fingers, otherwise, the hand will move upward when the finger depresses the key. And although this many not seem crucial, the hand must recover its initial position before the next key can be depressed, which takes time and therefore diminishes speed. So, each time students bounce the hand in reaction to a finger movement designed to depress the key, they are displacing the base of a lever.

When playing slower passages, pianists exploit this lever behavior to their advantage as slow-arm *legato* technique. This technique, where the arm is picked up after each key has been played, works because when the base is displaced in a slow tempo it is possible to return the base to playing position and then release the key from the keybed. However, as the tempo increases, the key release is begun at the same time that the base begins to return to its original position. This means that the key is down for a shorter period of time, and this affects control over *legato*, since an important concept in good piano playing is the ability to keep the key down for the maximum amount of time possible before the next key is depressed. For this reason, students put themselves at a disadvantage as regards speed and control of the key when they displace the hand, wrist, and arm in fast piano playing.

STABILIZING THE BASE

To keep the base from being displaced during each key depression, it is necessary to fix the base just enough to withstand the force the playing unit exerts during key depression. This means that whatever joints are behind the fulcrum must be fixed, which in our utilization of this type of movement, includes the wrist, elbow and shoulder. As the finger depresses the key, these joints behind the fulcrum must be fixed just enough to keep the base from reacting upward – *and no more*. A major area of difficulty in teaching this motion is the problem of *excessive* fixation of the base; because any amount of fixation beyond the amount needed to stabilize the base is wasted energy.

Here is an exercise that can be used in teaching this coordination:

- Place the second, third, fourth, and fifth fingers of the left hand on the top of the right hand behind – *not on* – the knuckles of the second, third, fourth, and fifth fingers of the right hand.
- Place the left-hand thumb under the back of the right hand (fig. 1).
- Place the right hand over the notes E, F-sharp, G-sharp, A-sharp, and C (fig. 2).
- Gently play the second finger on F-sharp.

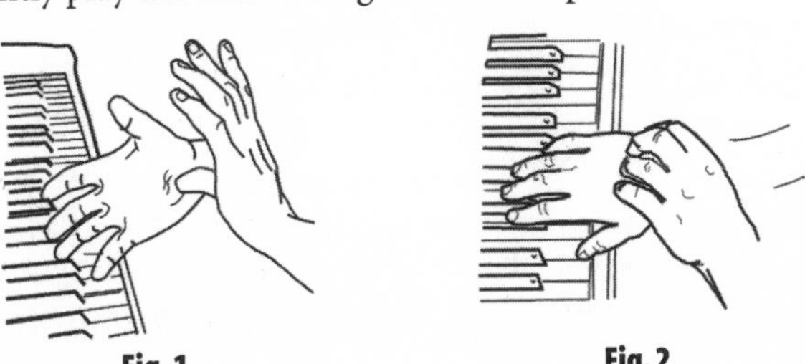

Fig. 1 **Fig. 2**

As the finger goes down into the key, you will notice the tendency for the hand to react in an upward direction. To counteract this upward motion, stabilize the right hand by exerting a slight downward pressure with the left-hand fingers. Repeat the exercise using each finger in turn. A crucial part of this exercise is making sure the right wrist is fixed only enough to withstand the action of each finger as it depresses its key. (The placement of the thumb of the left hand on the right wrist serves to monitor whether or not the right wrist begins to tighten unnecessarily.) This exercise teaches the right hand the feeling it will experience when it stabilizes itself as the base of a third-class lever.

The exercise should be done only in a dynamic range of *pianissimo* to *piano*, as the coordination is one requiring finesse and skill rather than sheer strength. It is important to remember that the small muscles one hopes to train are capable of great velocity, but not great force. The purpose of the exercise is to acquaint students with the very subtle feeling that exists within the hand when the fingers are working off the hand as their base. When this finger action is performed correctly, the forces of the muscles depressing the key and the forces of the muscles fixing the base should be in equilibrium; the resulting feeling in the wrist is 'neutral', with no strong sensation of effort. The arm should feel light; its weight supported at the shoulder joint. The hand may feel as if it is not attached to the arm, since very little action of the flexors or the extensors takes place across the wrist.

Some students tire quickly at the shoulder during this exercise. This is because the playing mechanism (fingers, hand, and arm) is being held in a very static position, without the normal lateral arm motions used in playing. If such fatigue is felt, the exercise can be moved from one area of the keyboard to another to provide a change from a static position. If the left had is monitoring excessive downward pressure in the wrist and arm correctly, this information can also help train the students to avoid positions which cause disproportionate stiffening.

When employing the quiet hand in practice or performance, there will be some degree of fixation in all joints supplying the base, including the wrist. This poses a dilemma for those who espouse a 'loose wrist' position because, as we have illustrated above, a totally loose wrist is not possible in this type of piano playing, nor, in fact, in almost all advanced playing. It is essential to think of the wrist as not fixed beyond the point needed to keep it from bouncing, rather than as loose. Since the tendons of the flexor muscles of the forearm pass underneath the wrist and the tendons of the finger extensors pass over the wrist, any pull by them in either direction will necessarily result in some fixation of the wrist.

The key factor in a feeling of fixation at the wrist is the *amount* of fixation occurring in the joint. Most pianists do not perceive the amount of fixation needed to play in a coordinated manner at the piano as fixation. It is better described as either a neutral feeling or a feeling of lightness and readiness to do something. This feeling of readiness is particularly important because it insures that the muscles around the wrist have some tone, and are therefore ready and able to move. A totally relaxed muscle lacks the tone necessary for readiness and will not respond well to neural impulses of motion. This parallels sprinters about to begin a race. As they start, they are not in a relaxed state. Rather, they go through the steps of acquiring tone, specifically 'on your mark–get set–go'. The 'get set' part of the expression is the period during which the sprinters' muscles acquire enough tone to react quickly.

Pianists who say that they are totally relaxed while they play are defying the laws of nature and physiology. A completely relaxed hand and arm will not remain in playing position. It will instead fall towards the body because muscular effort is required to keep it in playing position. What these pianists mean is that they are playing in a coordinated fashion, using integrated motions that enable them to feel free while playing. Once again we have an example of perception being different from physical fact. The important thing to be learned from this is that coordinated motions at the piano feel 'right' or even 'effortless'. They also are smooth due to the fact that they do not put the playing unit in an extreme range of motion; nor do they result in extreme contractions of the muscles.

The quiet hand offers the most efficient way of moving across the keys when speed counts. It also enables the pianist to introduce integrated motions involving the arms and shoulder into the playing. This use of the entire playing mechanism allows for the constant re-adjustments that are required by the reactive forces that tend to displace the playing unit upwards.

INTEGRATING VARIOUS PARTS OF THE PLAYING MECHANISM

Nothing a pianist does at the piano is unrelated to finger coordination. Since the finger is the part of the playing mechanism that has contact with the keys, its use and position must always be considered when technical matters are being discussed.

There are two basic uses of the finger: active and passive. Active use of the fingers occurs when the finger depresses the key acting off the hand as a base. Passive use of the fingers occurs when the fingers become a part of a larger playing unit that depresses the key, the entire unit moving downward for key depression and the entire unit then moving upward for key release. In other words, the fingers do not move up and down at the knuckle in passive use. Instead the separate joints are fused together and then join up with the hand, forearm, and upper arm as needed to become a single playing unit.

Scales represent active work of the fingers moving down into the keys integrated with lateral movements of the arm. Chords represent passive use of the fingers; in chords the fingers move into the keys molded into the particular shape of a chord and being moved downward by hand, arm, or both hand and arm as part of a larger unit. When the fingers are used passively, they support another playing unit: it can be the hand; the hand and forearm; or the hand, forearm, and upper arm. Pianists learning advanced technical skills must therefore become familiar with these combinations, which are more commonly known as:

- Wrist stroke – fingers and hand move as a unit with wrist as fulcrum
- Forearm stroke – fingers, hand, and forearm move as a unit with the elbow as fulcrum
- Whole-arm stroke – fingers, hand, forearm, and upper arm move as one unit with shoulder as fulcrum

Of great importance in the forearm and whole-arm strokes is the ability to lift the playing unit from the keys without a break in any one of the intervening joints. If an intervening joint breaks or falls inward, the playing unit is divided into two parts and time must then be spent in regaining the fused or one-piece position, which puts the pianist at a disadvantage when playing speed is a factor.

The breaking-in of the wrist as part of a larger playing unit can be problematic and deserves more explanation. In all playing that uses the arm as the playing mechanism, relaxation of the wrist on the upstroke is very common. It is also advocated by many teachers for musical and psychological reasons because a relaxation of the wrist on an upstroke tends to release excessive tension from that joint, thus aiding endurance. But when a passage, such as a series of fast chords, does not allow time for both the breaking-in of the joint and the repositioning of the wrist, another coordination is needed. Therefore the advanced pianist must learn how to lift the entire playing unit off the keys *in one piece*. The key factor in acquiring this coordination is the ability to keep the joints from breaking using just enough fixation of each joint to keep it from breaking-in, and no more.

The following is a helpful exercise to help develop this skill:

> With the student seated at the piano and in position to play, place a 3-by-5 envelope, a small, light piece of cardboard, or another such light object on top of the area of the back of the hand in such a way that it is also touching the wrist and forearm (fig. 3). Now ask the student to lift the hand, wrist, and arm – *as a single unit* – straight up, so that the envelope remains in place.

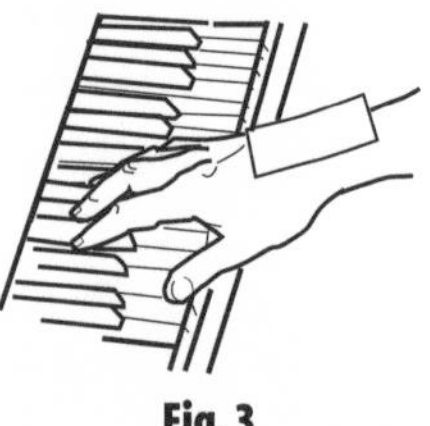

Fig. 3

The student should be advised to lift the playing mechanism *from underneath*, imagining arrows under the hand and arm that serve to show it the way up. This teaches the student to lift the mechanism of the hand, wrist, and forearm in one piece without a break in the wrist joint and without causing stiffness. The student must now be made aware of the fact that it is not necessary to break a joint in order for it to remain relaxed, nor is excessive fixation necessary. Rather, the ideal amount of fixation in the joint should feel neutral.

The above exercise will also help the student get a sense of how light the arm should feel in this one-piece position, especially when it is properly supported by the shoulder. If the playing mechanism is or feels heavy, students will be at a distinct disadvantage in fast playing, in part because of another basic principle of physics – velocity is inversely proportional to mass. Said another way, the heavier the playing mechanism is (or feels) the slower it will move. And while it is not impossible to play this way, it will only be in an uncoordinated manner. It is this lack of coordination that leads to the excessive tension so many teachers see in students who try to play fast chordal passages without proper coordination of the one-piece position.

MINDSET IN ADVANCED PLAYING

At this point it is necessary to address another important element in piano technique: mindset. It has been my experience in teaching piano technique that while many students work hard at the piano to acquire a proficient technique, they encounter difficulties in dealing with the actual *feel* of an advanced technique.

This is the result of many elements in their own personal relationship with the piano, including the inability of many students to let go of the real psychological need to feel each and every note they play. While it is of course necessary to *study* each note of a piece in order to assimilate and memorize it properly, it is not possible to *feel* every note that one plays in a virtuoso composition. Students must learn to 'chunk' groups – many times, large groups – of notes together in order to play at a very fast tempo. This skill can be practiced in scales and arpeggios, with eight-note groups as a good starting point. Again, the importance of a sound knowledge of structure (thinking in phrases), rhythm (thinking of strong and weak beats, more complex groupings such as *hemiola*), harmony (knowing which are the primary harmonies in a passage and which ones are to be glided over), and tone color cannot be bypassed or overemphasized.

If a student has the psychological need to feel a strong contact with each key played, the teacher must wean the student away from this mindset because it often translates into a heavy playing mechanism. How does one accomplish this? The first step is to emphasize the importance of having an *aural image* of the sound that one wishes to produce before a single note is played. When helping students develop this skill, try giving them an easy piece that has a light, floating character (such as the easier Debussy preludes) to practice. Through a combination of a strong conviction of their own interpretation and a preset (thoroughly practiced) aural image, the teacher can begin to make progress with this type of student.

Mindset can also impact physiological aspects of playing. Take for example the lifting of a finger. Although this is a physical action, if students think of picking up the finger from the underside of the tip (the last joint containing the fingernail), it will keep the bridge knuckle from becoming tight. It is also helpful to have them picture the fingertip as being slightly weighted. This serves the purpose of keeping the finger from feeling weightless, in which condition it is incapable of getting the key down.

WHY PRACTICE IS BENEFICIAL?

Students who wish to obtain a brilliant and secure technique must also perform as often as possible. This is because it takes considerable routine to work out the fine points of really difficult pieces. For example, there is a pronounced tendency for pianists to play too heavily into the key during initial performances, which calls to mind the previously mentioned relationship between velocity and intensity.

It must also be stated that musical and technical comprehension does not take the place of repetition. Although a detailed study of any composition is a prerequisite for a good performance, the playing mechanism must be exercised enough to make pianistic movements automatic because the mind does not have enough time to think of the details of practice when we perform. By the time a piece is performed, automatic functions must be in place so that the mind can give its full attention to the listening to and unfolding of the piece.

A student who is frustrated in his or her attempts to play because of the aforementioned problem (playing and thinking of every note) can also be helped in the following manner: let them play using a larger-than-needed motion on each note. As they play in this manner, usually with success, the teacher can then ask the student to reduce the size of the motion used on each note in each successive playing of the piece. As the size of the motions is reduced, the tempo can be increased and the student is given a chance to make a technical transition to the way that the piece must actually be played. I have found this method, while time-consuming, to be very useful.

HOW REPERTOIRE RELATES?

I believe that the progression of piano literature – from beginning pieces to the most advanced works – resembles the levels of a pyramid. At the bottom of the pyramid are all of the pieces that do not call for great speed or endurance. They allow the pianist many choices as to how to use the playing mechanism. Furthermore, these easier pieces enable beginners to use a larger playing unit at first, rather than an isolated finger stroke, which requires a good deal of complex and subtle motion. Then, as scales, arpeggios, and four-note chords are studied, the student discovers that certain motions are more advantageous and efficient than other larger motions in passages encountered at this level. As the pianist approaches the advanced literature, there are fewer options available. At this point the pianist needs strong, independent fingers supported by a playing mechanism that serves to guide the fingers to the keys that they will play.

Most advanced pianists come to discover that all parts of the playing unit must participate in efficient playing of virtuoso literature. This is an important revelation. It means that, while they may spend a great deal of time working on finger exercises, advanced playing is not possible without the participation of the hand, arm, shoulder, and torso. These added elements further emphasize that some areas of technique are much more difficult to master than others.

The Chopin etudes are a good case in point. Without strong fingers, it is not possible to play them, particularly at concert tempo. But each etude reinforces the fact that a successful performance of the etude involves a synthesis of finger, arm, hand, and shoulder. More specifically, take for example the *Winter Wind* etude. Even pianists with very strong fingers cannot successfully perform this piece until they have realized that the shoulder must support the arm, which then has to carry the fingers to their notes, as they cannot move there unaided. Examples in the repertoire abound. Liszt's *Feux follets* contains double-note passages that require not only independence of the fingers but also the knowledge that it is the hand, arm, and also the shoulder that aid the fingers in a successful performance of this etude. The hand and arm move the fingers into playing position; the shoulder takes all excess weight out of the playing unit so that the fingers can depress the keys very lightly with the least possible expenditure of effort, using the intrinsic muscles of the hand as much as possible.

BALANCING EFFORT AND MUSICALITY

The harder a pianist tries to play a difficult piece, the worse it generally goes.

A pianist who reaches the top of the pyramid comes to realize that sheer muscular effort on the part of the pianist will not result in an advanced technique – quite the contrary. The harder a pianist tries to play a difficult piece, the worse it generally goes. Why is this the case? It is because will power is often translated into muscular tension, more specifically, *excessive* muscular tension. Advanced pianists must use their minds to develop the kind of control over their bodies that enables them to do less, not more, thus freeing the body to engage smaller muscle groups for activity that would cause a larger muscle to tire rapidly. A good example is any passage in double notes that must be played very rapidly. If the pianist is tense (perhaps nervous) he or she will likely use the long flexor muscles to play this passage. Although this may work for perhaps a few bars, the longer muscles cannot sustain this effort for an extended period of time. The immediate result is excess tension, which, over time, can lead to tendinitis. This explains the great difficulty of pieces such as the double-thirds and double-sixths etudes of Chopin and also why they are so seldom performed publicly.

It becomes clear that advanced piano technique is not based upon sheer strength, although this is certainly an asset. Rather it is based on a sound knowledge of the mechanics of motion as they relate to the keyboard; economy of motion where necessary; the ability to form a strong aural image of the piece before it is to be performed; the ability to choreograph complex motions to match the musical intent of the passage; and the ability to let the mind control the hands while playing. This frees the pianist to let all the musical ideas in a score come to life. Such a reward is the justification for a life's work in developing an intimate knowledge of the piano.

The Musical

Mind Over Muscle

Robert Mayerovitch

THE APPARENT PARADOX

What is truly impossible need not be attempted, since it is impossible; what masquerades as impossible must be reinterpreted so that it can seem possible.

Music strives to communicate, to convince the mind and heart with musical forms and gestures and moments. In an ideal musical world, performers respond to the intellectual and emotional demands with a refined vocabulary of physical gestures that guarantees that what *needs* to be expressed *will* be expressed. Yet music often makes significant demands on our bodies. And when those demands are not met with a confidence born of experience and conviction, we allow ourselves to be overwhelmed by a sense of difficulty and fear. The result is dysfunctional music making, music thwarted by jerky, strained, uneven motions, and music containing broken lines, unbalanced voices, wayward tempi, and uncontrollable tone.

But the too-well-kept secret is that music making, and especially piano playing can be easy. We can learn to use our bodies in ways that are sensual, organized, and dependable; in ways that allow us to trust that when we want to express ourselves musically, we will have the musical words available to us. One of the most efficient ways to overcome our sense of limitation and fear is to organize what we know about playing in a fashion that alters the seeming complexity of our task by simplifying what we think about. When we make war with our music, we need an attitude adjustment to allow us to find ways to embrace it instead. We need to liberate ourselves from the tyrannies with which our false assumptions subjugate us.

MUSICAL TYRANNIES

THE TYRANNY OF NOTATION

Here is a simple premise: What is truly impossible need not be attempted, since it is impossible; what masquerades as impossible must be reinterpreted so that it can seem possible. Our notational foundations have numerous seeming impossibilities built into them. The innocent and the unconscious sometimes try endlessly to accomplish what they never can, or assume that by trying hard they will get a reassuring pat on the back. But when the flaw is in the very way in which we capture musical thought, we need to learn to *interpret* clearly what the composer is *intending*, not necessarily what he or she is specifically requesting.

For example, the score asks for two successive quarter notes on middle C. What is being asked *literally* is for the pianist to hold the C for the time it takes to measure a one-quarter-note duration, and then play the same note, starting exactly a quarter note after the first note began. That is impossible! Truly, completely, *impossible*. The solution is usually conscious for a good orchestra member: shorten the first note as needed to articulate the second one in time. The same solution occurs to the uninitiated because there is no other choice. Why the solution needs to be conscious, however, is because the performer must be in control of deciding how much of a break is appropriate for the musical moment. When repeated notes increase in speed and become technically challenging, they employ the same solution, not because it is difficult to get back to the note, but rather because it seems difficult to *leave* the note in the first place. A repeating gesture that does not include a trustworthy releasing element will never succeed.

Another similar way in which notation misleads us is in the skipping from one note to a distant one with no time for the migration allotted in the score. A quarter-note middle C followed by another C two octaves higher is again impossible, unless another hand plays the second note or the first note is shortened. But by how much? Inexperienced pianists will assume that no time is best, and breakneck speed is second best. Experienced artists know that the time taken is dependent on the musical context. Pedal can help where appropriate, a bending of tempo to highlight the skip may be expressive, but most often the first note is shortened so that the skip is secure and graceful. Inexperience, by contrast, leads to desperate, and often inaccurate lurching around the keyboard.

THE TYRANNY OF THE ORNAMENT

A specific notational difficulty arises when what is intended is not clearly indicated. This situation arises regularly when twenty-first-century musicians play from eighteenth-century notation. Ornament realizations, so much a part of the oral tradition of the time, become a mystery of often significant proportion. Pianists uncertain of the placement and rhythm of notes regularly attempt the impossible. Grace notes, often written in a smaller script than that used for the normally metered and counted notes, are played as if no time is allotted for their execution. The logic of standard counting seems to bear this out: no time in the meter is available for grace notes. As a result, pianists tend to go to great lengths to attempt the impossible, to rush the execution as if to come close to using no time at all. Of course, *all* notes do take time. It is up to thoughtful musicians to realize that the difficulty lies in the false assumption that no time is available. Rather, an appropriate amount of time must be determined; one that permits secure execution and musical results. Whether the time taken comes from a preceding or subsequent note may be a stylistic choice, but the awareness of the need to *take* time from the surrounding note or rest values is an essential precursor to any technical solution.

The same strange attempt to resolve the irreconcilable differences between reality and the misperception of technical demands occurs in the execution of trills and tremolos. When a trill is defined as a continuing oscillation executed as quickly as possible between two adjacent keys, what often results is a trill executed too quickly to allow for clarity, evenness, balance with the other hand, or ease. Why so? Again because the attempt is driven by a false assumption – that it is technical extremism or perceived difficulty rather than clarity, control, and consistency that defines an appropriate attempt.

Turns written over dotted rhythms are not normally considered to be inherently fast; nonetheless, pianists tend to stumble over them simply because the realization is uncertain, the rules of execution are unclear or unknown, the presumed time available is uncertain or insufficient, and any coordination with the rhythms of the other voices seems inherently ambiguous.

The solution in all these cases is simple – *write out the offending ornament.* Find an appropriate realization and work out the way the small notes would be notated if the composer allotted specific metrical time to them. Decide on the number of notes or repercussions in a trill or tremolo that would lead to a convincing musical moment, and then practice accordingly. There is rarely an inherent difficulty in playing the notes that make up an ornament, only a difficulty in knowing what those notes are, and when they can most persuasively be executed.

THE TYRANNY OF THE GROUP

Too often, we allow the way in which notes are grouped together on the page to dictate the physical gestures that we use. It is essential to note that our grouping conventions have absolutely nothing to do with technical ease, and often do not even reinforce persuasive artistic goals. Too often, teachers and students alike do not recognize that it is usually not the composer's primary responsibility to ensure that the music is easily executable as printed. Some of our most revered masters, like Bach and Brahms, do not seem concerned with the relative discomfort of a work conceived for its musical essence alone. So it is up to us to reorganize notes as necessary to ease execution and clarify artistic goals.

The Horizontal Group

We all know about the tyranny of the barline, the tendency to hammer a downbeat just because it is there, or to break up a phrase just because it is divided into measures. The result is that we often react to such groupings with an instinctive physical response, one that may not provide the ease necessary for proper execution. Take the following series of letters:

IT	SVE
RYG	RAYO
UTSI	DET
OD	AY

Read as grouped, it is an interesting bit of gibberish at best. Read with the recognition that it is English, albeit English that is obscured by inappropriate grouping, we can suddenly recognize "It's very gray outside today."

Most beats do not start a musical gesture, they complete it.

So too, we often play four-note sixteenth-note passages by beginning our gesture (and our thinking) with the first note. In fact, most beats do not start a musical gesture, they *complete* it. An obvious example of this phenomenon is dotted rhythms, which are usually heard, felt, and played as short-long elements in spite of the fact that most are written long-short. Unfortunately, other rhythmic patterns are not so intuitive. The example that follows is a familiar sequence that uses as its recurring cell a four-note group consisting of a rising third followed by a three-note descending scale. As typically found as a right-hand sixteenth-note pattern with a quarter-note beat, the notated passage suggests a contraction of the hand between the thumb and fourth finger in order to span the interval of a third.

The same notes, grouped to emphasize the simplest *physical* relationship, as well as the likeliest musical effect, use the resulting four-note descending scale as their basic sequence element.

Were we to go one step further, and reorganize our notation to mirror the gestures we prefer, we could make the four-note descending scale the group that we first see in the score, and even go so far as to move the barline, if it tends to obscure the true musical meaning or obstruct the discovery of a simple pianistic solution.

Of course a comfortable hand position alone does not guarantee musical truth, for artistic rendering does not simplistically follow what is inherently natural. Often the demands of beat groupings, inflections, articulations, and intensifications collide with the comfort of hand-based note groupings and efficient arm gestures. For example, the Chopin C-sharp Minor Etude, Op. 10, No. 4 demands beat inflections on the third notes in each four-note ascending scale group. In the right hand, that requires a stress delivered through the third finger, and in the left hand, the fourth.

F. Chopin Etude in C-sharp Minor Op. 10, No. 4

Accelerating the arm toward the appropriate key is a standard and effective solution; but a simultaneously constricted hand that mirrors the closeness of the two notated ascending seconds will thwart the body's ability to deliver a comfortably held hand and finger to the key. If the hand mirrors the grouping of the notes on the page, we accept the inherent awkwardness as a given. If instead, we search for an optimized comfort level, we *allow* our hands and bodies to dictate the nature of the physical solution.

The Vertical Group

When dealing with small hands playing extended chords, densely packed counterpoint, or passages involving awkward coordinations of the hands, we often put at the top of our checklist of available solutions a redistribution of the notes between the hands. With the help of a penciled loop in the score, one note gets reassigned to the other hand, *et voilà,* an immediate and trustworthy cure. What continues the difficulty is often the distraction of the score itself: the fact that the printed music may not then be reflecting the organization of the music in the mind and body of the pianist.

When the score is no longer serving its purpose, to facilitate and expedite learning, it can be simply changed. Where loops and brackets add additional layers of complexity, we can rewrite the score to mirror exactly the grouping that best reflects the physical and musical reality. We can easily copy the revised passage onto removable paper like Post-It™ and place it on top of the original, so that the printed music *reinforces* the efficiently learned gesture rather than obstructing it. Memorizing the new grouping provides another freedom from the implacable nature of a difficult score.

Music is full of apparent difficulties that can be easily overcome with regrouping and renotating solutions.

Music is full of apparent difficulties that can be easily overcome with regrouping and renotating solutions. Books can and have been written on the importance of recognizing the appropriate grouping that refines and simplifies the physical process. We must constantly be vigilant so that our assumptions about the musical notes *as written* do not negatively impact on our physical decision-making. Our bodies must be allowed to play efficiently, even if that means rewriting the way the notes are *seen* so as to better reflect the way the notes can best be *played.*

THE TYRANNY OF CHOICE

What is often most difficult is when two solutions present themselves and one seems like the more appropriate because the gesture or the skip is smaller. A moderate-sized hand reaches for a tenth. The owner of said hand knows that the score indicates a legato line, and is anxious to reach the second note before releasing the first; knowing that it is just at the outer limits of his capability, but assuming that there is nobility in the attempt. This student is wrong! The extra effort stiffens the hand, reduces control over tonal quality, and quite possibly begins an insidious and temporarily undetected buildup of tension. The choice was to make the effort because the stretch was manageable. The better choice would be to support the comfort of the body and have the arm move the hand to its appropriate position.

Often, the choice does not seem evident, because the solution seems obvious. A right-hand fourth finger plays an F, the fifth finger, an F-sharp. The notes and fingers are adjacent. The obvious solution – pick up the fifth finger and play the note. The physiological reality is a little different. It is hard to play the fourth and fifth fingers in sequence in the best of circumstances. When the fourth is lower and further to the outer edge of the key, the difficulty is exacerbated. The short fifth is effectively jammed against the raised black note, and therefore has limited mobility. A gesture involving the arm *delivering* the fifth to its key is faster, more efficient, and significantly more dependable. Faster? The small muscles that control the fingers can redo their efforts fairly quickly as compared with the arm muscles, but the larger muscles move through space much more quickly. Replacing an uncomfortable fifth-finger motion with a comfortable larger arm motion will seem counterintuitive to the pianist-innocent, but the difficulty is not in the pianist's execution, it is in his or her knowledge. The lack of a common-sense body of choices for the typical situations found in playing the piano often results in solutions that *seem* simple, but *are* unnecessarily effortful and insecure.

THE TYRANNY OF LEGATO

From an early age, pianists are taught how to play in a smooth, connected fashion. One of the first Italian terms we learn is *legato*, and we learn it while turning our thumbs under our third and fourth fingers when we play our first scales. We learn it again, often with great discomfort and awkwardness, when we try to play arpeggios over more than one octave, and twist our hands in an effort to cross the thumb under the third or fourth finger and stretch to intervals of a third or fourth. Hanging on to the preceding note is stressed and even applauded, as it may provide the only reasonable simulation of an unpedalled legato when the tempo is slow. But the moment that speed increases to the level where the twisting hand and swinging arm detract from the consistency of the scale or arpeggio, we become aware of the problem inherent in this solution.

Reaching, twisting, and quickly reversing direction all become much more difficult as the tempo increases, so we are forced to look for different solutions. The arm must *deliver* the hand to the appropriate key and finger. It can do this efficiently only when it is not impeded by a resisting gesture on the part of the finger. *Knowing* this is at the crux of virtuosity. If we believe we must hang on, then we must practice against the resistance that we assume is a part of the experience. If we *know* that we can look elsewhere, that we can think outside the box, that we can trust our bodies to tell us what they can do, comfortably, dependably, and accurately, then we can achieve technical results without constantly fighting ourselves. Philosophers and psychologists have long discussed the so-called 'mind-body' split – the war between the presumed parts of ourselves. Nowhere is this more obvious than in the abortive attempts of an uncomfortable pianist trying to control multiple lines and coordinate multiple gestures, all while insisting that dogged determination is the best way to tame a recalcitrant body.

Trusting what you learn about the natural capabilities of the body is the better solution. This is an extension of my central belief about technique – *technique is discovered, not imposed.* Imposing your uninformed will gives far too much control over your musical destiny to the insistence of the mind, rather than to its wonderful ability to catalog and categorize what it has learned, cooperating with the body in optimizing the physical aspects of music. This purification of effort provides musical results that cannot be achieved by determination, dedication, and diligence alone.

Trusting the body allows you to let go of the keyboard where necessary, to shorten notes to have time to move comfortably, or to sustain an important line without stiffening. Use the pedal as musically appropriate and necessary to reduce the need to hold notes uncomfortably in the name of a pure legato. Know how the piano can help you by solving the mysteries of the piano.

MYSTERIES OF THE PIANO

How trite the best of maxims often sound: "*Knowledge is power.*" But there is a reason why many sayings and clichés have staying power. In some simple way, they capture some elemental aspect of truth. Knowledge of the instrument itself, combined with a discriminating understanding of the workings of the body, provides a powerful and focused means of making music at the piano.

THE MYSTERY OF THE MISSING DAMPERS

One particularly unnecessary struggle involves playing *legato* in the upper registers. The often unexplained fact that the piano does not have dampers all the way to the top of its range results in pianists working just as hard to accomplish a finger *legato* here as they do in lower registers. The reality is that their efforts may be psychologically useful, but are physically totally unnecessary. From the second-highest E on in many instruments, there are no more dampers. Striking these keys will result in strings vibrating until the sound decays naturally. No finger release will stop the tone because no dampers will damp. As a result, an uncomfortable attempt at finger legato in this register fulfils no useful musical purpose, because the effort creates a tonal edge or unevenness that could easily be avoided by releasing the troublesome keys in a graceful fashion at a convenient time after they have been depressed. Too many pianists have never thought about what an absence of dampers means to the choices they make.

THE MYSTERY OF THE WHITE NOTES

Look at the pictures in beginning piano method books. Almost all of them have at least one graphical representation of the keyboard. At least 90 percent indicate that the shapes of the white notes D, G, and A are the same. Those same 90 percent are misrepresenting the piano. We also assume too often that the black notes cut into the white notes symmetrically such that all white notes bounded on both sides by black notes are alike, i.e. D = G = A. Even experienced performing pianists and teachers often make this assumption. The truth comes out on close scrutiny of the keyboard. D's *do* look symmetrical, but they *don't* look like G's or A's. In fact, G's and A's are usually mirror images of one another, with the small left-side cutout of G equal to the right-side cutout of A. The adjacent middle cuts are larger. The biggest cuts are on C and F (on their right, accommodating C-sharp and F-sharp) and on B and E (the reverse, cut deeply on their left). Some older pianos are even more varied, with D obviously asymmetrical (the left side cut less than the right), G like D, only with the left cut smaller than that on D. The A on these pianos has a left cut almost as big as that on B and E, and the right cut is therefore smaller than that on D.

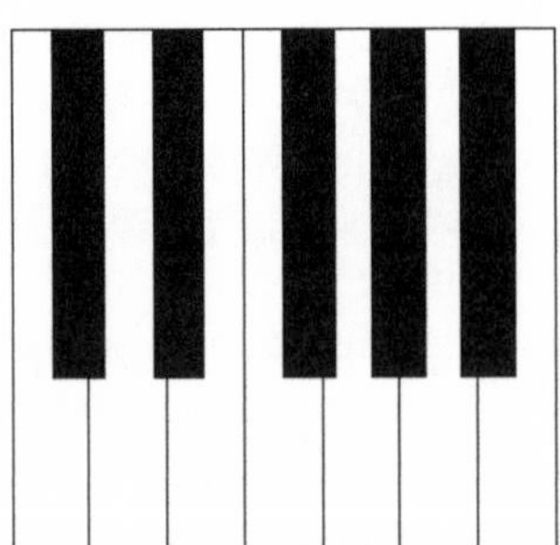

What difference does this knowledge make? It describes reality better and makes playing more dependable. On a contemporary piano, the interval from C to F-sharp, from D to G-sharp, and from E to A-sharp is musically the same: a tritone. However physically and spatially, this tritone gets *bigger* from left to right. The more typical major third, whether from white note to black or black note to white, offers similar discrepancies in size. Accurate pianists will accommodate for those differences unconsciously, but less experienced musicians will often fight a mysterious insecurity, missing notes, or losing grip because their minds expect one sensation, their hands experience another. Knowledge of these idiosyncrasies of the keyboard empowers pianists to practice to control the changing sensations.

Knowledge turns a slippery slope into a simple series of steps, and an improved technique evolves from those steps.

SIMPLE STRATEGIES FOR TECHNICAL SUCCESS

It is an irony of nature that one of the most important and one of the most often overlooked components of a good technique, of the physicality of playing, is not efficient motion or balanced posture or hand position or even finger stroke. It is the mind. It is our ability and willingness to think clearly about the task at hand, to recognize the physical demands placed on us by the music and the musical environment. It is our experience that allows us to recognize the situation and thence know and trust the solution. It is our confidence level, born of the proof that comes from repeated demonstrations of value and dependability, which enables us to trust that our strategies will bear physical and musical fruit. It is the assurance of technical security and simplicity of attitude that empowers us to explore the depths and breadths of creativity through the enlarging of our physical palette.

This might seem self-evident, but in practice (no pun intended, but one willingly celebrated) we need to do most of our explorations as musicians and pianists and teachers to foster a sense of clarity, self-confidence, ease, and trustworthiness. Yes, we can do this with well-conceived exercises both at the keyboard and away, both within a musical context and without. Yet there is an enormous value in developing simple analytical tools that allow the quick recognition of technical demands, often before the physical perception of difficulty even occurs.

ACCURACY

Often this involves the restatement of the obvious, because it is a quirk of human nature that we often forget to consider the obvious because it is too obvious to consider. For example, all good musicians know that playing the right notes honors the composer and the composition. Still, we regularly struggle, well beyond the sight-reading stage, with playing at high levels of intensity and low levels of accuracy. When the inaccuracy comes from sloppiness, we are reinforcing physical behaviors that allow the wrong notes to take up residence. When the inaccuracy comes from uncertainty, then that insecurity itself produces emotional conflict and physical tension. Technical solutions to the challenges of a passage require an understanding of what the notes are.

Musical accuracy, however, is often defined solely as the playing of the 'correct' notes. So what are the correct notes? The pitches represented in the score? Their rhythms? What is more accurate, a phrase with all the right pitches and many of the wrong rhythms? A phrase with all the right rhythms but many of the wrong pitches? Obviously, we cannot look up in a table the appropriate mix of musical parameters in a performance to determine which is the more accurate, though we can arbitrarily define one. But what about other elements? To do justice to a composition or even a portion of one, must we not honor its intent or motivating forces as well? Does not the shape of a phrase, its sense of balance, of climax, of direction help to determine whether an interpretation is *accurately* capturing the intent of the composer? If this is so, then part of our preparation in practice must be to find the musical and *physical* gestures necessary to represent the music properly.

For this to occur, we must have a judgment standard. I have chosen to base this standard on the concept of *continuity*. This is a simple word, used in many contexts. Here it implies that technically well-prepared music must have a sense of flow, a linkage from moment to moment that offers a persuasive involvement in the intent of the composition. When this element is missing in music, even at an early level of preparation, then the musicality of the experience is thwarted.

THE TECHNICAL MAGIC OF SIGHT-READING

Many musicians have had the peculiar experience of sight-reading a difficult composition with a sense of total involvement. Though they may be missing many of the correct pitches and rhythms, they play with a shapeliness and persuasion that demonstrates their understanding of the musical intent. The energy level is high, the color is vibrant, the musical experience can be convincingly shared with a performing partner or listener. What makes this result possible? It is because the performer has *accurately* captured the motivating elements of the music, those qualities of line and structure, of *meaningfulness* that allow the essence of the music to come alive in spite of the incompleteness and approximation of the rendition.

Why is this significant to technique? Because that kind of reading represents musical continuity at its best, a sense of musical gesture that emanates directly from a refined sense of physical gesture. Applying an appreciation of this kind of reading to the art of practicing is an essential aspect of piano technique, and probably of the technical development of most refined neuromuscular skills.

If gestural accuracy becomes an essential element of preliminary work, the resultant physical and technical dependability very quickly supports the reinforcement of all the other accuracies.

PRACTICING FOR CONTINUITY – VERBAL ANALOGS

Too often, it seems to be standard practice (another one of those doubly delicious usages) to assume that the slow rendition of notes in a score has a mystical connection with a good final product. Of course we must play the proper notes. But we must play them idiomatically, in context. A favorite exercise I use in my studio is to associate modes of musical communication with verbal ones. My students and I have conversations at the word level, emphasizing the individual quality and importance of each word:

How (3-second pause) *do* *you* *dooooooooo?*

I'm *fine,* *thank* *you!*

It does not take long (especially if the pauses between words are long and significant) for the conversation to sound totally ridiculous, for the intent of the words and their relatedness to be thwarted by the absence of continuity. 'How do you do' is an idiom that cannot even be examined word-by-word without sounding inane at best. 'How do you do *what?*' is a reasonable reaction. Persons learning to speak a new language rarely rely on word-for-word translations to develop fluency (another word for continuity). Rather, they practice full phrases (thus the ubiquitous phrase books in lieu of dictionaries for most typical tourist situations).

If word communication does not drive home the analogy dramatically enough, we communicate in letters, sounding each one out:

Hhh Ah Wh Duh Ooo

Yuh ooo Duh Ooo ?

The word play is akin to playing in isolated small musical figures: a partial motive, a broken chord, a two or three-note scale fragment. The letter talk is of course just like playing isolated notes. Neither form of verbalization provides effective communication. Rather both obscure meaning quite handily. Try playing *Mary Had a Little Lamb* at one-sixteenth of the original tempo to find out how quickly a lack of connection and continuity destroys meaning.

But this is a discussion of *piano* technique, so how is the above relevant? That is the easy part! Continuity requires at least two points in space or time. One note cannot show tempo or shape. So we select somewhat larger elements that require a sense of integrity, and then we practice to discover and maintain that indivisible quality. We find the smallest useful physical building blocks that will guarantee ease, tempo, clarity, and shape, and work to incorporate them so convincingly into our systems that we trust them whenever they appear. That is how idiomatic language works, and that is exactly how idiomatic, continuous playing works. A fearful pianist will concern him or herself self-consciously with all the little elements that are not dependable. A confident one know that the important elements are always available, and are thus not thrown by the surprises of performance. We can all sign our names even when fearful. We must be able to sign the pianistic equivalent of many names no matter what the musical setting.

TONGUE TWISTERS

Both language and music can have traps that disguise the awkwardness of the passage and inhibit the sense of flow. In speech, tongue twisters set up an expectation of a certain pattern and then interfere with that pattern. The result is usually a curious and often hilarious dysfunction in which ordinary words become the equivalent of polysyllabic monsters. One of my favorite tongue twisters is:

Unique New York

Said quickly ten times in a row, it allows very few people the sensation of ease or flow. An analysis of the phrase reveals why.

Spelled out phonetically for a typical American pronunciation, Yoo Neek Noo York shows the expectation and destruction of parallel patterns. A standard mispronunciation is Yoo Neek Yoo Nork, during which our linguistic performer comfortably and incorrectly weds the 'y' sound with 'oo', while maintaining an alternation of 'y' and 'n'. One aspect of the trap is the seemingly necessary separation of Unique and New York. The adjective and its proper noun are understood as separate entities and consciously treated so. The problem is that our bodies are stuck with making the appropriate sounds, and our physical needs are different from our mental ones. If we regroup the syllables as Yoo Neek-Noo York, we discover a linkage without the preceding challenge. Two syllables starting with the same consonant are no more difficult to say than it is to play C D C E on the piano.

Practicing the three elements in isolation – Yoo • Neek-Noo • York – is a simple matter. Combining Yoo with Neek-Noo adds no particular complication so long as the original association of Yoo with Neek (remember, we started with unique) is seen as weaker than the new association of Neek with Noo. York gets added when the other three syllables make a trustworthy and indivisible whole. At first, the middle two syllables are linked, then the anacrusic Yoo is added and finally, separated by as much space as is necessary and comfortable, the concluding York.

Many teachers will recognize the space needed to add the last syllable. I call it the *mental breath* and consider it to be one of the most important practice tools. It is, in essence, the permission we give ourselves to take the time necessary to guarantee the comfortable and accurate execution of that musical moment. Usually it takes place where some kind of transition happens, where a pattern changes significantly, where a leap follows a series of steps, wherever notes (or words) that we are unaccustomed to linking together require that very linkage. In the case of our tongue twister, so long as the final syllable is seen as separate from the preceding verbal/physical gesture, it can be linked with ease. As the two elements become more comfortable, the mental breath shrinks until it is inaudible. It is always available as a safety valve (Yoo Neek-Noo York), but its value is not in the time taken, but rather in the possibility that the time *may* be taken. It provides the sense of permitted breath rather than panic, a condition in which action and time are antithetical.

In musical situations, the mental demand is often identical. Tricky passages tend to be so because expectation and reality collide. The body follows its expected path. The mind tells it to play the recognized notes. Without comprehension of what the true physical challenge is, the system is trapped in a bind – what feels good provides wrong notes (funny in a tongue twister, frustrating in piano practice). What is necessary is to rearrange the way in which we perceive the passage so that the body's natural capabilities are exploited. Barlines, beats, metric braces, sequences, all can mislead us by suggesting an obvious execution that never quite fits. We must be vigilant to allow the body to suggest its own way. The body has a mind of its own.

THE ROLE OF MEMORY

Memory in music almost always implies the memorization of a score, often to satisfy an externally imposed standard. Contests, competitions, juries, and concerts usually demand a memorization component. Countless lives have been affected by the turmoil induced in the hearts of pianists who need to fulfill this demand. In fact, pedagogues and critics have for years devoted energy to debating the value of a performance element that perhaps takes up more practice time than any other, and that certainly affects the emotional well being of many pianists. However, that debate is not what is relevant to technique. True memory – the fully internalized understanding of the makings of a piece of music that is portable and does not require reference to its source – is, however, a *requirement* of good technique.

The mathematical world provides a fine analogy. Young students learn certain math facts, like multiplication tables. They also learn deductive reasoning and manipulation techniques that enable them to multiply large numbers together. They need ready access to the math facts in order to make the larger calculations work. For example, multiplying two multi-digit numbers on paper depends on the ability to multiply single digits, like 9 x 9, mentally. So too, pianists need to know basic facts about what they are learning to play in order to find an effective and dependable strategy. Just as 9 x 9 = 81 must be an automatic and accurate answer when a student is solving 19 x 29, performing a complex musical passage depends on the ability to recall, for example, a C-major scale clearly, quickly, and confidently. When one combines a clear understanding of what is contained within a piece of music and a recognition that the means of expressing it are always available, the result is a partnership of mind and body that is unassailable by fear.

THE CHOREOGRAPHY OF ATTENTION

One additional strategy that deserves some mention is what I call the choreography of attention the consciously planned ways in which we determine what, where, how, and when to think about events in the music while both learning and performing. Ponder for a moment the amazing ability that cocktail pianists have to maintain an easy and flowing performance while carrying on a conversation about someone's life story. Every so often they will look at one hand or the other, withdraw from the discussion to assure good aim or a secure hand position, and then return to the topic without skipping a beat either musically or conversationally. How is this possible? Do cocktail pianists have superpowers? Are mortal pianists doomed to live a life pondering only one thing at a time?

Consider all we do in daily life. We can walk down a street in intense conversation, dodging obstacles as we go while balancing a coffee cup in one hand and a lo-cal doughnut in the other. We can adjust our stride, stop for a red light, avoid a hole in the road, and still maintain our animated involvement in the topic. It is not that we perform all of these activities with equal conscious involvement. Instead, we prioritize our tasks and trust that what we can do with little mental effort will maintain its automatic dependability until circumstances signal the need for corrective action, or what computer people call multi-tasking. We learn the mechanics of walking so well that we only need think about the technique of locomotion or the placement of feet when mud or snow requires a different gait, or suddenly changing traffic patterns demand attention. Mortal or otherwise, piano playing is no different.

We can play with the same automatic ease that we use while walking (imagine any easy vamp figure); and we can also think so hard about everything happening that we are physically and mentally thwarted by the effort (visualize sight-reading a complicated Bach fugue at performance tempo while trying to be note accurate, bringing in all voices clearly, balancing and shaping them as you go). For a Bach fugue, we know the learning drill separate the voices and hands. We practice them until they can be played confidently and securely with little conscious effort so that when they are combined with other parts, we can concentrate on only the one thing that is the new challenge. By definition, concentration requires that we choose one focus point, so it becomes necessary to know when to trust our fully assimilated skills and when to divert our attention to them.

Without that selectivity of attention, we simply cannot play certain music well. We may also miss finding the solution when we choose to concentrate on the wrong thing. Typically, melodies and parts in higher registers win out. Faster, harder passages demand our involvement. That is fine when it works, but we must recognize that it is often the innocuous-looking supporting line that requires our conscious effort.

Consider the beloved Chopin Minute Waltz. Students learning the delights and challenges of playing the right hand quickly may be confused by their lack of success when playing hands together. If they are concentrating on the running right-hand part, they are unlikely to succeed because the left hand jumps around, requiring either visual attention or an extremely well-developed and well-calibrated ability to leap accurately by feel. A pianist aware of the different demands of the two parts will learn to play the right hand accurately without having to look at it. Then the attention can be diverted to the left, where seeing the keyboard quickly improves security. In essence, though the right hand plays the musical melody, the psychological melody the prime voice of attention is in the left. An awareness of the simple need to know where to look and what to think about provides a powerful tool and antidote to frustration. Many pianists put too much effort into a kind of generic concentration in which thinking hard about everything they are doing passes as a useful working strategy. Instead, it is important to choreograph that attention, shifting concentration from place to place as the needs change.

Many pianists put too much effort into a kind of generic concentration in which thinking hard about everything they are doing passes as a useful working strategy.

A perceived technical difficulty is always difficult, but when the perception is focused on the elements of the solution, difficulty ceases to be the issue. As pianists we must be able to discriminate between potential minefields and meadows. We must know when we have to watch our step, even know how to take that step, and know also when to allow our bodies to go ahead and do what we have taught them or allowed them to do so well.

RULES OF PIANISTS' THUMBS

Many musicians simply do not have a large enough vocabulary of easily available strategies and tools for technical problem solving at the piano. When we practice forming the shapes of chords, or working to ensure dependable, accurate, even scales or arpeggios, we are practicing what could be called *musical primitives* – the basic elements of an extended piano technique that are always available. So too, we must collect simple observations about what makes certain motions more efficient than others, certain strategies more fruitful than others. All humans use basic maxims or aphorisms as a reminder that similar situations have been encountered before, and will be encountered again. Successful daily living often depends on an understanding of these behavioral rules. Driving during rush hour tends to take more time than on Sunday morning. Phoning to find out whether a store is open or has the item you are looking for is a strategy that saves time and frustration.

In life, philosophers and others like the fabulist Aesop have addressed these kinds of recurrent situations rather concisely and effectively. Musicians need their own sets of standard guiding principles, and pianists in particular need help in simplifying and ordering the rather complex demands they regularly confront. Not just students, but performing artists of all skill levels benefit from succinct and memorable observations about movement, learning principles, and identifiable mental and physical traps that disappear when recognized. And while most teachers tend to collect these sets of general principles that represent their experiences and allow them to help their students recognize recurring pianistic challenges and apply proven solutions, few take the time to write them down. Every time the teacher or student makes a technical discovery or finds a succinct way of explaining an important principle, write it down!

Any initial concerns that basing technical teaching on sometimes-humorous musical maxims will result in simplistic instruction will be quickly allayed. For it provides an enormous confidence-booster, a feeling that students develop a foundation and superstructure of understanding that allows both for the quick, score-based recognition of most pianistic demands and for the accessibility of strategies to deal with more complicated situations in which the solution is not immediately apparent. It is also worth noting that the more colorfully illustrated the principle, the more likely it is to be remembered.

The same philosophy stands for the verbal analogs discussed previously, which are not just appropriate spoken parallels to musical demands; they are also vivid experiences for students. Non-musical and non-pianistic adventures that entertain while teaching, and that weaken defense mechanisms against improvement through their use of disguises. For whatever reason, principles that apply to the whole body; to efficient movement as it is invoked everywhere, not just at the piano; to learning in the so-called real world; these tend to be persuasive precisely because they have universal applicability. And they tend to be invoked regularly because they associate the pianistic experience with all others.

Throughout this chapter are a number of aphorisms, designed not to be contentious, but rather the restatements of commonly held truths about learning and the ways of the body. What follows are two others, one witty, one not, provided to demonstrate how easy it is to teach piano technique with a free and curious attitude about technical problem solving. They show that learning at the keyboard is a natural extension of observing ways in which the world around us operates. The first states what would probably seem obvious to most people, musicians and non-musicians alike:

Wherever possible, use hand positions involving fingers
comfortably positioned next to one another and
not extended, compressed, or crossed.

Ridiculously simplistic, right? Of course, we prefer being comfortable to being uncomfortable, right? Not always. Pianists will often assume that suffering for their art is appropriate and necessary. So they will stretch to reach notes at the limit of their physical capability, or they will reach their thumbs uncomfortably under their third fingers when playing arpeggios, or compress their fingers while playing chromatic scales. Armed with a guiding principle that they accept as representing common sense, comfort, greater security, and persuasive musical shaping, they can start to let go. Literally. The arm can carry the finger to the note that is almost out of reach of the extended hand. The comfort, dependability, and duplicable nature of that maneuver link the two notes in a legato fashion far better than can an awkward reach. Thus is the tyranny of legato thwarted.

Advanced pianists will all recognize that their arpeggio execution changed when they started playing more quickly. A comfortable arm motion that delivers the finger to the key without strain replaces the necessary stretching under of the thumb to reach a fourth away. Again, the musical aim, a flowing legato line, is enhanced rather than diminished by the new choreography. Even chromatic scales benefit from an awareness of comfort levels. Keeping fingers over the notes they are responsible for playing results in a compression of the hand into a position of relative discomfort. When we allow the hand to open up in the opposite direction from that of the scale, continually relieving the compression, the resultant ease makes the scale much more dependable. It is also likely to be faster and clearer, because the finger strokes are not being resisted by the awkwardness of the hand position, and because the arm is better able to deliver the hand to each new position.

These are observations well known to informed students of the body and the piano. The risk, however, is that the unstated but obvious principle will not be invoked in the early preparation of a passage, or when frustration builds. When it is not only readily available but also invoked as a basic element in an always-present checklist, it gains a power and a utility otherwise unknown.

A second rule-of-thumb deals with dependability and standards while practicing:

Hope is a four-letter word.

This is not a rant against hope in the powerful way it can inspire humans to survive in the grimmest of situations. Rather it addresses all the times (at or away from the piano) in which we do not conquer a problem, yet continue to assume that the situation will right itself. We must recognize that invoking hope is an avoidance strategy where clear thinking and real problem solving are more appropriate. A maxim referred to regularly, even daily, about the dangers of hope should set off an alarm whenever a musician recognizes during practice that the current solution is not working and has not worked consistently. It is not just the F-sharp that has not miraculously metamorphosed into the correct F-natural over the last two weeks and three lessons. It is also the passage first tried today in which the proposed solution does not feel right, nor sound right, and shows no indication that it is bound to provide a breakthrough over time. For safety and for efficiency of practice, invoke instead a corollary: repeating a mistake three times is a mistake.

These suggestions are not meant to denounce experimentation or temporary failure. Instead they provide a reminder that practice is regularly filled with traps, traps that lead us to simply will fixes for our difficulties while not examining why they exists in the first place. These aphorisms also give us courage to look for another fingering, a different gesture, an unexplored way of dividing the elements of the challenge, an untried way of focusing attention on visual or aural or tactile cues.

Reliance on common sense develops self-reliance. Trusting that the body has naturally efficient and graceful ways of moving leads to trustworthy solutions to pianistic challenges.

The essence of these aphorisms, indeed the core principle of this chapter and of my teaching of technique, is that playing the piano is simple. Reliance on common sense develops self-reliance. Trusting that the body has naturally efficient and graceful ways of moving leads to trustworthy solutions to pianistic challenges. Understanding how we learn has a fundamental effect on how well and how quickly we learn.

Understanding language helps. If we have confidence in our ability to communicate in non-musical ways, and if we examine the nature of language, we develop a deeper kinship with how that knowledge affects the ways we assimilate and project musical ideas. Developing a free and accessible technique means developing virtuosity or, as its origins indicate, the display of musical virtue. This ability to state what we need to in a succinct and persuasive fashion is this purpose of technique: to enable our musical voices. Technique emerging from the unity of mind and body provides the ultimate vocabulary for the musician. From that vocabulary springs the ultimate communication, heartfelt and full-voiced human expression.

Musicality

Seymour Fink

From a purely musical point of view, the piano is too easy to play. Students do not have to worry about intonation or breathing, intervallic distances, or real sustaining. In addition, there are skills we can teach students that sound impressive to some, but at the same time have little to do with the expression of a musician. The training of a true musician concerns listening, singing, and moving. It includes inner hearing and audiation skills, discrimination, memory, continuity in movement and rhythmic control, recognition of rhythmic, melodic, and harmonic patterns, cognitive understanding, and awareness of tonality. Truly superior training promotes musical imagination, improvisation, musical decision-making, and joy in performance; thus inspiring a highly personal involvement with music. Like a singer or dancer, the pianist's instrument should be his or her body, breath and vocal cords, muscles and joints, emotions, and gray matter. Ultimately, the piano becomes the outlet for expressing one's personal musicality.

Unfortunately, musicality is an illusive concept to define and, therefore, to teach. Although listeners (be they professional musicians or untrained appreciators) will generally agree that a given performance was either musical or unmusical, they may not be able to tell you what captivated them (in the case of the former) or where it fell short (in the case of the later). When we as teachers hear a student perform musically, we often feel that he or she is blessed with an innate, almost genetic, capacity to communicate beyond the notes on the page. These feelings may further reinforce our frustration when a student's performance is unmusical. While many unmusical students are serious, worthy piano students who may excel in other ways, their lack of musicality will be a constant barrier to their maturation as a performer.

It is our responsibility as teachers to resist the desire to throw up our hands, and, instead, to forge ahead armed with the knowledge and understanding to encourage and improve the essence of music making; essentials found not in score reading and technique, but in the body's linkage to song and dance, in ear training, inner hearing, and audiation, and in a deeper emotional grasp of the musical values relating to performance.

NOTATION CAN BE PROBLEMATIC

It is often during the normal course of study when students are unwittingly taught to be unmusical.

A great paradox of teaching is that while we recognize the ultimate importance of musicality, jump at the chance to reinforce students' natural musicality, and leap at the chance to teach others the musical values they lack, it is often during the normal course of study when students are unwittingly taught to be *unmusical.* By concentrating our curriculum primarily on the teaching of notation, lines and spaces, and rhythmic subdivisions – score reading – and the mechanism and ways of manipulating it – technique – we ignore, or worse, even obstruct, the true musical development of a student. Although indisputably important, if literacy training and instrumental technique form the major focus of a student's studies, he or she will often become frustrated and loose any personal and musical sense of accomplishment and joy. When students are not trained to listen, play by ear, or improvise, they feel alienated from the spontaneity of music making, playing dutifully as though raking leaves, not as though they were expressing inner feelings. By not teaching the essentials of musical meaning and its communication, we doom them to experience music as a foreign language spoken only as perpetual outsiders.

Notation's impact on musicality is even more disconcerting when one realizes that none of the requisite skills needed for a musical performance have anything to do with the written symbol. Consider that much music of this world has never appeared as symbols on a page, having been handed down aurally, one generation to the next, from master to apprentice; good jazz players realize this. More apropos, the traditional teaching of notation can be musically inhibiting. We must alter our thinking, and accept that notation refers to specific melodic and rhythmic content *within* an aural environment: an environment that must be solidified and experienced within a player's mind and body before it can have any personal meaning. If we introduce notation before a student has this grounding in listening comprehension, we end up teaching symbols for things students have no experience with. It would be like teaching a child the word 'cat' before they had any experience with a real cat. The child may be able to use it in a sentence, but it may be "We sat at the cat for dinner," as he or she would have no personal experience to distinguish it from a table. Notation is a wonderful, if limited invention; it can be a powerful memory and ensemble aid. But the traditional study of note reading often interferes with the freedom of the ear to focus on pure sound, and of the freedom of the body to create and respond to rhythm. We set students up for failure as musicians when we deny them these freedoms because they will never find joy in transferring music from the printed page to the levers of the keyboard without an intermediary, audiated, musical experience.

Few unmusical players are aware to what extent they have been victimized by the notation system. I refer here to concerns from the perceived tyranny of the bar line to the packaging of music into measured segments or into conventional beaming systems; and to the over-reaching importance given to meters, with their implied accents. It is not surprising that students who have had no experience with internally processing a musical gesture (most of which go over the bar line and rarely start on a beat), would feel almost compelled to stop and start with each measure or beat pictured on the page. These disruptions are responsible for causing the breaks in musical continuity that are the hallmarks of unmusical playing. As we present notation, we must teach its limitations and misrepresentations along with a sprinkling of musical skills, like the ability to hear tonal patterns or to hear a kinetic beat (the foundation of musical continuity), so that the false pictures propagated by the notation system will not mislead them.

Music is an aural art existing purely in the world of sound. Written music does not do justice to those organized sounds, which originated in the composer's head. We must teach the symbols on the page in ways that insure that students experience the live sounds being symbolized – the intervals and tonal patterns, the feel for a wave-like beat, and the like – things that must be perceived internally by singing and moving rhythmically. Ideally, teaching the symbol should come *after* students have some aural recognition of patterns; this is how language reading is taught. We need to always reinforce our students' inner hearing and their feeling for musical and physical continuity.

THE FIRST RULE OF PIANO TECHNIQUE

Technique is best defined as *purposeful movement towards musical ends* and must be presented in ways that reinforce music's existence only in perceived or actual sound. It follows from this that the first rule of piano technique is to audiate musical intention before moving – to project in the mind what one wants to create before any attempt to do it. It is this projection of musical understanding and intention that triggers the physical movement. Otherwise, technique becomes a dull, precision-building, muscle-building exercise related more to typing quickly than to music making. The union of aural image and activating movement is what lends authenticity and authority to a performance, both important ingredients of musicality.

Early technical training lays the groundwork for a lifetime at the instrument. Its presentation should be carefully sequenced as follows:

- Instill the experience of grace, expressive freedom, and joy in pure movement before concerning students with notes and levers.
- Focus on listening carefully to the types of sound that various movements produce. Harping on rounded hand position and broken nail joints does nothing for the ear, and has a proven history of locking shoulders and wrists, hobbling future development.
- Coordinated movement linked to musical intention is the essence of technique – not static position. Larger elements of the playing mechanism should be dealt with first. General posture and graceful movement in the shoulder girdle, shoulders, upper arms, and wrists are extremely important. Generous arm motion fills in both physical and temporal space, ingredients necessary for rhythmic understanding. A pulling arm stroke (in continuous, pulsating form – like petting a cat) is an appropriate first coordination.
- Students should be encouraged to explore the entire length and depth of the keyboard. Cement the relationship between

students' movements and the sounds they create, between kinesthetic feel and carefully monitored end product. Slower or faster swinging arms change tonal dynamics; extending upper arms outward affects the alignment of the fingers with the keys, which also affects the tonal result. Understanding these relationships and experimenting with the variables empowers students to take an active role in their own development.

- A pure finger technique should be taught only after several years of study, when the technique is needed for increased speed. The premature introduction of the complex coordination often creates unwanted tension. Beginning students get along quite nicely with arm strokes for which the fingers are supple landing gears. Independent finger action is usually not necessary before the sonatina level of study, when the ability to use the arms efficiently will ease the learning of new coordination. It is important to remember that technical training should not outpace the musical sophistication of the students.

Practicing should be thought of as wiring the sounds heard inside the head to the physical motions necessary to create them. Training that follows a course of slowly building skill upon skill, in the proper order, with little tension and strain, monitored by the ear, and always in response to expanding musical demands will insure that this all-important connection is never severed. New skills require new habits; specifically the ability to perform new, useful, and automatic movements that demand minimal mental effort. These are acquired through thoughtful repetition, inner awareness and well-considered feedback. Practicing should ultimately take us from self-conscious, deliberate, and effortful behaviors to goal-oriented, automatic ones. As we move from conscious factual knowledge (knowing what to do) to procedural knowledge (knowing how to do it), we become freer to concentrate on the goal-oriented purpose of the behavior – producing an imagined musical idea.

THE RULES THAT GOVERN ESSENTIAL MOTION AND GROUP TONES INTO MEANINGFUL GESTURES

The creation of a musical conception is accomplished by first focusing attention on the bedrock, indivisible components that come into play at a level below that of the phrase. By narrowing the focus within this aural milieu, we can bring the innate musicality in some to a conscious level and cultivate musicality in others, even during the first lesson. Hopefully the following focus areas will take some of the guesswork out of the road our average students must travel to develop necessary musical skills.

FEELING A KINETIC BEAT

In contrast to popular thought, a beat is not a dot of time. In actuality, it is the basic unit of the forward-moving, wave-like impetus of music. Accomplished physically by pulsation within recurring gestures, it is an extended wave shape consisting of a forebeat, a center, and an afterbeat. Students can discover this by swinging a relaxed arm in a half circle in a broad, pendulum arc. The center of the beat is at the point of fastest motion, the bottom. Beat separation occurs when the arm is highest, almost suspended; there the previous beat ends and the new one begins. The division, most emphatically, does not occur at the point of the note head, nor, for that matter, at the bar line. To reinforce a notation system that encourages students to cut the musical fabric into measures and to conceive of things beginning with downbeats is like teaching someone to mechanically stop at the end of each line when reciting a poem, regardless of the punctuation or meaning. This single misconception, more than any other, causes the breaks that interfere with musical continuity. And while the discontinuity is often very subtle, creating only a vague feeling of annoyance, it will still register in the listener as a lack of musicality. When we teach note values, meters, and bar lines, we must do it in ways that transcend the limitations of the notation system and enhance the body's ability to create a kinetic beat.

It is also easier for students to create a kinetic beat if they can physically experience a similar sensation in a larger context. This can be accomplished by alternately speeding up and slowing down the motion of a circling arm, creating a pulsation. Swaying the whole body side-to-side, or bending the knees as though dancing a waltz are other ways to feel a basic beat. Mastering a large, well-coordinated conducting motion is also fruitful.

PRESERVING MUSIC'S INNATE FORWARD MOTION

The life force of music is the performer's internal engine, which propels the music forward in an unstoppable flux, a state only fully perceived by the body. The following will help to keep the music flowing:

- Continuous, evenly subdivided metric units should be organized to begin anywhere except on the beat.
- Upbeats generally begin new musical ideas, and progress to the beat on a downward slope. In other words, they approach the beat point on the forebeat side of the wave, sliding directly to and through the center dot to the afterbeat area.
- Any particular note should be treated as the end of a previous beat's follow-through or as the beginning of the next upbeat.
- In complex music, special care must be taken to integrate rests, embellishments, skips, and special expressive devices in such a way as to maintain the temporal thread.

Unbroken forward motion is the natural extension of the kinetic beat. Students must learn to experience this as early as possible, so they can generate their own continuously moving waves. Even if higher-level musical elements – like an impeccable handling of the structure, lovely contrasts, or beautiful piano sonority – are in place, the listener will remain dissatisfied if there are interruptions in the musical continuity, for these create a feeling of weightlessness and discomfiture. It is essential to remember that although you can stretch the rhythmic thread, make it elastic; you can never break it without paying the piper.

FEELING LINEAR MOVEMENT

By itself, playing *legato* on the piano is not a prerequisite for linear thinking, nor does it insure it. For this we must look beyond the continuity implied by a kinetic beat to the musical matter residing in the spaces between note heads.

Musical meaning calls for intervals to be lumped into small coherent groupings, which then become the building blocks of the larger, melodic units. It is reminiscent of the numbered dots in children's puzzles; the numbers and dots have little visual coherence until they are joined, and then, suddenly a meaningful picture emerges. Conceiving and singing a melodic line is similar. When students learn to fuse tones into meaningful small groups, suddenly a living phrase shape clicks. A meaningful gesture is born, which can later be expressed at the piano.

The understanding of these melodic shapes is determined by their harmonic and tonal context and by the feeling in our throats when we sing particular intervals. One of the best ways to understand and project linear movement is to imitate the breathing and sound of trained singers on your instrument. For example, the physiological reality that vocal chords slide easily in step-wise motion but need time and space to articulate wider skips or changes of direction should have ramifications on one's interpretation of disjunct musical lines. For this reason, and many others, it is very important for students to experience the elements of music vocally. And while some students have a natural ability to sing lines, others have never listened critically to the pitches they produce and therefore lack this ability. Unlike trained singers who always imagine a particular pitch *before* making a sound, non-singing students hear and think nothing before their attempt.

It is very important for students to experience the elements of music vocally.

How can we help this kind of student? Students must first learn to match pitches, to hear both inside and outside at the same time; this will demand a new kind of concentration. They must then learn to move from one adjacent matched pitch to another, and to focus on the size and direction of the interval. The general rule when practicing this skill is that the discrete pitches must be subsumed, that is accomplished *within* the context of something larger that moves steadily. If five successive pitches are sung by someone who moves his or her head and body five times, they will not be perceived as a line, even if they are sung perfectly *legato* and all in one breath. The key is that the experience of musical line is primarily cognitive. Students should establish a fluid arm gesture (while holding the rest of the body still) and then begin singing the five notes. With concentration, most students can do this without bouncing their heads or interrupting the arm's flow. This is the physical experience of musical line. The arm's steady movement acts as substrata for the changing pitches, having a psychological sustaining power akin to a bow stroke or breath. The next step is to sing simple phrases that cover increasingly distant intervals, but always within the context of a tonality and gesture.

The vocalization of groups of discrete pitches within a smooth, continuous body movement leads naturally to an internal understanding of line, musical gesture, and phrasing. One can develop a convincing lyricism on this foundation, which can be further refined in some of the following ways:

- While singing without head movement or interruption of the arm's movement, do not allow surface articulation, like rests or accents, to interrupt the cognitive experience of line.
- Pianists must also remember to concentrate through to the end of long, held notes in order for subsequent notes to make melodic sense within a phrase.
- Two-note slurs should be presented as the expressive binding

of two notes in a way that encourages students not to separate them from each other or from the surrounding musical context. Generally speaking, two-note slurs are held together just as the five notes were in our example, by a larger gesture. Contrary to standard instruction, the second note of a two-note slur should often be played earlier and at times louder to enhance the binding action. Second notes can sometimes be played softer, but almost never late.

- Occasionally a single, extended moving line makes the best musical sense if viewed as representing several lines. Interpreting faster notes as embellishments of a slower moving primary line may occasionally also make the best musical sense.
- Good posture at the piano can go a long way towards providing the smooth background movement required for the binding of tones. Most good musicians will also sway gently when they express lyric materials. The physical cycles tend to bind the many discrete intricacies into a musically coherent whole. Line is projected in this manner, whether a performer is consciously aware of doing so or not.

Performers must take the composer's written notes off the page, vocalize them, organize them into meaningful gestures, and then physically produce this at the piano. Every step of that process is manageable and teachable. And while it is truly hard, time-consuming work that requires effort and patience, once musically disadvantaged students internalize the proper skills and habits, their disability simply disappears. Most students have the potential for this transformation and are able to acquire the essential skills that their more fortunate, naturally musical colleagues have.

UNDERSTANDING SYNTAX

Our last consideration is the rules of musical grammar by which certain tones are grouped together melodically and rhythmically, forming the building block of musical meaning from which phrases are constructed. Although decisions about which tones are grouped together and which should be separated are often obvious, we occasionally confront ambiguous situations that require additional thought and experimentation. This is what practicing should be about – deciphering the composer's puzzle, deciding a personal conception, and developing the physical wherewithal to project it through our instrument.

Think of melodic invention as an exciting one-way journey in which the intervals between successive pitches have meaning only in the context of scale or harmony. The path can imply a chord (like an arpeggio), circle around important tones (like turns and upper or lower neighbors), or serve to pass from one note to another. The journey can take you through highly charged leading tones or through stabilizing bridge tones. Complex melodies often imply several voices or levels of operation. Tonality, primarily a closed system with its own rules and relationships, always exerts a significant, if not decisive pull, on melodic activity. These factors determine the melodic shaping and grouping rules that make musical gesture meaningful. It is the performer's duty to discover these kernels of musical meaning, and to build upward and outward from there, to a larger design.

Rhythm is the irregular, temporal element of syntax, whose notes and rests of differing lengths are organized into coherent groups. The rule of rhythmic syntax is surprisingly simple: a faster note usually begins a new rhythmical group. This rhythmic-impulse rule attunes students to an awareness of where faster motion begins. If a group of eighths is followed by a group of sixteenths, the first sixteenth begins a new rhythmic grouping that will last as long as note values remain the same or become slower. Rests, in this scheme, are added to the previous note value. Were the situation reversed, with eighth notes following sixteenth notes, these would be conceived of as within one rhythmic grouping.

These rhythmic groupings have little to do with meter, measures, or braced groupings of note-heads oriented to the beats. They are instead governed purely by contrasting note values, which, by themselves, can become a most important and useful organizing tool. In dotted or long-short triplet patterns, the short note belongs to the next note, not the previous long note. In dactylic patterns it means that the first of the two quicker notes begins a groups that ends with the longer note, no matter how it is braced. In long upbeat patterns, it means that you do not cut the upbeat into metric accents nor do you separate and/or accent the longer downbeat note. Accents should be used sparingly, only for special expressive purposes, for they tend to interrupt the line and break continuity. Metric accents should be avoided all together, as they cut musical meaning into a one-size-fits-all tedium. Rhythmic-impulse organizations can also be separately applied to each voice of a polyphonic work, which will enhance the individuality of the separate lines.

Rhythmic-impulse thinking dictates that upbeats, not downbeats, begin syntactical units. Just as interval distance and direction are the crux of melodic thinking, so too are the time-intervals between beats, upbeats, and wave-like movements, the critical areas in rhythmic thinking. When approaching music, students should first establish a kinetic beat that does not require attention, and then search for faster motion beginning in any voice. Ultimately, those two elements will become interlocking energy renewals that keep the whole fabric moving smoothly forward.

LITERATURE AND ITS PERFORMANCE

Any workable definition of musicality calls forth a description of the attributes of music itself; for it is in performance that musicality, or the lack thereof, is most exposed. We violate, in some critical way, what music making should be when we perform unmusically; we have erred in the way music works, or misunderstood something in a particular composition, or bungled something in the performance process itself. Whatever the reason, we have failed to make ordinary, satisfying, musical sense to the listener. The music we deal with is the product of the imagination and thought of one human who, working with the raw materials of music and within the parameters of the art, writes down an approximation of his or her aural image. We could call it an *auralism*. More specifically, we might describe a composition as organized, patterned tones moving through and creating the flux of time that exist purely in the world of hearing, and which, unlike language, denote nothing but themselves. These tones are dynamic; they reach beyond themselves in an implied context of shape and relationship.

One pitch is a mere sound, nothing more, but with two pitches and the space between, we have a beginning. The smallest ingredient of music is the interval between two tones, its size, direction, and its implication within tonality and the local context. Several intervals will tend to coalesce as they move toward or away from particularly important tones to form a contoured arrangement of meaning beyond the mere sum of parts. These small musical gestures become segments of melody. Dynamic melodic forces tug in the spaces between the pitches even before we add meter and rhythm. For instance, we hear C as the restful tonic in the key of C. However, our hearing of C when in D-flat is antithetically to the latter, because C is now the restless leading tone. Students need this kind of generalized music education to enrich their music comprehension and enhance the student's ability to conceive and project music intelligently – *to audiate.*

Rhythmically, we have interplay of the regular and irregular as performers generate the flux of time. Beats imply a regular, wave-like motion whose sense of forward motion is fundamental. Even more than that, it is music's natural state. Meter is a regular grouping of these wave-like beats (inaccurately illustrated by the bar line and other notational conventions), which should be subordinated to the most salient facet – rhythm. Rhythm is the irregular, the freely created, the most engaging element of music in the temporal dimension. Based purely on the interplay of long and short note values, it can galvanize a composition to a helter-skelter pace, or sustain an extended melodic line.

Rhythm is the irregular, the freely created, the most engaging element of music in the temporal dimension.

With harmony, we become aware of the relative tensions of sounds occurring simultaneously, and of the slower moving background structure of the music. Bass lines, which underlie harmonic movement, are also linear themselves and contain properties of melody and rhythm. Chord progressions have strong implications for tonality, phrase structure, and modulation.

Music is intensely alive in its own aural world, an amalgam of dynamic forces coexisting on many planes at once. These tonal forces are the result of one person's considered thought. We respond physically – somatically if you will – to this living, pulsating organism that is music because it mirrors the subtleties of our inner life. Students can be led to discover this excitement by connecting it to their bodies and to their feelings, by discovering the miracles of the tonal system, and by attending to the patterns of the written notes that the composer provided. Students will discover that music can reach places where words cannot go.

Our palpable attachment to music is through the inner ear and through an inherent, if not latent, ability to sing and dance. Students are able to understand melody to the extent they can be taught to sing musically – in tune and with melodic inflection. They are able to understand rhythm to the extent they can be taught to experience rhythmic motion kinesthetically, that is, through their bodies. The same holds true as we teach inner ear awareness of harmonic tension and release, of harmonic progression, rhythm, and phrasing.

CONTINUITY, PHYSICALITY, AND COHERENCE

Ultimately, musicality is impacted by three general and teachable skills, which ease and reinforce the learning of one another:

- Students must internalize the physical concept of a kinetic beat, and to reproduce the compulsion of musical *continuity*.

- They must connect all musical events to a personal experience of song and dance, to *physicality*.
- And they must gain the tools to understand the smallest and next smallest elements of music, and to move up the cognitive ladder to musical *coherence*.

Must piano lessons be turned into eurhythmic classes, singing lessons, and solfège classes to achieve these powerful anecdotes to unmusical playing? At times, certainly. When possible, piano teachers should farm much of this work out to the choral, eurhythmic, dance, and theory professionals, but we can never wash our hands of it completely. We must still insure that when seated at the piano, in front of us, students function as real musicians. I cannot overstate just how important musical authenticity is to the success of students. They must project intended pitches before they push levers. They must sense the rhythmic flow of the music with their entire body; counting, in the traditional sense, will not suffice. They must be helped to feel at one with the music, connected to the performing process. And then, within this framework, we can teach them about literature and style, and about how to best manipulate the instrument so that they will no longer feel on the outside looking in, wondering what they are missing.

Though desiring impressive results, we must guard against the quick fix, guard against leading our students down a path of disconnection, alienation, and eventual disillusionment. We must help them realize that the instrument is the vehicle for expressing the inner *musical* impulses, and we must show them what this means. We must also remember that these students will require great encouragement to overcome their shyness and fear. Our job as piano teachers is to bring students along as total musicians, training them to think, experience, and audiate music in ever more sophisticated and independent ways.

The Healthful

Spirit, Ego, and Music

Dylan Savage

This article is for all musicians, particularly pianists, who have not yet found any sustainable happiness with their life's work; specifically, those for whom the joy of music making has become elusive, whose inner struggles with negative, unproductive energies have become dominant. For many, the answer to this problem may lie in the balance between the roles of the spirit and ego.

THE BASICS

All expressions of human emotion are rooted in one of two primary emotional areas: love and fear. These two opposing forces speak to us through our thoughts and feelings. Love-related thoughts and feelings speak to us through our spirit. Fear-related thoughts and feelings speak to us through our ego. One can think of the spirit and the ego as separate agents that promote their respective belief system, be it love or fear. In the music-making process, struggle and conflict arise out of our moment-by-moment decision to listen to one internal voice or the other.

At the core of the ego – "the sense of oneself as contrasted with another self or the world"[1] – is the fear of not measuring up. When we choose to listening to this fearful, defensive, and competitive internal voice, the result is negative thinking that is disruptive to our artistic selves. This negativity stems from the belief system of the ego, whose primary goal is to defend its need to continue to exist, to watch out for 'number one' at all times. This defensive stance gives rise to all fear-related thoughts.

The spirit is the true essence and totality of you apart from your body, "an animating or vital principle held to give life to physical organisms."[2] The spirit is the activating force within you, the inner energy that delights in the creative process. The spirit promotes thoughts rooted in love. Not romantic love, but rather, a more generalized quality of love – a free, expressive, and abundant thought system that brings about feelings of joy, affection, devotion, and cherishing. These are all

[1] Webster's Collegiate Dictionary (1994), s.v. "ego."

[2] Webster's Collegiate Dictionary (1994), s.v. "spirit."

emotions that pianists might use to describe their relationship with the piano. It is your spirit that primarily shapes your music making into its unique voice.

The difference between ego-related thoughts and spirit-related thoughts about music can be identified by the emotions they evoke. As intoned by Shelley, in *The Sensitive Plant*, "For love, and beauty and delight / There is no death nor change."[3] This suggests that our spirit's joyful feelings about piano music are not influenced by our ever-changing abilities or levels of accomplishment. Ego-based thoughts focus on these assessments about one's playing, which change moment by moment, creating polarized feelings of self-worth that alternate between pride and censure. Spirit-based thoughts are unconcerned with such assessments, and create feelings of satisfaction at any level.

IMPLICATIONS FOR THE PIANIST

It is a spirit-driven energy that usually attracts young children to the piano; the same spirit that enables tones from randomly struck notes to instill such delight and wonder in the beginning pianist that the stage may immediately be set for a life-long journey with the piano. At this point, the most innocent and honest way one can approach the instrument has taken place – an attraction yet unaltered by any external forces. The spirit's attraction to the piano has no expectations, it is just an energy that exists and telegraphs a kaleidoscope of feelings. Some of these feelings defy articulation and others present clearer meaning such as the sense that this union will provide one's life a sense of meaning and fulfillment. At this early stage, few outside demands, pressures, or expectations are brought to bear on the quality of piano playing.

Some young pianists will make a conscious choice to make music their life's work; they sense the spirit will provide a conduit for its fullest expression, and thus, for themselves. They have found that artistic expression is perhaps the most meaningful and fulfilling part of life. In its purest state the creative spirit can exist quite happily and healthily by itself without any external input – it does not need praise nor peer respect to be fulfilled, it does not react negatively to criticism, pressure, or failure. However, at this level, the quality of one's playing becomes important and, as we all know, piano skills do not fall from the sky and careers are not made in isolation. Refined pianism is gained through constructive criticism, failure, struggle, and meaningful training. The pianist wishing to become involved in the professional arena is subject to the all the scratches and bruises that come as part of the professional music schools and music marketplace experience. It is in these kinds of competitive and highly selective arenas that the ego becomes most active and reveals its biggest downside: its capacity to take the spirit out of the music-making process.

The role of the ego (the part of us that traffics in fear) usually develops in young musicians after their music making becomes intertwined in the external world of teachers, recitals, auditions, competitions, and positions, to name a few. The ego voice can manifest itself in many ways: the first feelings of envy at something you feel you do not have; feelings of superiority when an accomplishment draws attention; how, when practicing and performing, it constantly tells you that you are not good enough; how defensive it may make you feel at even mild criticism of a performance; or that it restricts the impulse to complement the fine performance of another because you felt it might diminish the perception of

[3]Percy Bysshe Shelley, *The Sensitive Plant* (New York: Haskell House, 1972).

your own ability. In and of themselves, these are perfectly normal ego reactions. Remember, one of the main functions of the ego is its defensive system; it wants to make you feel good about yourself and does not like detractors. The danger is that the ego can progressively take over from the spirit and effectively smother it.

Scarcity, the fear that there is not enough for me, is a common ego theme. The ego reasons that there is only so much 'pie' available, and a slice given to another musician is one less slice available for itself. When you become dominated by the omnipresent sense of scarcity, you lose sight of all the possibilities for abundance for yourself. This last thought is important – although there will always be perceived scarcities, abundance, too, is *always* present.

Another ego belief and function is comparison. Comparison is such a common practice that there is hardly a person who has not engaged in it. At first glance, belief in this practice seems a logical, natural, and helpful thing to do. A look behind this belief, however, shows that the ego usually compares in order to *manipulate* judgment into praise for one's self, or criticism of another. Also, comparison can lead to crippling self-doubt and insecurity by magnifying the sense of one's own shortcomings, be they real or imagined, and it can cause yet-to-be accomplished goals to balloon out of proportion to take on an inflated sense of importance.

Fulfillment should come mainly through one's own personal experience and journey with the piano, and not be so dependent upon external successes.

Identity loves to commune with the ego. The ego wants to believe that its version of you is your true identity. To let go of the ego is to let go of a false identity, ending most conflicts. This undertaking may seem impossible for many, and the ego will indeed fight tooth and nail when steps are taken to banish it from being a dominant force. It will struggle to preserve itself at all costs, in large part because identity and self-value are, for many musicians, defined entirely by their abilities and successes as a professional. It is quite natural to want to define oneself as a successful pianist, and certainly logical and appealing for anyone pursuing a professional music degree. However, a major concern with identifying oneself with accomplishment (or lack thereof) lies with an insidious element of the ego: its astounding ability to never be satisfied with *any* accomplishment. This has disturbing ramifications. Left unchecked, the ego works to convince you that you are never quite good enough and that you always need to do more (a common trait from the ego's above-mentioned tendency to compare). A famous pianist once remarked that he felt he never had the career he deserved because he never attained the status of Rubinstein or Horowitz. One can only wonder what affect that mindset had on his playing and whether he ever truly celebrated his incredible gifts.

SUGGESTIONS TO HELP MINIMIZE THE ROLE OF THE EGO AND MAXIMIZE THE EFFECTS OF THE SPIRIT

TRY PLACING LESS IMPORTANCE ON THE EXPECTATION OF SPECIFIC RESULTS OR GOALS

Surprisingly, this is not counter-productive. When inroads are made in lowering expectation (not to be confused with standards), you will experience less turmoil and more inner peace, especially as it relates to your music. You will start to enjoy the process of making music again, which is a process of the spirit. The twentieth-century Irish poet Seamus Heaney said, "art is the process." This suggests that fulfillment should come mainly through one's own personal experience and journey with the piano, and not be so dependent upon external successes. Heaney's statement reveals what many of us, at our very core, honestly feel or have a sense of – that we would play the piano even if we were not paid for it and if no one ever heard us, and we would work no less hard at playing it. This, in turn, reinforces the earlier observation that the spirit voice within you, in its profound wisdom, sensed a deep attraction to the piano, somehow knowing the meaning it would add to your life.

Few of us actually internalize Heaney's perspective and put it into practice during our professional lives. Instead, we are more often caught in an irrepressible script, driven by ego that resoundingly proclaims the world's mantra that accomplishments are the only way to prove success, to ourselves and to others. It mimics a bad dream with a familiar narrative – despite an endless succession of accomplishments, nothing we do ever seems to be enough or gives any lasting satisfaction. Turning away from this script and claiming Heaney's perspective as your own will strip all power and function from the ego. This may be a frightening thought for those who fear that they will become soft and unambitious, lose their drive and vital perfectionist qualities, reduce their competitiveness, and lower their standards. These reactions are reflective of the ego-driven fear voice, and we can choose not to listen. Choosing, instead, to listen to the spirit voice will encourage our music making to grow more fully, enhancing those very elements the ego would have us worry about, and thereby negatively affect. By listening to the spirit voice, the primary motivation force is transformed from ambition to inspiration

LESSEN CONFLICT BY ADOPTING A DEGREE OF DETACHMENT

As Westerners, we may well equate this notion with not caring, but this could not be further from the truth. In Angeles Arrien's, *The Fourfold Way*, she wrote, "Linguistically, however, the word detachment is most often defined as the capacity to care deeply from an objective place."[4] Another way of looking this is what Timothy Gallwey, in his book, *The Inner Game of Tennis*, calls "Control by letting go"[5] and "Excellence by not trying."[6] Detaching yourself from the practice of valuing who you are *as it relates to your professional accomplishments* is a good first step. Piano practice and performance are not degraded in any way by this step and there are no negative effects if one applies the same exacting standards. For example, this step means that when something is not to one's liking in performance or rehearsal, by all means, correct it as always, but do so *without* emotional attachment or making a personal value judgment. When the propensity for negative judging is minimized, the spirit becomes more involved in the music-making process, freeing a path to potentially greater musical accomplishments.

TRY BECOMING MORE COMFORTABLE WITH UNCERTAINTY

How often have we labored long and hard for a specific outcome, only to have it derailed by circumstances beyond our control? Realizing how little influence we actually exert on our surroundings, and on the outcome of the future, takes time and requires a bit of humility. Not only does the uncertainty leave many feeling unsettled, it is the feeling of not getting what you deserve that causes much of the unhappiness along a career path. Countering these effects of uncertainty begins with minimizing expectations, a far cry from minimizing hard work and goals. By doing this you become more at ease with uncertainty and more apt to experi-

---

[4]Angeles Arrien, *The Fourfold Way: Walking the Paths of the Warrior, Teacher, Healer, and Visionary* (San Francisco: Harper, 1993).

[5]W. Timothy Gallwey, *The Inner Game of Tennis* (New York: Random House, 1974).

[6]Ibid.

ment and take chances, both of which often produce opportunities that exceed prior expectations. In some African cultures, a person is highly respected when they are comfortable with uncertainty. They are described in poetic metaphor as "walking the land of gray clouds."[7] So, work hard, persevere, *but* do so for the joy of the process. Success will come with this approach and its definition will take on new meaning.

REJOICE IN THE MOMENT; LIVE IN THE PRESENT!

Many people adopt this philosophy for their 'everyday' lives, but tend to ignore it in regards to their musical lives. An understandable shift, as one's musical life is often seen as elevated and separate, but the effects can be profound and the transition is worthwhile. The key is to start simply. Try spending a few minutes at a time during piano practice by being acutely aware of each moment, but, regardless of what happens, do not dwell on or negatively criticize what has occurred. Try, instead, to react in positive, constructive ways to situations over which, in the past, you would have berated yourself. This positive mindset will enable you to leave a practice session or performance where things may not have gone as you wished with equanimity instead of anguish. Do not confuse this equanimity with apathy. Becoming more comfortable with the present also means taking stock of all that you have accomplished to this moment *and* finding satisfaction in it.

STOP THE PRACTICE OF COMPARISON, FOR IT HAS NO REDEEMING VALUE

The ego does its best to find ways in which to boost its own level of esteem, creating continual fluctuation between the highs of self-aggrandizing and the lows of self-doubt. Comparison is done as a self-praise gathering mission, to see how you measure up. Remember the phrase 'you are unique,' because it plays a large roll in freeing the spirit in the music-making process. You are the sum total of a myriad of elements: your talent, instruction, discipline, environment, circumstance, etc. When you compare yourself to others you devalue your own accomplishments and retard your progress.

STOP BEING OVERLY SELF-CRITICAL AND GIVE YOURSELF PERMISSION TO ENJOY YOUR PLAYING

Years ago I made a breakthrough in my music making when I made the conscious choice to stop constantly berating myself for all that I perceived as wrong or not up to par with my playing. Up to that moment, I had been hypercritical of every note I played; earnestly thinking this approach would help me improve. The harder I tried to improve, the tighter my mental knots became. Instead of providing a climate that would allow my playing to grow at its fullest, I merely became a master at trying harder. The inner turmoil caused by my self-criticism could reach such a fever pitch during practice sessions that it was extremely uncomfortable. I felt no enjoyment in what I was doing, just chronic disappointment.

One day (in an act of desperation) I simply decided to enjoy what I was doing. It was not until later, thanks to Eloise Ristad's description of "inner judges"[8] in *The Soprano On Her Head*, that I understood what I had done – I had kicked all the "inner judges" out of my head, the ones that provided a constant litany of criticism on every note or phrase I played. I had been, with the best of intentions, effectively stifling my music-making ability. (The spirit retreats quickly in the face

---

[7] Arrien, *Fourfold Way.*

[8] Eloise Ristad, *The Soprano On Her Head* (Moab, Utah: Real People Press, 1982).

of ego criticism.) My negative self-judgment (a function of the ego) had worn me down and took the joy out of my music making. My turmoil was due entirely to the involvement of my ego – it had expectations and was constantly raising the bar.

By making this choice, I made peace with my piano playing and myself. Yet, I resolved never to stop trying, working hard, and challenging myself. I vowed to never again criticize myself in such a negative manner. A magical thing happened after taking that big step a few years ago: my playing immediately rose to a whole new level...and I began to enjoy making music again!

Choosing to listen to your spirit voice brings freedom to your music making. When your spirit is in command of your playing, your music making will no longer be fettered and will soar. Taking chances will become more attractive and easier, and you may find yourself doing things that you never considered (or had the nerve to do) before.

When you release yourself from the ego's energy and spirit-obstructing tendencies, you will give your music making the ability to find its fullest and most comfortable voice – its *mirabile dictu*. And this is, after all, what we were all striving to do in our practice and performance all along.

So, try switching over to your spirit voice instead of allowing the ego voice to dictate. Take a few steps at a time. If you have to, pretend at first. Take a leap of faith. Give yourself permission to enjoy your music making, as it is right now! Recapture the joy you felt as a child by remembering how wonderful it is to be able to play the piano the way you do.

An Introduction to Cognitive Strategies and Skills for Practice and Performance

Phyllis Alpert Lehrer

Most performers have suffered from some level of performance anxiety during their studies or careers. While anxiety may manifest itself physically, as sleeplessness or illness for example, it is the cognitive manifestations of performance anxiety that are often the most unsettling. Because of worry, self-doubt, distraction, and inability to concentrate in practice and/or performance, some pianists may choose to postpone, avoid, or even cease performing. Pianists who do not face such impediments to focusing on the music describe themselves as free from intrusive thoughts and feelings about themselves, other people, the piano, or the hall. For them, effective musical connection and expressive projection occur easily because they are totally involved with the performance. As psychologist, educator, and author Csikszentmihalyi writes:

> When goals are clear, feedback relevant, and challenges and skills are in balance, attention becomes ordered and fully invested. Because of the total demand on psychic energy, a person in flow is completely focused. There is no space in consciousness for distracting thoughts, irrelevant feelings.[1]

While many pianists are able to use intuitive methods to build confident, focused performances, others need to learn skills and strategies to do so. The private teacher plays a paramount role in integrating these strategies and techniques into the fabric of lessons and dress rehearsals. Parents also play an important role. Educating them about the relevance and usefulness of these skills and strategies will enable them to become positive and active influences, helping their children to build healthy mental attitudes and habits for practice and performance. Fortunately the relatively new body of literature and research on performance anxiety includes discussions of cognitive skills and strategies related to practicing and performing. Some of these emanate from studies of performance enhancement

[1]Mihaly Csikszentmihalyi, *Finding Flow: The Psychology of Engagement with Everyday Life* (New York: Basic Books, 1997) 31.

for athletes through sports psychology, while others are derived from research and development in the fields of stress management, music education, and piano pedagogy.

COGNITIVE TECHNIQUES STUDIED IN ATHLETIC PERFORMANCE

In the *International Journal of Sport Psychology*, Charmaine De Francesco and Kevin L. Burke described their investigation (through questionnaire) of the most common mental performance enhancement strategies used by professional tennis players (mean age of 25 ½). These included imagery/visualization, the use of consistent pre-service or pre-service return preparatory routine (i.e., mental preparation), as well as relaxation, goal-setting and self-talk. The players reported that their motivation to compete, and to maintain concentration and self-confidence all had important effects on their performance.[2]

There are obvious parallels to musical performance. For example, in studies involving tennis players, swimmers, and golfers, elite and non-elite athletes were compared with regard to their experience with anxiety, specifically its intensity and its debilitating and/or facilitating effects. Both groups experienced cognitive and physiological anxiety symptoms, but elite athletes reported that both kinds of anxiety were helpful (facilitative) to performance. In separate studies involving children just beginning to studying music and college musicians, the anxiety both groups experienced tended to be more facilitative to performance the longer the student had studied an instrument.[3]

At the Olympic Training Center in Colorado Springs, Colorado, elite athletes are instructed by their coaches in various stress management approaches, including progressive relaxation and breathing strategies. For many weeks in advance of the event or competition, these athletes also spend a great deal of time visualizing perfect movements. They also have sessions with a psychologist to discuss the dynamics of their relationships with their coaches. After the event, detailed de-briefings are held, during which player and coach discuss the positive aspects of the player's performance and the goals that will be set for future events. Music teachers and students might benefit from considering this as a model to be included in their performance preparation.

Discussions and rehearsals of progressive relaxation,[4] regular practice of a breathing method, and repeated visualizations of all aspects of the performance situation help quiet the body and focus attention. While it is unrealistic to imagine piano students with psychologists on board to evaluate the positive and negative aspects of the teacher-student relationship before a recital, teachers can use this

---

[2]Charmaine De Franceso and Kevin L. Burke, "Performance enhancement strategies used in a professional tennis tournament," *International Journal of Sport Psychology* 28, no. 2 (1997): 185-195.

[3]Donald L. Hamann, "An Assessment of Anxiety in Instrumental and Vocal Performances," *Journal of Research in Music Education* 30, no. 2 (1982): 77-90; Donald L. Hamann and Martha Sobaje, "Anxiety and the College Musician: A Study of Performance Conditions and Subject Variables," *Psychology of Music* 11 (1983): 37-50.

[4]It is important to note the combining of these techniques with Progressive Relaxation training, which is a technique invented by Edmund Jacobson and comprehensively described in his book, *Progressive Relaxation*, first published in 1929. Jacobson's premise was that the body responds physiologically to thoughts and events that provoke anxiety. The muscle tension that results from anxiety also increases it, creating a vicious spiral. He reasoned that learning deep-muscle relaxation would cancel out the anxiety, thus allowing a habit of muscle relaxation to replace a habit of muscle tension in the face of stressful events or situations.

model as a reminder of the impact their behavior can have on a student's performance. Indeed, the stress of performance can play upon a teacher's unresolved needs. For example, if the student's performance is connected to the self-esteem of the teacher, the teacher may become impatient, severely critical and exhibit other destructive behaviors as the time of a student's performance draws near. The upcoming performance of a student is a good time for teachers to step back, reassess, and reformulate the short and long-term goals they have for the student.

When preparing students for performance, it is also important for teachers to have a plan to address those students who are truly unready or too fearful to perform, but are hesitant to postpone or cancel a performance. This may be a time to use 'tough love' and insist that the student reschedule or indefinitely postpone their performance. Issues such as choosing to perform new or previously performed repertoire, setting realistic goals regarding the date and place of recitals, managing practice time wisely, testing thoroughness of practice preparation, and exploring strategies for performance anxiety may need to be considered. Pushing a marginally prepared student to perform sets the stage for failure and creates psychological tension in both student and teacher.

Finally, a musical parallel to the routine at the Olympic Training Center might suggest that it is important to have some immediate contact after a performance, a de-briefing, for example, between teacher and performer. Too often, a pianist goes directly to a reception or party after a recital; the teacher goes home, and the next contact between them is a week later. The student awakens the following morning wondering where the weeks or months of preparation went, barely remembering the performance experience. A teacher can help the performer continue to enjoy the afterglow of performance, while setting a time to meet by phone or in person within a day or two to set new goals for repertoire and to discuss the positive aspects of the performance. If there are many negative issues, it is also important to put these in perspective. The teacher should not deny what did occur. Rather, the communicative aspects of the performance can be emphasized. This is a good time to make plans for how teacher and student, together, will analyze and practice particular skills that will improve future performances.

Sports psychologist Kenneth Ravizza, who has worked with Olympic athletes, summarizes the ephemeral but gratifying goal of peak performance in his chapter "Qualities of the Peak Performance Experience in Sport."[5] He describes peak experience as "the fusion between the perfect nature of the movement and the willingness to dispense with the usual caution of not making an error. The athlete is in charge of the situation. Comments or congratulations from a coach, another player, or spectators become unnecessary because the perfect quality of the experience is irrefutable."[6] Equipping our students with the tools necessary to have such satisfaction in piano performance should certainly be one of our primary goals as teachers.

WORRY, JUDGMENTAL ATTITUDES, AND COPING STRATEGIES FOR PERFORMANCE ANXIETY: A PSYCHOLOGICAL STUDY OF MUSICIANS

Psychologists Paul M. Lehrer, Ph.D., Nina S. Goldman, Ph.D., and Erik F. Strommen, Ph.D. reported on the results of a questionnaire study of performance

---

[5]Kenneth Ravizza, "Qualities of the Peak Experience in Sport," *Foundations of Sport Psychology*, ed. John M. Silva and Robert S. Weinberg (Champaign, IL: Human kinetics, 1984) 452-461.

[6]Ibid., 457.

anxiety in the journal *Medical Problems of Performing Artists*.[7] Three aspects of anxiety designed into the questionnaire were:

1. "The tendency to worry about various possible performance disasters,
2. to be overly rigid and judgmental about the possibility of their occurrence, and
3. to avoid planning how to cope with them, should they occur."[8]

The subject populations included musicians giving concerts in the major halls of New York and Philadelphia, as well as those giving faculty, senior, or graduate recitals at several university music departments in the United States, Britain, Canada, and Australia.

The investigators found dimensions associated with debilitating anxiety to include:

1. High standards and judgmental attitudes toward performance
2. Worry about feeling anxious and how that might affect performance
3. Planning, or not planning, to cope with anxiety symptoms
4. Concern over distraction, either created by oneself (i.e. worry about memory, congratulatory or critical internal dialogue) or the audience
5. Concern about negative reactions of important others (i.e. critics, teachers, parents, and peers)

A variety of approaches can help pianists deal with these cognitions. *Inner Game* strategies and skills are specifically designed to eliminate mental interference such as judgmental thinking, distractions, and worry.[9] (The *Inner Game* master skills were first discussed by Timothy Gallwey in *The Inner Game of Tennis.*)

APPROACHES TO COUNTERACT THE ABOVE COGNITIONS

APPLYING STRESS MANAGEMENT TECHNIQUES

There are many techniques for pianists to borrow from the vast literature of stress management. These include ways to help recognize and then 're-frame' self-defeating thought patterns and irrational thoughts. For example, one way in which some performers express being anxious before a performance (dimension 2 above) is to feel depressed several days before a performance. Rather than interpret these feelings as 'bad', or indicative of an underlying desire to stop performing, pianists can accept that depressive feelings and thoughts are part of their pre-performance expression of anxiety and have no greater significance than that.

---

[7]Paul M. Lehrer, Ph.D., Nina S. Goldman, Ph.D., and Erik F. Strommen, Ph.D, "A Principal Components Assessment of Performance Anxiety Among Musicians," *Medical Problems of Performing Artists* (1990): 5, 12-18.

[8]Ibid.

[9]Barry Green with Timothy Gallwey, *The Inner Game of Music* (New York: Doubleday/ Anchor Books, 1986); Barry Green and Phyllis Lehrer, *The Inner Game of Music Workbook for Solo* Piano (Chicago: GIA Publications, 1996).

Another technique, described by psychologists Beck and Emery, involves becoming aware of anxiety.[10] This technique can be summarized as:

- *Accepting* anxiety as a natural part of responding to stress
- Achieving distance from your anxiety by *watching* it come and go (some people even give a pet name to their anxiety)
- *Acting* with anxiety, knowing that it may be appropriate to be anxious, but still possible to perform
- *Repeating* the first three steps may be necessary before the effects of anxiety become less (as with any new skill, repetition is important to mastery)
- *Expecting* anxiety as a natural part of life and certainly as a natural part of performing, rather than an indication that there is something wrong.

These five basic concepts, which form the acronym *AWARE*, can be a helpful reminder for performers, teachers and parents to keep a healthy perspective on the occurrence of performance anxiety. This technique might also help those who worry about planning to cope or planning not to cope with anxiety (dimension 3 above), as well as those worried about feeling anxious (dimension 2).

Pianists can begin to deal with worries about the negative reactions of important others (dimension 5 above) by using a technique called self-assessment, which involves the articulation and evaluation of the thoughts that underlie the pianist's anxiety and are used to justify it. The technique helps pianists restate their aims and goals for performing and can also help them discover how they handle their reactions to anxiety.[11] Concerns with the reaction of others can often generate negative self-talk. Albert Ellis, a well-known psychologist who developed a system to explain how irrational ideas or beliefs could contribute to our feelings about ourselves, suggests that self-talk produces unpleasant emotions, rather than actual events. This can be particularly useful and even comforting to the pianist who becomes increasingly anxious as he or she imagines the thoughts or reactions of others.[12]

Professionals in the already discussed field of athletic performance have developed other stress management techniques. Sports psychologist Don Greene suggests rather than internalizing every 'what if?' and allowing it to snowball and consume your attention, use it to reinforce what you need to do for a solid performance instead. In other words, every time you hear the 'what if?' respond either with a positive statement or challenge it, rather than buying into those

---

[10]Aaron Beck and Steven Emery, *Anxiety Disorders and Phobias: A Cognitive Perspective* (New York: Basic Books, 1985).

[11]An excellent resource to learn more about self-assessment is "The Psychology of Coping with Performance Stress," chapter 2 of the following: Paul G. Salmon and Robert G. Meyer, *Notes from the Green Room: Coping with Stress and Anxiety in Musical Performance* (New York: Lexington Books, 1992).

[12]Clearly described means of dealing with stress-producing thoughts can be found in the following: Ibid., 159-168; Martha Davis, Ph.D., Elizabeth Robbins Eshelman, M.S.W., and Matthew McKay, Ph.D., *The Relaxation and Stress Reduction Workbook* (Oakland, California: New Harbinger Publications, Inc., 1995) 135-155.

doubts. Answer the externalized voice with a very conscious, logical and knowing response. Consider this musical example: a pianist is worried about arriving at a passage for which a fingering was changed. Even though ample time has elapsed to enable the passage to be played automatically, the pianist is feeling distracted by worries about what might go wrong. Greene would suggest giving the distracting thought a name, maybe Bob. Then, have the pianist remove Bob from his or her head, externalizing Bob as the one behind the 'what if?' voice. The pianist might explain, *consciously and logically*, to Bob that the passage feels more comfortable with the chosen fingering, and ample time has elapsed to make it comfortable and successful. Greene further recommends that this technique should become part of a performer's daily routine.[13]

In some circumstances, difficult underlying issues relating to past experiences, parental expectations, or unique personal styles and circumstances may require the assistance of a counselor or therapist. That assistance may enable the pianist to identify and solve the problems of irrational beliefs and negative self-talk.

MENTAL REHEARSAL: AUDIATION AND VISUALIZATION

It is often stated that the mind does not distinguish between what is real and what is imagined. In other words, when we imagine playing something on the piano, many of the same neural pathways are activated as when we actually perform it on the instrument. Just as elite athletes spend weeks before an event picturing themselves executing perfect movements, pianists can practice visualizing the precise fingerings and arm and hand movements at the keyboard that will be used to play passages, phrases, and eventually entire pieces. Imagining the keyboard topography associated with these movements and picturing the musical form as it unfolds on the page can provide other visual cues. It would be helpful to introduce and practice this kind of visualization at a lesson, with the teacher instructing the student to close his or her eyes, visualize a particular passage or phrase, and picture the hands moving over the keyboard while also hearing each note. Another step might be to have the student slowly play the passage or phrase again, this time looking intently at every note on the keyboard and listening to its sound. The student might then be instructed to return to the music and look at every note of the passage or phrase and imagine its sound and feel. These steps enable pianists to test that they are truly audiating. Audiation being the ability to hear music silently, when it is not physically present, but more than just inner hearing, the musician must hear meaningfully and intelligently.[14]

When we imagine playing something on the piano, many of the same neural pathways are activated as when we actually perform it on the instrument.

A final step might be to imagine visually and aurally specific analytical details. Some examples might include:

- The shape and direction of every phrase.
- The relative tension and repose in the harmonic progressions within particular sections of the formal structure.
- Character and mood changes and their expression through changes in articulation and dynamics.

---

[13]Don Greene, Ph.D., *Audition Success: An Olympic Sports Psychologist Teaches Performing Artists How to Win* (New York: ProMind Music, 1998).

[14]Edwin E. Gordon, *Learning Sequences In Music, Skill, Content, And Patterns: A Music Learning Theory* (Chicago: GIA, 1988) 7-18.

This kind of work is painstaking, but well worth the effort to build trust in the visual mode, its relationship to sound, kinesthesia, musical understanding and intention. These steps will also prove useful for strengthening musical memory.

Many professionals, including Susan Bruckner, have addressed increasing the visual representational system in both learning and performing. Bruckner describes how the performer can use the visual modality to see exactly what it will be like to be in a performance situation. She refers to three positions or visual perspectives that can be used, and suggests that the performer:

1. Imagine being on stage, allowing his or her body to go through the 'motions of performing' and checking on what is seen while in the performance situation. In this position, the pianist would also be aware of what is felt (kinesthetic) and what is heard (auditory).

2. In the second position or perspective, the performer visualizes being a member of the audience and watches the performance. The pianist then imagines walking on stage, bowing, sitting down at the piano, experiencing every phrase of a piece, and playing a satisfying and expressive performance.

3. In the third scenario, the pianist imagines being at the back of a hall, perhaps in a lighting or recording booth, seeing him or herself in the audience, watching the performance on stage which is done confidently, accurately and expressively. Awareness of the audience connecting to the beauty of the music is emphasized in this final step.

This is a technique that teachers might assign to students for practice; in addition, teachers might include it in rehearsals with their students in the weeks preceding a recital.[15]

In addition to enhancing learning and performing, "visualizations or mental sense impressions that you create consciously can train your body to relax and ignore stress."[16] A technique called guided visualization enables the pianist to set a goal, and then visualize a scene in which a guide helps give support, wisdom and/or advice, which, in turn, helps the process of attaining the particular goal (in this case, a focused, confident and fully expressive performance). Pianist Mary Ann Hanley's article "Creative Visualization: Antidote to Performance Anxiety"[17] summarizes the guided visualization technique detailed by Shakti Gawain.[18] Hanley's article cites the work of hypnotherapists and counselors, and provides other useful references about creative visualization. She also describes a guided visualization that might be used by pianists before a performance, which is paraphrased below:

> Imagine a beautiful scene, a place which can be considered your personal sanctuary. You feel serene, at ease, happy. You may walk through a mountain pass, a path to a lake or some other scenic place. Imagine all aspects of the natural environment: breezes, birdcalls, the sound of water. Soon a place such as a mansion or

---

[15]Susan Bruckner, *The Whole Musician: A Multi-Sensory Guide to Practice, Performance and Pedagogy* (Santa Cruz, California: Effey Street Press, 1997).

> cabin is discovered, with a beautiful concert grand piano inside. There is also a guide or counselor to nurture, support and give guidance and inspiration. You visualize this guide as a brilliant musician and/or great teacher. As you play with great confidence and artistic mastery, you are aware of the encouragement of the guide who may even be providing helpful comments.

Most forms of mental rehearsal, including guided visualization, should be *preceded* by some sort of whole body muscle relaxation method, which is practiced as a strategy for reducing physiological tension. They are then *followed* by slowly counting to ease the way back to reality. It is suggested that, as with any new technique, visualization will only become a useful skill when it is practiced three times a day. For this particular skill, it is especially beneficial to practice while lying in bed in the morning and evening. With experience, pianists will become able to use visualization whenever and wherever they find it may be helpful.

VISUALIZATION: LEARNING AND MEMORIZING THROUGH MAPPING

Educators and psychologists who study cognitive processes have asserted the importance of students learning ways to organize new material in their own way, connecting this information to what they already know. In 1977, author Tony Buzan described a way of organizing the thought process in the form of diagrams or "mind maps."[19] Buzan's technique was aimed at helping readers understand and retain material read or heard in lectures through arranging key words visually on a page in order to indicate their relationship.

More recently, Rebecca Shockley applied this organizational tool to musical learning and memorization. The pianist is advised to study the music away from the piano, paying particular attention to form and recurring patterns. A map is then made, using graphics, numbers, colors, or any kind of representational notation. A typical map might include:

- A time line divided into measures or phrase lengths
- Numbers indicating interval size or chord symbols
- Dots, dashes, and/or wavy lines that indicate rhythm and/or melodic shape
- Abbreviations for repeated patterns, slightly contrasting patterns, continuous or foreshortened patterns

Teachers may introduce this technique to students at any level of study, from beginner to advanced, and it may be also used effectively at any stage of learning or memorizing. Mapping is also an effective tool for transposing, sight-playing, improvising, and composing, and can be used in private and group settings. It is also essential to urge pianists to experiment with mapping, because the most important goal of this technique is to create a map that organizes the musical material in a way that is *personally* useful. While some will respond to the chal-

---

[16]Davis, et al., *The Relaxation and Stress Reduction Workbook*, 56.

[17]Mary Ann Hanley, "Creative Visualization: Antidote to Performance Anxiety?," *The American Music Teacher* (June/July 1982).

[18]Shakti Gawain, *Creative Visualization* (San Rafael, California: New World Library, 1978).

[19]Tony Buzan, *Use Both Sides of Your Brain* (New York: E.P. Dutton, 1977).

lenge of working away from the instrument right from the start of learning a piece, others may choose to map portions of their pieces while doing some practice in more traditional ways.[20]

I have observed this process among a group of experienced piano teachers and graduate performance majors. Each member of both groups created a map for the same piece. Pianists were very different in the way they expressed their perceptions through mapping. Several people from both groups were amazed at their ability to memorize the new piece, given their propensity for fearing and avoiding the process of memorization.

INSURING A SECURE PERFORMANCE

In his chapter "The Performance of Music: Rehearsal" Sloboda writes, "... experts insist that secure knowledge of a piece of music involves forming multiple representations of it."[21] Traditionally, pianists have considered visual memory as one of the four standard multiple representations that help to insure a secure performance – visual, tactile/kinesthetic, analytical, and aural:

- In the visual representation, a pianist visualizes the music on the page and the look of the hands as they move across the keyboard to form visual representations.
- The pianist imagines the feel of fingers, arms, and hands and can reproduce fingerings mentally, on a tabletop, or in the air, for tactile security. Dancing or using movement to express sequences of musical events is also helpful.
- In the analytical representation, the pianist makes a formal, harmonic, and melodic analysis of the musical score, writing in chord functions, keys, noting passing tones, circling patterns or notes which change in similar patterns, coloring voices, and making indications of mood or character over portions of the music. Singing and verbally describing musical events further enhances comprehension of structural and musical details.
- When visual, tactile, and analytical memory become automatic, the most powerful representation remains, the aural representation. Now the pianist can just listen. It is extremely helpful to mentally rehearse the *sound* of the music, without the presence of the piano. Playing the piano with eyes closed is another way of testing aural security.

The teacher may suggest steps that have the pianist spend a few minutes each day sitting with the music in a relaxed environment, away from the piano. The pianist will check on his or her ability to imagine the sound, sight, and keyboard feel of the music. We have seen how mapping formalizes and helps secure the separate or combined aspects of memory. This can be the intermediate step before the pianist removes the music, and practices with eyes closed or in a dark

---

[20]Rebecca Payne Shockley, *Mapping Music: For Faster Learning and Secure Memory, A Guide for Piano Teachers and Students* (Madison, Wisconsin: A-R Editions, 1997).

[21]John A. Sloboda, *The Musical Mind: The Cognitive Psychology of Music* (New York: Oxford University Press, 1985).

room. Trust has been built in the analytical and visual skills, which become part of the memory back-up system. The most salient musical skills for performing by memory – the aural and tactile/kinesthetic – are now securely available. The pianist can focus on serving the composer and projecting the music.

Some or all of the ideas for mental rehearsal may be included in the process of preparing for performance. Teachers can guide students to include them as part of consistent practice routines and thoughtful pianistic preparations, which take place during the months before performance. During the more immediate rehearsal period (weeks or days before), visualizations should be emphasized which incorporate positive feelings and expectations about the upcoming performance:

- Qualities of the concert instrument
- Acoustics and visual aspects of the particular hall
- Placement of bench and piano
- Choice of lighting
- Members of the audience or jury
- Clothing, shoes, and jewelry
- Mood, pacing and order of pieces
- When to bow
- Whether to go off stage after every piece

Many performers also find it helpful to practice a pre-performance mantra which will be said or backstage or though en route to the piano. Some examples might include the short phrases: Have fun. Be musical. I'm ready. These too can be part of the visualizations as a performance draws near.

Mental rehearsal will aid teacher, student, and professional in helping to make practice and performance preparation creative and focused. The inclusion of cognitive strategies and skills in all the stages of a pianist's preparation can contribute significantly to building confident and focused performances. Their inherent applications to managing performance anxiety make them powerful tools. Acquiring and applying these special cognitive strategies and skills can lead to more productive practice and more gratifying, inspired performances.

Coping with Performance Anxiety: Inner Game of Music Strategies

Phyllis Alpert Lehrer

A pianist despairs over the awkwardness of a passage from Beethoven's Sonata, Op. 10, No. 2. She has played the passage in every conceivable rhythmic pattern. When her teacher asks her to experiment using awkward and unusual motions, the student's initial giggles give way to a tactile and visual awareness of a pattern that is the key to executing it. No longer fighting the awkwardness, the pianist has found that using more physical movement facilitates playing the passage. When her inner critic stops judging both her pianism, and Beethoven's 'awkward' writing, she connects to the music and plays it with conviction.

Another pianist searches for a way to get a dependable left-hand trill in the first movement of Schubert's B-flat Sonata, D. 960; she knows the number of trill repetitions she is making and has practiced daily trill exercises. However, as soon as she puts hands together, the trill sounds stiff or uneven. When her teacher suggests she play the same section two octaves higher, suddenly the trill comes out perfectly. The new registration has enabled the student to listen more closely; she has become aware of the sound of the trill in a new way and she finds a coordination that works, hands together, in both the high register and the low register in which Schubert wrote it.

A third pianist describes worry over getting tense while playing the A-flat 'Harp' Etude of Chopin. He has practiced varying the patterns and playing through the etude at different tempi with eyes closed; he has found no way to be free from the fear that tension may creep into his performance. When his teacher asks him to play the etude and rate his muscle tension on a scale of one to ten, he admits to eight. He is asked to repeat the etude and finds that amount of muscle tension has clearly decreased to four. *Allowing* tension to be present has put it into a different perspective. Paying attention to the *amount* of tension, rather than fighting its existence, has enabled the tension to decrease.

Paying attention to the amount of tension, rather than fighting its existence, has enabled the tension to decrease.

The way in which the pianist is *thinking* about tension now has a different framework. Psychologists call this strategy paradoxical intention. Deliberately inducing a fear eventually reduces or eliminates it. By seeming to separate it from the person, i.e. objectifying the fear, the individual gains more control over it. Pianists who worry over trembling hands or legs have used the same technique. They practice deliberately shaking their limbs or even specific fingers while they play; the trembling stops.

In each of the three examples, the teachers helped the students find non-judgmental 'awareness' instructions, substituting these for the more traditional problem-solving approaches that the students chose previously. The students' choices, while valid practice techniques, were aimed at finding the *correct* practice technique for getting something *right*. The teachers' suggestions were directed at student exploration: awareness of the *feel* of a passage; awareness of the *sound* of a trill in a new place; awareness of the *quantity* of a physical sensation and a different *way of thinking* about it. Rather than tell the students exactly what to do, or criticize them for not having success, the teacher used suggestions that illustrate the Inner Game master skill of awareness.

DEVELOPMENT AND OVERVIEW

Developed by professional athlete, coach, and educator, Timothy Gallwey, the Inner Game was intended to give athletes new ways to achieve a state of relaxed concentration and learn more naturally, thus reducing mental interference. In collaboration with double bassist Barry Green, applications for musicians were explored and developed.

The following Gallwey formula summarizes the aim of the athlete or the musician to perform at one's best:

P = p − i

Performance equals potential minus interference

Potential (**p**) stands for the sum total of talent, training, and experience; interference (**i**) includes the cognitive and emotional opponents of concentration and listening: self-doubt, judgmental thinking, irrelevant thoughts, and feelings.[1]

Barry Green investigated the Inner Game techniques through his own playing in the Cincinnati Symphony Orchestra, teaching double bassists, and giving workshops to singers, instrumentalists, and ensembles at the University of Cincinnati Conservatory of Music. *The Inner Game of Music,*[2] written with Gallwey, reflects that investigation.

Derived from these workshops for singers and instrumentalists, I collaborated with Green in developing *The Inner Game of Music Solo Piano Workbook*[3] to apply the Inner Game skills to the teaching, studying, and performing of piano repertoire specifically. I selected seventy piano pieces with the student, teacher, or performer in mind; providing two levels of repertoire for each Inner Game exercise, one quite easy, the other more advanced, from which the pianist may choose.

AWARENESS

Inner Game awareness instructions help pianists pay attention to what they hear, see, feel (emotionally or physically) or understand. For example, there are numerous ways described in the workbook to become aware of muscle tension,

---

[1]These are among the same dimensions of performance anxiety that were explored in the psychological study by Paul M. Lehrer, et al, quoted in "An Introduction to Cognitive Strategies and Skills for Practice and Performance."

[2]Barry Green with W. Timothy Gallwey, *The Inner Game of Music* (New York: Doubleday/Anchor Press, 1986).

[3]Barry Green with Phyllis Alpert Lehrer, *The Inner Game of Music Solo Workbook for Piano* (Chicago: GIA Publications, Inc., 1995).

in addition to the way mentioned above (the pianist playing the Chopin A-flat Etude, Op. 25). One exercise invites the pianist to select and slowly play either Gigue by Arnold (Level 3) or the more challenging Bach F-major Invention (or choose a similar piece, such as a gigue from a Bach suite or a fast prelude), noticing where in the body tension is found.

The pianist who is unaware of tension might deliberately create tension in a part of the body where tension often does occur: the shoulders, thumb, jaw, or neck, for example. The exercise is then repeated at a faster tempo, and again, the experience of tension is noticed. During the next repetition, pianists noticing tension would be instructed to put some kind of movement in its place. For example, if tension occurred in the forearm, the pianist might focus on gently moving the arm to a pulse while playing. If the pianist noticed tension in the neck, the suggestions might be made to move the shoulders or lower back while playing. Sample dialog questions for the muscle tension awareness activity might include:

- How did your focus change when you substituted movement for tension?
- Repeat this exercise with your attention on your breathing as your play. Is your breathing steady or irregular?

As will be seen when the master skills of will and trust are explored, these applications not only link teaching with performing, but address performance anxiety as well.

Inner Game coaches focus on non-judgmental approaches to learning. Exhortations to 'try harder' are avoided. *Gestalt* psychologist Fritz Perl is frequently cited for his saying, "Trying fails, awareness cures;"[4] or, as guitarist Joseph O'Conner has stated, "the key to teaching and learning is where to place your attention."[5]

WILL

Defined as giving direction and intensity to the performer's intention, this second master skill helps pianists clarify their musical intentions and goals. While awareness skills involve monitoring sights, sounds, feelings, or understandings *while* playing, will skills influence decisions *in advance* of playing. These might include basic decisions pianists make when practicing, such as deciding upon fingerings after listening to and/or reading through a piece of music.

An example is the will activity "Commit to Pitches and Fingerings." This activity may be applied to an early level piece, such as Tony Caramia's "The Scrambler," from *Sounds of Jazz, Book 2* or to the more advanced J.S. Bach Prelude in B-flat from Book I of *The Well-Tempered Clavier*. The pianist is directed to focus on one thing at a time. Reading the notes at a steady tempo; studying the key signature and accidentals; or listening to the music on tape, following it without playing and getting the pitches in the ear. The next instructions are to play with the hands on an imaginary keyboard or silently 'play' the keys on the piano to explore fingerings that might work in the new piece. Blocking or noticing the interplay or trade-off of melodic material between the hands is another possible step; playing through the piece at a steady tempo, on an imaginary keyboard, with eyes closed might complete this phase of learning.

---

[4]Fritz Perl, *Gestalt Therapy Verbatim* (Utah: Real People Press, 1969).

[5]Joseph O'Conner, *Not Pulling Strings* (London: Lambent Books, 1987) 130.

The corresponding dialog exercises will help pianist clarify their practice goals:

- Were you able to stay with the exercise step-by-step, or did you find you wanted to combine any of the steps? If so, which steps?
- Did you find yourself rehearsing what you intended?
- What was the effect of practicing the fingerings without actually pressing down the keys?

New decisions are made for polishing musical details as a performance date nears. Decisions for dynamics might be investigated, asking such questions as: Where might the loudest passage be? The softest? What should *crescendo* or *diminuendo*? When phrasing is decided upon and marked in, the relationship of phrasing to dynamics might then be explored.

Not meant to elicit 'right' answers, the questioning process is intended to clarify intentions and explore them. The same can be said of another suggested part of the dialog:

- Imagine yourself explaining this way of practicing these pieces to a friend or colleague. How would you explain the benefits of this approach?

Being given the opportunity to further clarify his or her performance decisions during practice will also give the performer confidence in remaining focused on the music during performance.

A performance application of will skills, once a piece has been polished, might follow this scenario. A pianist preparing a rag by William Albright has made detailed musical decisions but feels self-conscious and constrained about communicating the style. A next step might be to imagine the most appropriate place or setting for playing this piece – café, concert hall, jazz club, outdoor festival, to name a few. Another decision to make might be about how the pianist wants to feel while playing – laid back, formal, at ease, communicative, relaxed. These kinds of decisions help formulate a commitment to a performance goal, which replaces worry and insecurity. Before the pianist plays, the *intention* is clear: to communicate the atmosphere or performance style of this piece.

TRUST

Trust skills are those that enable a pianist to be focused and at one with the music. They assume that the basic hard work of a pianist is done: getting the music into the ear and fingers, solving any technical problems, and formulating basic musical intentions. When trust skills are mastered, there is little room for fears about being prepared for the task of performing, meeting the expectation of critics, teachers, parents, or peers, or worrying about distraction and memory. As Mildred Portney Chase wrote in *Just Being at the Piano*:

> ...each time seek to reach that place where the only thing that exists is that sound and moving toward the sound. The music on the page that was outside of you in now within you, and moves through you; you are a channel for the music, and play from the center of your being.[6]

[6]Mildred Portney Chase, *Just Being at the Piano* (Berkeley, California: Creative Arts Book Company, 1985) 3.

Barry Green designed a non-musical trust exercise that illustrates the difference between performing a task with a critical inner voice versus performing it by letting go to the activity, becoming one with it, trusting it: Performers are instructed to work in pairs. After finding a partner, one pianist gives the other an expert massage, trying to use fingers correctly to work their partner's tense muscles, impressing the partner with an awareness of where tension resides and with the quality of the massage. After the roles are reversed, another back massage is given. This time the instructions are different. The person giving the massage is to imagine that the partner's back is a large lump of pizza dough. The instructions are to knead the back, to use the whole hand, to dig in, remembering the image of pizza makers to guide the massage. (Again, each partner should experience giving and receiving this second massage.)

Participants in this exercise are guided to answer questions about their feelings during each massage. These have no correct answers, but help convey the difference between doing something with a focus on being an expert and making an impression versus trusting and letting go to a playful image of an activity. The earnest and serious tone of a room full of masseuses trying to give 'correct' massages contrasts markedly with that created by the same group of people turned into a convivial, un-self-conscious crowd of pizza makers.

Much of music study involves being in control of technical, stylistic, and interpretive details. An inspired performance, though, makes the audience feel that the performer has, in some sense, relinquished control and trusted some essential aspect of the music – its feeling, idea, imagery. Self-consciousness and inner obstacles can again hamper the communication of those essential aspects. By working through the following trust activities in preparation for performance, though, it is possible to minimize these obstacles:

ROLE PLAYING

Pretend to be the great pianist with whom a piece is associated – Argerich playing Prokofiev's Third Concerto, Horowitz playing *Traumerei*, Periaha playing Mozart's D-minor Concerto, K. 466. Then play a recording of the artist you choose, close your eyes, and join the artist performing.

Turn off the recording and imagine the playing. Listen to the sound. Imagine watching their hands. Notice their confidence and superb concentration. Feel you have their experience, technique, confidence, and musicianship. If you were this person playing this piece, you would sound like this.

Now play it as if you actually were the performer. Throw yourself into it. Let the artist play through you.

TRUSTING TO THE CHARACTER AND POTENTIAL STORY OF A PIECE

Copland's *Cat and Mouse* has been a favorite for students and teachers. Scenarios can be specific, with students providing detailed images describing the activities of the cat and the mouse for each section of the music. Ask them to consider how assuming the qualities of the cat and mouse influenced tone, expression, freedom, or gracefulness.

Remind that them in performance, one would likely oscillate between awareness of the animal character – constantly comparing your sound and character to the images and feelings evoked by these animals – and trust in just being these animals. There is nothing wrong with this, as most musical performances are not merely transformations of a character. It is also likely that in a lengthy piece such as *Cat and Mouse* it will be necessary to depart at certain moments from the character portrayal to attend to details of rhythmic accuracy.

Once the performer develops and trusts this strong connection to the music and its program, worries about the speed or precision of the sixteenth-note passage become unlikely.

TRUSTING TO THE QUALITY OR FEELING OF A PIECE

The final movement of Schumann's Phantasie, Op. 17 provides a poignant example. In this nostalgic and hauntingly beautiful piece, dream-like, wistful sections alternate with more intense, impassioned ones. Forming an image of Clara and Robert dancing through eternity has been helpful to me, particularly since ending the athletic coda of the second movement often makes it difficult to begin the dramatically contrasting final movement without a transformative image and change of feeling.

TRUSTING THE BODY

A pianist was about to begin the second half of a recital, but was unable to remember the first notes of the piece. She decided to ignore doubt and worry, and let her hands find the notes. Trusting her kinesthetic sense helped her avoid an awkward and embarrassing memory block.

Pianist and author, Charles Rosen, has written about improvisation:

> It may not be completely true to say that the fingers of the pianist have a reason of their own that reason knows not of, because improvisation is not exactly unconscious, but it is clear that the fingers develop a partially independent logic which is only afterward ratified by the mind. In playing a Chopin ballade, an interpretation can be as much an instinctive muscular reaction of the body as a reasoned approach.[7]

Other activities involving trusting the body might involve playing an etude as fast as possible, without worry about controlling the fingers; conversely, playing a slow movement slower than would ever be its chosen tempo. In each case, the pianist may play beyond expectation. Trusting to exaggerated tempi may lead to a feeling of freedom and competence. A quotation from the *Inner Game Workbook's* "Trust Dialog" seems appropriate here: "Often our fingers, wrists or arms can do things we didn't expect them to do – when our mind doesn't limit the speed of our muscles."[8] New insights about the music's shape, groupings of patterns, spaciousness and breath, balances, voicing, and coloristic possibilities are likely to occur as non-judgmental explorations that trust the body are made.

THE BENEFITS

The application of the Inner Game and its master strategies can help pianists and piano teachers facilitate creative explorations and self-generated learning. It is not meant to provide a new set of rules or 'shoulds' for concentrations. Rather, having worked with techniques for awareness, will, and trust, teachers may find

[7] Charles Rosen, "On Playing the Piano," *The New York Review of Books* XL VI (October 21, 1999): 16.

[8] Green, *The Inner Game of Music Solo Workbook*, 167.

their students more active participants in listening and making musical decisions. Also, pianists will feel more confident in focusing their attention, should they need to regain concentration as they practice, rehearse, and perform. The relaxed concentration achieved through meeting the challenges of the Inner Game will enable pianists to enjoy the freedom to connect with the music and express it fully.

Strategies for Handling Performance Anxiety

Gail Berenson

Performance is not life threatening, but for many the stress that surrounds it can threaten a future of successful music making. Sweaty and shaking hands, and the inability to eat, sleep or function normally are common symptoms of a problem that can become so significant that a number of students may choose to quit their lessons due to their overwhelming fear about an upcoming recital. For some, it is any upcoming performance, regardless of its relative significance, even a weekly lesson. What would appear to be a minor performance to one person can pose almost insurmountable difficulties to another.

Today's pedagogues are finally beginning to recognize that students do not simply become accustomed to performing, and are promoting strategies to deal with the serious problem of performance anxiety. Though wanting to lessen the debilitating effects of stage fright, entirely eliminating the anxiety is not the goal; for it is the very same elements that create the stress that make the performance exciting and memorable for the performer. Rather, the objective is to prevent the feelings of apprehension from derailing the performance and allow the electricity of the moment and the connection with the audience to combine for a thrilling performance that can surpass anything achieved before.

It is the very same elements that create the stress that make the performance exciting and memorable for the performer.

Be it with exercises to reduce feelings of performance anxiety or strategies to acclimate them to performing, helping students discover ways to channel these emotions to work in their favor is where teachers can be the most effective. With an arsenal of techniques at their disposal, teachers can work with the unique circumstances of a given individual to help make them more comfortable with performing, or even strengthen the performance skills of those students who already enjoy performing. What follows are strategies designed to help ensure that a student's performance more accurately reflects his or her capabilities. They can serve as a guide for teachers and students; using a trial-and-error approach, each can experiment and personalize their own performance routine.

LOWER YOUR HEART RATE

One of the most common and alarming things that can happen before or during a performance is the sudden awareness of your pounding heart. To some, it seems to be beating so fast and so loudly, they feel certain that everyone present can hear it. While this is obviously an exaggeration, the heart rate can increase tremendously when the individual perceives that he or she is under duress, even when there is little physical exertion involved. When this occurs, there is a feeling of being out of control that can lead to or increase anxiety. This can be combated in two ways: achieving a lower overall heart rate, and mastering ways to lower pre-performance heart rate.

By scheduling aerobic exercise four or more times per week for at least twenty minutes, students can achieve a minimum level of cardiovascular fitness and reap the benefits of their efforts, including stress reduction, injury prevention, and a reduced resting heart rate. The latter is a significant benefit because as a performer begins to acclimate to the situation and relax, the return to his or her normal resting heart rate will be faster. This translates to a feeling of greater control and will help to greatly reduce anxiety.[1]

For even the most fit individuals, the moments just before a performance can be particularly stressful. The heart rate can skyrocket and breathing can become fast and shallow, causing students to hyperventilate and begin to feel faint. Controlled breathing is the quickest way to achieve control over these reactions, which, along with the many physiological symptoms that can be so troublesome in a performance situation, are produced by the autonomic nervous system. To this end, there are numerous exercises, found primarily in books that deal with stress management, with which teachers and students may experiment in preparation for a stressful performance. One such example, as described in the book *Superlearning*, follows:

> The objective of this exercise is to learn to breathe in rhythm, and through rhythmic breath control, to slow down body/mind rhythms. Sit comfortably in a chair or lie down on a couch or bed. Put yourself into a very relaxed state. Make sure all parts of your body are relaxed. Close your eyes and take a very slow, deep breath through your nose. Inhale as much air as you can hold comfortably. Try to take in just a little bit more air. Now exhale slowly. Feel a deep sense of relaxation as you exhale. When you think all the air is out of your lungs, try to force out a little bit more. Practice taking these very deep breaths for a few moments. Inhale as much air as you possibly can. Distend your abdomen. Slowly exhale. Pull your abdomen in. Take another deep breath, as much air as possible. Hold it for a count of 3 and exhale very slowly. Relax. Try to inhale the air in a very even, continuous breath. Now, try to make your breathing rhythmic. Inhale to a count of 4; hold to a count of 4; exhale to a count of 4; pause to a count of 4.
>
> Inhale – 2, 3, 4; Hold – 2, 3, 4; Exhale – 2, 3, 4; Pause – 2, 3, 4. Repeat four cadences of this rhythmic pattern. Relax. This time, try to slow down your cadenced breathing even more, by trying a count of 6.

---

[1]The methods and benefits of basic fitness are addressed in more detail in "Benefits of Fitness," page 143.

> Inhale – 2, 3, 4, 5, 6; Hold – 2, 3, 4, 5, 6; Exhale – 2, 3, 4, 5, 6; Pause – 2, 3, 4, 5, 6. Repeat four cadences. Now try to slow down your cadenced breathing even more by using a count of 8, etc.[2]

Some musicians may prefer to use meditation or yoga to become more centered and to slow their breathing, and they should be encouraged to find a exercise in that discipline that feels comfortable to them. Once mastered, the exercises can be done just prior to the performance, or whenever experiencing symptoms of stress, to lower the heart rate, enabling the individual to relax and focus his or her concentration.

RELEASE EXCESS PHYSICAL TENSION

The stress of an upcoming performance will often manifest itself in physical tension, which can throw students into a very dangerous stress cycle, which is illustrated below. Once immersed in this pattern, it is extremely challenging to escape, so it becomes particularly important to work with students on strategies to release excess tension. This includes incorporating relaxation and stretching exercises into lessons or performance classes to promote the concept of relaxation.

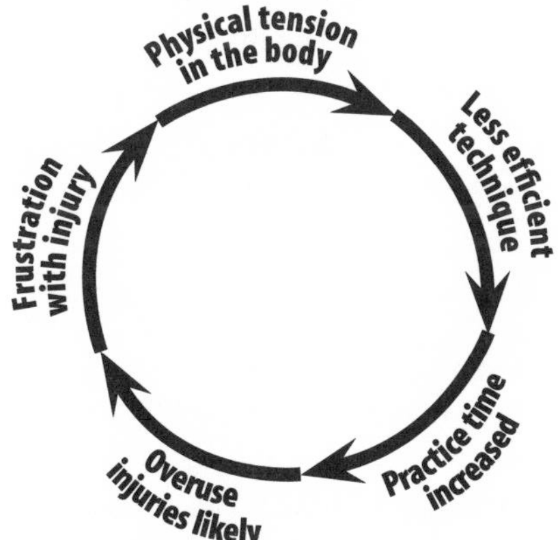

One technique used frequently by psychologists is progressive relaxation. A type of tension-release exercise, the technique involves working systematically through the different muscle groups, tensing targeted muscles, holding for ten seconds, and then releasing these muscles. Experiencing the contrast between tension and relaxation helps identify the muscle group and allows students to focus on specific areas that are especially prone to holding tension. This is particularly beneficial because even in the presence of other people backstage, it is possible to do some of these tension-release moves and to release tension without drawing undue attention. For people who have difficulty getting to sleep prior to performances, working systematically downward through the body, beginning with the forehead, can provide a feeling of release, enabling the individual to sleep.

It is important for teachers to carefully observe their students to ensure that posture and technique are being executed in a relaxed and efficient manner. A number of movement techniques not traditionally associated with pianistic instruction can also be employed to enhance a student's overall comfort and security at the instrument. These include Feldenkrais, Pilates and the Alexander Tech-

---

[2]Sheila Ostrander and Lynn Schroeder, with Nancy Ostrander, *Superlearning* (New York: Delta /The Confucian Press, 1981) 105-106.

nique, and teachers should be encouraged to take advantage of the many available books and videotapes.

MAKE CHANGES IN COGNITIVE THINKING

If the mind perceives a performance as a threat, it will engage the body's natural response to fear – the so-called 'fight or flight syndrome'. By changing a person's perception about performing into something positive, as opposed to the enemy, we can reduce the symptoms of the body's response system, and thereby, minimize anxiety. Several strategies to accomplish this goal follow:

TRUST IN SELF

If performers do not have trust in themselves and they begin to question their ability, they will have difficulty believing that they are capable of making it through the performance successfully, thereby creating a self-fulfilling negative prophecy. To combat this, quiet the internal negative voices and replace them with thoughts like, "I've done it before," "I know I can do this!"

SET REALISTIC GOALS

Musicians are notorious perfectionists and more often than not, if one wrong note is played, the performer will become distraught, lose concentration and give up on the rest of the performance. This can be magnified if the performance is seen as 'do or die'. Recognizing that a perfect performance is an unrealistic, possibly unachievable goal is an important first step in countering this reaction. The next step is equally important – creating more realistic goals: to make it through the performance, to play as well as possible, and to gain something from the experience that will make the next performance better. Being more attentive to the valuable information that can be gleaned from each performance and using it to identify and clarify the places that need more attention will be more beneficial in the long run. Ultimately, students should be encouraged to think of each performance as one of a long string of performances, each a vital link in the learning chain.

STAY IN THE PRESENT

Some performers are so preoccupied with judging themselves as they play that they are not listening or aware of what they are doing at the time. If a mistake is made, they are consumed with figuring out how it happened rather than focusing on the ongoing music. Irrelevant thoughts like, "Oh, no! What's the next note?" "What if I forget and can't go on?" "What if I make a fool of myself?" creep in. Performers must transcend these distractions not only to ease anxiety, but also because responding to the music as it is created provides the most spontaneous and exciting kind of performance. It is when the performer is so involved with the music, the sound and the connection with the audience, that a sense of *flow* occurs, enabling one to play with amazing clarity of thought and physical ease. A state of being that athletes are familiar with and strive to reach, musicians can try to attain this same feeling if they immerse themselves in the music and the composer's intentions. Focusing on their physical senses can help performers achieve a desired sensation of *mindfulness*, which can help in this pursuit: *hear* the music unfold in a natural way, *listen* to the melodic line and the way the other voices support it, *watch* your hands move effortlessly across the keys in fluid gestures, and *feel* your hands relax into the keys or move briskly from key to key.

Anticipating potential pitfalls prior to a performance can be equally detrimental. Focusing on questions such as "On what note does the next fugue entry begin?" can result in sudden panic when thought of in isolation, without any other cues, and the answer is "I can't remember!" Music is learned using aural, kinesthetic and visual senses. Attempting to remember a specific note, when under stress and without the presence of all of these sensory cues, can lead to disaster. Students often unwittingly orchestrate the likelihood for memory slips to occur by thinking through their pieces backstage without any sensory cues, relying only on their analytical memory. With their concentration scattered due to all the activity backstage that is typical prior to a performance or their own heightened inner excitement, they suddenly draw a memory blank. This last-minute panic can undermine their confidence and, ultimately, the performance. While backstage, it is more prudent to use the music when thinking through different passages just prior to performance.

PERCEIVE PHYSICAL SENSATIONS AS POSITIVE INDICATORS

It is possible that the day of the performance will bring some unusual or unexpected physical sensations, including dry mouth, queasy stomach, or cold, clammy hands. With a severity often directly proportional to the perceived importance of the performance, these symptoms are typically met with dread or fear. Unfortunately, this negative reaction and intense focus will only magnify the symptoms and be detrimental to the performance. Students should instead view these sensations, a result of signals from the brain to the body brought on by the excitement and adrenaline from the occasion, as something that can heighten awareness and enable the performer to achieve a more spontaneous, electrifying performance. Viewed in this positive way, the performer can then focus on the task at hand, resulting in the diminishing or disappearance of these symptoms.

VISUALIZE YOURSELF SUCCEEDING

For many years, athletes have been working with sports psychologists to visualize their movements and rehearse a positive outcome in situations where they have only one chance to accomplish their goals. And just as the competitive events for which these athletes are preparing parallel performances for musicians, so can this training strategy.

Some ways in which these visualization techniques can be adapted for musicians follow:

VISUALIZATION AND PRACTICING AWAY FROM THE INSTRUMENT

Sitting in a comfortable, quiet location and using their music, students can visualize themselves performing a composition or playing through a recital, deriving many of the same benefits as if physically executing the activity. It is important to experience every musical and technical detail, and to also imagine that one's playing is effortless, technical issues are problem free, and the sound is glorious. When fully utilized, mental practicing can help create a more secure performance and can offer students another option when playing time is limited due to an injury, or when no instrument is available.

Mental rehearsal can also be an effective tool immediately before a performance situation.

Some researchers have investigated the use of mental rehearsal just prior to performance of a skill. In their studies the subjects used brief mental rehearsals of the immediate task (rather than imagine actions that might happen later on in the performance). The results showed that in addition to preparing the nerves and muscles for action, the mental rehearsals promoted concentration and helped many performers to maintain a sense of confidence.

Therefore, just prior to playing, project your ideal mental model of the opening measures of music. In the course of playing a piece, mentally prepare entrances that follow rests. By engaging in such mental activity your mind remains focused on the task at hand, thereby reducing distracting thoughts. Furthermore, the knowledge that you are mentally in command may generate some extra self-assurance.[3]

THE POWER OF VISUALIZATION

As psychologists have discovered, individuals have such a strong mind-body connection that they can control a number of physical functions through their thoughts. While this is a skilled dynamic that must be developed, the potential to counteract some of the physical symptoms that arise in a performance situation certainly exists. An example: stressful thoughts can cause one's hands to become cold. Visualizing sitting near a fireplace with a glowing fire, feeling relaxed and enjoying the cozy warmth of the room can raise hand temperature. Many of the physical symptoms arising from stress that create problems for performers can be significantly reduced through a combination of relaxation exercises and visualization.

VIRTUAL PERFORMANCE

For those students with little performing experience, or a succession of negative experiences, visualizing themselves successfully completing a performance can build confidence that will transfer to the actual performance, making it less foreign and threatening. The first step in this exercise is to achieve a totally relaxed state, which, for many, comes best in the evening, before going to bed. Once relaxed, begin mentally playing through the composition in the manner discussed in the mental practicing sectioning above. While going through each composition, immerse yourself in every musical detail and nuance in the score, and simultaneously envision being in the performance situation, performing well, and enjoying the experience.

To help students mentally create a performance setting, students can create a personalized guided imagery that describes their particular performance circumstance. Mentally seeing themselves successfully complete the upcoming performance helps build security and self-confidence. The sample below can be used as a template:

---

[3] Malva Freymuth, *Mental Practice and Imagery for Musicians* (Boulder, Colorado: Integrated Musician's Press, 1999) 62.

Positive Thought
Guided Imagery for the Day of a Performance

Written by Gail Berenson

I look up at the clock — time to get up. Then I remember what day it is — today is my recital! It seems only yesterday that it was a month away. I feel excited and ready as I start this special day.

I move at a relaxed pace all day. After breakfast I spend some time warming up at the piano.

As I continue my warm up, I feel my muscles grow more supple. I start each composition and slowly play through some of the more difficult spots. I will go through this process several times today. I will play just enough to feel comfortable since I want to save my energy for tonight, not wishing to wear myself out in rehearsal.

As the day progresses, I feel more and more exhilarated. The day passes quickly, and soon I begin to dress for the performance.

As I dress I feel a flutter of nervousness. It is okay for me to be a little nervous - it is heightening my self-awareness and will allow me to present a more sensitive performance. I have learned to relax. I can control my nervousness and turn it into a positive factor.

Warming up at the piano in the recital hall, in my performance clothes, I am very aware that my recital is merely minutes away. This is my night! Having practiced for those short periods spaced throughout the day, I already feel warmed up. Now I begin to feel even more flexible and comfortable as I try out the piano this last time. The sound of the piano in the empty hall resounds in my ears. It is a new sound enhanced by the excitement of this moment.

The microphones have been put in place, the lights adjusted, the piano positioned. The stage manager has just told me that he is ready to unlock and open the doors. This is it!

I retire backstage and visit for a while with a few close friends until they leave to find their seats. Now, while I'm alone is a good time to take one last look at my music and to rethink my first piece, focusing on what I want to express in this composition. All the little details and decisions I made in my practice have become an integral part of my conception of this piece. I have special feelings about this music that have grown since selecting it, and I want to share these feelings with my audience.

Five minutes to go and then the door is opened for me and I'm walking onto the stage. I feel a charge of excitement and anticipation. I move with ease and purpose toward the piano. All my practice and hard work has brought me to this moment where I can communicate my feelings about this music.

As I acknowledge the applause of the audience, I am aware of their energy and support. The warmth of the lights and the sound of the applause make me feel welcomed to the stage.

I feel comfortable as I sit down at the piano. I have spent so many hours at the piano, it now feels very much like "home". I look out at the expanse of the instrument - the bare strings, the open lid, and I feel a sense of power and mastery. The keys feel warm from the lights. The cone of light makes me feel as if I am ensconced in a cocoon - warm, safe and secure.

I position my hands, take a deep breath and begin to play. Sinking deeply into the keys, I feel assured by the solidity of the bottom of the key bed. My arms are relaxed, my hands steady. I know I am well prepared.

Although I feel a rapport with the audience, my concentration is on my music - listening, allowing the piece to unfold by itself, through me. Memory will remain intact since I will allow one musical idea to naturally follow another. Ideas unfold like the telling of a musical story I know very well.

My hearing is sharper now than it has been in my practice. The presence of an audience creates a heightened awareness and sensitivity toward my playing. As I respond to the sounds I am creating, I feel as if I am hearing the music in a new, fresh light, stimulating a more intense interpretation of the music. My hands feel very supple. I play with ease and fluidity. It seems as if my hands are dancing on the keys.

Each piece is over so soon! What took so long to prepare is going by so quickly, first one piece, then another. I can hardly believe that it's already intermission with only half the program remaining. As I wait backstage, I am eager to get back on stage. My hands are tingling - I can feel the blood surging through my hands. I feel hot and flushed. I can hardly wait for the stage manager to turn off the house lights. I'm ready to begin the second half!

Back on stage, I realize that as I complete each piece I grow nearer and nearer the end of the recital. I wish it could go on forever. And then, it's suddenly over! I hear a burst of applause and it feels wonderful. The sound rolls toward me like a wave enveloping me. It is as if the audience is reaching out to me.

Very important to me is knowing that I have played as well as I can at this moment. This was a good performance! I greet my friends and relive the excitement of the performance with them. I know why I play recitals - it's because I love to perform! Another reason is because I love the celebration afterwards!

SCHEDULE A VARIETY OF PRACTICE PERFORMANCES

Students that challenge themselves to play in front of others and succeed receive a tremendous boost to their self-esteem, often followed by the powerful realization that they are capable of doing anything they want to do if they work at it. It is the challenging responsibility of teachers to find ways for all students to experience this fulfillment.

Desensitization, when coupled with relaxation techniques, is a powerful behavioral technique that is often used to relieve fears of flying or heights. It can be equally powerful when assisting a fearful student in feeling more comfortable playing for others. Because what is stressful for one may not be at all stressful to another student, it is helpful to have each student create a personalized progressive hierarchy of performance activities, from the least stressful to the most stressful.

Rather than forcing students into performing, which is never a recommended strategy, the challenge becomes matching the student with a series of options that enables them to begin to share their music making with others. Lower-stress performance options can include small group, partner or overlapping lessons or playing duets with a fellow student. For students who are still uncomfortable, tape recording practice sessions might be a non-threatening first step. Young students might choose to perform for their family pet or their teddy bears. As students progress, some options including taking them to nursing homes to perform or suggesting that they play for their family or in their church or synagogue. Featuring a teacher/student duet on these early performances may also be advantageous. Higher on the stress hierarchy, teachers might arrange recitals or offer the chance to participate in non-competitive adjudicated events, and so on up the list, gradually increasing the stakes, until the student establishes a degree of performance comfort and, ideally, discovers that performing can be fun.

THE IMPORTANCE OF PRACTICE PERFORMANCES

Because it is often only in pressured situations that slips of memory or glitches in technique will occur, it is also vital to eventually test the performance in a situation that replicates as closely as possible the performance stress. Working through a composition or recital in a performance setting will help reduce any fears of the unknown and allow students to become comfortable playing in front of others. A minimum of four performance practices is recommended, but some students may need many more to begin to feel comfortable. These dry runs will also help focus upcoming practice sessions by revealing any weaknesses.

BECOME EDUCATED ABOUT CURRENT MEDICAL ADVANCES

In years past, it was not uncommon to learn that famous performers used alcohol or tranquilizers to enable them to face their fears, sometimes inadvertently sabotaging the quality of their performance. Educators and doctors certainly frowned upon this behavior, then and now, but recently a new class of prescription medication has found itself at the center of a similar controversy. Beta blockers, normally prescribed to patients with heart and blood pressure problems, have also been found to eliminate the physical symptoms of stage fright without the dangerous physical side effect of drugs and alcohol. For a number of years, physicians have been prescribing them, off-label, to help people cope with performance anxiety.

Beta blockers like propranolol or Inderal (brand name) work by preventing adrenalin from combining with specialized beta receptors in the autonomic nervous system, eliminating or alleviating the anxiety responses that would ordinarily occur. On the surface, this can seem like a terrific solution because a single small dose (10-20 mg) taken 60 to 90 minutes prior to a performance will give you the desired effect, while at the same time entering and exiting the blood stream quickly and posing no threat of *physical* addiction.

More careful consideration, though, reveals that these medications are not the quick fix that some hope for. It is important to recognize that beta blockers will not eliminate any of the psychological thoughts that can occur before or during a performance and negatively affect a performance. It is helpful only to a person who is well prepared, has discovered ways to control his or her thoughts, and is primarily concerned about some specific physical stress symptoms. For example: a string player who is auditioning for a position with a major orchestra might fear that her bow arm will shake, producing a wobbly sound. Ultimately, she feels more nervous about the possibility of the bow shaking than the performance itself. In this instance, beta blockers might be useful. They might also help those individuals who are caught in a vicious cycle of becoming nervous only because in previous performances their nervousness has caused them to emotionally and pianistically fall apart.

It is this author's belief that, for most individuals, performance anxiety can be overcome through combining and experimenting with the behavioral strategies listed earlier. If this is proving not to be the case, though, it might be useful to seek a medical professional specializing in performance anxiety to help discover what is at the root of the anxiety. Often, if individuals are experiencing anxiety in musical performance situations, they are dealing with excess stress in other areas of their lives as well, and bringing resolution to these stressors will be much more beneficial in the long run than camouflaging the true problems with medication.

That said, there will be those students who decide to incorporate beta blockers into their performance routine. In this situation, it becomes the teacher's responsibility to see that the decision is made in consultation with a physician, who will check for any contra-indications that might prohibit them from taking beta blockers, and, in the case of younger students, with their parents. For teachers who utilize beta blockers themselves, please remember that this is a prescription medication and teachers must not give out their own medication to students, under any circumstances.

MISCELLANEOUS TIPS FOR TEACHERS

Since teachers play such a vital role in helping students cope with performance anxiety, it is important to be aware of several practical things that they can do to give students the best chance for successful performance experiences.

1. Select appropriate repertoire that is challenging, but within a student's range of ability, and assign it far enough in advance to allow ample time for security and mastery of material.
2. Encourage thorough preparation, for without it there is no performance strategy that can save the performance.
3. Assist students in developing self-confidence. A positive self-image will transfer to performance situations.
4. Provide a variety of performance opportunities that enable

students to build a foundation of positive experiences; making sure to include low-stress options on a regular basis.

5. Encourage, but never force performance. Often the best encouragement comes by serving as a role model as one who enjoys performance.

6. Assist students in working on concentration and relaxation skills. Use studio or performance classes to introduce and experiment with these concepts.

7. Practice stage presence and provide opportunities for dry runs. Try out concert clothing, especially shoes for women and jackets for men.

8. Focus on the naturalness of the music unfolding and conveying the meaning of the music. Place less emphasis on mistakes or wrong notes.

9. Encourage students to take good care of themselves, emphasizing healthy diet, exercise and adequate rest. Reduce caffeine several hours prior to a performance.

10. Emphasize the joy of performing and having fun!

Just as teachers can be and often are the vital link in help helping students overcome performance anxiety, they are also capable of making statements that can negatively affect students. Often done with the best intentions, it is nonetheless important to avoid the following:

1. Forcing students to perform.

2. Telling students they should not be nervous.

3. Criticizing a student's performance just prior to the recital when adequate time is unavailable for the student to act on the feedback. Comment only about what can be comfortably corrected in the time that remains.

4. Offering negative feedback immediately, even though constructive. Allow the student to bask in the glory of the performance.

It is to every teacher's advantage to explore the rapidly expanding body of work on the subject of performance anxiety. In recent years, a large variety of books addressing current trends have proliferated in the marketplace. One outstanding source of information is the journal *Medical Problems of Performing Artists*. Music Teachers National Association (MTNA) also offers an excellent, current, and well-annotated wellness bibliography on their website, *www.mtna.org*.

THE LIFELONG REWARDS

Although pleasure can be derived from playing or singing in private, there is something very special and exciting about sharing this experience with others. It can be a joyful experience and, to those students who accept the challenge to perform, it can bring a sense of accomplishment and increased self-worth. It is not uncommon for students to discover that if they can handle the demands of a performance situation, the other stress-provoking events that life presents are easier to overcome.

Taking a test in school, standing in front of a class to give a presentation, playing for one's family over the holidays, going for your first job interview, or performing on the stage of Lincoln Center. The measure of anxiety is not about the specific event; rather it is about the degree to which the apprehension interferes with accomplishing one's goals. With the help of a sensitive and knowledgeable mentor, performing at the instrument and in life can eventually become an expressive outlet, free of anxiety, and a means to enhance self-confidence, positively affecting all aspects of life.

The measure of anxiety is not about the specific event; rather it is about the degree to which the apprehension interferes with accomplishing one's goals.

Benefits of Fitness

Gail Berenson

Musicians rarely define themselves as athletes, but it is an image that should be seriously considered. Given the long hours of practicing, the concentration required, the physical demands placed on the body when sitting properly, and the scrambling to meet rehearsal and performance deadlines, it becomes clear that the life of a musician can be physically and mentally challenging. Meeting these challenges requires a strength and endurance that can be improved by adopting fitness strategies.

Beneficial to musicians of all ages and skill levels, fitness is an important key to unlocking the potential of all pianists. The greater the fitness level, the better equipped they are to handle stress, to focus concentration, to enjoy increased stamina, and to avoid injury. Musicians need not train as intensely as athletes to reap these benefits. Rather, simply perceiving themselves as athletes may help to promote a greater attentiveness and appreciation of the body, and encourage them to integrate small amounts of consistent, moderate exercise, coupled with a healthy diet.

AEROBIC EXERCISE

Medical research continues to document multiple benefits from incorporating exercise into one's daily routine and stress that it is an important factor in ensuring a healthy future. To enjoy these benefits, one can schedule as little as twenty minutes of aerobic exercise, four times per week. While it is always wise to check with a personal physician before beginning any exercise program, any continuous activity that involves the entire body will work, including activities such as walking, running, swimming, rowing, cross country skiing, or bicycling.

To realize cardiovascular benefits, exercise physiologists recommend achieving and maintaining a target heart rate of 55 to 75 percent of one's maximum heart rate, provided it is not so strenuous that one cannot carry on a conversation. Less fit individuals should work at the lower end of the range, while those who wish to achieve a higher level of fitness may choose a workout objective that brings them closer to 90 percent of their maximum heart rate.[1]

Benefits for musicians are wide ranging, beginning with a strengthened immune system, which reduces the need to cancel performances and minimizes time away from work or school due to illness. A boost in endurance is another important benefit. It is common for pianists, both students and professionals, to practice and/or perform for hours at a time. Aerobic activity appears to strengthen the entire musculoskeletal system and can become an important element in helping musicians endure extended practice sessions and avoid injury.

The mental benefits are also a tremendous asset in both practice and performance. Due to the increased blood flow that is the natural result of aerobic exercise, concentration is improved. Exercise can also help improve sleep quality and reduce feelings of anxiety, and its ability to manage stress is touted throughout the medical community.

> Exercise is one of the simplest and most effective means of stress reduction. Vigorous physical exertion is the natural outlet for the body when it is in the 'fight or flight' state of arousal. Exercise returns your body to its normal equilibrium by releasing natural chemicals that build up during the stress response.[2]

Increased ability to handle the stress and anxiety that often accompany performance is yet another reward. When under the pressure of performance, it is not uncommon for the heart rate to extend well beyond what the physical circumstance demands, particularly at the start of a performance. If, however, a pianist has achieved a reasonable level of cardiovascular fitness the time is takes the heart rate to return to normal after exertion decreases. So as the heart rate rises early in a performance situation, the likelihood is that it will drop back to normal levels more rapidly, enabling the performer to feel more at ease and in control of the performance.

STRENGTH TRAINING

Strength training represents another component within a fitness profile. As with aerobic exercise, working with weights will increase endurance and help in avoiding fatigue. In addition it will strengthen and tone muscles, offering individuals a significant injury-preventive benefit. Appropriate for students of high school age or older, this activity should be seriously considered by older students in an effort to develop a stronger foundation of bone mass, helping to prevent osteoporosis in the future.

Musicians need to be especially cautious while performing this activity, making sure form is correct and that the amount of weight lifted is not more than what can be handled safely. It is also important to "strengthen muscles in a balanced way. For example, if one performs bench presses for strengthening the pectoral muscles, he or she should also perform a rowing exercise to pull the shoulders back and prevent a round-shouldered posture."[3] When working with

---

[1]The American College of Sports Medicine advises individuals to compute their maximum heart rate by subtracting their age from 220. Heart rate can be determine by measuring the pulse with the tips of the index and middle fingers of the opposite hand at the radial artery on the thumb side of the wrist for ten seconds and multiplying that number by six.

[2]Martha Davis, Elizabeth Robbins Eshelman, and Matthew McKay, *The Relaxation & Stress Reduction Workbook*, 4th ed. (Oakland, California: New Harbinger Publications, 1995) 251.

[3]Sheila Mark, licensed physical therapist, Athens Physical Therapy, Athens, Ohio.

weights, there should always be a day of rest in between strength workouts, giving muscles the chance to recover. To assure safety and to better determine which exercises are most appropriate for an individual, working with an experienced and certified personal trainer is recommended.

NUTRITION

Any discussion about fitness is incomplete without mention of diet. Eating a balanced diet is important in maintaining good health and takes on special meaning for musicians. Making sure that adequate nutrients are consumed to fuel the muscles is crucial. Although nutritionists differ in their recommendations, it should be noted that the United States Department of Agriculture (USDA) offers the following nutritional specifications, while noting that a focus on whole, unprocessed foods is especially encouraged:

- 55% carbohydrates, emphasizing complex carbohydrates
- 15% protein, emphasizing sources of protein that are low in saturated fat
- 30% fat, emphasizing mono-unsaturated fat

The food pyramid developed in 1992 by the USDA and the United States Department of Health and Human Services is also an excellent resource for determining an appropriate balance of nutrients, servings, and serving sizes. Research in this field is ongoing, so it is wise to be on the look out for any new models that evolve, including the Mayo Clinic's Healthy Weight Pyramid,[4] a recent arrival. Meanwhile, recognizing that it may not always be possible to achieve a well-balanced diet, it may be prudent to consider taking a daily multi-vitamin/multi-mineral pill.

Keeping the body hydrated at all times is another dietary consideration that is often neglected. Essential to achieving optimal performance, nutritionists recommend that people drink six to eight glasses of non-caffeinated fluids, preferably water, each day. During times of physiological stress, high temperatures and high humidity, even more water is needed to avoid dehydration.

The content of meals and their timing prior to performance is especially important for musicians. Smaller meals that avoid high-fat foods and emphasize complex carbohydrates, combined with a small amount of protein, should be eaten two to four hours prior to the performance. Eating candy or other simple sugars for energy creates a temporary rise in vitality but can quickly turn into an energy drain.

Coffee is another stimulant that can promote alertness, but it can also increase feelings of anxiety. Although individuals accustomed to drinking coffee should not eliminate it entirely on the day of a performance, due to the possibility of caffeine-withdrawal headaches, caffeine should not be consumed after 2:00 p.m. on the day of an evening performance. The same constraints apply to other sources of caffeine like tea, sodas, and chocolate.

WARM-UP AND COOL-DOWN

As with any kind of strenuous physical activity, a period of warm-up and cool-down is important. Previously, exercise physiologists recommended that

[4]A detailed explanation of the Mayo Clinic's Healthy Weight Pyramid can be found at *www.mayoclinic.com.*

everyone stretch prior to beginning any demanding activity. However, it is now believed that gradually raising the temperature of the body and the muscles even prior to stretching will help prevent straining or tearing of the muscles.

Whether exercising or practicing, begin with slow movements and carefully increase speed, allowing the muscles to slowly warm. A wide variety of books and videotapes that recommend and demonstrate stretching exercises are available, with some specifically designed for musicians.[5]

INCLUDING FITNESS IN ONE'S PEDAGOGICAL ARSENAL

Basic injury-preventive wellness methodology should become part of every teacher's pedagogical repertoire. By serving as both role models and vocal advocates of fitness, music teachers can bring yet another helpful strategy to their students that will serve to enhance all aspects of their physical and mental well being at and away from the piano.

[5]A listing of suggested warm-up exercises from the Rehabilitation Institute of Chicago Medical Program for Performing Artists can be found on page 219 of *A Symposium for Pianists and Teachers.*

Pushing the Physiological Envelope

Jacqueline Csurgai-Schmitt

In an ideal world, pianists would be able to instantaneously realize their musical ideas in sounds – an example of perfect mind/body coordination. In the real world, the musical idea, conceived mentally, must first be sent through a neuro-muscular-skeletal-circulo system (the body), which is functioning more or less efficiently and in a more or less-coordinated manner. Physiological, psychological and emotional barriers to efficient functioning will directly determine the amount of practice time required before a pianistic action is able to be finely tuned and coordinated by the body; if, indeed, the action takes place at all. Moreover, the swiftness and accuracy with which a body is able to translate a musical idea into sound has been, in the past, part of the criteria for determining musical talent or genius. In fact, the remarkable ease with which the virtuoso performs is a true indication of his or her superior, physical coordination.[1]

Until recently, physical ability at the piano was considered innate – either you had it or you didn't. However, within the last twenty years tremendous progress has been made toward demystifying the entire realm of psycho-physiological functioning at the keyboard. We have found new techniques for improving peripheral facility by increasing inner awareness, with many of these methods now taking place away from the piano. The musical passages that, in the past, may have taken many hours of practicing to perfect, now may often be refined in much less time. The reason: other, non-pianistic activities have removed some of the internal barriers to efficient movement.

It is an exciting by-product of this information age that human potential is viewed, not as a static condition, but as a dynamic and changing state, improvable by direction of will and intent. Boundaries of all kinds – mental, psychological, physical, and emotional – are capable of being expanded, and even broken, if the individual's will and desire are strong enough. The pianist who wants to dissolve the limitations to complete musical freedom of expression in his or her own playing will explore each of these areas.

---

[1]Otto Ortmann, *The Physiological Mechanics of Piano Technique* (New York: E.P. Dutton & Co., Inc., 1962) 99.

While the phrase 'getting in touch with the body, mind and emotions', sounds very 'new age' and may turn many pianists away, the fact is that the pianist can use awareness techniques to great advantage in expanding his or her own physiological boundaries.[2] The number and type of techniques available are extensive. The Alexander Technique, the Feldenkrais exercises, Hatha Yoga – all have much to offer in helping the pianist become more consciously aware of the level of tension in the body. One has only to select the right technique(s) that works for him or her.

The pianist can apply yogic stretching to muscles that are operating within a short range of motion and increase the efficiency of their performance. One can use controlled, rhythmic breathing to change and modify the internal muscular resistance that limits the physical level of functioning. Or, one can apply meditational techniques to dissolve mental and emotional barriers that prohibit the pianist from reaching his or her full potential. Moreover, there are numerous health care providers who will work with the individual to correct, modify, and improve the way in which the body and mind operates.

It is usually rare for muscles to be exhibiting only the tonus needed for efficient functioning. Lack of physical exercise (a particular problem with pianists) and the stress of a professional career, which can often include public performances prepared with an inadequate amount of practice time, is enough to cause excessive tension in the muscles. At any given moment, our physiology is usually holding some degree of extraneous muscular tension, the manifestation of which changes from day to day. Most pianists have had the experience of playing a particular passage at the piano with ease and facility one day, only to find the same passage awkward and difficult the next. The body may feel 'out of sorts' and uncomfortable on these days; these signals should not be ignored. After all, "incoordinated movement results from excess relaxation as well as excess contraction."[3]

TENSION RELEASE

This dynamic condition of surface muscles can overlay and hide chronic states of tension associated with trigger points in the deeper muscles and fascia of the body, because the mind's pharmacoepia of chemicals is capable of shifting the awareness of deep myofascial tension to a subconscious level. The resulting chronic muscle tension can become acute when the involved muscles are overloaded through sudden, heavy practice sessions or unusual stress in one's everyday life.[4] In a concrete way, these deeper layers of tension can and do limit the pianist's overall potential for speed, endurance, and control of the instrument, which interferes with his or her innate musical creativity and talent.

Pianists should know that, after many hours of practicing at the keyboard, muscles begin to retain a certain amount of tension, which, if not released through stretching every day, will accumulate. Since pianists are known for their long hours at the instrument, it is not surprising that, after years of such practicing, the muscles will normally store so much extraneous tension and become so shortened that they begin operating in a limited range of motion. The great

---

[2]Several contributors offer various techniques to improve mental well-being at the piano. Their chapters are included in *The Heathful.*

[3]Ibid., 100.

[4]These ideas are expanded upon in "Overuse, Pain, Rest, and the Pianist," by Dr. Norman B. Rosen, page 156.

majority of people, not just pianists, carry extraneous tension in their bodies, so it is helpful to know that physical therapies that release deep, myofascial tension are extraordinarily useful in reducing pain and enhancing freedom of movement.[5]

Accumulated tension in the deep muscles and fascia usually needs to be released by an expert in myofascial release. When these muscles are released, technical improvement at the piano, in the area of speed and endurance, is dramatic. Many pianists do not know that releasing chronically tight muscles in the back or shoulders, for instance, will increase flexibility, allowing fingers to move more freely and, therefore, faster. Hands-on techniques for myofascial release include such modalities as ischemic compression (also known as trigger point myotherapy),[6] spray and stretch technique,[7] trigger-point injection therapy,[8] Osteopathic Manipulative Technique, Strain-CounterStrain, Acupressure, Acupuncture, Rolfing, Reiki, Trager, Meilus Muscular Therapy,[9] and therapeutic-massage therapy.[10] (Remember, the ultimate responsibility for healing lies directly upon the pianist's shoulders. Finding the appropriate techniques and suitable practitioners is as important as finding the right piano teacher – each must be explored and experimented with to know what will eventually fit the individual.)

For the initial success of these methods to become long-lasting and enduring, the following will be required: retraining of the body systems through body awareness techniques; re-education of the muscles through stretching exercises; and reduction of chronic tension patterns through breathing techniques, similar to those taught in The Art of Living Workshops[11] and available in most cities.

Proper breathing – contracting the diaphragm to allow the lungs to fill fully – has a direct and positive effect on the muscular and circulatory systems. Unfortunately, pianists do not usually have to think consciously of about it because of the nature of the instrument. The addition of such yogic breathing techniques as Ujjayi breath to one's stretching postures, for instance, will greatly deepen the muscles' tendency to let go of excessive tension. Using the Bhastrika breath as an energizer can enhance one's daily activities, including piano practice.

STRETCHING

Playing the piano, while a strenuous activity, does not move the fingers, hands, arms, torso, and legs through their full range of motion. Indeed, if the pianistic movements are finely coordinated, the range of motion of the involved muscles will be minimal. By stretching, we maintain and enlarge the range of motion of our muscle, making them freer and more coordinated. This biomechanical fact has been accepted by most pianists and teachers, and has helped encourage most pianists to do some kind of warm-up *before* they begin their heavy practicing.

However, not all pianists stretch in an optimal manner. Most do not take the time to stretch their muscles *after* they have spent hours at the keyboard. Potentially

[5]The myofascial pain and dysfunction syndromes are addressed in the chapter, "Muscle Pain and Pianists: The Myofascial Pain Syndromes and Fibromyalgia."

[6]Janet G. Travell and David G. Simons, *Myofascial Pain and Dysfunction: The Trigger Point Manual*, 2 vols. (Baltimore: Williams & Wilkins, 1983).

[7]Ibid.

[8]Ibid.

[9]For more information, visit www.meilus.com.

[10]American Massage Therapy, 820 Davis Street, Suite 200, Evanston, IL 60201-4444, (708) 864-0123.

[11]The Art of Living Foundation, P.O. Box 50003, Santa Barbara, CA 93150, (805) 453-6396.

more damaging than failing to stretch after time at the keyboard, many pianists do not know that it is important to warm the muscles even before beginning to stretch. (This can be done by doing some simple warm-up exercises or by taking a warm shower or bath.) Another common occurrence is for pianists to jump right into a stretching routine without investigating the proper way to stretch without injuring the muscles. This should never happen given the number of books about stretching on the market (and the willing input of one's physician).

The suggested exercises that follow are simple stretching postures, limited to the upper body. They can be incorporated into a general stretching routine that includes the whole body. If they are performed before and after the practice session, they can help to keep the muscles flexible, thus increasing their strength and endurance. Along with the above caveats, keep in mind that not of all the exercises need be done every time. Pick and choose the areas that need the most attention.

WARM-UP

Prevents damage to the muscles by increasing their temperature prior to any stretching.

Walk in place or around a room for five minutes, arms swinging forward and backward.

Breathe.

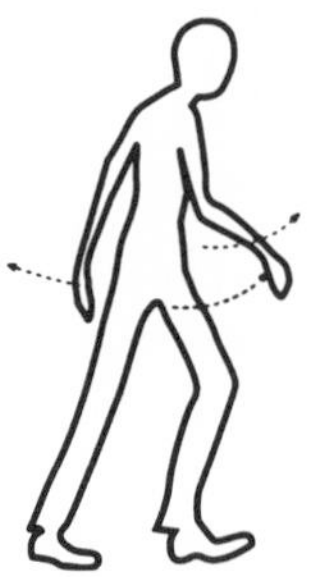

BODY SWINGS

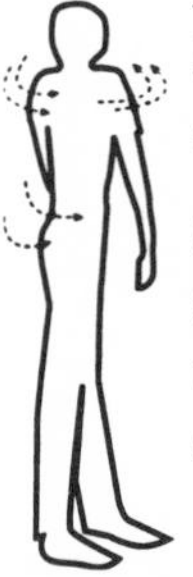

Increases circulation to the upper body and arms, frees the shoulders, and eases restriction throughout the upper torso.

Swing the upper torso to the right and to the left, allowing arms to swing freely from the body. Keep the feet in place but do not lock the knees. Breathe in while going one direction; breathe out in the other, alternating in-and-out breath.

SHOULDER SHRUGS

This tightening and relaxing of the neck and shoulder muscles increases circulation and releases tension in this area.

Lift shoulders, one at a time, up to the ears.

HEAD ROTATIONS

Stretches the muscles of the neck, releasing neck tension and allowing full rotation and freedom of movement.

Rotate the head on the spinal axis to the left and the right. If you have problems with tension in the neck, continue stretching in many different directions.

HEAD ROLLS

Reduces tension in the shoulder and the neck.

Slowly lower the head forward, moving the chin toward the chest. Continuing a slow movement, roll the head sideways in a semi-circle. If you encounter any pain or tightness, remain in that position and breathe through the tension. (This is an important stretch and should be done often throughout the day.)

SHOULDER AND ARM CIRCLES

The following four exercises move the shoulders and arms through their full range of motion and leave them in their strongest skeletal position.

Starting with one shoulder, make circles, forward and backward. Using a backstroke motion, gradually increase the range of motion of the arm. Repeat with other shoulder.

ARM LIFTS

Lift a straightened arm away from the side of the body to a position straight up, overhead, keeping the palm facing forward. It is impossible to do this lift if the shoulder remains in a forward rotation, or rounded.

Breathe.

ARM SWINGS

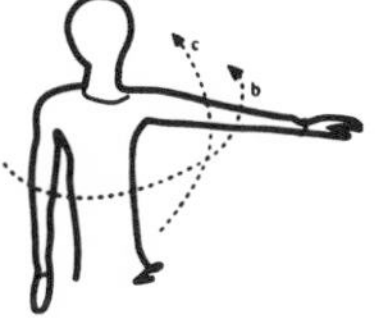

Lift arm away from body, with palm facing the floor, and swing the arm forward and backward along a horizontal plane (line b). *Do not attempt this without proper warm-up.*

ARM ROTATIONS

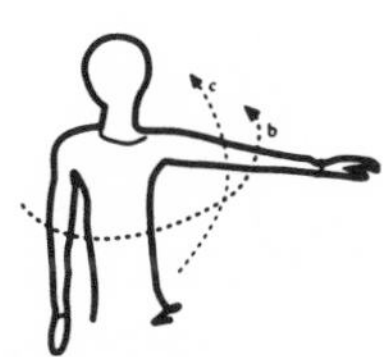

Extend one arm out to side of body, palm facing the floor, and rotate arm forward and backward along its axis (line c). Repeat with other arm. Now, extend both arms out to side of body, and rotate simultaneously in opposite directions. (This is a good stretch for all the muscles of the arm.)

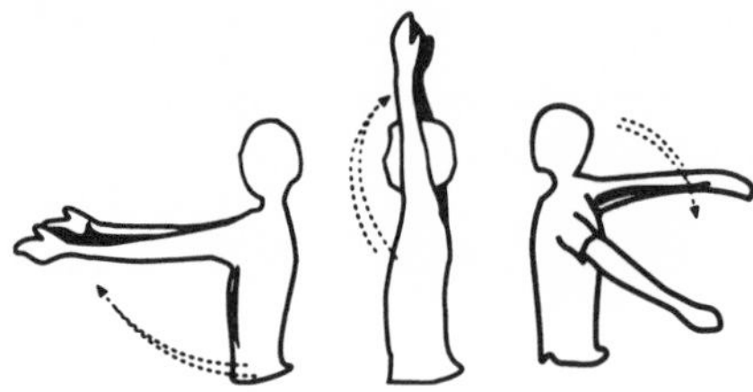

ARM STRETCH

Strongly moves the muscles of the chest, back and arm in a direction opposite to that used in playing, thus strengthening those muscles while stretching the playing muscles.

Lift arms straight in front of the body with palms facing each other and begin to reach forward stretching the arms away from the body. Slowly begin lifting the arms up until they are overhead, always stretching away from the body as much as possible. Continue moving the arms backward past the ears with the forearms in extreme supination. Follow through the circle with the arms as far back as possible, eventually returning to a position by the side of the body. Relax.

SHOULDER PUSH-UP

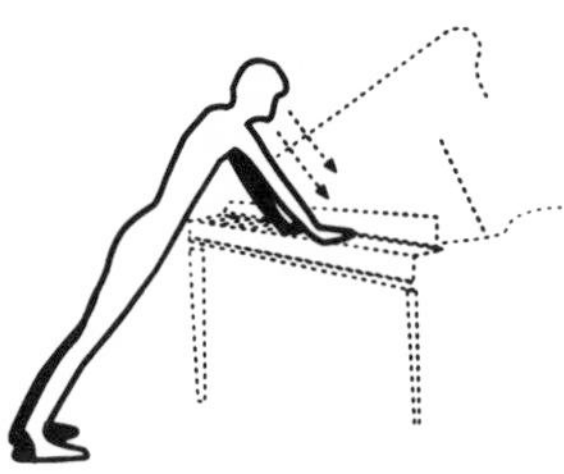

Helps to stabilize the muscles of the shoulder girdle and flatten the shoulder blades.

Using your grand piano or a convenient countertop, stand a few feet away with hands reaching out to the surface. Do partial push-ups against the surface, keeping your body straight and heels on the floor.

BACK CURL

A wonderful stretch for reaching muscles that are tight after sitting at the piano for a long time.

Bending the knees in a short crouch, curl forward by bending the spine. Think of bringing the navel toward the spine. Rotate shoulders forward and grasp the left forearm with the right hand, pulling the left hip away and increasing stretch. Repeat on other side.

TIE SWINGS

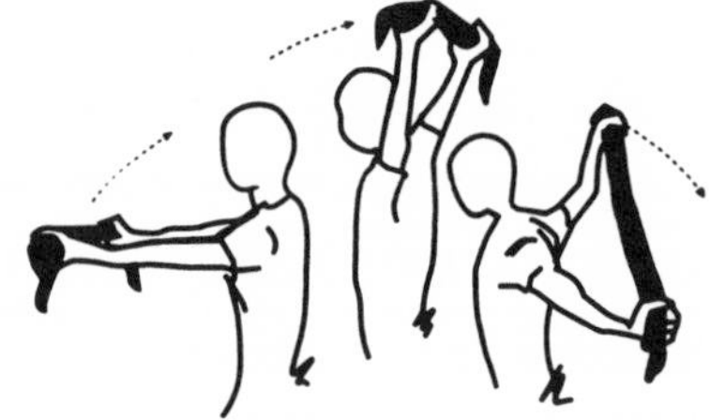

A real strength builder for the muscles of the shoulder and the arms, this exercise also reinforces a larger range of motion than is used at the piano.

Hold a tie or scarf between hands extended outward, palms down (pronated), and swing arms overhead and behind the body. Swing back in front of body. Repeat several times, and then rotate palms into upward position (supinated) and do again. This exercise should not be done without proper warm-up.

Breathe.

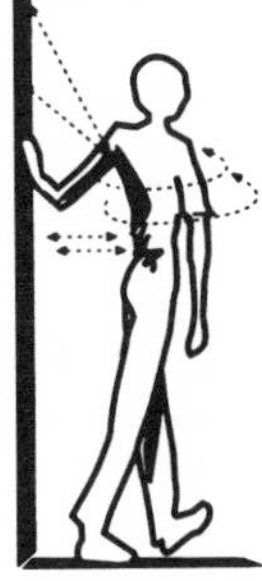

IN-DOORWAY STRETCH

A spectacular stretch for the adductors in the chest and the internal rotators in the shoulder.

Place right arm, bent at the elbow, flat against a doorjamb and in line with the body. Extend the either foot forward. (Each foot creates a different stretch.) Slowly move the body forward through the doorway, feeling the stretch in the chest and shoulder. Select several different positions along the height of the doorjamb, feeling the stretch move different fibers of muscles. Finish with fully extended arm, feeling the stretch in the armpit. Repeat with opposite arm.

The following exercises should be done with extreme caution. Individual flexibility will account for very large differences in movement. Do not push.

FLEXOR STRETCH

Eliminates the tightness that causes pain in the forearm, and can return the finger flexors to their full length after a great amount of work.

Stand in front of a chair or the piano bench, arms hanging down in front of the body. With palms facing forward (supinated) and fingertips touching the chair, slowly lower the palm toward the chair surface until the muscles halt your movement. *Do not push past the point of comfort.* (Some individuals will be able to flatten the hand completely on the surface. Others may be able to stretch only a little.) After stretching in supinated position, rotate the right hand counterclockwise from a 6-o'clock position completely around to a 6-o'clock position. The left hand can be used to hold the second position as the arm stretches on the fifth-finger side of the hand. Repeat with the left hand. (The first flexor stretch is one of the most important stretches one can do for the finger flexors. It should be done before *and* after all practice and playing periods; if no other stretching is done, this and the extensor stretch that follows should always be done.)

EXTENSOR STRETCH

Maintains full range of motion of these finger muscles, thereby helping to avoid injury and dysfunction in this area, particularly when done in tandem with the previous stretch before and after all practicing and performing.

Stand in front of a chair or the piano bench, arms hanging down in front of the body. With palms facing backward toward the body (pronated) and fingertips touching the chair, slowly lower the back of the hand toward the chair surface until the muscles halt your movement. *Do not push past the point of comfort.* If you feel little or no tightness nor stretch in this position, curl the fingers into the hand and again stretch the back of the hand toward the seat of the chair. (This and the flexor stretches described above are to be considered maintenance work for the muscles of the forearm. It cannot be stressed enough. If nothing else is done, these should be done.)

Breathe.

HAND MASSAGE

Massaging the fingers helps to increase the circulation before practice, and to loosen and relax muscles after practice.

Use a hand washing motion and knead individual fingers. To release acupressure points, begin with the thumb, gently press from base to tip of finger, holding a few moments in each position. Do all sides of the finger. Stop at base of nail and press, then gently pull the end of finger.

To reach the muscles in the hand, the pianist may apply pressure to tender spots with the eraser part of a regular wood pencil. Applying pressure along the entire line of the muscle will achieve the maximum benefit.

FINGER STRETCH

The small muscles of the hand have the ability to harbor trigger points, which are most difficult to release except by injection. It is not an agreeable experience, and these exercises can help avoid this prospect.

The individual fingers and thumb can be stretched prior to and after all practice and playing. It is an effective way to warm up the fingers backstage when no piano is available. Each finger, including the thumb, can be gently stretched in all directions: backward, forward, and sideways. It is important to stretch the thumb in directions away from the hand. With the help of the thumb and index finger of one hand, the both the fifth-finger and thumb sides of the other hand can be stretched backward, inverting the palm.

TIE TWIST

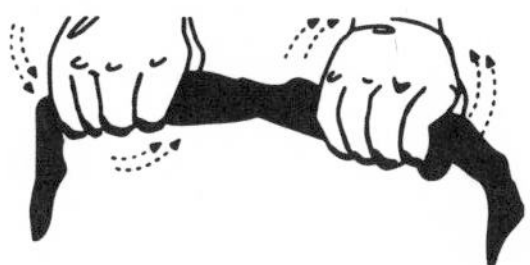

Both this and the next exercise are especially good for injured, dysfunctional or arthritic hands.

Twist a tie (or some other suitable material, like a strong scarf) as if you were wringing a washcloth. Twist both away from and towards the body.

TIE GRAB

Hold one end of a tie in your hand and let the remaining material dangle towards the ground. Using your fingers, 'make the tie disappear' by gathering the material into your hand. Do not rotate wrist. Repeat with each hand. Drop tie down and shake wrist, pretending the tie is a yo-yo.

Breathe.

Overuse, Pain, Rest, and the Pianist

Norman B. Rosen, M.D.

Having a medical problem is stressful enough for most people. However, for pianists, medical problems can be devastating from a professional, artistic, and financial standpoint, as they can affect the ability of pianists to practice and perform. It is imperative to treat such medical problems rapidly and appropriately in order to restore the players' functioning and allow them to resume meeting their artistic and professional responsibilities.

Medical problems among pianists can be subdivided into two categories:

1. Those that occur coincidentally to playing the piano. These include the myriad of conditions that are purely medical in nature and include such diseases as diabetes, stroke, rheumatoid arthritis, liver disease, kidney disease, cardio-respiratory and GI diseases, and even cancer. These are conditions where the pianist has little ability to affect the outcome, and must rely entirely on the directives of his or her physicians and caretakers.

2. Those that occur either as a direct or indirect result of playing the piano, and include problems caused by faulty technique, poor environment, substandard quality of instrument, stress, and overuse.

Although the vast numbers of disorders in the first category are beyond the scope of this discussion, the problems associated with the second category are important for the pianist to understand, because most of them are avoidable.[1] These conditions are primarily neuromusculoskeletal in nature, and include damage (or apparent damage) to the nerves, muscles, tendons, joints, ligaments,

[1] See Table 1 *Common Medical Problems of Pianists* on page 165 for a thorough listing of many of the problems in this second category.

and related neurocirculatory system. Although non-keyboard-related skeletal and bony problems can certainly impact a pianist's abilities and playing habits, actual bony or skeletal damage is highly unlikely in a pianist.

OVERUSE INJURIES

Those problems that occur as a direct or indirect result of playing have, for better or worse, been labeled overuse injuries. This term is, however, a misnomer, since 'overuse' applies to only a small percentage of the total number of cases so labeled. Furthermore, true 'injuries' occur only if pianists ignore their pain and fail to get prompt, appropriate medical and pianistic advice to correct the various factors that led to development of the problem in the first place.

In actuality, bodily dysfunction generally occurs not from simple overuse but rather from other factors, including: abuse of the body, particularly when muscles are weak or fatigued; use of improper technique; or the occurrence of inappropriate *loading* of the involved tissues and/or their supporting parts. For pianists, this concept of *overload*, as opposed to overuse, is an important one because 'load' can be redistributed in various ways, including taping, wrapping, or strengthening and balancing the load through other parts of the body. All of which allow the pianists to continue playing. (Overuse suggests that the problem is in 'using' the body, which therefore leads to a therapeutic response of rest; certainly not the ideal for most pianists.)

It should also be mentioned that weakness or tightness of the shoulders, trunk, and supporting parts, as well as fatigue, can contribute to overloading the fingers, hands, and wrists. This is a particularly harmful aspect of overloading because although the pianist reports pain in those latter areas (the fingers, hands, and wrists) the dysfunction, and therefore the area that actually requires treatment, is in the trunk or other supporting part. Fatigue contributes to overloading in a different, but equally detrimental, way. It lowers the *threshold of use*, resulting in the development of symptoms or injuries at lesser loads than those that would otherwise cause problems. These factors that cause mechanical inadequacy of the upper extremities are important to understand, both from the standpoint of (1) minimizing the disability that often occurs after a pianist sustains an injury (or apparent injury) at the keyboard, and (2) learning how to better prevent future problems.

Additional factors can also precipitate dysfunction. These include:

- Physical and emotional stress
- Postural mal-alignments
- Inadequate rest
- Environmental conditions, such as playing in a cold room
- Undertaking new or complicated repertoire
- Extended time and stress at the keyboard spent in preparing for performance
- Lack of pacing

All of these factors may combine to contribute to a lowered threshold of use and, by extension, the development of symptoms. Worse still these dysfunctions may develop or lead to true injuries if playing is continued.

MYOFASCIAL PAIN AND DYSFUNCTION

Weakness and tightness of muscles predispose muscles to injury and cause, in turn, other muscles to become weak, inefficient, and more prone to other injuries. This cascade of muscles (and their fascial containers) becoming progressively tighter and more dysfunctional has been called *myofascial dysfunction (myo-* referring to the muscles and *–fascial* referring to the connective-tissue envelopes or fascial linings surrounding the muscles). Tight tissues physically limit the mechanical efficiency of muscles and affect the nutritional supply to muscles as well as their efficiency in removing the toxic by-products of metabolism. This interference with nutritional supply and waste removal then causes a superimposed physiological burden on the muscles, which further compromises their ability to function. Muscles then become increasingly vulnerable to injury as a result of both physical and physiological limitations and this, in turn, interferes with joint efficiency and safety. The muscle-joint complex becomes more prone to release premature protective-reflex mechanisms in response to movement or stretch, which paradoxically interferes with joint and muscle function. This response also creates even more muscle tension, thus initiating a vicious cycle:

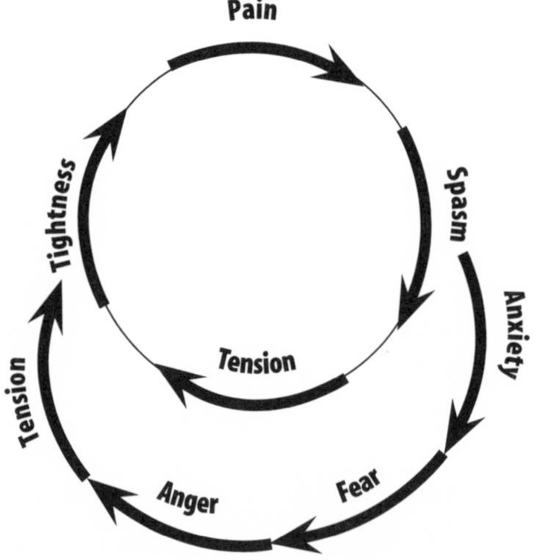

Once these areas of myofascial dysfunction become manifest, they further develop into a variety of superimposed painful syndromes known as the *myofascial pain and dysfunction syndromes.* These syndromes are important to recognize because the localized areas of tightness not only perpetuate the local dysfunction but also develop the ability to trigger symptoms elsewhere, often times mimicking more serious pathologies. In fact, pianists are often more aware of these areas of *referred pain* and tenderness than they are of the trigger area actually causing the problem. By complaining primarily about these areas of referred pain (i.e. pain in the hands and wrists when the problem may be in the muscles of the shoulders and arms), pianists may inadvertently mislead clinicians from the true source of the problem, particularly if the clinicians are not sufficiently sophisticated in the detection and management of these myofascial pain and dysfunction syndromes.

In addition, muscles will start to loose their range-of-motion and, since they work in pairs, they not only become tighter and less efficient, they also cause compensatory adjustments to occur in other adjacent muscles, precipitating similar dysfunctional dynamics (reflex spasm, pain, tightness, and/or weakness) to occur in these adjoining muscles. These maladaptations, in turn, further adversely affect the ability of the initial or primary offending muscle to function. Together the dysfunctional muscle pairs or groups cause secondary joint dysfunction. This then causes still further dysfunction in the muscles controlling the joint, thereby setting off a vicious cycle of pain and dysfunction involving both muscle and joint, which, in turn, further increases the pain and the dysfunction. With the passage of time, these compensatory patterns lead to the development of maladaptive habits, which become more fixed by repetition and learning. With continued activity and repetitive playing, the fixed bad habits expose all of these tissues to premature damage, coming even from loads that are actually less than those ordinarily required to cause injury.

There is a window of time, prior to when the tissue damage actually occurs, when continued playing despite pain can occur safely, so long as active treatment and conscious retraining of bad habits is occurring simultaneously.

Once tissues are strained or overloaded (overused in terms of the muscles' capacity to withstand loads) they are rendered more vulnerable to injury through a variety of subsequent events, including damage occurring from additional loads and usage, even in amounts less than that which would normally cause injury. The body, through the proprioceptive nervous system, perceives that injury may be occurring and responds to this perceived threat of damage by developing a variety of compensatory protective responses, which, ironically, then puts these compensating tissues at risk for premature strain or injury.

It is important for pianist to use pain as a signal that their muscles are at risk for injury and take the appropriate steps towards treatment. If not, the recovery process is much slower because of increased emotional distress and secondary deconditioning. And even more perverse is the fact that if the underlying myofascial dysfunction is not recognized quickly, alternative diagnoses are often made and improper treatment regimens introduced. In the worst cases, these may include inappropriate or unnecessary surgery. There is a window of time, prior to when the tissue damage actually occurs, when continued playing despite pain can occur *safely*, so long as active treatment and conscious retraining of bad habits is occurring simultaneously.

PROPRIOCEPTIVE NERVOUS SYSTEM

Just as pianists sometimes develop bad pianistic habits, so too they sometimes develop bad medical habits that may subtly 'reset' the exquisite proprioceptive balance normally existing between the various muscles that move, stabilize, and adjust muscle (and joint) motion. The *proprioceptive nervous system* is responsible for the body's awareness, control, balance, and coordination. It perceives changes in load, gravity, and motion, and then works through the muscular system to respond to these factors. Dynamic adjustments occur continuously, and are essential for the body to move and to perform effectively and efficiently in a rapid, flexible, and coordinated fashion.

Initially, these dynamic adaptations made by the body are temporary and result in no permanent structural joint or muscle changes. However, with continuous bombardment of aberrant information, as occurs with acute or chronic overload, overuse, sustained activity, sustained unusual postures, or fatigue (to name a few) the body makes a series of compensations and adjustments, mediated through the proprioceptive nervous system, to maintain coordinated and balanced movement. With repetitive input, these compensatory responses will become more fixed, regardless of their maladaptive nature. If stretching of the involved part is not performed, subtle or mild (*subclinical*) tightness in the tissue will actually start to set in. With the passage of time, that part of the body that has become tighter will be predisposed to injury because of the initial compensations.

PAIN

While the medical problems addressed above may often result in pain; it need not be a signal to quit playing. Nor does pain necessarily mean that damage is occurring or will result. Rather, it is a signal that something must be assessed and perhaps modified, from either a medical or a pianistic standpoint. Some pain may be an inadvertent by-product of attempting a new repertoire or playing for extended periods of time, in which case the solution may merely be to suggest a change in repertoire (sometime temporary, other times permanent) or ways to alter the intensity or duration of practice and playing sessions. Alternatively, assessing a player's technique and giving instruction in pacing one's efforts may be necessary. Playing on a new or stiffer instrument, or exposure to environmental changes (particularly cold or an intense preparation for an upcoming program or recital) can also lead to mild or nagging pain. In time, these discomforts will likely subside spontaneously. Clearly, time away from the keyboard is not desirable in these circumstances, and the pianist needs to remain focused and confident that playing can be continued safely, despite some pain.

TREATMENT

There are a variety of simple measures that often help treat pain. These include using some over-the-counter analgesics or anti-inflammatory medications. In addition, pianists should make some common-sense practice or playing modifications:

- Pace playing sessions to avoid fatigue.
- Institute shorter periods of intense play.
- Alternate aggressive passages that feature *forte, vivace*, or *staccato* sections with softer passages, often at an *andante* tempo or in a *legato* style.
- Stretch before, after, and even during the playing sessions.
- Perform some simple exercises away from the piano to improve strength and endurance. The "Significant Seven Exercise Regimen" that we use is an excellent example of such wellness exercises.

The "Significant Seven" exercise regimen

Posterior glide and neck stretches

- Tuck chin, glide head and neck backwards. Hold 7 seconds. Repeat 5 to 7 times throughout the day
- Side stretch, each side, by gently pulling head and ear to the same shoulder using hand over head resting on opposite ear. Hold 7 seconds. Then do opposite side. Repeat 5 to 7 times a day.

- Rotate head to each side. Hold 7 seconds.

'Think tall & up'

- Elevate your head, shoulders, and chest, in proper posture position.
- Head and shoulders pulled back.
- 'Float up' with head, spine, and diaphragm and 'think tall'.
- Pelvic tilt position (tighten buttock, abdomen, bladder)
- Breathe in and hold, then exhale while still maintaining muscle tension in buttocks, abdomen, bladder and chest.

Shoulder stretches

- Doorway stretch – Lean through doorway with elbow on frame.
- Shoulder raise and reach – Raise arms overhead and reach.
- Towel stretch – Grab towel with one arm behind back and one arm above hear. Pull with upper arm. Alternate arms.
- Tricep Stretch – With one arm bent over the head, reach out with opposite the arm and grab the bent elbow. Pull across the body. Alternate arms.

'Rusty Gate'

Just as a rusty gate need to be moved in all directions after oiling, so must we move our backs to keep them flexible.

- Bend forward with knees locked, place hands on knees. Hold 7 seconds.
- Return to standing position and 'think tall & up'. Hold 7 seconds.
- Lean backwards, placing both hands on the small of the back, and lift one segment at a time. Hold 7 seconds.
- Repeat 7 times per session, several times daily.

Knee-chest stretch and prone press-ups

- Lying on your back, pull one knee up to your check and hold 7 seconds. Relax. Alternate knee and hold 7 seconds. Repeat several times a day.
- Lying on your back, pull both knees up to your chest. Hold 7 seconds. Relax. Repeat
- Lying on your stomach and propped up on your elbows, press the upper body up and arch the back. Hold 7 seconds.

Push-ups

- Perform push-ups again a wall, table or countertop, or on the floor (either bent knee or military style). Perform 7 repetitions, 7 times daily. (After the first week, increase the number of times per day.)

Aerobic exercise

- Perform at least 40 minutes of aerobic exercise at least 3 times per week (and make it fun).

It is important to note that *persistent* pain is always a signal to stop in order to allow adequate assessment and the institution of corrective interventions, especially if the pain continues beyond playing at the keyboard. It is always better to err on the side of caution, however, than to risk future disability and the inculcation of bad habits by continuing to play with pain.

REST

Rest continues to be the safest way to treat pain, as long as it is done on a limited basis. When a keyboard-related injury has occurred, it is likely that bad habits (both pianistic and medical) have already set in, and may have become relatively fixed and hard to remove. In these cases, a pianist requires de-training to extinguish these bad habits and then they must embark on proper re-training. As continued improper playing will serve only to reinforce the previous incorrect patterns and habits, it is often beneficial for some pianist to take an extended period of time away from the keyboard.

Time away from the keyboard may also be creatively and spiritually beneficial for many pianists and is well warranted for emotional or spiritual reasons, including burnout or stress. It also promotes good pacing and a pursuit of alternative activities and routines. The resulting emotional or mental rest may also improve physical problems, as psychological distress can often masquerade as physical symptoms and worsen the underlying physical symptoms. It can also cause an increase in tissue tension, which may create or aggravate other physical problems at the keyboard.

Most experts do, however, agree that treatment should be comprehensive and should result in essentially full recovery, with *only* minimal time away from the keyboard. From a strictly medical standpoint, extended time away from the keyboard is usually not necessary, and recommendations to stop playing may be paradoxically damaging to the pianist from a physical, psychological, and spiritual standpoint.

Rest causes joints and muscles to become tighter, and thus puts them at a mechanical and physiological disadvantage when use is resumed. Tight joints do not allow adequate shock absorption or flexibility, and this, in turn, causes the muscles that move the joints to work harder. Prolonged rest also results in the muscles themselves becoming weaker, tighter, and less efficient, because muscles have an inherent tendency to contract when not used. *Excess* rest sets the stage for developing a variety of use-abuse syndromes, including overuse and premature fatigue, at lower levels of use. It also causes tissues to become both tighter and weaker. Excessive rest will often lead to physical and spiritual de-training and *deconditioning,* thus promoting fear. This fear will become even more debilitating if pain recurs following a prolonged period away from the keyboard.

Whenever time away from the keyboard is recommended for medical reasons, management techniques must include reassurance, specific alternative exercise programs (including both stretching and strengthening for the involved and uninvolved body parts),[2] and mental retraining. When rest is the only treatment, the pain will like reoccur (along with superimposed fear and anxiety when the pain recurs after a period of rest) because the factors that caused the pain were not adequately treated during the period of rest. Ideally, learning proper technique, coordination, balance, and efficiency allows the ceiling of practicing to be raised without rest, despite symptoms.

STRETCHING

Stretching allows the muscles to function more efficiently because it restores a more balanced and responsive environment for pairs or groups of muscles to work in. Gentle stretching can generally be done to the involved part following most injuries (except for fractures), and it should certainly be encouraged for all uninjured parts of the body. While some caution should be exercised in individuals who have loose joints or *hyperlaxity*, stretching is, for the most part, very important to maintain optimal muscle health.

Simply stretching a muscle prior to using it will actually result in that muscle becoming stronger and will increase both its efficiency and strength. This phenomenon is called *preload stretch*. A common application of this phenomenon is the initiating back swing in golf or tennis, or the stretch prior to a pitcher throwing a baseball. It is this important motion that gives the follow-through its strength.

Unfortunately, playing the piano does not allow for a full range of motion, either initiated or followed through, because of the joint motion and speed required. However, many pianists, despite significant joint laxity, have empirically discovered that by stretching the joints of their hands prior to playing, and at other times throughout the practice or performance, they actually feel better, stronger, and looser – *and less vulnerable to injury.*

RELATIVE REST WITH STRETCHING

Thus, the prescription for rest should be modified to advocate relative, as opposed to complete, rest. Some form of stretching should be performed while at rest, both for the injured part and for the rest of the body. In addition, some mild strengthening should be performed whenever possible. At the least, an isometric muscle contraction (a muscle-tightening contraction that occurs without joint motion) of an involved part can be performed.

Relative rest allows continued movement of muscles, within limits, and counteracts the most detrimental aspects of inactivity: tightness and weakness. From the standpoint of both the muscles and the joints, some muscle contraction is desirable even if either is injured. This is because muscles lose tone and develop wasting, or *atrophy*, from disuse. In addition, some gentle stretching is desirable in most instances to counteract the normal tendency for muscles and joints to get tighter when not used.

The prescription of activity and use must also be modified in those cases where involved joints are arthritic or poorly aligned. In these instances, the external mechanical stresses are clearly deleterious to the health of that joint, particularly

---

[2]See Table 2. *Types of Exercises for Pianists,* page 166, for an outlined training regimen.

on a long-term basis. However, whereas exercise is excellent for the spirit, soul and muscle, exercise and use is not in the best interest of the joints, particularly a mal-aligned or arthritic joint. Nonetheless, when joints are mal-aligned (truly involved in a pathological process), a balance between use and rest must be achieved, and all efforts to ensure proper use should be made. The use of functional splints and external supports (including taping), particularly when engaged in non-critical activities, may increase the longevity of those joints. It is particularly important to gently stretch joints that are arthritic or mal-aligned *along their longitudinal axis.* Otherwise, injured joints may become progressively deformed and placed at a mechanical disadvantage, incompatible with continued play.

Learning more about the proper and efficient use of body tissues (*load control*) will also help pianists feel more comfortable about continuing to play in those instances where pain would otherwise interfere with the ability to play. Understanding the true pathogenesis of injuries will also help them develop a better sense of control and power over a disability, should it occur. This enables a more rapid and successful rehabilitation effort and a quicker, fuller restoration to maximal function, despite a disability.

KEYBOARD INJURIES AND TAKING RESPONSIBILITY FOR THEIR PREVENTION

Injury avoidance is primarily a function of recognizing poor mechanics and correcting them before they become ingrained into the individual's unconscious playing technique. Understanding the various factors that lead to injury, and to its avoidance, should be part of the basic piano-pedagogy curriculum. Bad habits should be diagnosed and corrected immediately, before they can result in medical – or pianistic – disability.

If, however, a pianist develops *any* medical problem that impacts on his or her ability to play at the keyboard, it is imperative that the individual seek advice from a competent clinician, one who not only understands the presenting medical problem but also is aware of the unique physical and emotional demands and pressures on the pianist.

It is also important for pianists to be informed consumers in matters of health and wellness, particularly in this era when cost-containment is pervasive in the healthcare industry. Professional pianists need to be especially aware that the problems they sustain at the keyboard are the very ones that, in most managed-care scenarios, are most likely to be *under treated* or treated with 'benign neglect'. From a managed-care standpoint, pain or numbness of a finger is perceived in general as a minor or minimal disability. From a pianist's perspective, however, it is a major disability that impinges on his or her employability, self-expression, and overall quality of life. Ultimately, it is the pianist's responsibility to see that others respect these problems in the same way.

In summary, by considering the concepts of muscle loading, joint protection, and proper use, rather than thinking in terms of simple overuse, pianists can better understand the pathogenesis of injuries and can continue to play, despite pain. When in doubt, medical consultation from an appropriately trained physician is appropriate to prevent further disability and allow continued playing with minimal time away from the keyboard. Having available a repertoire of treatment options dedicated to the preservation of the physical, mental, and spiritual aspects of playing is also crucial, particularly if a medical problem or injury does develop. Equipped with this information, pianists are more likely to avoid injury or limit time away from the keyboard.

Table 1. Common Medical Problems Affecting Pianists

I. Postural and mechanical (dynamic) abnormalities of the spine, shoulders, or upper extremities

Scoliosis

Curvature of the spine, including neck and low back and thoracic spine

Arthritis

Weakness of muscles

Disease related

Disuse related

Tightness of joints and muscles

Predisposing to "overload" syndromes

Hyperlaxity

"Loose-jointedness," predisposing to "overload" syndromes

II. Abnormalities of the joint-ligament-tendon-muscle complex

Underlying arthritis

Usually osteoarthritis

Other forms of arthritis, including rheumatoid, lupus, Lyme disease, FIIV, and metabolic arthropathies are rarer and require special consideration

Ligament tear or sprain

Tendonitis *(also tendinitis)*

Inflammation and degeneration of tendon, due to direct injury (partial or complete tear); indirect injury due to overload (faulty posture, overuse, muscle dysfunction; see next)

Muscle problems

Weakness

Disease-related – systemic, infectious, metabolic, neurological, endocrine

Disuse-related – deconditioning, muscle imbalance syndromes, myofascial pain and dysfunction syndromes)

Injury

Direct – rupture, partial tear, or bruise

Indirect – overuse, overload, myofascial dysfunction

III. Nerve entrapment ("pinched nerve")

Neck or lower back ("radiculopathy")

Thoracic outlet

Extremity entrapment

Median nerve – at the wrist (carpal tunnel syndrome) or in the forearm

Ulnar nerve – at the wrist, elbow, or at the thoracic outlet

Radial nerve – at the upper arm

Sciatic nerve – in the lower buttock; can be entrapped within the piriform muscle

Peroneal nerve – at the fibular head

IV. Circulatory problems

Arterial – Raynaud's disease/phenomenon

Venous – edema

V. Cutaneous problems – eczema, dennatitis, scleroderma

VI. Systemic Medical Conditions

Table 2. Suggested Exercise Regimen for Pianists

Breathing

Relaxed and full inhalation and exhalation affect the muscle spindles and muscle tone.

- *Inhalation causes muscles to stretch.*
- *Exhalation allows muscles to relax.*
- *Maximum relaxation occurs during a full exhalation.*
- *A full inhalation followed by a full exhalation allows even greater relaxation.*

Posture

Posture awareness is critical in ensuring maximum efficiency and economy of effort, particularly with sitting and standing and changes in positions.

Relaxation

Lowering tension reduces muscle tension both in the muscles and central nervous system.

Stretching

All muscles tend to get tighter with both use and inactivity.

- *Simply stretching a muscle will increase its strength and mechanical efficiency.*
- *Caution must be advised in those individuals with loose joints (hyperlaxity).*

Strengthing

Use two primary types:

- *Isometrics – muscle contraction without joint movement*
- *Isotonic – muscle contraction with joint movement*

When weights are added, this is called *resistance-strengthening exercises.*

Endurance

Exercises involving repetitive activities should be done continuously for a minimum of 20 to 30 minutes. (The "Significant Seven" outlined earlier is an excellent routine to follow.)

Balance and coordination

Having fun

This is the most important ingredient of any good exercise program.

Points to remember

- *Exercise should become a way of life.*
- *To have a higher quality of life, remember the adage 'No pain, no gain', but don't act insane.*
- *Maintain perspective.*
- *Exercise is work. And for exercise to work, you must consistently work.*
- *It is better to exercise more frequently throughout the day than to engage in one intensive workout, and this is particularly true when initiating an exercise program.*
- *It takes persistence and desire to have a more efficient body.*
- *We exercise as much for tomorrow as for today; if you don't use it, you will lose it.*

Muscle Pain and Pianists: The Myofascial Pain Syndromes and Fibromyalgia

Norman B. Rosen, M.D.

Developing an awareness of these syndromes will better enable pianists to alert their physicians to particular aspects of their discomfort and question their clinicians more effectively.

A variety of medical conditions can interfere with the ability of the pianist to perform comfortably and artistically at the piano. Many of these illnesses or conditions have become part of the vernacular of most individuals (arthritis, tendonitis, disc problems, and carpal tunnel syndrome, for example). However, those are only part of a series of conditions involving the neuromusculoskeletal system. Others include: neuritis, bursitis, entrapment neuropathies ('pinched' nerves), and overuse (or misuse) syndromes. Although they may not be part of the common vocabulary, their occurrence in pianists is sadly frequent and physicians are normally aware of the standard diagnoses and treatments. The same cannot be said of myofascial pain and dysfunction syndromes.

Relatively few pianists are aware of this group of surprisingly common syndromes, which often coexists with, mimics, or complicates other medical conditions, including those listed above. Unfortunately, pianists are not alone their lack of awareness of these conditions. Many clinicians and/or other medical personnel frequently overlook myofascial dysfunctions, as they are not well understood.[1] This should be particularly disconcerting to pianists, since myofascial pain and dysfunction is often part of most cases of persistent or refractory physical and/or physiological problems involving the neuromusculoskeletal system.

Developing an awareness of these syndromes will better enable pianists to alert their physicians to particular aspects of their discomfort and question their clinicians more effectively. Ultimately, pianists can become better partners in the quest for a more precise diagnosis; one that properly recognizes and treats these syndromes, thereby avoiding (1) alternative diagnoses that may be wrong, or only partially correct, and (2) the prescription of inappropriate treatment, including, in some instances, unnecessary surgery.

---

[1]For a more thorough bibliography, see Norman B. Rosen, "Myofascial Pain: The Great Mimicker and Potentiator of Other Diseases in the Performing Artist" *Maryland Medical Journal* 42/3 (March 1993): 261-266.

THE CHALLENGES OF GETTING A PROPER DIAGNOSIS

When a clinician faces a patient who has widespread pain and dysfunction that cannot be readily explained, the physician may, unfortunately, tend to impugn the patient's motivation for wellness, or question his or her psychological balance. Unfortunately, some patients have inadvertently used musculoskeletal pain as a way to express and satisfy other needs, but to restore the individual to a functioning lifestyle, it is necessary to resolve these components in a manner more effective than blaming the patient! Once myofascial pain and dysfunction is recognized and treated, it is easier to put into proper perspective any emotional disability that might accompany the physical problem. A successful clinician must recognize and treat both the physical and emotional components in his or her patient's presentation, and it is especially important to understand and diagnose the underlying physical disability before ascribing residual disability to emotional factors alone.

Once that hurdle is crossed, the nuts-and-bolts challenges of clinical diagnoses enter. One such factor that makes diagnosis difficult for physicians is the century-long confusion of terminology for describing diffuse or widespread musculoskeletal pain.[2] In 1904, the term *fibrositis* was coined to apply to a localized form of musculoskeletal dysfunction involving the low back.[3] However, over the years, the term became associated with a more generalized form of musculoskeletal pain and dysfunction, including a variety of psychophysiological pain syndromes in which no objective physical problem could be found. Indeed, most medical textbooks of the 1950s and 1960s considered fibrositis to be a purely psychogenic disease. Today's research reveals this to be inappropriate, and we now recognize several subgroups in patients who have both localized and generalized (widespread) muscle pain and dysfunction.[4] There is also a relatively new term for this latter group: in 1981 fibromyalgia became the common term used to describe the generalized form of muscle pain.[5] While this may seem to simplify the process, the reality is far different: the medical profession is still trying to solve the problem of enigmatic musculoskeletal pain.

THE COMPLEXITY OF MYOFASCIAL PAIN AND DYSFUNCTION SYNDROMES

More localized areas of pain *(myofascial pain syndromes)* continue to be thought of as conditions separate from those listed above.[6] This name was coined by Travell and Rinzler in 1952 and has its linguistic roots in *myo-*, which refers to

---

[2]Robert M. Bennett, "Fibrositis/Fibromyalgia Syndrome: Current Issues and Perspectives," *American Journal of Medicine* 81 (1986): 3A.; David G. Simons and Janet G. Travell, "Myofascial Origins of Low Back Pain," *Postgraduate Medicine* 73 (1983): 66-77.

[3]William R. Gowers, "Lumbago: Its Lessons in Analogues," *British Medical Journal* I (1904): 117-121.

[4]For more information on recent research, see Norman B. Rosen, "Physical Medicine and Rehabilitation Approaches to the Myofascial Pain and Fibromyalgia Syndromes," *Bailliere-Tindall Clinical Rheumatology Series: The Management of the Fibromyalgia and Myofascial Pain Syndromes* 8 (1994): 881-911.; Idem, "The Myofascial Pain Syndromes," *Physical Medicine and Rehabilitation Clinics of North America* 4 (1993): 41-63.

[5]Mohammed Yunus, Alphonse T. Masi, et al., "Primary Fibromyalgia (Fibrositis): Clinical Study of 50 Patients with Matched Normal Controls," *Seminars in Arthritis and Rheumatism* 11 (1981): 151-71; Mohammed Yunus et al., "Primary Fibromyalgia," *American Family Physician* 25 (1982): 115-21.

[6]Janet G. Travell and Stuart H. Rinzler, "The Myofascial Genesis of Pain," *Postgraduate Medicine* 11 (1952): 425-34.

muscle and *-fascia,* which refers to the linings of muscles, more specifically the envelopes of fibrous tissue that surround the muscles and allow them to function as coordinated masses of tissue.[7] The syndrome occurs when injury, overload, or fatigue cause pain in the muscles and their fascial linings. The pain then causes the nervous system to reset the tone of the involved area of the body.

To complicate matters further, myofascial pain and dysfunction can present as:

- Single-muscle syndromes, which, as one would expect, involve one muscle.
- Localized (focal) syndromes, which usually involve two or more muscles around a single joint.
- Regional syndromes, which usually involve three or more muscles and two or more joints within a single area (or region) of the body.
- Multi-focal syndromes, where two or more regions of the body are involved (i.e. right leg and left shoulder).
- Generalized syndromes, which present with diffuse pain throughout the entire body. (Typically fibromyalgia and superimposed myofascial pain syndromes exist together.)

When the involvement is more generalized, one should suspect, in addition to myofascial pain and dysfunction, the presence of an underlying fibromyalgia or some other generalized disease, such as: thyroid or vitamin deficiency; other hormonal, nutritional, or endocrine dysfunction; various mechanical and postural factors; and sleep deprivation. The double-edged sword of this problem is that when widespread muscle involvement occurs, the more easily correctable multi-focal or multi-regional myofascial pain and dysfunction syndromes are often misdiagnosed as fibromyalgia. The resulting treatment, which focuses on fibromyalgia, will be unsuccessful (unless the treating physician recognizes and treats the concurrent myofascial pain and dysfunction problem properly). As a result, the underlying muscle pain and dysfunction gets worse, and the patient is left disabled. This might not have occurred had the correct diagnosis and treatment been rendered in the first place.

The following is but a partial list of the multiple conditions that physicians must consider when a patient presents with muscle pain.

Possible Diagnoses of Muscle Pain

Fibromyalgia

A widespread disease of muscle, of unknown cause but presumed to be of primary, central origin. That is to say, the muscle pain in this disease is due to physiological events that are occurring in the brain and spinal cord, and not in the actual muscle itself.

Myofascial pain syndromes, true muscle pain syndromes

- ***With secondary joint dysfunction***
- ***Without secondary joint dysfunction***

---

[7]A more fundamental discussion of myofascial pain and dysfunction syndromes is included in "Overuse, Pain, Rest, and the Pianist," page 156.

Primary *articular* (joint) dysfunction with *secondary* muscular dysfunction

- *Inflammatory*
- *Mechanical, structural*
- *Autoimmune, connective tissue, vasculitis*
- *Infectious*
- *Metabolic, endocrine*

Rheumatic pain modulation disorder (i.e., sleep deprivation)

Metabolic — endocrine, electrolyte, or inherited genetic defect

Infectious

Inflammatory, autoimmune

Neurological

Trauma

Neoplasm

Toxic

Psychogenic (i.e., true tension myalgia, conversion reaction, psychophysiological reactions)

Reactive

- *Tendinitis*
- *Bursitis*
- *Spasm*

SPREAD OF DYSFUNCTION: FACTORS TO CONSIDER

The myofascial pain syndromes are generally initiated by a variety of events (trauma, overload, fatigue) that have as a common denominator muscle imbalance and muscle overload. If this muscle imbalance is not corrected, the problem persists. The persistent factors which cause and extend the process are called *perpetuating factor*s. Therefore, physicians must look for perpetuating factors that may have caused the problem in the first place.

Another cause of limited syndromes becoming more widespread is due to peripheral and central *sensitization*. Sensitization refers to pain spreading throughout a region, or occurring in multiple sites when brain is forced into 'fight or flight' mode. Designed to prevent future injuries, it ratchets both mental and physiological systems into a heightened state of alertness. In this state, the muscle tightens when it perceives pain, but if this protective reflex malfunctions the muscle does not release, creating more pain and further sensitizations.

This ever-expanding cycle is difficult to detect, and therefore to break, in large part because of the numerous and diverse factors that can suggest myofascial pain:

- History of muscle pain, tenderness, stiffness, aching, gelling, tightness, numbness, tingling, weakness, or coolness that may be localized or generalized.
- Localized areas of muscular 'ropiness' (taut or hard bands)
- Trigger points or localized areas of tenderness within the taut band
- Referred pain and tenderness, as a result of compression of the trigger point, to areas remote from that trigger area; local tenderness is also possible
- Local twitch response elicited on snapping or needling the taut band
- Characteristic pattern of referred pain and tenderness for each trigger point
- Some weakness, which may be subtle, of the involved muscle or muscles where trigger points are located
- Loss, which again may be subtle, of range of motion in the joint
- Immediate reversal of weakness and an improved range of motion following inactivation of the trigger point
- Vasoconstrition or vasodilation locally and vasoconstrition in the area of referral (autonomic components)
- Nerve, tendon, or blood vessel entrapment, which may occur as a result of compression of the taut band of the muscle
- Physical deconditioning, often resulting from lack of exercise
- Disuse and other factors, including pain, fear, stress.
- Psychosocial dysfunction, including anxiety, depression, or fear of activity (actophobia or kinesophobia)
- Epiphenomenona accompanying the pain (emotional, spiritual, fear, anxiety, stress, frustration, anger, helplessness, hopelessness)

TRIGGER POINTS AND REFERRED PAIN

One of the more unusual aspects of the myofascial pain syndromes is the phenomenon known as the "trigger point."[8] A *trigger point* is a tender point found within an area of spasm in the involved muscle, which has developed a taut band (an area of localized muscle spasm). The trigger point is so named because compression of the trigger point will send pain and tenderness to more remote areas of that region of the body. For example, numbness, pain, or tenderness in a hand may not necessarily be coming from pathology involving the hand, but may be

[8]Ibid. Also see Janet G. Travell and David G. Simons, *Myofascial Pain and Dysfunction: The Trigger Point Manual*, 2 vols. (Baltimore: Williams & Wilkins, 1983).

referred from a trigger point in one of the muscles of the shoulder or arm; thus *referred pain.* (The clinician who is sophisticated in the diagnoses of myofascial pain knows which trigger points in which muscles can cause the various referred syndromes.) The existence of a trigger point and a taut band also interferes with the ability of muscles to move in a dynamically balanced, coordinated fashion, wreaking havoc on any hope pianists' have of efficient functioning.

MYOTATIC UNITS

Although any underlying pain and dysfunction typically comes from the same process, muscular pain and muscular dysfunction are two separate issues, and while they may coexist, they need to be addressed as independent variables. Pain can be disproportionate to the underlying dysfunction, and there can be significant dysfunction without any pain whatsoever. That said, any dysfunctional unit is at risk for injury unless the underlying dysfunction (usually tightness or weakness) is corrected. Thus stretching and strengthening are essential parts of any program of piano wellness – and the piano professional must understand the kinesiology of efficient muscle functioning.

At the core of efficient muscle behavior is the functional *myotatic unit.* The myotatic unit is those groups of muscles that work together in order to achieve a purposeful movement. The members of the myotactic unit include:

- The *agonist*, or primary mover.
- The *co-agonists*, which are the muscles or co-movers that assist the primary muscle in achieving a purposeful movement. (Their particular function is to spread the load, allowing the primary mover to work with less energy and more efficiently.)
- The *antagonist* of movement, which provides the necessary braking and decelerating forces that slow down and better control the movement of the primary movers. (Without antagonists, the primary movers would operate with less control, and be more prone to injury.)
- The *proximal stabilizers*, which are found closer to the spine (in relation to the primary mover). Effective muscle activity depends on a stable base being established. It is the function of the proximal stabilizers to establish an adequate base of support from which the desired activity can be performed by the more 'distal' elements (those further away from the spine). Thus, the forearm muscles are the proximal stabilizers for the fingers; the shoulder muscles are the proximal stabilizers for the arm, the forearm and the hand; and the trunk, itself, is a proximal stabilizer for all upper extremity activity, hence the importance of truck support. The proximal stabilizers must be both strong and flexible in order for the distal movers to function maximally and to minimize the propensity to injury.
- These muscle groups must work together in a synergistic fashion, and are thusly called *synergists.*

In order for muscles to work efficiently and in a controlled and coordinated-fashion, they must communicate with each other. Muscles communicate with each other through the central and *proprioceptive* nervous systems. The central nervous system provides the necessary nervous control to move, or to stop from moving, any particular muscle or muscle group. The proprioceptive nervous system lets the central nervous system know where the specific joints and muscles are in space, and functions as a sensory feedback mechanism to modulate movement. This interaction is best thought of as 'muscle talk'. This talk, mediated through the nervous system, allows muscle to move together in a smooth coordinated fashion. When the agonist contracts, there is reduced contraction in the antagonist; when the antagonist contracts, there is reduced activity in the agonist, and so on.

In order for muscles to contract, they must have some *internal tone.* Without tone, muscles would be floppy and unable to move efficiently. This tone is influenced by multiple factors, including the level of conditioning of the pianist, the presence or absence of other diseases, the circulation to and innervation of the muscle, and the level of physical and emotional stress, which is present. This internal tone is called the muscle *set.* Each muscle of the myotatic unit has its own set, which must be in balance in order for the members of the myotatic unit to work in a coordinated, efficient, and effective fashion, with an economy of effort, and minimal strain.

The myotactic unit becomes strained in situations of stress, overload, overuse, speed, poor environmental conditions (particularly cold), and, most importantly, fatigue. As muscles get fatigued, the 'muscle talk' becomes less efficient, subjecting muscles to less coordinated and balanced action, which then leads to strain, further imbalance between all of the synergists of function, and injury.

The primary cause of dysfunction in the musculoskeletal system occurs where there is an imbalance of forces between the agonists, and antagonists, or when there is weakness or tightness of any member of the myotatic unit, including the proximal stabilizers. Injury, overload, or *perceived* injury, leads to a reflex muscle *spasm,* which normally releases after the perceived (or real) threat to the muscle is removed, or as the injury heals.

In the case of myofascial dysfunction, this protective spasm does not subside; rather it persists in the form of a taut band. This taut band develops as a result of an internal 'energy crisis' within the involved muscle which biases the ability of the muscle to contract normally. Further, the taut band sends a subtle message to the nervous system that something may be awry in the peripheral muscles. This then triggers a heightened alert to the other muscles of the myotatic unit to increase their internal muscle tone, which now biases the ability of these other muscles of the myotatic unit to contract normally. This has been called the 'fight or flight response'.

With continued input of the adverse factors listed above (stress, overload, overuse, speed, poor environmental conditions, particularly cold, and fatigue), which caused the taut band in the first place, adaptive changes occur in other muscles in the myotatic unit. These other muscles now become less flexible and less efficient, predisposing themselves to the development of their own 'energy crises', and eventually developing their own taut bands, as well. This not only results in interference with their own efficiency, but further provides feedback information to the other members of the myotatic unit that resets the entire system geared not to release and expression but rather to one of control and being on guard. This is a normal protective mechanism. In the case of myofascial dysfunction, this protective reflex persists, setting the stage for the development of the myofascial pain syndromes.

The taut band, because of a variety of factors, sets up a trigger point area within itself. This trigger point develops the ability to not only persist as a local generator of pain and dysfunction within the muscle, but also to act as a autonomous pain generator for symptoms elsewhere, through the mechanism of referred pain (which was discussed previously in this chapter).

Another factor that can disrupt the delicate balance of the muscle system is overload. Occurring when the load is not distributed throughout the muscle group, overload causes the muscle to break down. Pianists should be aware of the factors that are likely to affect the critical load on their muscles:

1. Alignment, structure, or posture
2. Static and dynamic loading forces
3. Use or overuse
4. Hyperlaxity
5. Balance between agonist and antagonist muscles
6. Internal environment of the muscle set
    a. Length-tension relationship
    b. Nutrition and energy supply
    c. Circulation
    d. Sympathetic nervous system
    e. Temperature and adequate warming of muscles
    f. Psychosocial modulators
7. External Environment
    a. Physical and emotional stress
    b. Temperature
    c. Coexisting entrapment neuropathy

TREATMENT

Stretching should be done throughout the course of the day, with specific target muscles being the low back, the neck and the shoulders.

The importance of having flexible but strong muscles cannot be overstated. This is the hallmark of any program of treatment. Stretching should be done throughout the course of the day, with specific target muscles being the low back, the neck and the shoulders. Because the pianist spends so much time sitting, a key exercise involves stretching the back backwards (extension exercises), although rolling the trunk into a ball while lying on the floor with the knees pulled to the chest is a good way to stretch the back as well.

Pianists need to be aware of proper posture: the role of strong abdominal muscles in supporting the back while sitting and standing, and the importance of proper head position. In the normal standing position, the chin should be straight back with the ears over the shoulders. Neck flexibility in all directions should be achieved.

The shoulders are typically the most overlooked area of the body in the pianist. Often these very important proximal stabilizers are weak or tight, which biases in a negative fashion the functioning of the more distal muscles. This is particularly devastating to the pianist. To counteract the problem the shoulders need to be stretched and strengthened.

MEDICATION

The use of medications is often a controversial area since all medications have some potential for side effects, including simple over-the-counter medications such as aspirin, Tylenol, and ibuprophen. Nonetheless, these are very easy and effective ways to minimize the pain and improve performance. The pianist should understand the way in which these, and all, medications work.

The primary medications that the pianist should be aware of are subdivided into two categories: those that treat both the pain and the inflammation, and those that simply treat pain. The former group includes aspirin, the entire class of medications called the non-steroidal anti-inflammatory drugs, and the steroids. The latter group includes virtually all of the preceding medications but also includes other medications such as Tylenol, and the various codeine-containing compounds.

In addition, since proper sleep is important and since 20 to 30 percent of the population or more have dysfunctional sleep, the use of a variety of sleep medications is important. Sleeping medication should be used with caution and should be cycled to avoid dependency and addiction. Some sleeping medications also are effective in treating pain, and others work also on anxiety or depression. Proper medical consultation is essential before using these medications, and, more importantly, proper sleep hygiene is essential to correct problems that are perpetuating the poor sleep. Thus caffeine avoidance, establishing a good sleep routine, and avoidance of stressful activities prior to sleep is ideal.

Other medicines of note to pianists include anti-histamines, the use of which, in some hands, has been found to be effective ancillary medications. Anti-anxiety and anti-depressants may also be helpful. The use of muscle relaxants often causes daytime drowsiness, and this limits their daytime usage. However, these medications may be helpful at night.

Understanding how and when to take medication is essential. As the purpose of medication is to increase activity or work tolerance, pain medication is best taken in anticipation of participation in activities that cause pain. Proper nutrition, stress management, taking time out of the normal routine for fun (or for a change of pace), and self-caring activities are also necessary recommendations for the pianist.

IN SUMMARY

It is important for the pianist to have a better understanding of all of the conditions that may interfere with his or her ability to play or perform. In particular, the pianist should recognize the existence of the myofascial pain syndromes, since a better understanding of these will result in less of a chance of sustaining an injury at the keyboard and an improved outcome if a pianist does develop a problem. The myofascial pain syndromes often lurk in the background of most persistent and refractory pain problems and the pianist needs to obtain appropriate consultation from physicians who are skilled in the diagnosis and management of these conditions.

Neurological Insight and Treatment for Practice and Performance-related Pain

Mitchell L. Elkiss, D.O., F.A.C.N.

In discussing the field of piano wellness, it is incumbent upon us to attend to the vexing problem of practice and performance-related pain. A highly prevalent disturbance for all musicians, from beginners to professionals, it includes the occasional acute pain, along with the cases of insidious and chronic pain, which are common and widespread amongst pianists. For those pianists who suffer from chronic pain, clinical experience reveals a high incidence of biomechanical dysfunction. This structural pathology of the neuromuscularskeletal system[1] is a hallmark of chronic pain. Regrettably, standard medical and neurological evaluation often fails to recognize, or under-recognizes, the damaging pathologic process, the diagnoses of which requires a meticulous, palpatory examination of the structural aspects of the musculoskeletal system.

MYOFASCIAL SYNDROME

Patients who complain of the chronic pain described above must be examined for general physical, neurologic, and biomechanical health. While general physical and neurologic examination techniques are fairly well standardized, it is the evaluation of the biomechanical aspects of the neuromusculoskeletal system that are typically under appreciated and under evaluated. Not only is this diagnostic process critical, it is also very heavily dependant on the physical examination, as there is no alternative way to do this type of evaluation. This process is very dependant upon palpatory examination of the soft tissues, evaluation of active and passive ranges of motion for the involved regions, joint segments, and muscle groups.

One particularly relevant observation I have made is the effectiveness of examining the patient in a simulated state of playing. In other words, I have found it effective to have the patient to act out the activities that cause him or her the biggest problem. What become clear under these circumstances is that

[1]A systems analysis recognizing the integrated and synergistic functions of the nervous system, the musculotendinous system, and the skeletoligamentous system.

there is a very high incidence of myofascial syndrome[2] present at the root of many of these disorders. Of course, there are neurologic entrapments, rheumatologic disturbances,[3] congenital deformities,[4] and a whole range of endocrine,[5] metabolic,[6] and general medical pathologies that must be considered.

The often-overlooked myofascial pain syndrome is diagnosed by way of palpatory identification of tender trigger points in affected muscles, which, when palpated, evoked a local reaction, as well as a referral of pain to a distance site.[7] These muscles may harbor painful nodules[8] and tender bands, which may act as trigger points. Muscles involved in this process undergo a shortening and, in the process, become weakened. They frequently become associated with pain, stiffness, and limitation of motion. Pathologic activation of trigger points is typically associated with trauma, or repetitive overloading. In the process of learning to play the piano, these traumatic forces are all-too-often brought to bear. Surprisingly, much of the traumatic process may go unnoticed by both student and teacher. In this way, the mechanism of injury may be promulgated, and efforts to consciously heal and repair may inadvertently be thwarted.

HOW IS IT THAT SUCH A CIRCUMSTANCE CAN DEVELOP?

When learning how to play the piano, a training of voluntary motor functions is required. This can be understood in terms of a typical neurologically mediated learning paradigm. This involves the control of posture, and stabilizing, synergists,[9] and antagonist muscles, as well as the fingers themselves. In the early stages of training for the complex and rapid movements of playing the piano, the student is highly dependant of feedback from the proprioceptive,[10] visual, and auditory sensory afferent input systems. In this way, the precise movements can be finely adjusted and honed to achieve the outcome of playing the piano successfully and accurately. At this stage, the teacher has a particularly prominent role in helping to establish the essential healthy behaviors of posture, coordination, effort, and intensity that become the first layer of learning upon which all others are subsequently laid. If the first layers are dysfunctional or maladaptive[11], one does not need a crystal ball to predict the future difficulties that might be anticipated.

In the beginning, these lessons must be performed slowly and with a good deal of requisite attention. If the student goes too fast, the error rate increases. At this state, the primary motor cortex is very much the active motivator, so students

---

[2]Myofascial pain is a large group of muscle disorders characterized by the presence of hypersensitive points, called trigger points, within one or more muscles and/or the investing connective tissue together with a syndrome of pain, muscle spasm, tenderness, stiffness, limitation of motion, weakness, and occasionally autonomic dysfunction.

[3]Pertaining to diseases that cause inflammation and pain in muscles and joint. *Webster's New Dictionary* (1989), s.v. "rheumatologic."

[4]Conditions that exist at (and usually before) birth.

[5]Secreting internally, specifically producing secretions that are distributed in the body by the bloodstream. *Webster's New Dictionary* (1989), s.v. "endocrine."

[6]The totality of all the physical and chemical processes in the body, and the transformation by which energy is made available for the body.

[7]Janet G. Trevell and David G. Simons, *Myofascial Pain and Dysfunction: The Trigger Point Manual*, 2 vols. (Baltimore: Williams and Wilkins, 1983).

[8]Small lumps, swelling, or collection of tissue.

[9]Muscle groups where the total effect of the combined action is greater than the sum of the effects of the individual muscles.

[10]Those parts of the body that regulate posture and coordination.

[11]An adaptive response of an organism which is counterproductive to its survival.

must think about what their hands are to do before music sounds. Frequently, the emphasis is in the fingers and hands at the end of the operator. A lesser attention is placed on the spinal postural balance, centering, rooting, and proximal stabilizing synergistic muscles, which are no less important in the performance of piano playing and, as we shall see, are often the culprit in many of the painful scenarios which develop over time. Again, the teacher can be helpful with little input, such as adjusting the height of the seat, correcting the posture of the student to sit straighter, relax the shoulders and upper arms, keep the elbows and wrists from locking, etc.

As the lessons are learned, an unconscious mechanism of sensorimotor[12] control begins to dominate. This type of ballistic motor control[13] is mediated through the basal ganglia[14] and cerebellum[15] and operates independently of external feedback. It is also not degraded by increasing the speed of performance. Ballistic motor control is also largely unconscious and allows the performance of highly technical, rapid fire, incredibly precise movement. It can be done with eyes closed and allows the performer to actually play faster than they can think. It accounts for the performance of the fine and delicate, as well as the forceful movements of the fingers, hands, forearms, and arms. It also provides the appropriate supportive tone of the proximal upper extremity muscles, in addition to the trunk and its postural stabilizing muscles.

When the sensorimotor system is functioning at a primary unconsciousness level, it can be difficult to recognize (much less change) any maladaptive neuromusculoskeletal behavior patterns. For that reason, it is most important for intervention to occur early at the most primary of acquisitional states, when the conscious mechanism is maximally engaged. Unfortunately, it is not until symptoms of dysfunction arise, such as pain, that sufficient attention to these dysfunctional behaviors may be manifested. It seems logical that screening for these problems and sensitizing teachers and students alike to these issues may actually help prevent such disorders from developing. When they have already developed, it allows for an early opportunity for therapeutic intervention.

RE-EDUCATION

When the pathologic process involves chronically acquired well-learned, maladaptive, and unconsciously mediated neuromusculoskeletal behavior, it should not be surprising that a single intervention may not eradicate such a process. Rather it is the re-education of the individual and the performance of a therapeutic regimen of neuromusculoskeletal re-education that can be expected to be successful. This involves work at the peripheral muscles and joints, peripheral connective tissues, more proximal stabilizing muscles, joints and connective tissues, the axial support muscles and spinal elements, and, most importantly, the central nervous system integrative elements.

---

[12]Reflects the essential linkage between afferent (sensory) and efferent (motor) functions in a systems analysis.

[13]Flinging motions. An unconscious system of motor control originating in the basal ganglia and utilized in the rapid performance of well-learned motor skills.

[14]Three large subcortical nuclei of the brain that, along with the cerebellum, participate in movement. Legions of the basal ganglia occur in a variety of motor disorders, including Parkinson's disease.

[15]The part of the brain that is concerned primarily with somatic motor function, the control of muscle tone, and the maintenance of balance.

More specifically, the process of neuromusculoskeletal re-education includes:

1. *Modification or elimination of occupations and avocational mechanical stressors* • This includes such things as the height of the piano bench, piano technique, excess tension in the shoulders, arms, forearms, wrists, and hands, and other activities the patient or musician might be involved in, including study habits, computer work, crafts that involve the upper extremities, and other hobbies and activities.

2. *Promotion of postural awareness with training and posture modification* • This begins with raising the awareness of the piano performer as to how their posture influences their playing technique, the various aspects of healthy and unhealthy posture, and the introduction of exercise designed to promote proper posture. These might include such ancillary techniques as yoga and tai-chi, but more particularly, specific guidance by the piano teacher on good playing position.

3. *Identification of specific biomechanical restrictors and the performance of prescribed therapeutic muscular stretching and strengthening exercises* • Beginning with the consideration of all the fingers, hands, forearms, arms, shoulders, neck, spine, rib cage, and finally the diaphragm; all these areas need to be assessed for their flexibility and free range of motion, any structural asymmetries that might exist on a congenital or acquired basis, and search for any signs of excess soft tissue or muscle tension. These then would represent direct cues for prescriptive exercise, to begin with, stretching those areas that are tight with customized exercises given by the teacher to the student for the regions of involvement, including those listed above, but might also include a formal inclusion of an adjunctive physical therapy program utilizing functional stretch, myofascial release techniques, and other physical therapy modalities such as heat and ultrasound. This type of stretching exercise is typically a precursor to any type of strengthening exercise, with the exception of those syndromes of hypermobility,[16] which are a rarity. The myofascial release techniques are particularly relevant to the myofascial pain syndrome, as they treat both viscoelastic properties of the connective tissues as well as the neuroreflexic properties of the muscles themselves.[17]

4. *The development of technically healthy practice and playing neuromusculoskeletal behavior* • Again, the teacher has a particularly great role to play, in both training the techniques that

[16]Joints that can move beyond the normal range of motion. This condition can result in pain and the tendency to sprain or dislocate.

[17]*Foundations of Osteopathic Medicines*, eds. Robert C. Ward, John A. Jerome, and John M. Jones, III (Baltimore, Maryland: Williams & Wilkins, 1997).

the patient exhibits at the piano, as well as a general assessment of movement along the learning curve, which would be unique to each individual piano student with regard to their inherent capacity, unique skills and motivations.

In all instances, the patient is viewed as the agent and vehicle of the healing process and all efforts are designed to enhance this process, including:

1. *Nutritional evaluation and counseling* • The body is constantly forming new muscles, tendons, and bony structures that are dependent upon proper raw materials. The service of those materials includes a proper diet, balanced in its ingredients, completeness, and in the basic substrates of cell formations and metabolism, including minerals and vitamins essential to cellular and organismic function.

2. *Evaluation and education with regard to therapeutic sleep hygiene* • Not only is it important to teach the patient how to practice and work hard, but this needs to be complemented with an understanding of the role of rest, particularly with regard to sleep, during which time the body does its general repair work. This becomes an important consideration and avenue for intervention.

3. *Instruction and description of appropriate relaxation and stress reduction techniques* • These include the relaxation of muscles during actual practice that are unnecessary for the performance of the functions of the hands, as well as the mental attitude of relaxation and depressurization of the atmosphere of learning. With stress reduction, certainly the lowering of sympathetic tone during the times when it is not important to performance is a worthwhile endeavor. Certainly there are times when sympathetic activation is appropriate to learning new skills and to performing, but often times it becomes an obstruction and an obstacle to the proper and restrained performance. Furthermore, even away from the piano, the emphasis on learning how to relax in between efforts and exertions is quite important, as the autonomic nervous system is intended to fire up, do its job, and then rest in between.[18]

Even away from the piano, the emphasis on learning how to relax in between efforts and exertions is quite important.

4. *The use of therapeutic exercises* • In addition to the specific exercises for the hands, arms, and restrictors that have been identified by the teacher and/or by the specialist during a medical evaluation of the musician, more general exercise programs have a place. These include both those that would enhance cardiovascular fitness, such as aerobic training, considering the endurance and intensity required for a sustained performance, and the general conditioning that promotes both strength and flexibility of the entire body. It seems clear that playing an instrument involves that whole body, and so those disciplines

[18]Hans Selye, *Stress Without Distress* (Philadelphia: Lippincott, 1974).

that offer systematic approaches to whole-body conditioning seem to have a particular value in this regard. These include such disciplines as tai chi and yoga.

5. *The use of positive visual imagery* • This is the notion that a student of music has an image of him or herself struggling to learn music, flourishing in the learning of the music and succeeding, or seeing themselves as failing and suffering. This image is maintained in the non-dominant hemisphere of the brain where an actual visual representation of self is maintained and can be modified through the use of appropriate visual imagery techniques. A positive shift in a patient's image of self is very important when trying to promote a healthy individual. The teacher may suggest some of these exercises of positive imagery and some may come spontaneously to the patient. Many of them may be learned as part of a general relaxation and physiologic enhancement program. The benefits of positive visual imagery have been well documented in recent years, with regard to the fields of psychoneuroimunology,[19] psychosomatism,[20] and psychophysiologic[21] dysfunction. In some cases, convincing the patient of their capacity for wellness and their ability to learn and master a material while feeling well at the time represents the most difficult and crucial of objectives.
6. *The promotion of a positive attitude through education about the nature of the problem and the formation of realistic objectives for therapeutic management* • Here is where the student and teacher work together to create a program based upon positive goals for the training, considering the skills, capacities and motivation of the student.

Consider the nature of students' painful problems and what both student and teacher alike might do about that with realistic objective formation, whether the patient has a severe rheumatologic disorder versus a more amenable tight muscle syndrome. Develop a management program with positive therapeutic goals that can be agreed upon. Finally, it should be acknowledged that involving patients as active participants in their own therapeutic objectives is an essential component in achieving true success in the most complex of endeavors.

---

[19]The well known and essential link between the mind and its neural substrate with its powerful effects on the immune system and its functioning.

[20]The effect of thoughts and feelings as manifested thru a concomitant expression thru the somatic or neuromusculoskeletal system.

[21]The effects of thoughts and feelings on the intrinsic physiology of all of the body's interrelated systems. Also, it relates to the physiologic basis of psychic phenomena.

The Pedagogical

The Role of the Teacher if an Injury Should Occur

Gail Berenson

While it is hoped that most problems can be averted with a knowledgeable teacher who stresses injury preventative practice and performance strategies, along with careful attention by the student, injuries still can and do occur. Since teachers are usually the first to hear if a student is having a problem, they need to be aware of the most common types of injuries and know what to do if a student becomes injured.

RISK FACTORS

At the piano, overuse or repetitive strain injuries are the most commonly diagnosed type of injuries, a frequent consequence of placing excessive demands on the musculoskeletal system. The following are some of the risk factors that individually or, more often, cumulatively initiate the circumstances that can precipitate an injury:

One's inherited genetic makeup can be a risk factor. This can include things as common as increased joint laxity (often referred to as being double-jointed) or having extremely small hands. These genetic variations may exist with or without the individual's knowledge, and when coupled with the physical demands of playing the piano, can sometimes lead to injuries.

Cumulative excessive tension is often a critical component of injury. It can be physical or psychological, or a combination of both. Psychological stress can lead to physical tension, sometimes making it difficult to distinguish between the two.

Poor practice habits can, over time, cause serious injuries. Lack of proper warm-up, excessive repetition of a physically demanding section, overplaying an instrument that is stiff or dull, or improper management of practice time (a common problem for young, dedicated students) can all be very harmful.

Faulty or improper technique can also cumulatively produce injuries. Inappropriate fingering and improper use of physical gestures are two of the most common examples. Excessive stretching of the hand is another. This is a frequent problem of students with small hands, but it can be equally problematic for a person with a large hand. Although they can stretch without difficulty, people with large hands often maintain an extended hand position, which can promote excessive tension.

Inappropriate repertoire is a problem for students of all ages. Selecting music that is too difficult or poorly suited to an individual's hand size and shape can make technical demands that go beyond what the student can handle, creating frustration and making physical overuse or misuse more likely.

An unhealthy lifestyle poses a more serious risk for teenagers and college students, who often have inadequate diets and are lacking in rest. College students in particular will also practice for long periods of time without taking sufficient breaks and are likely to practice late at night when tired.

An instrument lacking in quality is often overlooked as a risk factor, but it can be the cause of serious problems if the action is stiff or if it has a dull sound, which encourages individuals to overplay.

Often it is young people who are most vulnerable to injuries away from the instrument because of their involvement in sports.

NON-PIANISTIC RISKS

Sometimes the injuries are playing related. However, other times it is a result of an accident or activity that has nothing to do with the piano. Activities such as lifting heavy boxes, spending an entire weekend painting the house, a fall on the ice, or jamming one's finger in a pickup game of basketball can promote an injury. Life need not be lived in a bubble but, like athletes, musicians use their bodies and must be particularly cautious about the extracurricular tasks they undertake. Eventually a decision must be made as to whether or not it is worth the risk to do these things. Often it is young people who are most vulnerable to injuries away from the instrument because of their involvement in sports. A word of caution: the most dangerous sports for musicians are those that use the bare hand as a racket, including volleyball, basketball and handball.

STAGES OF OVERUSE

Evaluating the seriousness of an injury early in its onset is important to insuring proper care and treatment and in minimizing the chances of prolonged or permanent damage. The following descriptions of stages of overuse, adapted from a similar listing by Dr. Hunter Fry,[1] are helpful guidelines for both teachers and students to consider when determining the best treatment options.

Stages of Overuse

Stage 1

Discomfort during *or* after activity but no performance disability

Analogous to post exercise muscle soreness. Pain is usually felt in only one site.

Stage 2

Discomfort during *and* after the activity but no performance disability.

The pain lasts for only a short period after the activity and can be felt in multiple sites. There is some pain during other activities of the hand. Palpable tenderness is present.

Stage 3

Discomfort during and after the activity and there is performance disability.

Pain will last for a period longer than two hours after the activity and will be present at rest and during many daily activities.

[1]HJH Fry, "Overuse syndrome of the upper limb in musicians," *The Medical Journal of Australia* 144 (1986): 182-185.

Stage 4

Discomfort that is incapacitating due to continuous pain, weakness, and inability to coordinate.

DIAGNOSING INJURY

If teachers are to serve as the first line of defense for students, an open line of communication should be encouraged. Students should feel comfortable telling their teacher if they are having problems. If a student indicates that he or she is experiencing pain, it is the teacher's responsibility to assess the seriousness of the injury and, if possible, determine the cause. In this instance, the teacher first functions as a detective, asking questions and trying to discover what caused the injury. A few sample questions are listed below:

1. Do you think your injury is due to a non-playing related activity or is it due to playing-related overuse or misuse?
2. Have you engaged in any different kind of physical activity prior to the beginning of the pain?
3. Since the onset of these symptoms, have you done anything to address this problem such as ice the area or take an over-the-counter anti-inflammatory medication? Have you altered your practicing routine?
4. Do you notice it more when playing specific literature? Can you relate it to a specific passage in your piece?
5. How soon does the pain begin after you start practicing? Does it go away when you stop playing?

It is important to monitor a student carefully since a stage-2 injury can easily progress to stage 3.

Although teachers play an extremely important role in helping students prevent injury, there are limitations. Teachers are not medical professionals. If a student arrives at his or her lesson describing injuries similar to those in stage 3, this cannot be ignored or fixed by the teacher. Insist that the student seek professional medical intervention as soon as possible.

TEACHING A STUDENT THROUGHOUT THE VARIOUS STAGES OF AN INJURY

While working with a student with any level of injury, carefully observe the student, making sure he or she is seated properly at the piano and approaching the instrument in a technically sound manner, playing in a tension-free, fluid manner. Before sending a student home to practice, impress upon him or her that pain, a dull ache or feelings of excess fatigue are signals that should not be ignored. Students should learn that if something hurts, they should stop whatever they are doing immediately!

Teachers also need to be especially flexible while working with an injured student. The first priority must be helping him or her recover and eventually return to normal activity. Depending upon the type of injury, a number of changes in practicing or repertoire might need to be adopted. Keeping the hand small and in its natural, closed position is a frequent requirement, so it becomes necessary to work around those pieces that have large stretches or other physically demanding elements. At times it is possible to continue practicing sections of a composition, the slow movement of a sonata, for example, or to slow down the tempo to reduce the physical demands. In some cases, though, it is advisable to briefly *or permanently* drop a piece.

If an injury is severe enough, it may be necessary to rest the hand and avoid practicing for a few days. Today, physicians rarely demand total rest for long periods of time since that creates weakness and an even more difficult and lengthy recovery period. If a student has been immobilized in a cast, it is critical that the return to previous repertoire be handled in a gradual fashion, building strength and flexibility in small increments. Frequently, physical therapy proves very helpful in recovery. Most physicians automatically prescribe physical therapy for musicians. Licensed physical or occupational therapists provide therapeutic modalities that will help the student recover more quickly and also strengthen the injured area to avoid future problems. There are some physicians who assume that students will heal and return to normal activity on their own. Playing the piano, however, goes beyond normal activity, so it might be necessary for musicians to ask about the benefits of physical therapy for their type of injury. In those cases where physical therapy is determined to be advantageous, students should request a physical therapy referral from their physician if it is not automatically forthcoming.

Sheila Mark, a therapist who has successfully treated many performers, offers this advice to musicians searching for a physical therapist:

> It is important for the therapist to have special training in performance arts or experience with performance artists so that they understand the demands of the instrument, as well as the appropriate practice schedule for the student's injury. Most physical therapists will welcome the opportunity to work with a piano teacher in helping to determine the cause of the injury and to design the progression of the student's return to full function.[2]

Helping the student design a strategy to return to normal practicing is an especially important responsibility for the teacher to assume. In most cases, the student should begin with very short practice periods. Even during these five to ten-minute sessions, it might be necessary to insert rest periods every few minutes. Have the student stand up and stretch, walk around, perhaps get a drink of water and then return to the piano. Continuous practice time during the initial recovery process should be limited to a maximum of fifteen minutes, with the possibility of repeating that time period two or three times, spaced throughout the day, as the recovery process progresses and if no pain reoccurs. It is crucial to make certain that the student increases his or her practice time gradually, and stops immediately there is any pain or excessive fatigue.

Patience is required of both the teacher and the injured student as the return to pre-injury practice routine and performance level may be rocky and take longer than anticipated. Out of necessity, students may need to shorten their practice time for days, weeks, or even months. It is important for the teacher to recognize that this does not reflect a lack of motivation or dedication on the part of the student. It merely reflects that the rate of recovery moves at its own pace and cannot be hurried.

---

[2] Sheila Mark, licensed physical therapist, Athens Physical Therapy, Athens, Ohio.

If the student is not allergic to over-the-counter medications, he or she may want to consider taking either aspirin or one of the many over-the-counter, non-steroidal anti-inflammatory medications on the market, in an effort to reduce pain. As with all medications, it is always safest to consult a physician before beginning, and it is a must if the use becomes prolonged. It is also important to remember that while they can help control pain, these medications may also mask pain, resulting in increased tissue damage.

To reduce inflammation after practicing, students should ice the injured area in a proper manner as relayed by their teacher. Licensed physical therapist Brigham Cooley, Athens, Ohio, recommends the following:

> Students should use ice or a cold pack for fifteen to twenty minutes after practicing if they suspect a tendon injury. Injured students should put a cloth the thickness of a pillowcase over their skin and then apply the ice or cold pack over the pillowcase. Most students will not have a problem with cold packs but a few cautions should be provided to students. Only apply cold packs to areas where the student has complete sensation, check the area regularly for the ability to feel moderate finger pressure and remove the cold pack if the area remains white after the finger pressure is removed.[3]

It is not uncommon to find injured students manifesting symptoms of frustration and depression, and the more serious and dedicated the student, the more likely this is to happen. Teachers need to be patient, supportive and understanding, finding ways to encourage the student and keep him or her involved in lessons. The assignment of a one-handed composition can give a student the opportunity to work on a complete composition, while still resting the injured hand.

Mental practice, which is executed away from the instrument, has also been found to be a wonderful practice strategy for injured students. Describing her use of mental practice during her recovery period from tendinitis, Malva Freymuth states, "by playing a few measures at a time and then practicing them mentally for several minutes, I was able to distribute five minutes of physical playing over an hour's worth concentrated mental work."[4] This practicing technique can also be advantageous to a student who is uninjured, as it encourages more thoughtful practice.

COMMUNICATION IS CRITICAL

Piano teachers are trained as neither physicians nor psychologists, but they still play a vital role in maintaining and, at times, improving the health of their students. Should an injury occur, it is essential for the teacher to take it seriously and to team with the medical professionals in the student's recovery process. Even before this, though, it is important to provide a supportive, non-threatening learning environment that motivates and encourages productivity, independence and self esteem and opens the lines of communication. With this in place, students will feel comfortable confiding in their teachers the problems that impact their performance at the instrument, including injuries. This is the key to helping students quickly resolve any problem before it becomes chronic and derails a future of enjoyable music making.

---

[3]Brigham Cooley, licensed physical therapist, Athens, Ohio

[4]Malva Freymuth, *Mental Practice and Imagery for Musicians* (Boulder, Colorado: Integrated Musician's Press, 1999) 17.

Keeping It Simple: Fundamentals of a Healthful Piano Technique

Barbara Lister-Sink

HEALTHFUL PIANO TECHNIQUE: A BRIEF HISTORY

> For the past five years I have had severe tension and nerve damage in my right arm. I've been to four or five orthopedic surgeons and was told that I would either have to quit playing the piano, or that I could have an operation, but that I would never play more than half-hour a day.
>
> – *Thirteen-year old, exceptionally talented, dedicated pianist*

This should not and need not happen. Healthful, injury-free piano technique is a skill which every pianist has the ability and right to acquire. Such a tragic state of affairs is the result of a confusing, inadequate, or misinformed definition of healthful technique, not to mention a lack of a clear, effective means of attaining it. An older pianist poignantly states the consequences of this dilemma:

> I graduated in 1978...with a profound love of the piano literature, and tendinitis and nerve damage in my right shoulder. I stopped playing altogether, and did not start practicing again until 1995! Playing seriously meant pain, and I avoided it for a long time.

For many, technique is seen as either a meaningless waste of time that promotes pain and injury, or a sure means of dampening musicality. Little wonder that many pianists throughout the twentieth century developed an aversion to it altogether. But one of the greatest musicians and teachers of that century, Nadia Boulanger, was emphatic about the role of technique in music making, declaring: "It is the only means we have for making music." If this is true, then we have turned away from an essential part of musical development.

What has led to such a disheartening state of pianistic affairs? To find answers, a look at the history of piano technique and its transmittal through time might be helpful. Promoting ease and avoiding injury is not a new pedagogical goal. In one way or another, it has been addressed – not always scientifically, but often successfully – for more than 250 years. C.P.E. Bach's *Essay on the True Art of Playing Keyboard Instruments* and François Couperin's *The Art of Playing the Harpsichord* contain helpful information on avoiding unnecessary tension and strain. From the accounts of his students and colleagues, Frédéric Chopin was himself also a stunning revolutionary in this area. His unique contribution to the evolution of keyboard technique was not only his legacy of superbly musical etudes, but also the way he asked that these studies be taught. The great Franz Liszt contributed to this revolution, amplifying Chopin's technical ideas.

In 1903, the renowned English pedagogue Tobias Matthay restated the basic principles, although in a more florid and expansive way. His method revolutionized piano technique and produced such offspring as Dame Myra Hess. Meanwhile, the so-called Russian School was developing its own special brand of powerful, free, and virtuoso technique. Its pianistic products are legion. In 1929, Abby Whiteside's *The Pianist's Mechanism* was published almost concurrently with the scientifically exhaustive *Physiological Mechanics of Piano Technique* by Otto Ortmann, both again revolutionizing the way pianists thought about technique – Whiteside with her model of the pianist as athlete imbued with a fundamental pulse, and Ortmann with his rigorous, rational scrutiny of the body and piano mechanisms.

Added to these were innumerable contributions by the great pianists and teachers of the first half of the twentieth century, as well as a number of more recent, updated technical perspectives. Reginald Gerig's *Famous Pianists and Their Technique* offers an encyclopedic and especially useful survey of the subject, although it does not directly address the questions of how to play the piano. By the late twentieth century, a number of videos on piano technique began to appear. In addition, beginning in the mid-1980s, the hybrid field of performing arts medicine was created, adding additional medical and scientific insight into injury-preventive technique.

NOT-SO-EVIDENT TECHNICAL TRUTHS

The truths embodied in several centuries of such injury-preventive technical training are as follows:

- Injury from playing the keyboard is unnecessary and preventable.
- Healthful technique is synonymous with natural ease, not difficulty.
- Technical ease is a skill, not a talent, and can be learned by anyone with the appropriate, hands-on instruction.

WIDE-SPREAD DISCOURAGEMENT

Injury-preventive, free, effortless technique is a very old concept. We have been told how to play well and prevent injury almost since the keyboard was invented. So, given this immense legacy of great teachers and effortless performers of the last several centuries, as well as the added help of the relatively new field of performing arts medicine and global communication technology, why is there an epidemic at the beginning of the twenty-first century of playing-related injuries and dysfunction? Why is there still so much pedagogical isolation, disagreement, and confusion?

Pain, discomfort, frustration, and even despair are rampant among pianists worldwide. "For far too many dedicated pianists of all ages and levels, playing the piano becomes a disappointing, discouraging activity, rather than one that is enriching, even healing. Many pianists stop playing simply because they see no other option, and they cannot find answers in time to rescue them from physical discomfort, pain, injury, and the accompanying emotional debilitation."[1] Why has knowledge and the ability to play in an unconstrained, injury-free manner repeatedly faded or disappeared, like some elusive comet? Perhaps, as one pianists reported her teacher had alleged, we just aren't practicing enough?!

MEDIUM DISTORTS THE MESSAGE

One reason may be quite simple. We have traditionally relied on words in written form to describe and convey very complex physical sensations. Noted neuropsychologist Howard Gardner, creator of the concept of multiple intelligences, might suggest that we have used one form of intelligence – the cognitive/analytical – to describe and teach another – the kinesthetic/physical.

It is like trying to describe the smell of a rose. Words and symbols cannot convey a smell or a sound or a kinesthetic sensation. They might evoke a certain physiological state, but they are notoriously unreliable messengers when it comes to training the body in specific, highly complex coordinations. Even so, throughout keyboard history, we have continually attempted to reduce the intricate, complex, neuromuscular event of piano playing to analytical descriptions. Witness the number of books written on piano technique. For centuries, outside of actual lessons, the written word has been the only means we have had of conveying the state of the mind and body while playing.

It is important that we see all contributions to this mode of conveyance (even those you are currently reading) for what they are – verbal explanations of a physical event – and take into consideration the ramifications of that reality. Even visual images on video are potentially misleading, although somewhat less so than words alone. We can at least imitate a well-coordinated gesture. However, imitating the *look* of a movement will not necessarily give us the all-critical *feel* of it. Countless anatomical descriptions and rational analyses of movement will fail *unless we convey them kinesthetically, physically to the student.*

THE ARTIST AS ATHLETE

A primary reason for our failure to embrace the physical essence or athletic nature of technique may be best stated by Howard Gardner:

> The divorce between the 'mental' and the 'physical' has not infrequently been coupled with a notion that what we do with our bodies is somehow less privileged, less special, than language, logic, or some other relatively abstract symbolic system.[2]

Or as noted neurologist and amateur pianist Frank Wilson states in *Tone*

---

[1]Barbara Lister-Sink, "Piano Technique, Plain and Simple," *Piano & Keyboard* (March/April 1999): 18.

[2]Howard Gardner, *Frames of Mind – The Theory of Multiple Intelligences* (Cambridge: BasicBooks, 1993) 208.

Deaf & All Thumbs?, "deep within our collective memory is the imprint of the bespectacled, frail, and passive kid instantly recognized as being musical."[3] But Gardner also reveals a more positive image for the musician, echoing recent scientific discoveries about the role of listening to and making music in enhancing intelligence: "It is worthy to note that psychologists in recent years have discerned and stressed a close link between the use of the body and the deployment of other cognitive powers."[4]

Of course, playing the piano is not only an activity of the body. At its best, it represents an exquisite combination of body, mind, emotions, and spirit. Again, Wilson declares that:

> Musical skill provides the clearest example and the cleanest proof of the existence of a whole class of self-defined, personally distinctive motor skills with an extended training and experience base, strong ties to the individual's emotional and cognitive development, strong communicative intent, and very high performance standards. Musical skill...is more than...ordinary manual dexterity, or expertness in pantomime...
>
> ... [it is] a whole *family* of physically and cognitively demanding, hierarchically structured, creatively rich human skills that have communicative content.[5]

Before we synthesize the emotional, interpretative, stylistic, intellectual, and spiritual planes of music making, we need to establish the most free, natural, efficient way to produce sound on the piano.

How is that for a morale booster?

However, before we synthesize the emotional, interpretative, stylistic, intellectual, and spiritual planes of music making, we need to establish the most free, natural, efficient way to produce sound on the piano. We simply cannot play the piano with our brains, emotions, or spirits alone. We must use our bodies, and use them as fluidly and naturally as well-trained athletes or cats. Pianists are athletes, using primarily the smaller muscles of the arms, hands and fingers. Beautifully coordinated pianists are first-class athletes.

Again, Dr. Frank Wilson is even more emphatic about the extraordinary athletic skill required of a pianist:

> Musical skill depends upon movements in which the entire body participates, but is built on precise control of the smaller muscles of the arms and hands...The musician, a small-muscle athlete, is not just a big athlete in miniature. No other activity in which we engage required that accuracy, speed, timing, smoothness, or coordination of muscular contraction exhibited in finished musical performance.[6]

Pianists often eschew this idea that they are athletes. After all, we want to play the piano because of our love for music, not mechanics or movement. Some of us even fear that focusing on the athletics, if only temporarily, might diminish our musicality. The joyful reality is that athletics and artistry can be intrinsically

[3]Frank R. Wilson, *Tone Deaf & All Thumbs? – An Invitation to Music Making* (New York: Vintage Books, 1986) 27.

[4]Gardner, *Frames of Mind*, 208.

[5]Frank R. Wilson, *The Hand* (New York: Vintage Books, 1998) 207.

[6]Wilson, *Tone Deaf & All Thumbs?*, 27.

linked while playing once pianists:

1. Agree on a definition of healthful piano technique.
2. Develop fail-safe paths toward its development.

HEALTHFUL PIANO TECHNIQUE: A DEFINITION

Nature's way is simple and easy, but men prefer what is intricate and artificial.

– Lao Tzu

The problems of pianists must not be too sharply differentiated from those of the dancer, the singer, the violinist. Indeed, all bodily skills have this in common: they always involve the whole body if the best results are to be obtained. The body is the center of all these skills...the center controls the periphery.

– Abby Whiteside

Pianists need a clear, universally acceptable, understandable, and consistent definition of technique, one which works for pianists and keyboardists of all ages and in all styles of music, one that allows a maximum of artistic expression with a minimum of effort. I would like to suggest such a definition:

Healthful piano technique occurs when there is good coordination of the whole body with the piano.

And while such a definition might seem too simplistic and general for some, it is that very simplicity and generality that make this definition so valuable. By paring the definition down to basic principles, which follow natural laws, we lessen the controversy over what is good and what is not.

Have you ever watched a cat cleaning its face with its paw? Or a world-class golfer swinging a golf club? Or a master carpenter hammering a nail? If so, you were observing healthful technique – the means of accomplishing an activity or task in the most natural, efficient, and well-coordinated way. It is a way of taking full advantage of the extraordinary design of the mind and body. It is, by definition, injury preventive.

Technique has also long had a double meaning for artists in Western society. Derived from the Greek *technos* meaning art and skill, and the early French *tekhné*, meaning art, these origins underscore the statement by Nadia Boulanger, "We can only be musically free if the essential technique of our art has been completely mastered." When one has truly mastered technique, the two – technique and art – become one. Music cannot come into being without technique.

HOW, NOT WHAT

For many pianists, the goal of technique has often been getting the right notes down at *any* cost to the body. At its best, this has led to a history of bizarre contraptions, ruinous exercises, and rigid systems antithetical to a healthful way of using the body, often led to discomfort, pain, injury, and malfunction. At its worst, this has resulted in a corrupt and destructive definition of techniques as *what* – playing the right notes in the right place with the right dynamics – rather than *how* – the particular physical coordination we use to accomplish all that.

Technique is not *what* we accomplish; it is *how* we accomplish it. It is not the clean fur, the driven nail, or the golf ball flying through the air. It is not the scales, arpeggios, exercises, or studies we play, it is *how* we physically coordinate our bodies with the piano to accomplish these activities.

Musicians, like athletes, are extraordinarily dedicated, disciplined, and committed to self-development in their art. Such characteristics are laudable, but they can lead to negative results if we do not attend to how we use the body. Hundreds, if not thousands, of hours spent accumulating muscle tension, misaligning our skeletal frame and stressing our joints, and the ensuing stress this physical state places on the mind and emotions, can lead to the loss of that which we hold dearest – our ability to make music.

WHOLE-BODY TECHNIQUE

Good physical coordination is the harmonious working together of all the parts of the body, with the mind as the director. This is how the finest athletes define technique. On the most fundamental level of each sport, it is called basic form. And the mind is an intrinsic, inseparable part of the athlete's or pianist's technique. It directs the activities of the body in an unending flow of communication from the brain through the sensory-motor nerves of the spine out to the muscles.

The whole body is part of that coordination. Just because the visible part of piano playing primarily involves the arms and hands does not mean that the whole body is not involved. For centuries we have labored under the false assumption that piano technique is a collection of isolated movements of the fingers, hands, and arms. Now we are finally accepting that the body is one beautifully integrated web of cells, fibers, bones, muscles, joints, tendons, ligaments, organs, fluids, nerves – approximately 700 muscles, 200 bones, and ten-million muscle cells, just for a start.

Most importantly, all of it is interconnected. A human being is a collection of exquisitely fine-tuned systems – musculoskeletal, sensory-motor, cardiovascular, neuromuscular, to name a few – each related to the other. The simplest movement or muscle contraction resonates, like ripples in a pond, throughout the whole body. We cannot isolate the movements of the fingers, hands, and arms from the rest of the body.

Let us now get more specific in our definition of good coordination of the whole body and turn, in our imagination, to the cat as it cleans its face with it paw, runs, or chases it tale. We can also envision the same characteristics of the superb natural coordination as we watch a world-class golfer swinging the golf club. It might even be easier to imagine these activities in slow motion. Both are demonstrating the two characteristic of a well-coordinated, injury-preventive technique:

1. Efficient, restorative muscle use
2. An optimally aligned, dynamically-balanced skeletal system

EFFICIENT MUSCLE USE

> In all activities of life, the secret of efficiency lies in an ability to combine two seemingly incompatible states: a state of maximum

> activity and a state of maximum relaxation.
>
> – *Aldous Huxley*

> Musical skill depends upon movements in which the entire body participates, but is built on precise control of the smaller muscles...No other activity in which we engage requires the accuracy, speed, timing, smoothness, or coordination of muscular contraction exhibited in finished musical performance.[7]
>
> – *Frank Wilson*

Learning to control muscles though the full range of total relaxation to total contraction is essential to a healthful technique. The lack of this control leads to accumulated, chronic muscle tension, which is one of the main causes of discomfort, pain, and dysfunction in most activities. A healthful keyboard technique allows for the muscles not only to contract at will but also to be continually refreshed and restored to their original state of release.

As Thomas Hanna clearly explained in *Somatics*:

> The chronically contracted muscle is like a motor that one cannot turn off. It continues to run and to burn up energy.
>
> This is why muscles with a high tonus [level of contraction] are always sore. The glycogen, which is stored in the muscle for the energy of contraction, is constantly being burned up. The combustion of glycogen creates contraction, and the glycogen is then turned into lactic acid. If there is constant combustion, then there is a constant buildup of lactic acid, and the more acid there is, the more the muscle's sensory cells become irritated. A 10-percent buildup will create enough activity to make the muscle feel tired. A constant 40-percent buildup will create so much hot acidity around the pain receptor cells that the bloodstream cannot flush it away, and the muscle will constantly feel painful.[8]

The muscle states described here by Hanna are typical of those of many pianists, not only in the arms and hands, but also in the shoulders, neck, and back muscles. In pianists, chronic, accumulated muscle tension can lead to fatigue, malfunction, and even paralysis of the arms and hands, as well as to neck, shoulder, and back pain. It blocks the free flow of weight and energy from the torso through the arms and impedes free movement of the joints. As a consequence, our movements at the piano become stiff, sluggish, and laborious. Speed and facility, which should be natural and easeful, are difficult to achieve. Learning how to avoid accumulating muscle tension by continually releasing muscle tension is essential to a healthful, injury-preventive technique.

To turn to examples of highly efficient muscle use, let us envision the cat and the well-trained golfer. Both are demonstrating efficient muscle use and, as a result, the natural suppleness that ensues. Both use the right muscles in the right amount of contraction at the right time and for the right duration to accomplish

---

[7]Wilson, *Tone Deaf & All Thumbs?*, 31.

[8]Thomas Hanna, *Somatics - Reawakening the Mind's Control of Movement, Flexibility, and Health* (Cambridge: Perseus Books, 1988) 14.

the task. When the cat is finished washing it face or the golfer finishes the swing, both relax the muscles so that they may return to their natural resting state and refresh themselves. In this way, neither is exhausting the muscles in unnecessary tension or movement, nor are they *accumulating* muscle tension. The joints are held in a fixed position, or stabilized, only when weight is being supported. When they are not stabilized, they are free of binding muscle tension around them, allowing for maximum freedom and speed of movement.

Well-coordinated walking is a simple example of efficient muscle use: the muscles of the supporting leg contract and stabilize the joints so that the leg does not collapse as we put weight on it. Simultaneously, the muscles of the non-supporting leg relax, liberating the joints and allowing the leg to swing through freely.

OPTIMALLY ALIGNED, DYNAMICALLY BALANCED SKELETAL SYSTEM

Healthful, well-coordinated technique is impossible without an optimally aligned skeletal system, from the center out to the periphery. And essential to that is the support of a dynamically balanced, flexible spine. It, together with the brain balanced on top of it, comprises the central nervous system and is the command center of the body.

Chronic misalignment of any part of the spine will very likely result in chronic muscle tension, nerve entrapment, and eventually, pain and malfunction, both in the torso and in the extremities. In addition to the physical problems resulting from spinal misalignment, problems such as performance anxiety, memory difficulties in performance, and a general lack of mental energy can be linked to the byproducts of skeletal misalignment – muscle tension build-up and inadequately functioning systems.

In their activities, both the cat and the world-class golfer will have beautifully flexible, lengthened spines. As they move and use muscular energy, their spinal vertebrae will be in a state of dynamic balance and internal flow. Forming the graceful, natural curves of the spine, the vertebrae will have adequate space between them for maximum flow of information from the brain through the spinal cord and out to the rest of the body.

If compressed vertebrae and the resultant nerve impingement blocked this flow, the muscles would not receive information from the brain adequately. As a result, the whole system would be compromised. Both the cat and the golfer would lose their muscular suppleness, timing and flow of movement. But thanks to a balanced and supported central axis, their heads, arms, legs, and paws can move easily and freely.

We were designed to enjoy happily functioning neuromuscular, sensory-motor, and cardiovascular systems. This can, however, happen only in the absence of chronically tightened muscles, compressed spines, and the resultant stressed joints or 'pinched' nerves. When a pianist learns efficient muscle use and optimal, dynamically balanced skeletal alignment, well-coordinated, injury-preventive technique is the result. And with this essential tool, our musicality can soar on unharmed wings.

MISUSE AND MUSICALITY

It should be mentioned that throughout most of pianistic history, many successful pianists have not demonstrated this type of healthful, natural alignment or efficient muscle use. Their success is a tribute to the ability of a dedicated, determined mind to dominate and ignore the cries of the body for help. And while we can respect and admire their artistry and ability to function under highly adverse physical duress, we should not use them as models for our teaching or playing. They are the exceptions. It is also important not to confuse mal-coordinated body-use patterns with superior musical gifts. Placing unnecessary stress on the body does not produce a better musical performance; it handicaps it.

THE IMPORTANCE OF A SOLID FOUNDATION

> I feel like when I play the piano I'm literally having to drag music out of it. I also feel like there are a million things happening inside my head and my body, and there are external distractions...resulting in uncoordinated, unfocused, non-musical playing.
>
> – *Twenty-year old student*

> Why is the piano so hard for me? A ghost whispers, "You can't do it." Rationally, I know I can. Emotionally, often I'm not sure. Then my attitude blocks the music, and it blocks the use of my arm. Fear is a very powerful force. As the music became harder, the fear shut down the music.
>
> – *A middle-aged teacher*

Both of these pianists were experiencing the consequences of faulty technical preparation. If a solid technical foundation of good mind-body coordination at the piano had been laid, the younger pianist would not have gotten to that point of mal-coordination and mental distractedness. The older teacher's fear was also largely the result of a faulty technical foundation, the unconscious realization that she was not really sure of herself at the piano.

World-champion athlete and coach, Dan Millman, states it well:

> If you lack a solid foundation, you compromise the entire structure. A strong foundation is based upon complete preparation of body, mind and emotions...In fact, nearly every difficulty you face in your chosen training can be traced to skipping steps in the past – to a weakness in your foundation.[9]

One of the most prevalent reasons that this fundamental stage is neglected is that there is rarely any evidence of discomfort or injury in the first several years of study. In fact, students often seem to progress rather well. But the problems begin to appear slowly and insidiously. Mal-coordination in a simple, slow melody or a simple movement is not so noticeable and will not lead to injury or dysfunction. However, with each new level of repertory, kinetic complexity, and speed – plus increased practice time – mal-coordination becomes potentially more harmful.

PERSONAL HISTORY

My own history, both as a pianist and tennis player, is a clear example of the previous statement and will serve to outline several training trajectories. I followed the same learning curve in both activities; the only difference was that I was largely self-taught as a tennis player. As a young pianist, I performed with

---

[9]Dan Millman, *Body Mind Mastery* (Novato, California: New World Library, 1999) 27.

great enthusiasm and few problems, playing with suppleness, velocity and ease. In early adolescence, competitions sapped some of the spontaneous joy out of playing. Predictably, as I advanced in repertory, developed self-consciousness as a teenager, and started making more technical and musical demands on myself, the weaknesses in my technical foundation began to influence my performances. I developed a debilitating case of tendinitis at age sixteen. The enjoyment of playing practically vanished; fear crept in slowly but surely and I had several emotionally traumatic memory slips on stage. I had outstanding, supportive teachers, but the learning curve had already begun its up and down flight. I came very close to quitting several times. The sadness of loss was matched only by my sense of helplessness.

My winning days in tennis tournaments were also over. My lack of a solid foundation in that activity led to increasing loss of physical control on the court as the stakes became higher. In the first semester of college, both my tennis and piano coaches, if you will, required that I go back to the very beginning and retrain my fundamental technique. The principle was good, but in both activities the retraining failed because of the lack of a clear definition of both the fundamentals and an effective method of training them.

Trips to the college infirmary were frequent; I was given enough cortisone to alter a cat's brain! Both the physical and the emotional problems associated with playing forced me to cancel a student concerto performance with a major orchestra. I knew I had no real control over my body or mind on stage, in spite of my level of talent, repertory, and performance experience.

I was one of the fortunate ones. In my early twenties I began studying with a teacher who not only understood the fundamentals of technique – including the mind-body-emotions connection – but who could train me in them, from the ground up. It took almost six months. During that time I was transformed from a perpetually injured, technically insecure pianist into a solid technician with a fundamental knowledge of well-coordinated, free, 'effortless' playing.

Millman refers to this trajectory as the "second wind"[10] we may get, if we are fortunate enough to meet the right teacher:

> If your preparation has been insufficient and you have been stuck on a plateau, you can duplicate the path of the natural athlete [pianist] by first going back for a time -- perhaps a few months – to do intense work on the 'talent foundation'.[11]

But the foundational stage of the journey was not easy, emotionally or psychologically. It took much longer to change the old habits than I had envisioned. I felt many emotions – failure, frustration, resentment, hopelessness, and mainly sadness at the temporary loss of the joy of making real music. Why me? Other pianists had not suffered the same fate of pain, injury, and cessation of playing. Of course, as my awareness of the piano world increased, I realized I was not alone. There were countless others.

But the journey was more than worth the temporary price. Initially, it required intense mental discipline as I replaced one set of habits with another. It also took almost a full year of concentrated work to return to my original level of

---

[10]Ibid., 29

[11]Ibid.

repertory. But the retraining and its result had a profound influence on my life, far beyond the concert stage.

MIND/BODY CONNECTION

Then, as fate would have it, one final injury occurred several years later; one that led me to the unequivocal realization that playing the piano was an activity of the whole body with the mind and emotions. It changed my destiny as a teacher, and my entire view of life. I experienced weakness in my right arm and was told by several doctors that I had, among other things, tendinitis, nerve damage, or carnal tunnel syndrome. The solutions suggested were more cortisone or an operation to reposition a nerve. Demoralized and distraught, I returned to my teacher.

She sent me to a physical therapist who had successfully treated numerous musicians, great and small, in Europe. My meeting with her was my first and most profound experience with a holistic therapist, one who wholeheartedly believed in the interconnectedness of the *whole* body with the mind and emotions in playing.

The therapist watched me play the piano in her studio and asked me several questions about my history and emotional state. To my amazement, she reassured me that there was nothing pathologically wrong with my tendons, nerves, or muscles. She then told me my spine was over-arched in the lower back and that my arms were too relaxed and unsupported by my torso. This unsupported looseness was placing undue stress on the elbow, wrist, and finger joints.

She also pointed out that I was housing my recent emotional stress in my right arm in the form of chronic muscle tension. As a result of this accumulated tension, I had cut the arm off, both metaphorically and literally, from the rest of my body. The coldness and weakness were a direct result of impaired circulation. The lymphatic system was also blocked, resulting in swelling.

I was a mess, but an understandable, redeemable one! Cortisone, painkillers, surgery, splints? Not in this case. Instead, I experienced the power of an insightful mind, healing hands, and a holistic view of playing the piano. The therapist gave me a lesson in dynamically balanced, optimal spinal alignment, treated me with lymphatic massage of the arm and with acupuncture to release muscle tension and restore flow and balance throughout the body. Perhaps as importantly, she listened sympathetically to my tales of woe, relieving me of much of the stress of stored-up negative emotions. My immune system received a much-needed boost.

After two magical, informational, and transformational hours with her, I flew home on my bicycle as if on wings. Over the next week, step-by-mindful-step, I applied her body-mind wisdom to my life and playing. I resumed a productive course of practicing and performing within a week.

Both of these experiences had a profound impact on my life. I realized that a disciplined, holistic approach – one that trains an alert mind, healthful emotions and the whole body – was the only way to insure a solid foundation and a joyous, injury-free journey.

HEALTHFUL TECHNIQUE: ONE PARTICULAR PATH

> The process by which a musician achieves a musical goal during performance requires the "painstaking composition of a neurophysiologic score to guide the physical movements on which

[12]Wilson, *Tone Deaf & All Thumbs?*, 33.

> the performance is built"[12]...It means that movement takes place because of muscular contraction, that muscular contraction is regulated by the nervous system, and that skilled movement is a process that requires advanced planning for optimal results.[13]
>
> – *Frank Wilson*

ONE SOUND

My particular method of building a healthful piano technique is admittedly radical, not only in comparison to past ways of teaching, but even to current, more inclusive and scientifically enlighten ones. I take the pianist back to the very beginning of the production of one sound, in all its beautifully coordinated, resonant splendor. Once the mind and body understand and master that seemingly simple but highly complex ability, we proceed to more and more sounds, and eventually back to music making.

Such a foundational approach is not for everyone. It requires tremendous attentiveness, mental stamina, and creativity from the teacher, as well as enthusiastic dedication from the pianist. But if the path is followed with integrity and joy, the rewards are abundant, technically and musically. (It is important to note that this particular step-by-step method, developed over many years of teaching, is only one of many possible paths to healthful piano technique.)

A PEDAGOGICAL AWAKENING: ONE CASE STUDY

I had always attempted to insure suppleness, muscle control, and good alignment, both of the whole body as well as the arms and hands. However, my teaching took a more revolutionary, radical turn in the early 1990s when I was retraining a very talented but technically hampered young man.

Initially, we did not return to the very beginning. I gave him the necessary technical information on an analytical, cognitive level and, to some extent, on the kinesthetic level, but we continued to work on advanced repertory, albeit in a more detailed manner.

I did not require complete mastery of each step of coordination along the way, as it would have been impossible because he had not even truly mastered the coordinations on the most fundamental level of sound production. In other words, we traveled an inconsistent, compromised technical path. The results were little real improvement on his part and much frustration on mine.

Then one day he came to me and declared that he was willing to do whatever it took to really get 'it' – the physical freedom and the healthy sound of well-coordinated technique. Prior to that moment of pedagogical soul-searching, he had been taking one lesson a week. We changed to a short lesson everyday for several weeks so that I could monitor his progress continually and not allow any side or backtracking.

1. The Basic Stroke – Sensations and Movement

As an experiment, we addressed the challenge of producing one sound freely. We broke the fundamental sensations and gesture of sound production down into four rather primitive components, similar to the components of a fundamental gesture in other activities, such as golf and tennis. I eventually called this the *basic*

[13] Ibid., 37.

stroke, not to contribute yet another confusing bit of jargon to the field, but for purpose of identification in plain English.

The basic stroke has four components:

1. Easy efficient lift of the forearm
2. Free fall onto the key (which will be modified to more refined forms of lowering later)
3. Optimal alignment of the arm and hand bones on landings
4. Instantaneous release of arm and hand muscle tension upon landing

In the initial stages, training the stroke involved movement primarily of the forearm as the primary lever. I had found that allowing the upper arm to be more passive led to greater freedom throughout all the joints of the arm.

2. The Role of the Whole Body

We stayed on each component and then combined them until the whole gesture seemed smoothly coordinated. Soon, however, he reported that he was having trouble fully releasing certain muscles of the upper and lower arm. We both realized his spinal alignment was partly to blame, so he immediately began to take private Alexander Technique lessons. These lessons resulted in a breakthrough in enhanced kinesthetic awareness and torso support of the arms. Nevertheless, the process required mentally intense, highly concentrated practice. I would often walk by the practice room, only to hear one note every thirty seconds or so. Such was his mental discipline and sense of direction.

After some time had passed he came into my studio and asked to play a very slow Chopin melody for me. I recognized instantly that our uncompromising diligence and patience had paid off in an extraordinary way. The sound was beautiful – healthful, warm and free. And, as pianists often describe it, the movements felt 'effortless'.

Once this solid foundation was laid, his progress was smooth and rapid. He applied this basic coordination to repertory, learning a piece in well-coordinated fragments – *up to tempo* – before linking them, step-by-step. Such a manner of study could be likened to making a crazy quilt. Piece by piece, the fabric is cut out, the design is embroidered onto each piece, and finally the pieces are carefully stitched together. After such disciplined, patient work on the foundation, the student reaped the results of a healthful, well-coordinated technique. He learned that it:

- Prevents discomfort, fatigue, strain and injury
- Promotes a sense of physical well-being while playing
- Enhances suppleness, speed and facility
- Increases tonal power
- Broadens dynamic range and tonal palette
- Promotes greater concentration
- Reduces performance anxiety

THE TEACHER'S CHALLENGES

The principles of good coordination on which this program is based – efficient muscle use and optimal skeletal alignment – are not in themselves difficult to understand. The challenges, however, lie in the nature of physical/kinesthetic learning and the means of conveying them to a wide variety of pianists.

1. A teacher must either already possess a free, well-coordinated technique, or he or she must go through a retraining period. Then and only then will the teacher have the qualifications to pass her knowledge on to another pianist.

2. Finding creative and appropriate ways to convey this knowledge to the various ages and levels of students also poses quite a challenge. Beginners, be they young children, adolescents, or adults, along with intermediate and advanced students of all ages, including seasoned performers, may all be in need of training. And while all must learn the same principles of healthful coordination, each pianist has a unique brain, body, psychological profile, history at the piano, age, and learning style, all of which must be taken into account when conveying the knowledge. Creativity and sensitivity become of paramount importance in recognizing the old patterns of faulty coordinations, ridding the pianist of them, and then programming into the brain and body another set of coordinations.

3. The third challenge is to understand and appreciate the necessary time and means required for training, or retraining, the new coordinations and body use patterns, the neurophysiologic score if you will. And because each pianist has a different brain, body, and current neuromuscular program, the time it takes to train or retrain well-coordinated, healthful technique varies from person to person, depending on many factors. These include technical history, receptivity to learning, and level of kinesthetic awareness.

   The process should never be pushed, but rather allowed to follow its natural course of organic development. The teacher must find the right balance between over and under challenging, always attentive to the student's real progress. The student needs to be engaged, encouraged, and affirmed, especially in learning mental discipline. Discouragement will occasionally surface, but it should never be allowed to last.

FUNDAMENTALS OF PEDAGOGY

Composing this neurophysiologic score can be accomplished in any number of ways, but all must take into account the basic principles of pedagogy:

---

[14]Jack Nicklaus, *The Best Way to Better Golf* (Greenwich: CT Fawcett Publications, 1967) 9.

1. Begin at the very beginning

As the great Jack Nicklaus stated in *The Best Way to Better Golf*, "No matter what you may accomplish in golf, regardless of how sophisticated your game may become, it will always rise and fall on your ability to master the fundamentals."[14] Musical training is no different, and while it might strike some as preposterous, going back to the rock-bottom basics is necessary, even for concert pianists.

The challenge of learning all of the other aspects of music making – theory, notation, interpretation – often prevents beginners from learning the healthful coordination needed to produce one sound. Each of these components requires different types of neurological activity – analytical, spatial, linguistic, emotional and kinesthetic. To attempt to train all or even several of these activities at once places impossible demands on the brain and body. It frequently leads to overload and even reversal of learning.

Dr. Suzuki was one of the few internationally known teachers of the twentieth century to actually recognize this tendency to overload the brain and get the musical cart before the technical horse, so to speak. The Suzuki method, when properly taught, is a proven and consistently successful means of attaining a healthy sound, natural coordination, and mastery of each step.

Returning to the basics must always remain engaging and stimulating. This occurs only if the student is fully informed, trusts the eventual outcome, and is able to focus on the sensations of each moment. Musical goals will be attained, usually far beyond what the pianist thought possible. However, those goals must be temporarily suspended as the pianist focuses exclusively on the building blocks of pure sound production – kinesthetic awareness, physical coordination, muscle control, overall skeletal alignment, and balance.

Going back to the beginning does not lead to frustration if it is done in a spirit of rediscovering our innate, natural, physical suppleness and freedom. Once the student has begun to 'free up' the body, he or she will often ask to remain on each step until the liberating sensation of beautiful coordination and true mastery has been acquired.

2. Proceed in a step-by-step manner

Again, I draw on the wisdom of a world-class gymnastics coach. In Dan Millman's *Body Mind Mastery* he asserts:

> Whether you are concerned with physical, mental, or emotional preparation, a step-by-step approach to the task at hand can assure success...
>
> ...Anything and everything in life can be broken down into its component parts. The more adept you become at the preliminary steps of preparation, the more you'll amaze yourself by what you can accomplish.[15]

This applies to developing healthful piano technique, either in the fundamentals or in advanced repertory. We continually over-challenge the body and train with inappropriate levels of literature. In our enthusiasm to advance, we move too

[15]Millman, *Body Mind Mastery*, 30-31.

quickly and compromise more and more the integrity of our technique and music making. Unfortunately, this has become an almost worldwide phenomenon that has cast a less exciting light on slower, but more effective learning. The only solution I have ever found is that the pianist must be disciplined and engaged enough to focus on the process of learning, rather than the goal, in order to achieve the sense of absolute joy and effortlessness that comes when the coordination has been truly mastered. Herein lies the creative challenge for the teacher!

3. Master one step before going to the next

Because technique is such a physical activity, the focus must be placed on only physical sensations and movements, at least until those new sensations and movements are mastered and become automatic. I might add that both Suzuki instructors and teachers in the traditional Russian system of teaching have also always emphasized mastery of each stage of technical, and musical, training before proceeding to the next. They have also been very clear in their definition of mastery.

Making music is not an inherently difficult thing to do, given the brain's remarkable ability to fine-tune motor skills, and the potential of the neuromuscular system. However, *how* we use that system is critical. If we misuse it, repeatedly programming in faulty coordinations and contradictory patterns, we will only confuse the body and brain. Consistent patterning is crucial to the learning process, whether in training technique or behavior. If children are given inconsistent messages, even ones as simple as "Yes, you can get ice cream after school" "No, you cannot get ice cream after school" without knowing why the message is changing, they will not know which path to choose after school.

Likewise, if we plow through notes on the piano inattentively, allowing our body to respond in varying degrees of coordination, our neuromuscular program will be confused and compromised from the start. All of our time and effort will show relatively poor and inconsistent results. Instead, we need to program consistently free coordinations with constant mindfulness each step of the way, until we sense that the movements are automatic.

Step-by-step mastery must also follow the law of organic growth. Living things require certain periods of time for gestation, growth, flowering, and rest. Allowing students ample time to experience these milestones is ultimately the quickest, easiest way of achieving the greater goal. If we do not provide this time, pollution of the coordination of the simplest gesture will eventually occur and lead to an undermining of general coordination. Proceeding to higher levels of repertory before mastering the coordination of the present level will increasingly diminish each new stage of technical development and possibly lead to dysfunction over time. In my experience, however, pianists will gladly discipline themselves in this way of training once they have experienced the phenomenal sensation of physical effortlessness. The challenge for the teacher is to maintain an enthusiastic, supportive and creative attitude along the whole path of learning.

CHOOSING A PIANO TEACHER

A fine teacher is one who not only has the knowledge of healthful, injury-preventive technique, but one who has the proven ability to communicate that knowledge effectively. With rare exception, pianists simply cannot learn well-coordinated, injury-preventive piano technique without the hands-on instruction and constant monitoring of a highly qualified teacher. Nor can we learn technique by reading about it, listening to a lecture, or even by watching a video. Although all three might enhance the kinesthetic learning process and satisfy our desire for a rational, scientific back-up system, none can convey the *sensations* of good coordination. Without hands-on physical and kinesthetic instruction, the pianist will be prey to misinterpretation, confusion, distortion of information, and even injury. This is, to say the least, an essential prerequisite to the learning process.

The teacher should be able both to demonstrate and effectively communicate the principles of good coordination, at least in the 'playing apparatus' – shoulders, arms, hands, fingers – if not throughout the whole body. I personally require all of my students to be trained concurrently by a qualified instructor in the Alexander Technique. Effective somatic, whole-body training of any kind can make the difference between a compromised and a superb technique.

A STEP-BY-STEP TRAINING PROGRAM

The following is a step-by-step outline of the method of training I use. Each of the steps in my particular program can take from one moment of insight to several months of awareness building and self-discovery to master. However, as the teacher, it is my responsibility to insure purity and mastery on each level of training. Otherwise, the training will not really 'take', and advanced levels of training will be sabotaged by a weak foundation. The goal is not only to develop a free, pure coordination on all levels, from simplest to most complex, but also to eliminate the traditional hit-and-miss approach to learning.

A fine teacher is one who not only has the knowledge of healthful, injury-preventive technique, but one who has the proven ability to communicate that knowledge effectively.

1. CULTIVATING KINESTHETIC AWARENESS: THE ESSENTIAL KEY TO HEALTHFUL TECHNIQUE

Healthful piano technique must be taught primarily through the senses, especially the kinesthetic sense, which monitors the state of our muscles and movements. It is the mind's most valuable tool in gaining control of the body. It is the mental bugle that awakens the unconscious body.

Kinesthetic awareness is the way the mind instructs the body in the easiest, most natural way to perform any activity. It performs two important functions for the pianist. First, it helps us unlearn and reverse old, faulty habits and inefficient body use patterns. Then it helps us awaken and rediscover the body-use habits of a happy, healthfully functioning body – the state of freedom of movement and suppleness of muscles that very young children enjoy.

Much is said of the important role of movement in piano technique, but it is the *state* of the muscles producing the movements that is even more important. Muscle state – relative contraction and relaxation – creates movement. Our kinesthetic awareness allows us to monitor the true quality of the movement. The eye alone cannot do this. For example, trace a beautiful S-curve with the arm in a graceful, well-coordinated gesture, allowing the muscles to be as released as possible. Then retrace the curve with the same apparent grace of movement but with tightened muscles. Both gestures would appear well coordinated and fluid; however, muscle contraction would vary widely. And even a trained eye would not be able to tell the difference. That is the role of the kinesthetic sense.

Training the kinesthetic sense, developing an awareness of ourselves in the world around us and inside our bodies, is the essential first step in training or retraining. I tell my students that the *world* is now their practice room!

2. UNDERSTANDING AND EXPERIENCING HOW YOUR BODY IS DESIGNED TO FUNCTION BEST THROUGH SOMATIC TRAINING

I cannot stress enough the importance of whole-body education to the success of the learning process. Even small children have often acquired poor postural habits and chronic muscle tension, not to mention inefficient coordinations in the arms and hands. Fortunately, young children may need only subtle physical cues from the teacher to correct these physical problems, as they are usually able to remember and retrieve their natural muscular freedom and suppleness in basic sound production.

Unfortunately, most adolescents and adults have often developed serious chronic muscle tension and entrenched skeletal misalignment. Most piano teachers, even those who have had considerable somatic training, are not adequately qualified to identify and rid the body of unnecessary, chronic muscle tension or structural imbalances. Freeing the body and mind of these habits and acquiring new ones require the expertise of a skilled, certified Alexander Technique, Feldenkrais, or other body-use education instructor.

I realize that finding a somatics instructor can be daunting. However, the Internet provides a wealth of information on the location of certified trainers. Even one lesson or a workshop is preferable to none. I personally do not work without this expertise and have found it to be essential and invaluable to successful technical training. In the absence of a trained somatics instructor, I would suggest several books. As I said, kinesthetic awareness, skeletal alignment, and muscle control can rarely be learned from a book. However, the following books are two of the most informative, accessible, understandable, and effective illustrated guides that I have found on the current market.

For a complete, easily understandable explanation of the dangers of chronic muscle tension, see *Somatics - Reawakening the Mind's Control of Movement, Flexibility, and Health* by the late Feldenkrais master instructor and pioneer in body re-education, Thomas Hanna. This is one of the most effective self-help books available for understanding the body and mind connection and for reawakening body awareness and regaining muscle control. Audiotapes of the valuable exercises are also available from Perseus Books, Cambridge, Massachusetts.

An informative, witty, and delightfully illustrated self-help guide to the skeletal system and how to maximize its use is, *What Every Musician Needs to Know About the Body,* by noted Alexander Technique instructor Barbara Conable. The book addresses the fundamentals of musculoskeletal design and optimal use for all musicians.

Body Mind Mastery, by world-class gymnastics coach Dan Millman, addresses any and all activities as a synthesis of mind, body, emotions, and spirit. In its succinctness and clarity the book goes right to the heart of the challenges, as well as the extraordinary achievement, of being a musician.

In addition, *The Musician's Survival Manual: A Guide to Preventing and Treating Injuries in Instrumentalists,* by Richard Norris, M.D., is invaluable for solid medical information in succinct, understandable form. It contains lists of performing-arts-medicine clinics and organizations, as well as a comprehensive bibliography.

For a look into the vast neurological complexities of playing the piano, I have found the book *Tone Deaf & All Thumbs?,* by noted neurologist and amateur pianist Dr. Frank Wilson, to be captivating and revelatory.

Happily, there has been a proliferation of helpful books, as well as video and audiotapes, on wellness and the promotion of good, overall health. Choosing among them all is the main challenge.

3. GETTING ACQUAINTED WITH THE PIANO

Learning to trust and feel comfortable with the instrument, from both scientific and psychological perspectives, is critical to developing a healthful, free technique. From the psychological standpoint, it is important that a pianist feel comfortable and at ease with the instrument. It should be a friend, not an adversary. This is not easy for many of us for a number of reasons.

Our built-in fear of wrong notes has led some of us to a state of psychological intimidation and its physical counterpart, unnecessary physical tension. Also, some of us simply do not trust that the piano can support us or be a safe landing field when we contact the key. We tighten muscles excessively before, during, and after sound production, losing our timing and efficiency of movement. Gaining an understanding of the piano mechanism might help us avoid that unnecessary, counterproductive response and will also make our indispensable colleague, the piano technician, very happy.

Our built-in fear of wrong notes has led some of us to a state of psychological intimidation and its physical counterpart, unnecessary physical tension.

Many pianists treat their instrument like the family car. Central to our lives and used frequently, we do have it tuned occasionally but we have little understanding about its construction or how it works. And like the car, when we explore the workings of the piano and increase our knowledge of its primary characteristics, we will find immediate insight into the best physical way to approach.

One of the piano's most important characteristics is also one of the most lamentable to many pianists – *the piano is a percussion instrument.* Sound is produced when felt-covered wooden hammers strike metal strings, an act accomplished by a complex mechanism called the *action*, which is constructed for maximum efficiency according to the laws of physics. And although we are not directly in contact with the string, we can be precisely connected with the movement of the hammer. The duration of sound production is so brief that the eye cannot even detect the moment of contact.

Embracing the instantaneous nature of sound production would save pianists a lot of unnecessary muscle use. Our muscles are required to stabilize the joints only at the moment of sound production. And even if we keep the key depressed or pivot from it, we need only a negligible amount of muscle contraction, about two or three ounces of pressure. Continuous over-pressing serves no real purpose and fatigues the muscles.

Moving side-to-side or up and down on the keyboard also takes relatively little muscle activity, and then only from the upper arms. The forearms need virtually no contraction during these non-sound-producing moments. Understanding this physiological fact alone would eliminate an enormous amount of excessive and accumulated muscle tension.

Another critical and this time helpful design characteristic is that the piano has a keyboard of levers on a *horizontal* plane. This is a marvelous advantage for the pianist because it allows us to take full advantage of gravity to produce sound. The structural design of the human body includes a set of levers and falling weights that enable us to easily activate the piano levers. In that regard, the keyboard design is intrinsically compatible with the body design. In a Darwinian sense, it would not have remained so popular for so long if it were not. This design takes advantage of gravity and requires a minimum amount of muscular exertion to play.

Ironically, there is a potentially troublesome contradiction lurking in all of this. We have noted that the piano is a percussive instrument, that its design takes full mechanical advantage of the human body, and that it is possible to play it with little muscular exertion. All of this should make the pianist happier, right?

Wrong. The dilemma comes when we must create musical, linear tension with a percussive instrument whose sound we cannot control from start to finish. Most piano music is both melodic and harmonic in nature and, as such, usually requires projecting great linear, harmonic, and musical tension. How can we project melodic linear tension or intensity when we have no control over the sound after its initiation? Every musician needs to feel somehow the ebb and flow of musical tension, the continuity of sound and line. The violinist can feel it in his or her bow arm, the flutist or singer in the breath. Where do we feel it?

This question is truly a paradox for the pianist and one that may be at the heart of accumulated muscle tension and injury. The answer is multidimensional and complex. To discover it we must first learn to play with some feeling of muscular continuity in the arms and throughout the body. Secondly, we must develop our aural feedback system – our ears – to monitor musical intensity.

Even before fully exploring this solution one thing must be certain – w*e do not need excessive, accumulated muscle tension to project or even feel musical intensity.* Meeting the challenge of this paradox is a fundamental component of training that follows the pianist's responsibility to celebrate and take full advantage of the design and nature of the piano.

4. DEVELOPING MUSCLE CONTROL AND JOINT FREEDOM, AWAY FROM THE PIANO

The phenomenal physical skill demonstrated in well-coordinated playing requires extraordinary control of small muscles, and the ability to contract and relax them in the subtlest gradations, at lightening speed. Dr. Frank Wilson notes that "there is almost an inverse relationship between the size of the muscles and the amount of brain set aside to regulate their actions."[16]

Various exercises involving stretching, selective relaxing and contracting, and the like can be used to develop this control. The ones listed below must always be done gently and with cautious attention to the sensations in the body. (As with most of these exercises, a written description is nearly useless, and may even be counter-productive without hands-on coaching. The purpose in listing these is more to inform than to instruct.)

Breathing and Progressive Relaxation

This requires about fifteen minutes and is done with eyes closed lying comfortably on a mat; face up, with appropriate head and neck support. First, the pianist simply observes his or her breathing pattern. Gradually, the breathing slows down as muscles relax and calm prevails. While lying quietly, the pianist then focuses on sounds, smells, and the surrounding tactile sensations. Finally, the kinesthetic awareness is used to discover and release unnecessary muscle tension, beginning at the toes and ending at the top of the head. The pianist is encouraged

[16]Frank R. Wilson, "The Full Development of the Individual Through Music," *Update* 5. This article is adapted from an address presented by Dr. Wilson in the Ergonomic Council of the Music Industry VI in Washington D.C., November 12, 1982.

by quiet guidance to envision an underground river system in the body, freely flowing, with no blockages or obstructions.

Lengthening

This is done on the floor, after the progressive breathing and relaxation exercise, to get the body moving again before standing. The pianist is asked to lengthen slowly, like a cat would, in whatever way feels most needed and comfortable.

Suppleness and Joint Mobility Exercises

These are done in a standing position. The pianist begins with gentle shoulder rolls, neck rotations, and overhead, alternating arm stretches. Exploring the mobility of the joints of the shoulders, elbows, wrists, and fingers is also important. Finally, the pianist softens the knees and allows the weight of the head to pull the body over gently, rag-doll fashion, as the arms hang. This gives the spine a good stretch. It also demonstrates the extraordinary mobility and pendulous quality of the arms in the shoulder sockets.

Arm Muscle Control Exercises

Learning to control the arm muscles begins by developing the ability to selectively and subtly contract and release muscles on command, at various speeds. These subtle sensations of contraction and relaxation must be taught through the kinesthetic sense. First, the pianist identifies the various muscles of the arm and shoulder area, including the deltoids, triceps, biceps, extensors, and flexors, by alternately contracting and releasing the various muscles. Then he or she explores the muscle pairs – agonist and antagonist – flexing and extending various units of the arms. This is done in graduated stages of muscle contraction, from extremely inefficient to the most efficient use of the muscles. Learning to have power over the muscles and to consciously direct them in activities is the end result.

Torso Support of the Arms

This is perhaps the most important of all the preliminary exercises in muscle control and efficiency. From it, the pianist learns the easiest, most efficient way to control dynamics. Many pianists support the arms with unnecessary contraction of the shoulder muscles (deltoids), fixing the upper arms outward, like flying buttresses. This form of support fatigues the upper arm muscles and disallows full mobility in the ball-and-socket joint of the shoulder. It also creates a blockage of energy flow from the torso out through the arms. Also, pianists may not realize that the arm structure not only includes the hand, wrist, and lower and upper arms, but the collarbone and shoulder blade as well. The arm muscles themselves do not actually end at the top of the arm, but wrap around the shoulder and extend to the sternum and shoulder blades. The sternoclavicular joint, not the shoulder joint, is the first joint of the arm.

This exercise is performed with a partner in two stages. First, with the upper arm simply hanging down and with the forearm parallel to the floor, the pianist learns to release the unsupported or 'sleeping' weight of the forearm into the hand of the partner. The wrist joint is fully released and the hand is hanging. This stage often requires quite a bit of coaching and gentle, kinesthetic work from the partner to get the pianist to release the arm muscles fully, which is a counter-intuitive state (unless one is sleeping!).

In the second stage, the pianist learns to take full advantage of the torso support of the arms. With the help of the partner, the pianist develops the ability to regulate, slowly and then more quickly, the weight of the arm, from the heavy weight of a stone to the lightness of a feather. Eventually, this will translate into the body's phenomenal ability to transmit weight into the key by transferring support of the arm from the torso to the keyboard and back in a split-second. It is a miraculous skill for which the body was perfectly designed. This exercise demonstrates the design of the torso and the shoulder girdle to support the arms leaving them free to move easily from the shoulder sockets. Once these exercises in arm muscle control are mastered, the pianist regains the natural, pendulous quality and power of the arms, and can prevent the build-up of potentially injurious tension.

Identifying the Arm and Hand Arches

This is a simple exercise performed in front of a mirror. The pianist stands, facing a mirror, with his or her arms hanging naturally by his or her sides. The teacher draws the pianist's attention to the natural, graceful structural curve of the arm and hand. Not only is this a form artists have loved for centuries, it is also the most advantageous structure for supporting the weight of the arm as it is transmitted into the keyboard.

5. PREPARING TO PLAY: ADJUSTING THE HEIGHT AND PROXIMITY OF THE BENCH

During this stage of training, we examine the appropriate bench height and proximity to the keyboard, both of which are determined by each pianist's individual height and the length of torso and upper and lower arms. In the case of tall pianists, the length of leg can also affect the spatial relationship. (An Alexander Technique instructor, or similar postural alignment instructor, is invaluable in this stage.)

The goal is to find a comfortable placement of the body on the bench that allows for the follow:

- Balance of the torso over the 'sitting bones'
- Ease of movement of the torso and arms
- Freedom of the head and neck
- A fully lengthened, flexible spine
- Pendulous upper arms, torso-supported, for maximum freedom in the shoulder and elbow joints and unhindered flow of weight through the arms and hands into the key
- Creation of the arch-span bridge of the forearm with the top of the forearm parallel with the ground and the underside arches visible. The apex of the greater forearm arch will be seen under the wrist and the apex of the hand arch under the knuckle bridge. (On landing, the top of the forearm will be level from the elbow to the knuckles and parallel to the floor.)

All of the above must be determined and demonstrated in a hands-on manner. Otherwise, the very kinesthetic sensations of balance and freedom necessary to determine optimal support and ease while sitting at the piano are missing. Also, misinterpretations of the information can lead to the opposite outcome – potentially harmful body use.

To prepare or center the body and mind for playing, my students place the following checklist or kinesthetic cue sheet on the piano rack before practicing:

- Balance torso on sitting bones
- Allow spine to lengthen
- Release shoulders
- Let arms hang like a pendulum, torso-supported, from shoulder sockets
- Release the neck
- Balance head lightly on the spine like a helium balloon
- Maintain kinesthetic awareness
- Breathe!

6. MASTERING THE BASIC STROKE: THE FUNDAMENTAL GESTURE AND SENSATION OF SOUND PRODUCTION

The basic stroke is the fundamental gesture that identifies a complex physical activity, whether it is hitting a golf or tennis ball, kicking a soccer ball or football, or depressing the piano key. In sports, this gesture is called a stroke or a swing, and it is the first thing well-trained athletes master. Conversely, if we as pianists cannot coordinate the simplest movement effectively, how can we expect to coordinate movements of increasing complexity? It is this realization that led me to insist on mastering the coordination of producing one sound first before adding more.

The basic stroke, when performed well, looks natural and free. In fact, one hardly notices it because the pianist is following natural laws of smooth coordination. However, learning it is challenging, especially if the pianist has produced sound in another, less efficient way. It is easiest to break the stroke down into four components and master them one at a time.

1. Easy, Efficient Lift of the Forearm

In the initial stages, one should isolate the forearm and allow the upper arm just to hang, like a pendulum, as the forearm is lifted straight up to playing height. The hand is also left hanging. (The hand should not feel heavy if the torso muscles properly support the arm.) The lift is the essential component. By building this lift into our coordination, the extensor muscles on the top of the forearm are continually refreshed and the wrist joint is freed. The lift eventually becomes more subtle until the release is almost invisible at times; but the mechanism for continuous release of the arm muscles is built in. The upper arm is, of course, eventually incorporated in playing, but in the fundamental stages of training the forearm is the primary lever. Also, the ability to maintain the pendulum-like motion of the upper arm is critical to joint mobility and free flow of weight and power through the arms.

2. Free-fall

Playing the piano does not always allow a simple free-fall of the forearm. But for purposes of learning to use the minimum of muscular effort, it is essential in the beginning stages of training for the pianist to be able just to let the forearms relax fully and fall onto the keyboard.

At first, the free-fall is not as easy to accomplish as it sounds, as it is counter-intuitive to fall. We are afraid of hurting ourselves, of a painful landing, or of missing notes. To being, try placing a folded towel on the keyboard to engender the confidence that the pianist can just let go and feel the gentle pull of gravity. This fall teaches the pianist the easiest way both to lower the arm and to depress the key. It requires that the neurological signal to the biceps be turned off. The resulting blackout allows the arm to fall, without effort, onto the keyboard. Eventually, more refined forms of lowering the arm are learned, the equivalent of placing a neurological 'dimmer switch' on the biceps. But beginning more simply with free-fall insures the development of full release and control of the arm muscles.

It is important to add that, while the pianist first focuses separately on the sensations of both lifting and falling, the two movements rather quickly become one smooth gesture.

3. Landing on Keys With Optimally Aligned Arm-Hand Bones, and Appropriate Muscle Contractions

The moment of landing is nearly simultaneous with the moment of sound production. It is crucial that the arm and hand be in the best alignment for supporting weight flowing through the arm and the hand. Fortunately, the best alignment for supporting weight is built into our system. The hand arch, together with the arch of the forearm (formed when the top of the arm is level and parallel to the ground from the elbow to the knuckle bridge) forms a beautiful arch-span bridge. This shape, as ancient Romans discovered, is the perfect form for supporting weight. When the forearm and hand bones are in this neutral alignment, both parts of the muscle pairs (i.e. extensors and flexors) are used equally. Neither is overtaxed.

In training, I have the pianist practice identifying the arch shape of the hand and arm away from the piano first. Next, he or she forms them, *with minimum muscle effort*, on the keyboard.

4. Instantaneous Release of Muscle Contraction

The body has a remarkable shock-absorption or shock-transmittal system built into it. This system incorporates the body's ability to relax muscles instantaneously, thereby releasing the joints and allowing shock to be transmitted freely from the object of resistance through the limbs to the spine. If the muscles do not release instantly, much stress and strain is placed on the muscles, bones, and joints.

Surprisingly, this instantaneous release occurs in the arms and hands naturally, once the pianist has mastered the preliminary stages of the training program, because he or she has already achieved a high degree of muscle awareness and control. It becomes instinctive and natural to release the musculature and to prevent stress and strain on the body. The result of the entire stroke is a healthy, free, resonant sound. Also, dynamics and tempo shadings eventually become easy and natural, once the simple coordination of producing one sound is mastered and becomes automatic.

In the training program, after these four components are mastered and incorporated into one smooth movement, the pianist works mindfully on a simple five-note scale. It is essential that enough time be taken between notes to allow for full kinesthetic monitoring of the body's musculoskeletal state, mental correction, and preparation for the next sound. In its entirety, the internal monitoring process often requires approximately twenty to forty seconds between sounds.

Once the basic stroke is mastered – when it has become an automatic, reflexive response of our body to the note – it is easy to coordinate increasingly more complex kinetic patterns and to reintroduce an added neurological challenge: reading notation.

7. INTRODUCING MUSIC

In all earlier stages of training the pianist has not read or played printed music. The rigorous requirements of undoing one neuromuscular program and learning another are too great. Reading music, a function of linguistic intelligence, would only detract from the kinesthetic sensations, a function of the kinesthetic intelligence. However, once the basic stroke has been grooved in, if you will, the pianist can begin using both intelligences in reading extremely simple music.

I personally prefer something as basic as *Progressive Sight-Reading Exercises* by Hannah Smith. These are one-line pieces that begin from the most elementary music (all whole notes) to increasingly but extremely well-graduated levels. Béla Bartok's *Mikrokosmos, Book 1* is also a good starting point for the pianist who can handle a slightly greater challenge. Whatever the repertory, it is important that the pianist play at a tempo which allows full mastery of the coordination at all times; for when allowed to work at his or her own pace, the learning curve is as smooth as silk.

8. INTRODUCING MULTIPLE NOTES-PER-STROKE, WITHOUT AND WITH MUSIC

By this time, the pianist has learned the sensations of suppleness, muscular release, and skeletal balance. The basic stroke is becoming automatic. It is relatively easy now to add more and more notes in one arm stroke. It is essential, however, that the muscles and joints maintain the same suppleness and freedom that they enjoyed in playing one note per stroke.

To insure this is the case, the pianist must now develop ease of coordination on simple scale patterns of two notes per stroke, without music. Then the pianist should apply this coordination to several simple pieces of music. Then I assign short pieces that contain two, three, and four notes per stroke.

Once the pianist has discovered how easy it is to combine two notes in one stroke, adding more and more notes, up to eight or even twelve, in one arm stroke, is not difficult. As each of these stages is mastered, I assign several pieces to allow time to *fully master* the coordinations. These pieces are learned first in fragments small enough to insure smooth coordination, and then the fragments are linked into ever-larger units. The purpose of this approach is to insure smooth coordination at all times.

To prevent any unnecessary muscle tension, loss of joint mobility, or structural imbalance, the teacher must scrupulously monitor each stage of learning. After all, speed and power result from efficient muscle use and liberated joints.

9. LEARNING RAPID, PERPETUAL-MOTION PASSAGE WORK

The ability to play rapid, perpetual motion passages without accumulating muscle tension is the highest level of coordination and is a natural outcome of the fundamental training. It is an outstanding example of the brain and body's ability to execute "ballistic movements," which are the most highly skilled muscular coordinations. Dr. Frank Wilson gives a revealing clue for learning virtuoso passage to the pianist, writing:

> The unique characteristic of ballistic movements is that, before the movement actually begins, all of the control signals to all of the muscles involved have been worked out in advance, and are sent from the brain in a single package before the move actually begins. Since there is no chance to correct mistakes after the move has begun, everything has to be absolutely right from the very beginning.[17]

This statement suggests that we use our time wisely by working out the smoothest coordinations and signals from the very beginning in practicing, rather than allowing a more haphazard approach. Certainly, it will cause less neurological confusion!

This ballistic principle of neuromuscular coordination has led me to a method of learning technique in the *actual tempo* of the piece. It would be very difficult to practice other highly skilled, rapid movement patterns in dance, gymnastics, juggling, or skating in slow motion. In these disciplines, movements are broken down into the smallest component parts, mastered separately, and then combined into larger and larger units. Why shouldn't the pianist use this efficient, logical approach as well? In this manner, we are learning the piece at tempo or in 'real time', and programming the body-mind from the very beginning to do what it will have to do in performance. The challenge for the pianist, however, is not physical endurance; it is rigorous mental discipline and attentiveness. But if the foundation for physical freedom is well laid, the pianist will seek out the appropriate coordinations and sensations.

10. APPLYING THE BASIC STROKE TO THE REPERTOIRE

By this time, smooth coordination in simple sound production is automatic for the pianist, yet the return to real music can be intimidating as well as exhilarating. We wish to maintain the wonderful, newfound sensations of physical freedom and true command, but the act of creating emotions with sound may, at first, distract from smooth coordination. Indeed, we now must call on our artistic and creative intelligence. The teacher also plays an important role in this step, for if he or she selects pieces carefully, a return to repertoire need not interrupt the flow of learning.

I re-introduce music making and repertoire through shorter piece, exposing the pianist to a limited number of kinetic and technical challenges while giving him or her emotional and musical gratification. We discuss very carefully how to organize practicing and learning. The piece is then usually broken down into manageable fragments. Once each fragment is fine-tuned, both musically and technically, fragments are combined and increased in size incrementally. The

---

[17]Wilson, *Update*, 5.

physical result can be likened to swimming a lap with the Australian crawl, as opposed to swimming under water. The crawl allows periodic breathing; likewise, this manner of practice builds in continuous muscular 'breathing' or release throughout the piece. The golden rule is to maintain smooth coordination and physical freedom of movement at all times, regardless of the musical challenges.

REDISCOVERING SOUND

Building kinesthetic awareness and good physical coordination requires discipline, patience, dedication, and time. The greatest challenge the pianist faces in the beginning is learning how to focus on sensations and sound production. Yet concentrating on the simple act of producing one sound in the most well-coordinated way allows our brain and body time to develop the tool of technique, without the added challenges of reading, interpreting, and expressing music. It also allows us to reacquaint ourselves with the fundamental element that originally drew most of us to the piano, *its sound*. Whether our piano was a console, a concert grand, or our grandmother's old upright, the sound was magical. We heard that sound at one point; *really heard it*, not just imagined it.

Training, or retraining, our bodies and minds in well-coordinated technique awakens that essential sense of *listening* to sound again. True music making has to begin with listening. And the truest listening occurs when we get out of our own way, when we remove the obstacles of mal-coordination.

This can be an exciting journey for both student and teacher, an exhilarating experience at every stage. Of course, the most well-coordinated technique in the world will not produce music. It is a tool, a means to an end, but it is the only means we pianists have. Once we have developed the body's potential for free, effortless coordination, we will be truly available for joyous, unfettered music making.

Healthy Practicing

Gail Berenson

The manner in which students spend the time between lessons is crucial to their development as pianists. At its most efficient, this time can evolve into an important growth opportunity that enables students to develop their independence and problem-solving abilities. At its worst, it can result in the formation and reinforcement of bad habits and detrimental techniques. In order to avoid these pitfalls, it is important for teachers to provide direction and guidance to students, who do not innately know how to practice and often lack the knowledge and experience to establish appropriate practice habits.

HEALTHY ATTITUDE

From the beginning of formal instruction, practicing quickly becomes a sizable and significant component of students' musical life. So much so that the bulk of their time in front of the instrument is spent alone, practicing. Too often, though, this time is seen as tedious drudgery, which often becomes the underlying impetus for either continuing or choosing to discontinue study. As with many facets of piano playing, it is attitude and mindset that set the tone for this critical activity and it is the teachers' responsibility to instill appropriate attitudes towards practicing in their students.

An essential first step in this process is helping the students learn to concentrate and creatively focus on the problem at hand as opposed to moving their fingers with their minds lost elsewhere in thoughts. Encouraging students to view practice as a time to experiment and to discover solutions to problems is also important because it nurtures their creativity and results in students who are active participants in their own learning. Teaching students to carefully listen and react to what is taking place within their practice sessions is an important step on the path toward achieving attentive and productive practice.

PRACTICING ENVIRONMENT

There are several pragmatic issues that need to be considered when teaching effective practicing strategies, including the placement and maintenance of the piano, either of which can be a motivator or a deterrent to practicing. A piano technician should regularly check over the instrument to ensure that it is in good working condition, in tune, and well regulated.

Placing the piano in a cold, inhospitable basement or adjacent to a frequently watched television creates a practicing obstacle that, with appropriate forethought, can be avoided by placing the instrument in a quiet location with good lighting. When working with younger children, it is important to remember that many of these needs become the responsibility of the parents and should be discussed with them.

POSITIONING AT THE INSTRUMENT

Helping students find a comfortable, ergonomically efficient, and injury preventive position at the instrument is another important element in developing healthy practicing habits. There are several issues to consider when working with a given student:

BENCH HEIGHT

The height of the piano bench should enable a student to maintain a level or slightly elevated arm when placed on the keyboard. To remedy a bench that is too low, the most commonly encountered situation, place carpet squares (readily available from carpet stores) on top of the bench to help raise the student to the appropriate height. If the bench is too high, the only options are to find another bench or cut down the legs.

DISTANCE FROM KEYBOARD

Students often sit too close to the keyboard and too far back on the bench. To allow for ease of mobility, the student should sit on the front half of the bench, making sure that the upper arm can move comfortably in front of the body. This will become especially important as students advance to more difficult repertoire.

FOOT SUPPORT

For those young children whose feet cannot reach the floor, it is important to find a box or footstool on which they can comfortably rest their feet. This provides support critical in helping students establish an appropriate sense of balance and stability while playing the piano.

POSTURE

There are several components of posture that need to be addressed:

Back

Teachers should help their students find the most natural position for their back by having them move through their range of motion, starting with an extremely rounded back with shoulders forward to one that is highly arched with the shoulders pulled back. After moving through both extremes several times, ask them to select the neutral position that feels most natural.

Shoulders

When under stress, it is very common for students to hold the excess tension in their shoulders, causing them to rise. This is especially true when playing difficult passages. Helping students become more aware of the position of their shoulders is an important first step in teaching them to remain relaxed.

Feet

Proper placement of the feet helps the student feel grounded and centered. The right foot is placed slightly forward, in preparation for resting lightly on the right pedal, with the left foot slightly back, forming a stable base.

The importance of proper posture at all times cannot be overstated. And while many students may have a tendency to ignore it during practice, the teacher must remind them often that their practice posture should be identical to that expected in performance.

In most cases, a student's posture will directly affect his or her ability to achieve an efficient technique. Consequently, the teacher has an enormous responsibility to see that students are using their bodies effectively. To this end, it is often helpful to look beyond resources geared only toward piano playing to other movement techniques, including the Alexander Technique, Feldenkrais, or Pilates, which can offer teachers the advantage of knowing more precisely what to look for in assessing a student's posture.

PREPARATION FOR PRACTICE

In addition to being mentally prepared, it is also important to be at your physical best when beginning a practice session, not only because your physical state of being can affect the ability to concentrate and think clearly, but also because playing the piano places physical demands on the body. In addition to having a good overall level of fitness, there are two basic physical needs that must be fulfilled prior to practice – nourishment and rest.

Eating a nutritionally balanced meal and avoiding the quick energy boost that comes from sugar and caffeine will best prepare the body for the upcoming work. Although some students, particularly those who are older, can manage practicing late at night or on limited sleep, it promotes a lack of attention to posture and hand position and an inability to think clearly. It is one of the teacher's many responsibilities to work with their students to determine appropriate practice schedules based on these physical needs[1]

WARM-UP AND COOL-DOWN

As piano playing is a physically demanding activity, there are certain needs that parallel those of athletes, including warming up and cooling down. Runners know that if they begin running at maximum speed without doing something to warm up their muscles, they place themselves at risk of a serious injury. Depending on the demands of the repertoire and the unique physical makeup of the individual, pianists are just as vulnerable to injury if they are not physically ready to play. Although there are varying opinions about the length and type of warm up, most music teachers agree that it is a good idea.

Some musicians choose to use less-demanding sections of their repertoire, often played at a slower tempo, to serve as warm-up material. Others choose scales or technical exercises beginning at a slow tempo and gradually increasing speed. Any of these choices enable pianists to gradually increase the temperature and flexibility of their muscles. Warm-ups can also be accomplished through exercises

[1]More detailed fitness information can be found in "Benefits of Fitness," page 143.

done away from the instrument.

Musicians are less likely to complete a cool-down at the end of a practice session. Yet, a brief time spent stretching the muscles can serve as an excellent injury-preventative strategy. For musicians who are recovering from an injury, the cool-down becomes an even more crucial component in their practice routine, enabling an injured student to stretch out the muscles worked during the practice session.

Below is a list of warm-up and cool-down exercises distributed to patients at the Rehabilitation Institute of Chicago's Medical Program for Performing Artists. It was developed and written by occupational therapist, Carol Brooks, OTR, and pioneering music-medicine physician, Alice Brandfonbrener, MD.

Warm-Up Exercises
Rehabilitation Institute of Chicago
Medical Program for Performing Artists

Always be cautious when trying out any exercises and, if any discomfort is experienced, stop and consult your physician.

Warming up

- The optimum speed of chemical reaction and metabolism is 102 to 103 degrees Fahrenheit.
- Evidence suggests that speed, strength, and efficiency of contractions are enhanced by a rise in temperature of muscle toward that range.
- The only efficient way of raising muscle temperature is by work of the muscle itself.
- Ten to fifteen minutes of active exercise for all upper-extremity joints are recommended.

Warm-up exercises

Avoid jerking motions. Perform each exercise smoothly and with moderate speed.

1. Shoulder flexion. Raise both arms overhead then relax at sides. (twenty repetitions)
2. Shoulder abduction. With both arms at your sides, raise your arms outward and upward overhead. Then relax to your sides. (twenty repetitions)
3. Shoulder shrugs. (twenty repetitions)
4. Pinch shoulder blades together. (twenty repetitions)
5. Elbow flexion-extension. Bend and straighten elbows fully. (twenty repetitions)
6. Shoulder circles. With arms at sides, rotate shoulders in circles. (seven repetitions clockwise; seven repetitions counterclockwise)

7. With elbows flexed and hands extended forward, palms up/palms down. (twenty repetitions)
8. With elbows flexed and hands extended forward, wrists up/wrists down. (twenty repetitions)
9. Bend wrist to little finger side then thumb side. (ten repetitions)
10. Spread fingers apart/squeeze fingers together. (ten repetitions)
11. Keeping the hand straight, bend fingers at the middle joint. The fingers form a hook. (ten repetitions)

Cooling down

- After vigorous activity muscles may tend to cramp or experience fatigue/discomfort.
- Stretching muscles their entire length, holding, and then relaxing them helps to alleviate these conditions.
- Ten to fifteen minutes are recommended. Hold each repetition for a long five count.

Cool-down exercises

1. Raise arms overhead. (five repetitions)
2. Touch opposite shoulder and hold. (five repetitions each arm)
3. Bend neck to the right then to the left. Hold each for a count of five. (five repetitions)
4. Hands behind head, elbows out to the side, push back on flexed elbows. (five repetitions)
5. Clasp hands behind hips and roll shoulders outward. (five repetitions)
6. Make a fist and bend wrist downward. (five repetitions)
7. Keep fingers extended and bend wrist backwards at the wrist. (five repetitions)
8. Spread fingers, then relax. (five repetitions)

LAYING THE GROUNDWORK

REPERTOIRE SELECTION

One of the major concerns in keeping students motivated to practice is making sure that they like the music that has been assigned. If it is no longer fun, practicing becomes an unpleasant chore, something to avoid. Ultimately, practicing music that they do not like will undermine the desire to spend time at the instrument. One solution to this problem is to involve students in the selection process.

The teacher should select, in advance, several compositions that are appropriate for the student and then encourage them to choose which they like best. When selecting these options, though, it is important to make sure that the compositions being considered are within the student's capabilities. There is nothing more disheartening to students than to be overwhelmed with the technical and musical demands of a composition for which they are unprepared. It is also important to consider the physical demands of a given selection. For example, it is equally frustrating for the student if a composition is not suited to his or her hand size. Not only will repertoire that constantly stretches the hand to its maximum prove difficult to play, it can be placing the student at risk for injury. As students get older, they should be encouraged to do their own research on possible repertoire, listening to several recordings while following the scores. (Borrowing their teacher's compact discs or going to a university library to find them on their own can help accomplish this.)

Assigning several pieces of varying difficulty, length and style is also important. For example, assign a shorter, easier composition that can be completed quickly; a longer, more challenging piece that stretches the student to reach a higher level of musical and/or technical proficiency; and perhaps a showy or popular piece that is just fun to play.

It is not unusual for students to hear someone else perform a piece and want to learn it, however, these works may be too difficult and beyond the ability of the student. If a student comes to a lesson with such a composition, the teacher has the difficult task of determining what is in the best interest of the student. A few possible options:

1. Encourage the student to work on similar repertoire and delay any work on this piece; it can be held for the future, a carrot, if you will, to achieve in time.

2. Work on portions of the piece, selecting sections that are within the student's reach and target the acquisition of specific skills.

3. Allow the student to work on it, with the understanding that this is just for fun and experimentation only, not a piece to be polished and publicly performed.

Selecting repertoire for a student's consideration is an art and skill that teachers develop over time, as their knowledge of a broad range of repertoire increases and their ability to determine a student's needs, goals, and preferences improves.

PREPARING THE STUDENT FOR PRACTICE

Once a student has selected a new piece, it is essential to provide adequate preparation during the lesson so that the student will feel successful and productive once he or she is at home practicing. Before sending a student home for the week, help him or her discover what the piece is about. This might include learning about the character and emotion represented, any pertinent or interesting information about the composer, including his or her overall compositional style, and details about the form and structure of the piece. And while every important detail need not be covered in this first exposure, it is important to address the technical issues and concepts presented in the piece and discuss which, if any, have already been learned in the form of etudes, technical exercises, or previous repertoire.

Finally, help the student establish how much of the piece will be covered within the week and exactly how it should be practiced. Setting musical goals and stressing the importance of careful listening is more important than setting duration or repetition goals like spend thirty minutes on the first line or play this through four times. Ideally, every student should leave the lesson eager to get home to explore a new piece, having a plan in mind about exactly how to approach it.

FINGERING

There are two extremes when it comes to fingering. The student who never pays attention to it, playing with whatever finger ends up on the note, and the student who adheres to exactly what is printed on the page, without exception. Neither extreme is ideal. A fingering that works for the teacher or an editor may not be appropriate for the student and insisting that he or she use either the teacher's fingering or the one printed in the score is not prudent nor in the student's best interest. It is, however, no more appropriate to allow a student to make random finger placements, as it will hamper his or her technical security.

Teachers should instead help students discover the principles behind good fingering and encourage them to make some decisions on their own. It is essential to discover these basic concepts early, even as soon as a student's repertoire extends beyond the five-finger range, because fingering affects both physical ease and musical fluidity. And although fingering is a very individual decision based on the person's hand size and shape, one fundamental concept is applicable to everyone – *keep the hand small.* Maintaining an outstretched hand for lengthy periods of time often results in increased tension and can ultimately lead to injury. Keeping students involved in the decision making process will promote independence and more efficient learning, and is ultimately the key to learning music quickly.

TIME MANAGEMENT

Today's society makes enormous time demands on students, so much so that it is no longer enough to simply expect students to practice outside of the lesson. Teachers need to be aware of what else is going on in a student's life and help them find a way to fit practicing into their daily schedule. Exploring ways to practice more efficiently should also be part of every music student's education.

Making sure the time at the piano is productive is an important facet of time management. This depends in large part on two factors – concentration and endurance. Students of all ages should practice only as long as their concentration can be maintained, which for younger students will be considerably less than adults. Very young students may only be able to work for ten or fifteen minutes at a time. Taking breaks to stretch and regroup is crucial, even for the most advanced, adult student. Many arts-medicine physicians suggest that three to five-minute breaks be taken every thirty minutes, although some advanced students may be able to extend their practice time to an hour. Teachers should stress the need for vigilance on the part of the student, emphasizing the importance of being aware of any excess fatigue or any kind of dull ache or pain anywhere in the body. This is a signal that excessive demands are being made on the body, and ignoring it can result in an injury.

It is also important to make sure more advanced students do not sharply increase the intensity or duration of practicing sessions, as that could lead to injury. This is an especially likely scenario for college students, many of whom take a summer off from their practicing and then return to extremely intense practicing in the fall. These young adults are most at risk during their freshman year, a time when they are working with a new teacher and often experimenting with new approaches to the instrument. Eager to do well and surrounded by older, more advanced peers who are practicing many hours a day, these dedicated students dramatically increase their practice time. Depending on their inherited risk factors, a number may be dealing with some kind of injury within six months. Another hazardous time for pianists is just prior to juries or major recitals. These events prompt dramatic increases in practice time, and are also frequently coupled with psychological stress. This combination results in increased tension while playing, putting the student at even greater risk of injury. A commonly recognized rule of sports is equally applicable to pianists in these situations – one cannot increase training in time or intensity by more than 10 percent per week.

One cannot increase training in time or intensity by more than 10 percent per week.

WORK STRATEGIES

How to utilize practice time is as pertinent a subject for a teacher to discuss, as is the amount of time to be spent.

THE MYTH OF REPETITION

A prevailing misconception amongst students of all ages is that learning is best accomplished through sheer repetition. While some repetition can help a musician achieve greater physical security, it often becomes a wasteful exercise because students play without listening. For repetition to be most effective, it should have a purpose that involves the full attention of the student, not just motion in his or her fingers. Perhaps the repetition is to experiment with a different musical nuance or to try a different fingering. Or, the student may choose to play the passage exactly the same way again, utilizing the repetition to focus on a different aspect of his or her playing (i.e. how the arm moves through the gesture). Listening carefully enough to determine which repetition is more effective enhances a student's ability to refine listening and diagnostic skills, encourages experimentation, and is ultimately a means to successful practicing.

The problem of repetition occurs on a larger scale when students play a piece or passage again and again, believing that if they play it enough, the problems will be solved. They rarely are, but for students who cannot think of any other way to improve the piece, repetition seems logical. It is the responsibility of the teacher to provide the students with other ways to fix problems and improve the piece, including problem-solving skills that can be taught within the lesson environment.

Rather than continue through a problem section, it is important for students to stop, isolate and analyze the problem. Have them break the piece into workable sections, perhaps as small as a measure or a phrase at a time, or work from cadence to cadence, utilizing the natural musical divisions of the composition. Encourage students to act as detectives. If a technical issue is encountered, they might try asking themselves questions: Could fingering be the problem? Am I using the wrong gesture for this tempo? Perhaps my tempo is wrong for the gesture that is required. Helping students learn what questions to consider will enhance their independence and ability to solve future problems on their own.

MENTAL PRACTICE

Practicing away from the instrument is a valuable and often under-utilized strategy. Research in the area of sports medicine has proven the effectiveness of using mental imagery or visualization as a tool to enhance concentration and focus and to mentally rehearse movements.

> Researchers have found that when movements are imagined very vividly, slight physical reactions are triggered in the body. The tiny responses occur in the same muscles and nerves that would be used during physical performance of the imagined movement. The responses are so minimal that EMG electrodes must be used in measuring the nerve and muscle activity.[2]

Pianists can reap these same benefits by visualizing playing through difficult passages. While working through the composition mentally, pay close attention to all of the detailed markings in the score, thus reinforcing these musical elements. This technique also can serve as a powerful tool to help overcome performance anxiety if students imagine themselves successfully playing through a composition. This experience can produce feelings of success and enhance the self-confidence of the performer, making the next performance easier.[3]

USE OF THE METRONOME

The metronome can be a helpful gadget unless used in a mindless manner. Although playing through a piece with the metronome set at a slow speed and inching it up one or two notches at a time is a relatively common method of using the metronome, it can promote boredom and prompt students to stop listening to themselves, a dangerous combination. A metronome is better used as a tool to help students discover tempo inconsistencies.

LEARNING TO PLAY AT ALL TEMPI

The ability to play accurately and cleanly at a specific tempo is a complex practicing issue. Many students are eager to play fast, but are reluctant to slow down to clean up messy passages. Others are uncomfortable playing fast and tend to practice slower than that which is necessary to achieve the ultimate tempo. Because fast and slow playing each require unique gestures and use muscles differently, it is important to do both types of practicing in differing proportions, depending on the tempo of the composition and where the student is in the learning process.

When tempo indications dictate slow playing, it is helpful to think from pulse to pulse, rather than note to note. This promotes a longer musical line, more fluid physical motions and greater direction to the music. It also helps eliminate the tendency to pump the wrists on each note, a common habit that often results in the production of pedantic, monotonous, and unmusical sounds.

When speed is required, it will be necessary to work slowly initially. However, it is also essential to try playing up to tempo early in the learning process, even if only for a few measures or a phrase. This is the only way to determine what

---

[2]Malva Freymuth, *Mental Practice and Imagery for Musicians* (Boulder, Colorado: Integrated Musician's Press, 1999) 61.

[3]Visualization is explored with more depth and specificity in "Strategies for Handling Performance Anxiety," page 131.

physical gestures and fingerings will work at a fast tempo. Having experienced a few measures at tempo, the student will return to slow practicing with the understanding and, more importantly, the kinesthetic awareness of what will be physically necessary to play faster. Once a student is capable of playing the composition at tempo, it will be equally important to periodically return to slow practice to maintain clarity, consistency and security.

THE IMPORTANCE OF WORKING SECTIONS

Students are notorious for wanting to play straight through a composition. Although this is an important step to take at different stages in the learning process, the importance of dividing the piece into small sections cannot be diminished. Plodding along at an extremely slow tempo or one hand at a time is not a productive use of practice time, and often results in a frustrating and musically unsatisfactory experience. Students need to discover naturally occurring musical stopping points, such as major cadences or the beginnings of new sections, and break these into small manageable segments. Within these small units, technical issues can be handled, tempo can be increased, and musical decisions will often become more apparent. Students will also end practice sessions with a sense of accomplishment that will help motivate them to continue working on the composition.

There is one caveat about working in small units. All the isolated elements must be worked back into the whole. Transitions from section to section need to be examined and smoothed out both technically and musically to eliminate the working seams. Finally, the entire composition, as a whole, needs to be thought through structurally.

HAND-SEPARATE PRACTICING IS NOT ALWAYS THE ANSWER

Young children begin learning to play the piano using one hand at a time, and more advanced pianists will require hand separate practicing to work out difficult passages. However, working an entire piece at a slow tempo one hand at a time serves no real benefit. In fact, as the difficulty inherent in many compositions is the coordinating of the two hands, it can serve to impede development. A better approach is to work a given, challenging section hands separately to see exactly what is expected of each hand. Then, practice very small sections – one measure or even half a measure – slowly, playing both hands together, noting how they coordinate with each other.

SIMPLIFY TO GRASP THE WHOLE

Extracting the major components out of a more complex composition and playing those separately from the rest of the composition is a very beneficial tool to use in the early learning stages of working a new composition. Identifying and playing the essential elements of the music, perhaps only the melody and the bass line, helps students attain a clearer idea of the musical content of a new composition. By eliminating elaborate chords, inner lines, big leaps, and other difficult elements, the student is able to pay close attention to important musical details at a much earlier stage in the learning process. Specific interpretive issues such as sound production, providing direction to the line, achieving the gestures necessary to shape the phrase, and attempting to play at or close to tempo now become the primary focus.

Attention to the music at this point would likely be impossible if the student was trying to play all the notes. However, this simplification process helps eliminate many of the difficult technical issues that can initially divert a student's attention and instead brings it to the musical content at a much earlier stage in the learning process.

MINDFUL PRACTICE

The most significant piece of information a teacher can impart about practicing is the importance of being present in the moment, hearing the sounds as they are being produced and responding accordingly. Productive practicing demands concentration and an approach to the instrument that results in an awareness of how things feel and sound. What separates practicing the piano from practicing any other physical skill is that this skill requires total concentration, coupled with creativity and artistry.

Whether practicing repertoire or technical exercises, there should be a continuing focus on sound production, phrasing and musical direction. There is *never* a time when unthinking and unmusical sounds are to be produced. Paying attention to gestures and fluidity of motion will enable students to feel relaxed, comfortable and at ease while practicing or performing.

A TEACHER'S ROLE

Because the lesson is such a small percentage of the total time a student spends at the instrument, it is important not to overlook the wealth of information that can be found by examining how students work when alone. Having students demonstrate at their lesson how they practiced a given section, make audio or videotapes of their practicing sessions for review, or maintain a practice log, perhaps including specific questions that have come up during the week, can be most useful in helping students develop more efficient practicing skills. Using lesson time to actually work through a problem can also provide students with a model for how to work at home.

When assigning tasks and goals for the next lesson, it is also crucial to remember that teachers serve as an important catalyst in helping students maintain a creative practice attitude. By offering new perspectives to approach a composition or a problem in lessons, teachers provide students with the tools to develop productive and enjoyable practice experiences and help them build self-esteem and feelings of success. Feeling successful provides powerful motivation for students to continue their study and enjoy time spent at the instrument, both now and throughout their lives. It is also important to remember that teachers are powerful role models for students. When students discover that their own teacher practices, and regularly works through the same difficulties with which they are dealing, they begin to realize that spending this productive time at the instrument is something they can do for a lifetime.

Orienting to the Keyboard: Middle D

Seymour Fink

Many factors influence the emotional connection individuals have to their instrument of choice – attitudes towards music, learning, practicing and performing; the instrument's size, monetary value, and portability; and tactile involvement. These all mold a musician's sensibility. String and wind performers cradle their instruments as they play in a comfortable, centered fashion to minimize strain, and to encourage the postural expansiveness that sustains good music making. When finished, they gently swab or polish them, put them in their cases, and tuck them under an arm for transport.

The piano, in marked contrast, never gets tucked under an arm and it rarely engenders such nurturing feelings. In fact, seated as they are, in front of a large stationary apparatus, feelings of intimidation at the sheer size or spread of the keyboard are a likely emotion. The task for pianists is to overcome these feelings by developing a comfortable, centered relationship with the instrument; beginning with a starting position that is consistently maintained. This central position creates the stable base on which all other physical habits are built, and allows for efficiency of practice and security of public performance.

PLACEMENT AT THE INSTRUMENT

Placement issues, such as seated height, location on the chair, and distance from the keyboard, are determined in common sense terms, taking into account an individual's body proportions. The following two principles govern:

- It is mechanically advantageous to use muscles and joints in their midrange.
- The body must comfortably reach the entire length and depth of the keyboard, and must be in position to set optimal alignments for the fingers, hands, and arms with each other, and with the keyboard.

Although final placement will require refinement, an initial guideline is that when upper arms are vertical and close to the body, elbows should be at the approximate height of the keys (or slightly lower) with thumbs reaching midway onto the wide part of the white keys.

Once seated at the piano, posture is decisive. A good seated posture minimizes muscular strain and allows for an easy, balanced, 360-degree body sway that helps one feel and express flowing musical lines. The spine, neck, and head are aligned and elongated, with the sternum held up. The resulting solid torso base permits the shoulders to relax downward and outward to gravity, positioning the arms to move freely. The straightened torso tilts subtly forward as the pelvis is tipped backward, accentuating the lower curve of the back; weight is thrown forward onto the thighs, as stomach muscles slightly tighten. Movement forward and back takes place in the hip joint, not at the waist or neck. The ball (not the toe) of the right foot is placed on the damper pedal; the left foot remains flat on the floor, slightly to the left. This position balances the body, reduces tension, and establishes stability for even vigorous movement. It also promotes upper arm freedom and dexterity, allowing them ample reach, and giving them the ability to lead with power and ease.

Students who become comfortable in the posture described above may progress to movement exercises. These larger, basic movements of the total body are the first step in teaching the body to move as a mature pianist does, gracefully, to both sense and support musical expression and to aid technical positioning. At first, it is best to do these exercises away from a musical context:

- While maintaining a centered balance, gently sway an erect torso side-to-side in large elliptical circles, rolling from one hip to another. This balanced movement establishes the precondition for experiencing and expressing musical line.
- One should then practice movements that support extreme positioning of the arms:
    - Slide the left foot far left, to counterbalance body mass when both hands move far right.
    - Place the left foot firmly on the floor, half left, to carry added body weight when both hands move to that side.
    - Bend forward from the hip joint (not the middle of the back or neck) to accommodate hands moving to opposite extremes.

Sitting centered on middle D permits the two bilateral symmetries – that of the player, and that of the keyboard – to be brought into synchrony.

The head-neck-spine alignment remains constant throughout, as the body, in a fluid equilibrium, moves with the flow of the music, poised always to help position the arms and hands; for they, along with the fingers, have their own work to do and must never be called on for help in holding the body up.

The final and often overlooked issue in establishing a central position is lateral placement. Choosing to sit in front of middle D provides a way of centering at the instrument that bestows considerable physical and psychological advantage. Pianists are bilaterally symmetrical beings, whose one side substantially mirrors the other. Middle D on the keyboard centers a pattern of keys in which the spatial relationships of black and white keys moving outward in both directions mirror the other. Thus sitting centered on middle D permits the two bilateral symmetries – that of the player, and that of the keyboard – to be brought into synchrony. No other lateral placement near the center of the piano will do this.

KEYBOARD KNOWLEDGE

Middle-D orientation, when exercised and followed to its logical conclusion, has a profound effect on performers, serving to center, root, and stabilize them. It revolutionizes technical training by enabling students to perform identical exercises at the same time, in both hands, in a mirrored, contrary mode. This training promotes equal development of both sides of the body, and helps to eliminate a common problem fostered by a staple of traditional training: left and right hands learning differing skills. The contrary-motion practice also establishes a distinct center-outward orientation. Unlike the parallel practice of scales and arpeggios, which fosters thinking in terms of high and low, or right and left, contrary practice trains one to think of movement as going from the center of the instrument and body outward and back. The synchronous two-handed pattern practice also encourages and speeds the kinesthetic perceptions necessary for keyboard knowledge – an intellectual mastery of the physical shape of the keyboard.

As with all skills at the instrument, keyboard knowledge is built slowly, from the ground up. In this case, the ground is adopting a new perception of the keyboard. A fresh, objective look at the keyboard reveals two tiers of levers stretching more than four feet wide. A higher, shorter, irregular tier of black levers rises above a row of longer, lower, white ones. Getting one's mind around this daunting form demands a structure, which can be found in a natural extension of the middle-D approach.

Suggest that students project an imaginary grid, much like the stripes on a football field, onto the keyboard, with the fifty-yard line denoting middle D, and the five-yard line markers denoting G-sharps and D's, the two tritone signpost notes that coincide in a contrary chromatic scale starting on middle D. These imaginary lines should be projected outward for three octaves and labeled from ½-octave G-sharp to 3-octave D.

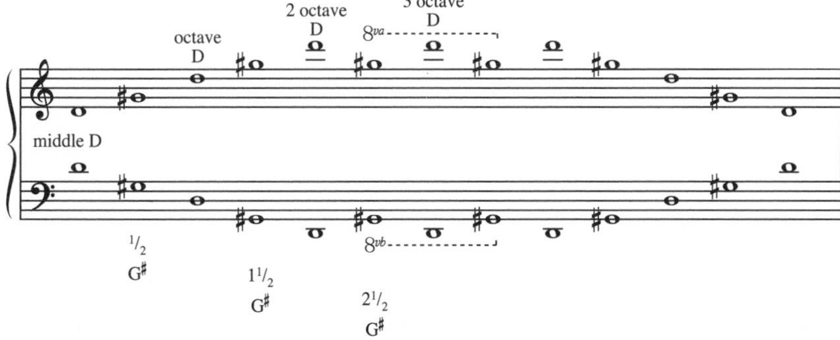

With this in place, the students have internalized a psychic map embracing a six-octave 'playing field' conceived in terms of a center-outward orientation and are ready to begin reinforcing this mental image with hands-on exercises. Starting on middle D, students should play a contrary chromatic scale outward and back for three octaves, employing smooth arm travel and identical hand and finger patterns. Their thumbs should play in the gray area along the front edge of the black keys, with the second and third fingers touching in the black area. The bridge of the hand should be low enough so that there is a straight line between the top of the wrist and the midjoints of the fingers.

This basic exercise allows students to experience how the mirror image relationship simplifies the mental imaging. Comparing this experience with the more difficult task of playing a four-octavo parallel D-major scale can further reinforce the concept. In the case of the latter, the hands and arms, using contrasting fingering, are forced into different, often conflicting coordinations. Also, the large parallel movement tends to throw the body off center. For students whose early instruction places an exaggerated emphasis on parallel playing, these offputting movements will lead to a tipsy feeling and overall sense of being ill at ease at the keyboard. Far more preferential is training in contrary motion, which requires far less cerebral effort, and which is the natural way our bodies work.

Looking further at the keyboard, students should take note of the comforting and fundamental octave-duplication pattern throughout the entire range. Within the octave, the asymmetric groupings of two and three black keys can be simplified by projecting two contrasting areas of the octave, one predominantly high and black (F-sharp major), the other predominantly low and white (C major). The signpost notes become markers: G-sharps center the groups of three black keys; D's center the groups of three lower-tier white keys; F's and B's are transition keys.

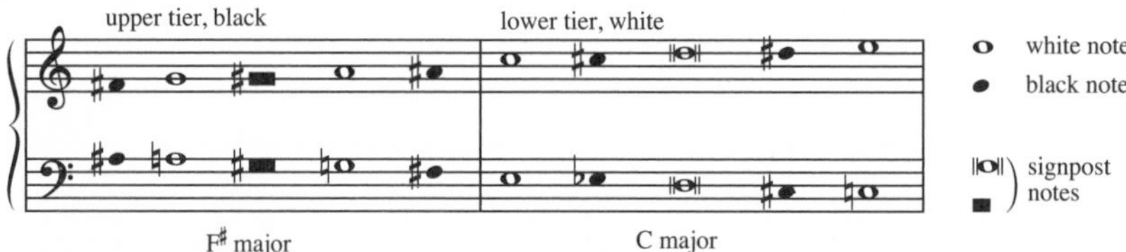

Semi-tone spacing is visually consistent only in the black area where all half steps, black or white, high or low, are roughly of equal width. The white area of the keyboard contains equally wide keys that disconcertingly stand for both whole and half steps. The divergence of physical from musical proportion, compounded by variations in key height, length, and depth, as well as the various shapes of white keys, all force bewildering complexities on the hands and fingers. This tangle can be largely resolved with systematic topographical training.

Topographical knowledge – sensing within exactly where the keys are – is the essence of technical proficiency. By exploring a myriad of contrary motion patterns centered on middle D, one discovers all the nooks and crannies of the full width and depth of the keyboard. It is also worth repeating that this bilateral synchrony speeds the spatial-kinesthetic learning and serves to root and center the player. It is prerequisite for expert sight-reading and greater overall accuracy with playing; and it also helps one to feel more relaxed at the instrument, resulting in increased confidence.

When adopting this approach, students should first train lateral movement of the upper arms, always aware of two basic rules:

- All playing is done touching and sliding in the black-key area.
- Hands play together in contrary motion, with right and left-hand fingers constantly touching, in mirrored fashion, keys that are the same distance from middle D.

Using continuously moving whole-arm circles, play straightened third fingers on single keys in each hand, moving outward on signpost keys to 3-octave D and back. Prepared fingers slide along the keys in the black-key area propelled by a pulsating, elliptical arm stroke, first in the pushing direction, and then in the pulling direction. Once the tritone lateral spacing is mastered, with bodies still and centered, students should move on to the spatial underpinning of other lateral distances – skips of octaves, thirds, fourths, and the like. Stepwise and chromatic motions are also useful.

As students progress, the exercises should also be expanded to include chromatic transposition of simple intervals like major thirds with 1 and 3, 2 and 4, and 3 and 5, or perfect fourths with 1 and 4, and 2 and 5. Exercises that transpose three-note chord patterns using a consistent finger pattern should follow. Fingers will learn to adjust automatically to the differing heights of the black and white keys. Once secure, the next step is to practice broken chords and other short melodic fragments, transposing them in the same fashion. Consistent practicing of these exercises will help students develop considerable expertise in playing in the black-key area, and greatly enlarge their general keyboard know-how.[1]

HAND VOCABULARY

Systematic, middle-D, contrary motion practice molds students' minds, arms, hands, and fingers to the shape of the keyboard from the vantage point of their own central position. This mirrored movement contributes profoundly to the development of an instinctual understanding of the keyboard, leading directly to increased technical sophistication. It also lays the groundwork for a hand-vocabulary approach to fingering – a consistent use of fingering that relates not to the black-white keyboard design, but to the intervalic structure of the musical contours.

Thus in chromatically transposing a major triad, the fingering never changes from 1 3 5 as one moves outward, regardless of the black-white relations. Longer fingers will just touch white keys in the black-key area as thumbs fall near the front edge of the black keys. As students apply hand-vocabulary logic, they quickly develop ease in handling the relatively tight quarters and irregular turf near the fallboard. Blacks become just higher, not further away; whites become lower and proportional to interval size. Any initial finger inconvenience is quickly overshadowed by the considerable amount of mental simplification and musical potential hand vocabulary offers.

Consider for a moment only the gain in directness and memory resulting from fingering the same musical shapes in a consistent way, regardless of the black-white configuration. Although many editors unfortunately discount this advantage by avoiding 1, and even 5, on the black keys, students need only discover the repetitive musical shapes of a composition and organize them into finger-interval equivalencies independent of any other indications. This applies to all patterns – repeated notes, motives, sequential writing, complete passages, and even to entire compositions.

The musical potential springs from the possibility for upper arm freedom and consistency. Because fingering patterns define the possibilities for arm movement, we are not just fingering, we are arming. The arms become free to faithfully

---

[1]For further explanation and a road map for orientating or reorienting to middle D, see the chapter on Keyboard Topography in *Mastering Piano Technique*, by Seymour Fink, published by the Amadeus Press.

choreograph the repetitive musical shapes. Picture the directness, simplicity, and power that the arms can bring to bear on such musical values as expression, consistency, facility, rhythmic pacing, tonal range, accuracy, shaping, and control. The logic of hand-vocabulary fingering ushers in this world, a world in which the full application of arm power, our most dependable and valuable technical asset, can flourish.

In spite of all its benefits, middle-D orientation does not enable pianists to cradle the instrument, nor tuck it under an arm when we are finished playing. However, it does provide an avenue for thoughtfully approaching the instrument, allowing it to become a faithful tool. One that we can comfortably use to search for, find and produce the kinds of sounds that admirably project our inner musical thinking. This cannot but lead to forming a very deep bond with our overgrown partner.

Video Camera Applications for Enhancing Piano Practice and Performance

Dylan Savage

Effective and efficient use of the playing mechanism (i.e. the hands, arms, etc.) is of utmost importance to all pianists seeking ways to improve their technique's ability to express musical intentions. But what is the best way for a teacher to help students achieve this difficult goal? For centuries, the most common and effective method of explaining how to solve musical or technical problems has been demonstration at the keyboard coupled with verbal descriptions. Unfortunately, demonstration of gesture and motion has a fleeting aspect to it that makes it difficult to recall accurately for any length of time. Particularly ineffective for fast passages, demonstration can further cloud the picture because the eye cannot follow the precise movements of the hand, and fast passages played slowly often do not replicate the motion found in the same passage played at tempo. Using language to accurately describe sound and/or the physical nature of a certain motion or series of motions at the keyboard, can be extremely time consuming, problematic, and inaccurate, thus impractical. Indeed, excessive description may be more confusing than helpful to a student.

The pioneering piano pedagogues came to realize this as well, and began to embrace the modified saying – an aural and visual picture is worth a thousand words. Books and articles containing pictures of arm, wrist, and hand motions (as found in Ortmann) and sequences of still photographs depicting anatomically correct motions by famous artists at the keyboard (as found in Gat) resulted. Helpful to a degree, these still images can be insufficient when a more comprehensive understanding is needed, because they show a single, static moment that is but a fraction of a second in a continuum of a series of complicated, interlinking movements.

The use of the video camera, on the other hand, presents a more helpful dimension in the study, analysis, and application of piano technique, as it can aid pianists in observing the piano-playing mechanism much more accurately and in greater detail than with the naked eye. Visual images of a particular motion, especially when seen in the easy-to-follow pace of slow motion, are much easier to recall and mimic than those presented through the use of real-time demonstration or descriptive words. It also addresses the two-fold difficulty students have when watching their teacher demonstrate a passage in question – *seeing* clearly what the teacher did, and *recalling* an accurate memory of that visual. Because this problem is rarely addressed in the 'watch, now copy' method, a considerable bit of misconception has been created. By using slow-motion replay, however, a teacher can dramatically reduce the misconception a student experiences while trying to recall a series of demonstrated motions solely from the mind's eye, and recapture much of the lost time in musical and technical development. Video replay may be even more effective today, as students are extremely visually attuned, due to the ever-present computer, video, television, and movie screens. Consequently, having today's students *see* a specific motion or series of motions is an especially successful method of teaching and learning.

IMPORTANT VIDEO CAMERA FEATURES

Video cameras (both analog and digital) are versatile, lightweight, and affordable, and therefore practical for use in enhancing piano practice and performance. While the list of features on most brand-name cameras is varied and lengthy, if one is selecting a video camera primarily for slow-motion analysis of performance, it follows logically that slow-motion playback and/or frame-by-frame replay is the most important feature. Both allow the user to replay what was just filmed as long as a television screen is present. (Although many video cameras now have small, attached screens that allow you to view the playback, they are generally too small for clear viewing of minute details.) If slow-motion replay is not a capability of your current video camera, there are a few options. Many VCRs have a slow-motion feature, which you can utilize after making a recording on VHS video cameras. (Please note that four-head VCRs provide the clearest picture.) 8mm video cameras often have a frame-by-frame advance feature that can be done manually. This feature provides viewing quite similar to slow-motion playback.

Other features to consider are as follows:

- Low-light capabilities, for filming indoors in low-light conditions
- Editing features
- High resolution
- Remote control operation

Increasingly affordable digital-camera technology, along with large, high-resolution monitors, offers additional options to those teachers (and performers) who wish to make the investment. In addition to creating high-quality images, digital cameras allow the user to download the results of filming directly to a computer. Once the files are saved to the computer, a wide range of possibilities exist for use: viewing moving images in real-time, slow-motion, or frame-by-frame; examining stills; printing color photos of stills; and editing, to name a few.

SLOW-MOTION VIDEO REPLAY AND FRAME-BY-FRAME VIEWING

Teachers are familiar with the difficulty in clearly seeing and recalling every element of movement of a student's hands and fingers. This is particularly true during fast passages, when teachers are unable to see the critical small and intricate motions. It is also during these fast passages when teachers may make diagnoses that are incorrect, because it is not within human capability to see clearly motions that exceed a certain speed. What teachers may think they observed when viewing fast and complex motion at the keyboard, and what actually took place are often two different things. This problem is solved with the use of slow-motion playback, which allows all motions made at the keyboard to be viewed in continuous motion with great clarity and detail. Most effective for showing the flow and exchange of interlinking gestures and a more coherent sense of the whole, further analysis offers the opportunity to adjust, if needed, the arm, hand, or finger motions, regardless of the speed or complexity of the original motion, greatly benefiting the playing mechanism and, therefore, the musical intent.

Though similar to slow motion, frame-by-frame viewing allows the teacher to stop the action at any point and is effective for examining, in detail and for any length of time, any one spot in the motion continuum. The frame-by frame method is so detailed that the lift of one finger from the top of the key to the apex of the ascent often requires three to five different frames. This enables one to fully examine the most exhaustive levels of movement, no matter what the speed.

It is important to mention that to benefit fully from either analysis technique, teacher and student must first know *what* kinds of movement at the keyboard will give good results and which ones will not. Although there are some basic, generally agreed-upon movements, there is significant variance from pianist to pianist as to what constitutes comfortable and efficient motion; unfortunately pianists do not have the benefit of a standard of weights and measures. Students and teachers may find it beneficial to view videos or films of expert pianists in performance (at both normal and slow speeds), especially pianists who play with little effort and minimal motion. Please note that while there is certainly much to gain and emulate from these observations, it is essential to proceed with great care, as looks alone are by no means the whole story in piano playing. Because the manner in which one pianist plays could be injurious to another, remember that there need not necessarily be wholesale adaptations of another's technique. Instead, simply tailoring certain elements of another pianist's playing to one's own technique may be very helpful.

MENTAL IMAGERY

Slow-motion replay permits passages of any difficulty level and speed to be viewed clearly and at reduced speeds, which allows all movements to be easily recalled for 'mental tracing', thus enhancing the beneficial practice of mental imagery. Excellent for reinforcing movement patterns and choreographed sequences, mental imagery of motion has been used for years with a great deal of success in many fields, including sports and dance.

The premise of mental imagery is that watching a movement pattern, 'playing' it in the mind's eye, and then physically practicing the movement will help secure memory. Pianists can use video to take advantage of this tool both by watching themselves, and by observing well-played examples of specific motions or gestures to study and emulate. A clear mental picture, aided greatly by observation in slow motion, translates to sure and secure applications of movement.[1]

[1]Seymour Fink's video, *Mastering Piano Technique: A Guide for Students, Teachers, and Performers* (Amadeus Press), is a superb source for the depiction of movement patterns at the keyboard.

MODELING AND AFTER-THE-LESSON VIEWING

The video camera is a useful tool to enhance modeling, an important, though often overlooked, part of a pianist's education. Teachers may record themselves demonstrating a passage, or series of passages, that best illustrate the keyboard motions, or a sequence of motions, a student is learning. Not only does this fulfill a core requirement of modeling – an effective model must direct the observer's attention to what needs to be observed – the video format enables students to consult as needed the visual and aural directives of the past lesson or lessons during the time they are away from their teacher.

Including the week's lesson along with specific teacher demonstrations is an effective way to make the most of the 'other six days', when the teacher is not present. Students may then study specific motions pertinent to their upcoming lesson as many times as needed, ensuring that bad habits do not encroach, reinforcing important points and shades of meaning, and insuring that the focus of the week is not forgotten.

AURAL REPLAY

Beyond examining physical and/or biomechanical problems, the video camera can also be used effectively for real-time playback (which, unlike slow motion, includes audio). In this situation, the teacher and the student may take equal roles in the most important aspect of performance – aural analysis. Certainly all musicians *know* that how a piece of music sounds is the most critical determinate of movement, but at times it is appropriate to offer a reminder, particularly when so much space is devoted to physical movement, and methods for its analysis. All examination and discussion of physical motion is for one reason: for musicians to express their musical ideas in the fullest way possible without injuring themselves in the process.

All examination and discussion of physical motion is for one reason: for musicians to express their musical ideas in the fullest way possible without injuring themselves in the process.

Documenting a performance on video is an excellent time to use video technology for aural analysis, especially because students, when caught up in the passion of playing a certain passage, will often feel and believe that elements of expression, such as nuances, dynamics, and *rubato*, were clearly performed, when, in actuality, they were not. Teachers then have the difficult chore of convincing students, whose recollections largely reflect what they felt emotionally and not what was heard, that their expressive intentions were not transmitted fully. However, when students are able to immediately view and hear their performance, they can much more accurately assess what they did or did not do during their performance.

An added benefit of a video recording is that it may be easily and quickly repeated as often as is necessary, allowing teachers and students to discuss different elements of the same passage or piece. Without the use of a video recording, a student would be required to play a passage repeatedly for evaluation and critique of different elements. In this event, it is likely that the elements in question would change significantly with each repetition. Those changes are enough to vary the outcome, possibly making the initial comments irrelevant.

SPEED OF LEARNING AND INDIVIDUAL DEVELOPMENT

Students should be encouraged, early on in the process, to routinely critique their performances through listening and watching video replay. (More beneficial then simply listening to an audio recording, students discover that sound it not divorced from physical movement and learn the important dynamic of cause and effect.) Through this practice of self-critiquing, students will become better teachers of themselves. Each moment of practice will be endowed with a greater sense of purpose, promoting quicker and more thorough learning. Ultimately, students will begin to listen with far more capable ears when they start to regularly critique their own performances.

Promoting the practice of self-critiquing also creates an environment for more advanced students to develop individually, especially if their interpretations are encouraged. This will minimize the time the teacher spends describing the playing of his or her students, an important step towards individuality, as students' reflection on their own playing will become less attached to any biases of the teacher. The resulting equality of viewing and hearing status creates more homogeneity between the points of view of the teacher and student. Both teacher and student will then have the potential to interact on more equal analytical and observational levels. This becomes increasingly important as students mature and become more able to function on their own. (This is not to say that teachers should become less involved as students' contributions increase. In fact, the reality is quite the opposite. Teachers must find new ways to guide students whose interpretations are considerable off the mark, often by shifting their approach by asking questions rather than providing answers.)

VIDEO CAMERA SET-UP

For private piano studios, one video camera will be sufficient for most recording situations. (In college or university settings, each piano studio does not need its own video camera for the technique's potential to be used by all. Rather, a schedule can be made out so that many may share. The weekly piano-class hour is an especially good time to use the video camera.) As mentioned before, for playback, a television monitor will be needed. Also, a good-quality tripod upon which to mount the camera is necessary for quick, easy changes of camera angles, general stability, and a long life. Another helpful tool is the hand-held laser pointer. It can direct the student's attention to things on the screen during playback with more accuracy and less blockage than one's finger, and reduces the teacher's movement between piano and monitor.

The placement of the video camera is dependent upon the desired type of motion (and, of course, sound) to be studied and analyzed. The following are some basic camera positions:

- For the best view of the tops of the hands for lateral (side-to-side) motion, it is recommended that the camera be mounted or suspended directly above middle C.
- To examine finger motion and the vertical travel of the hands, arms, and fingers, place the camera level at keyboard (and hand) level.
- To explore rotary motion, the camera should also be at keyboard level. Placing a black dot on the wrist can focus one's viewing.
- The camera is again placed at keyboard level when looking for a flexible wrist, however in this situation, draw a black line from

the knuckle of the fifth finger to an inch past the wrist joint.

- Rotary-type motions and independent finger motion can also be examined by placing the camera below the keyboard.
- If both lateral and vertical motions are to be examined simultaneously, then the camera should be set to a 45-degree angle above and to the side of the hands. This is the best position for all-around viewing.

The side of the piano on which the camera is to be placed will depend on which hand should be filmed. The treble side is usually the predominant filming spot, because the right hand is usually faced with the most troublesome passagework. Both hands of the pianist can be viewed more clearly and with less obstruction when filming from angles above the keyboard level.

It is important to film the whole playing mechanism of the pianists – remember to make sure that the arms are uncovered at least to the elbows, although it is ideal to have the shoulder uncovered as well. This allows for many critical elements above the wrist to be observed, such as forearm and upper arm position, mobility, inflexibility, or tension. A mirror (or stick-on reflective film) can be placed on the left side of the keyboard for a more complete view of the left hand when filming from the right side. This allows both hands to be viewed on a fairly equal basis, at the same time.

The camera should always be set as close to the piano as possible, and yet be able to include all the critical movements of the playing mechanism within the camera's viewfinder. 'Critical' movements can include anything from close-up analysis to full-body filming, which is especially helpful for finding out if or how tension manifests itself on parts of the body. Viewing the pianist from the perspective of the teacher or audience can reveal certain quirks, such as gestures and facial expressions that may be eliminated or modified.

In my teaching experience, the video camera has been a particularly beneficial teaching tool. Its use has been instrumental in helping to correct a large number of chronic or previously unsolved problems for students and master class participants alike. Hopefully the information provided here will help make other teachers comfortable with incorporating this technology in their own teaching.

An Introduction to Learning Styles

Phyllis Alpert Lehrer

Can piano teachers benefit by learning:

- How students organize their practice?
- How students' thoughts about themselves influence their learning?
- Whether students favor one sensory modality over another?
- If their teaching style matches the learning style of all their students and, if not, what the best ways to adapt to these differences in style are?

As with most rhetorical questions, the answer is yes. And for each question, some of the answer can be found by exploring learning styles.

THE PIONEERS

In the past decade, much research in music education has focused on teaching and learning styles. This research has largely built upon theories promulgated in the late 1970s, which described individual preferences and differences in human learning. Two prominent theories were David A. Kolb's "Experiential Learning Theory" and Carl Jung's "Theory of Psychological Types." (Malcom J. Tait's book, *Teaching Strategies and Styles* followed a few decades later, but continued in a similar direction.)

Kolb's model identified perception and processing as distinct learning activities, each with its own subcategories. He theorized that events could be perceived through the senses – concrete experiences – or though mental or visual conceptualization – abstract experiences. The processing dimensions are fourfold: concrete experience, reflective observation, abstract conceptualization, and active experimentation.

Jung considered the two dimensions of thinking to be perception and judgment. Within those dimensions are two subcategories. For perception they are sensing and intuition; for judgment they are thinking and feeling. Upon this foundation, four dominant learning styles are identified: sensing-thinking, sensing-feeling, intuitive-thinking, and intuitive-feeling. It is this terminology that has been carried into the work of other researchers.

BROAD-BASED RESEARCH

Initial research on learning styles was focused primarily on the at-risk learner in the classroom. For example, researchers Natter and Rollins, in their 1974 study, ascertained that sensing-thinking tended to be the predominant style of leaders of government, business, and schools. They also found that 99.6 percent of those students dropping out of high school were sensing-feelers.[1]

Sensing-feelers as a group rank second highest on the Longeot Test of Reasoning, which measures levels of intelligence within the theoretical context of Jean Piaget's work. In marked contrast, they tend to score poorly on such standard measures of achievement as the California Achievement Test. On these more traditional tests, geared to memory and algorithmic skills, sensing-thinking and intuitive-thinking learners tend to score higher. Perhaps this reflects the nature of the objective test and its appropriateness for the sensing or intuitive-thinker, who tends to have a more objective impersonal response to externally imposed situations such as achievement tests.

Sensing-thinking and intuitive-thinking learners were also found to adapt well to traditional learning styles. They demonstrated that they knew how to ask the 'who, what, when, and where' questions, which enabled them to do their work correctly; they cared about getting good grades. Their teachers and leaders at school tended to have a relatively authoritarian approach, stressing drill, repetition, effort, and fundamental skills.

Of the intuitors, intuitive-thinkers were found to be the most academically advanced. Researchers Myers and McCaulley used a group of merit scholarship winners as evidence: 83.5 percent of merit-scholarship winners were found to be intuitives, with the thinkers being the more successful students.[2]

The intuitive-feelers, the highest scorers on the Longeot Test of Reasoning, were found to be academically weaker than their thinking counterparts, making them an at-risk group. Interestingly, this is not because they could not do their academic work. Rather, they did not feel challenged by the curricula, and needed to find different ways of learning successfully. Hanson, Silver, and Strong report that John Lennon was just such an intuitive-feeler. He wrote the following about his alienation at school:

> ...I always wondered...Why has nobody discovered me? Didn't they see that I was more clever than anybody in school? That the teachers are stupid too? That all they had was information that I didn't need? It was obvious to me. Why didn't they train me...Why didn't anybody notice me?[3]

---

[1]F. Natter and S. Rollins, eds. *The Governor's Task Force on Disruptive Youth: Phase II Report* (Tallahassee, Florida: Office of the Governor, 1974).

[2]Mary McCaulley, Majors of study selected by the 1972 Class of the University of Florida, Gainsville, Florida, Center for the Application of Psychological Types, 1975.

[3]J. Robert Hanson, Harvey F. Silver, and Richard W. Strong, "Learning Styles of At-Risk Students" *Music Educators' Journal* (November, 1991): 84.

Authors Hanson, Silver, and Strong point out the appropriateness of the study of music and other arts, for they speak more directly to the emotions of feeling-oriented students. The arts involve the student in a more subjective world. The authors hypothesize that there is greater likelihood that music teachers may understand those students and share the learning styles of the sensing-feelers. (It will be interesting to see if continuing research on the learning styles of music teachers confirms this theory.)

KEITH GOLAY – FOUR TYPES OF LEARNERS

One contributor to the body of early study who was not mentioned previously is David Keirsey. He linked the nature of personality to distinct types of learners, resulting in four distinct temperaments: Dionysian, Epimethean, Promethean, and Apollonian. Keith Golay, whose recent work in this field was discussed at the National Conference on Piano Pedagogy with application to piano students, renamed Keirsey's temperaments to correspond to the learning patterns described above. The result:

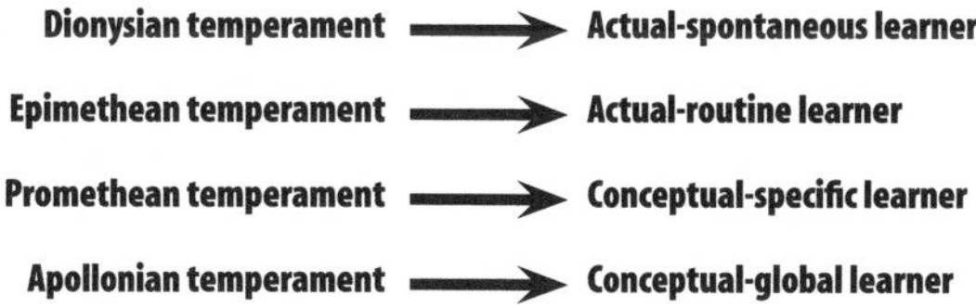

ACTUAL-SPONTANEOUS LEARNER (ASL)

This describes someone less interested in theoretical concepts or abstractions; who prefers to learn by sensing and watching. For this learner, experience is the best teacher. Planning or logic does not motivate the ASL; doing is the motivator. In music, this style might be found in the child who will spend time at the piano picking out tunes, and playing back what the teacher played at the lesson. Learning to read music might be intolerable unless it 'clicks' immediately. Teaching a child to play songs by rote, and deducing how to write it out together so the child can show his or her family how the piece looks might be a way to motivate the ASL to learn to read music.

ACTUAL-ROUTINE LEARNER (ARL)

This student thrives on knowing what is expected for accomplishing a task. Practice steps are a must. Improvising would likely be anxiety producing. Practicing with prescriptions for solving particular technical problems would feel more comfortable to the ARL than would projecting imagery, experimenting with color and voicing, or finding a story in the music. The ARL needs to please the teacher and, in turn, needs to receive praise for specific accomplishments. This student also does well in a group, provided the members are very supportive and give one another approval.

CONCEPTUAL-SPECIFIC LEARNER (CSL)

Golay characterized this learner as "the little scientist." The CSL wants to understand what is behind ideas and looks for answers to the many questions he or she has about people, sounds, the workings of the instrument, and the reasons for articulation, *rubato*, or decisions of tempo. This type of learner is usually a high achiever and always seems interested in self-improvement. Teachers of this type of learner should not overload him or her with too much new music, and should help the CSL to avoid commitment to playing difficult works before being technically prepared to master them. CSLs are usually not very socially aware and may prefer to work alone, rather than play in ensembles.

CONCEPTUAL-GLOBAL LEARNER (CGL)

This type of learner loves to achieve and tends to do well academically. Tending towards perfectionism, this student may often feel that performances are a reflection of self. Therefore a less-than-perfect performance may lead to a loss of self-esteem. On the other hand, the CGL is a fine communicator and enjoys sharing ideas with others, writing well, listening perceptively to others, and will often give inspirational musical performances. Nurturing this student happens easily in a non-competitive environment where it is clear that teachers and peers feel approval and act in a caring way.

In his article on *Four Types of Learners*,[4] Golay cautions educators to put these kinds of descriptions into perspective. Teachers must still apply their knowledge, experience and understanding of a particular child to an assessment of the way that child learns. These classifications are meant to be a helpful tool for observing and investigating the learning patterns of students.

BERNICE MCCARTHY – 4MAT SYSTEM: TEACHING TO LEARNING STYLE WITH RIGHT/LEFT-MODE TECHNIQUES

Recently, Bernice McCarthy combined theories of learning styles (Kolb's Learning Styles Inventory in particular) with the philosophies of teaching toward the right and left brain to formulate the 4MAT System for Teaching, Learning and Leadership.[5] Similar in structure to Golay's portraits describing learning patterns, McCarthy proposes the following four learning styles:

IMAGINATIVE LEARNERS

Working together, sharing ideas, and connecting with their music teacher are enjoyable for these learners. In the music class they will volunteer to play for the class and participate enthusiastically in singing activities, or music games. As piano students, they enjoy performing in accompanying, ensemble, and studio performance class.

ANALYTIC LEARNERS

These learners enjoy working by themselves and are usually well-organized, using time wisely, having good habits for study and practice, and performing well on listening tests, sight reading, multiple choice exams, and research projects. They prefer to watch their friends rather than participate themselves in musical games or group activities. They practice well on their own, but may become anxious under the pressure of solo or collaborative performance and even consider quitting piano lessons rather than be forced to play in a recital.

COMMON-SENSE LEARNERS

Common-sense learners enjoy solving problems, discovering how things work, and giving hands-on applications to new concepts. In their musical environments they are easily frustrated with ideas that do not seem to affect their performances. For example, these learners might find doing four-part harmony

---

[4]Keith Golay, "Four Types of Learners" *Keyboard Arts* (Spring, 1988): 3-7.

[5]Bernice McCarthy, *4MAT Coursebook I: Fundamental Training* (Barrington, Illinois: Excel, Inc., 1999).

exercises in theory class totally irrelevant despite loving to practice Baroque keyboard compositions. They enjoy asking their private teachers questions, applying their experiences in the studio to other musical experiences. They are often the students who keep playing the piano in the piano lab when the teacher would like the class to listen to instructions for the next activity.

DYNAMIC LEARNERS

These learners love to take risks and find new ways to learn things. They enjoy experimenting and working on their own, and often feel comfortable improvising and composing. They may not seem to use logical or organized approaches to practicing or studying, and do not want to establish set routines for either. They tend to rely on more intuitive processes that involve analysis and reflecting on their own experiences. They typically excel in performance, improvisation, and composition. They are the students who will arrange their Haydn sonatina for horn, violin, and bassoon on their keyboard synthesizer, write their own cadenza for a Mozart concerto, or add melodic ornamentation to the Bach works they are studying.

McCarthy's 4MAT System has found considerable favor among music educators, in large part because the four learning styles she puts forth "embody the comprehensive nature of music education...In a typical classroom or studio we often find students who perform comfortably in one or more of the areas."[6] Consider the following musical attributes:

- Innovative thinking – that which is required for the expression of artistry, whether as a solo player making sense of the musical score or as an ensemble player working with others to create an artistic experience.
- Analysis – the way in which students learn to read, write, listen to, and evaluate music.
- Common sense – the way in which students relate or integrate music with other arts or disciplines.
- Dynamism – that quality in music which is alive, to which we connect and then project to others.

(Several informal ways of assessing the learning styles of students and teachers, as well as descriptions of practical scenarios to introduce readers to each of these styles through fictitious students are presented in the Tanner and Stutes article cited above.)

FRANK ABRAHAMS – A LEARNING-STYLES APPROACH FOR AT-RISK STUDENTS

From the perspective of musicians and music educators, the most on-point research comes from Frank Abrahams. Using the goals of the general music classroom, he illustrates how a learning-styles approach can help all students become involved in music activities, bringing both "strengths as well as vulnerabilities to the classroom."[7]

---

[6]Donald Tanner and Ann B. Stutes, "Teaching With a Practical Focus: Developing Learning Styles Awareness," *American Music Teacher* (August/September, 1997) 20.

[7]Frank Abrahams, "A Learning-Styles Approach for At-Risk Students," *General Music Today* (Fall, 1992): 22.

He gives an example based on McCarthy's instructional model to show how teachers might encourage middle-school students to make judgments about the music they listen to. Each learning style, along with an example for right-mode and left-mode processing, includes an objective, an activity, and an evaluation. In one of Abraham's examples, an objective in the imaginative learning style, right mode, might be to have an unfamiliar 'sonic' listening experience. The activity would involve student teams listening to Subotnick's The Wild Bull. They would then spend fifteen minutes organizing their arguments for a debate on the question "Is this music?" The evaluation consists of hearing the class reaction to the recording and the quality of the presentations made by the student teams.

In the article, as well as in his book, *Case Studies in Music Education*, Abrahams uses the McCarthy 4MAT System categories discussed earlier for learning styles as the basis for his teaching models. He incorporates McCarthy's interest in hemispheric thinking by giving suggestions for engaging each learning style through both right and left modes. He reiterates McCarthy's urging to teach to the learning style of the student, but also urges teachers to help stretch the student's ability to learn by providing each individual with learning opportunities outside of their preferred style and hemisphere type.

In faculty development workshops given at Westminster Choir College of Rider University, Abrahams asks teachers to consider several important questions, including:

- Is my teaching authentic?
- Does it promote substantive conversation?
- Do I, focus on the depth of knowledge rather than breadth?
- Promote higher thinking?
- Make connections to the world beyond the classroom?
- Provide students with support when they achieve?
- Engage a variety of learning types and honor multiple aptitudes/intelligences?
- Allow students to construct their own meanings?
- Provide multiple assessment strategies?

DIRECT APPLICATION TO PIANO PEDAGOGY

Influenced by McCarthy and Abrahams, colleagues and I helped our pedagogy students design piano lessons that teach to the strengths and weaknesses of particular learning types. Recently my undergraduate pedagogy class spent eight weeks teaching two beginners. It became evident that one was an analyzer, the other a dynamic learner. These students were paired in weekly partner lessons. The dynamic learner always volunteered to play a new piece first, while the analyzer chose to be the listener first, willing to comment on how her partner played specific musical concepts, such as articulations or dynamics. Yet the analyzer was better coordinated and tended to play correctly after waiting her turn, while the dynamic learner would dive in only to find problems with coordination.

The class profited by its perception of the difference in learning styles. Pedagogy students found ways to involve the analyzer by having her suggest preparatory technical activities for the dynamic learner to do before playing a new piece. In turn, he was encouraged to make verbal suggestions or illustrate sounds or topics for improvisation to the analyzer. She enjoyed meeting the challenge by making up a phrase or piece at her piano and did so without hesitation.

When teachers understand the learning preferences of their students they can plan teaching strategies that will accommodate both strengths and weakness.

When teachers understand the learning preferences of their students they can plan teaching strategies that will accommodate both strengths and weakness. It is also important that teachers determine their own learning styles. Clearly, expectations and goals based on the teacher's learning style may not suit every learner. The hope is that better learning can take place when teachers are aware of their own learning styles and those of their students, and can use these differences to expand the possibilities for learning.

There are many self-observation mechanisms for helping both teachers and learners become aware of their learning styles. Among the type indicators showing learning tendencies is the Myers-Briggs Type Indicator (MBTI).[8] Based upon Jung's theory of psychological types, the MBTI measures individual preferences on four bi-polar scales: extraversion or introversion, sensation or intuition, thinking or feeling, and judgment or perception. Another type indicator is McCarthy's Learning Type Measure, which scores the test taker for learning styles consistent with her 4MAT System, described above.

It is important to note that there is no inherent judgment involved in determining a student's learning style. The above-mentioned tests have no high or low score. The outcome is simply information that can sensitize the teacher to various characteristics of students, which can help in fashioning a more effective teaching approach.

SENSORY MODALITIES

In addition to personality and behavioral characteristics that are indicators of learning style, each of us has a preference for concrete, musical perceptions: aural, visual, or kinesthetic. Understanding our preferred sensory modalities for learning music, determining what modalities are favored by each of our students, and being sensitive to the sensory biases in the beginning materials we use can also contribute significantly to the healthy development of our piano students.

For example, if a child is a strong visual learner, will lessons with a Suzuki teacher broaden the learning style or create frustration? A creative teacher in this situation will find ways to encourage the visual preferences while at the same time introducing the beginning student to the aural and kinesthetic experiences that the Suzuki approach advocates. Similarly, can the teacher of a strong aural learner, one who picks out tunes easily and has good coordination, insist on the exclusive use of an interval or landmark approach? While this approach emphasizes sound and feel before symbol, its materials include many pages that present the learner with tunes to be played between the hands, rather than within the hand. The visual recognition of intervals is an important part of its orientation. The teacher who is sensitive to a child with a strong aural/kinesthetic learning style will need to provide opportunities for aural and kinesthetic satisfaction, including learning rote pieces and playing and transposing of tunes within the hand, while taking

[8]Isabel Myers Briggs and Katherine C. Briggs, *MTBI Manual: A guide to the development and use of the Myers-Briggs type indicator*, 3rd ed. (Palo Alto, California: Consulting Psychologists Press, Inc., 1998).

advantage of the strong developmental approach to interval and landmark music reading.

Susan Bruckner has written about the importance of the teacher's understanding of the preferred learning style and sensory modality of the student as a means of creating rapport and matching communication styles. Influenced by studies in neuro-linguistic programming and psychology, she describes the characteristics of each modality and how to identify each type of learner, and gives suggestions for creating rapport between student and teacher. These include mirroring facial expressions, voice and language patterns, using metaphoric language, and becoming aware of the breathing patterns of your students. In the chapter "Increasing the Auditory Modality," Bruckner suggests that students barely touch the keys, making sure to not sound the pitches, of a dramatic passage requiring dynamic control. This "ghost play(ing)"[9] gives students the opportunity to hear that expression of the passage internally. For expanding kinesthetic control, Bruckner asks teachers to suggest that their students "feel their body as being light, heavy, watery, dry, soft, sharp, muscular, prickly, smooth, etc. to interpret a passage. Then imagine that your instrument is made of soft rubber, liquid, a hard rock, a furry rabbit…"[10]

An experience of my own in the area of sensory modality occurred when I developed tendinitis and sought the help of pianist Paula Kessler Hondius. Ms. Hondius pointed out that my music reading was so fast that my physical motions were often uncoordinated; I attempted to play music that I had only seen in the measures ahead, but had not heard yet. Despite years of training with many fine teachers, Ms. Hondius' own fine ability to sight-read and her fascination with coordinating the sensory modalities allowed her to diagnose my problem. An aural and technical retraining period that required consciously hearing and feeling everything I read before playing it immediately solved the tendinitis problem. This new sensory awareness enabled me to listen and play in ways that I had not previously thought possible.

From the theories, studies, and anecdotes described, it is clear that the topic of learning styles is one with enormous implications for improving the quality of both teaching and learning. Although the last decade has seen some decline in the amount of research on cognitive styles, the research on learning styles and their relevance to musical understanding and successful learning and teaching of music has burgeoned. The last fifteen years have seen an increase in the appearance of studies on pianists, their skills, practice habits, teaching methods, use of appropriate piano method books, modality preferences, relationships between musical learning style and non-musical or cognitive learning style, and teacher/student relationships.

SUGGESTIONS FOR FURTHER READING

To learn more about research done in the areas of sensory modalities and music education in general, it will be helpful to consult dissertation databases, RILM Abstracts in Music Literature, ERIC, and IIMP. These sources offer excellent opportunities in print and on-line to survey the literature.

Some of the questions posed at the beginning of this chapter have been widely explored; others are only beginning to be researched. Nevertheless, the potential applications for the healthy learning and teaching of developing pianists seem very rich indeed.

---

[9]Susan Bruckner, *The Whole Musician: A Multi-Sensory Guide to Practice, Performance, and Pedagogy* (Santa Cruz, California: Effey Street Press, 1997) 47.

[10] Ibid., 54.

The Importance of Lesson Environment

Gail Berenson

For students of all ages, learning to play the piano is only one of the benefits of piano study. Along with piano mastery, students can simultaneously develop attitudes and beliefs about music, learning, and themselves. And while musical potential will differ widely between students, depending on their talent and their interest, there are meaningful goals that are realistic and applicable to all students:

- The cultivation of an appreciation and love of music
- A satisfaction in learning new concepts and an excitement about problem solving
- The desire to do one's best
- A joy for learning

By encouraging an intrinsic reward system, best accomplished within a nurturing, non-threatening environment, many obstacles to learning are removed. Students become free to explore and challenge themselves, striving to achieve their true potential.

Establishing an environment of trust is paramount in providing a productive learning environment and forging a teacher/student team approach is one of the major contributors to it. When students adopt high standards as their own, it is often because the teacher believes that the students can succeed. This in turn encourages the students to work hard so that they may validate that belief. The realization that the teacher is on their side also offers the kind of support that helps motivate students to work even harder to reach their goals.

It is also important to address some of the students' fundamental psychological needs. When we do this, we can help them achieve a love of music, joy in music making, and a physical ease at the instrument.

ACCEPTANCE

A student's feeling of acceptance by the teacher must never be at risk. Students must feel that the teacher cares about them as individuals. Even though a teacher may not be pleased with a student's performance or behavior, the student should always know that he or she is accepted and respected as a individual. When students feel that their acceptance is not in jeopardy, they are more likely to experiment and risk undertaking a challenge. They are also more likely to feel good about their lessons and be motivated to practice.

SELF-ESTEEM

With the student and teacher working together as a team, self-consciousness and the likelihood of defensiveness is reduced. While lessons provide ongoing opportunities to build student's self-esteem, they may also be full of pitfalls. For example, always avoid making verbal comparisons about one student to another. Students feel insecure enough about their abilities without teachers belittling them.

SUCCESS

Honest feedback from a teacher is crucial.

Honest feedback from a teacher is crucial. Although students want to hear that they have done well, they know when they have not, and will distrust the teacher if positive comments are forthcoming when they do not deserve them. Teachers need to differentiate between rewarding effort and praising product. Feedback is most beneficial if it builds on the efforts of the student and recognizes the hard work that has brought their performance to its current stage of development, while raising the benchmark and establishing a higher performance standard to be reached.

INDEPENDENCE

Teachers who encourage students to develop problem-solving skills will also be nurturing their independent thinking. Providing guidelines for decision-making and then assisting students in discovering appropriate solutions will provide autonomy and self-confidence. Teachers must also always ensure that students possess the skills to handle a challenge *before* asking them to tackle it. This will avoid frustration on the part of the student, and ensure their success.

The lesson environment established by the teacher can significantly influence students' perceptions of their lessons, and when we utilize the time to address some of their non-pianistic needs, we can affect their desire to continue their music study and maintain a long-term connection to music and music making.

A Child's First Lessons

Jacqueline Csurgai-Schmitt

"Don't worry about the technique. Just think about the music and the technique will take care of itself." How many times have we, as students and teachers, heard this? Given the huge number of talented pianists who have become injured from playing the piano, we know that this statement is untrue. Technique is developed by a comprehensive and thorough pedagogy, and the order in which these musical and pianistic skills are presented to young children is crucial in determining the lifelong success, or failure, of their musical activities.

TECHNIQUE FOR THE BEGINNING STUDENT

Method books with the title "Piano Technique" abound, and suggest to the teacher that all a student need do to perfect essential physical skills is to study certain finger patterns or exercises. The concentration seems to be on *what* notes the fingers are playing, instead of *how* they are moving.

If there is physical direction at all in these books, it usually takes the form of instructions to pre-set the hand into a rounded shape (apples and oranges come to mind) with all the fingers curved, including the thumb. In truth, the natural form of the hand can be found by dropping the arm to the side of the body. In this position, the bridge is not high, the fingers are not particularly curved, and the thumb (if it has not been trained to curve through a lifetime of piano playing) is straight. To force the hand into an unnatural rounded shape interferes with a successful technique in two ways:

1. The muscles of the hand and fingers must contract to hold this shape, which wastes energy and creates unneeded tension before the student has even moved a finger. (This is especially true of the thumb, where there is no need, in normal piano playing, to curve its distal (nail) joint. In fact, curving this joint actually shortens the length and range of the thumb considerably.)

2. There is a tendency to line up the nails of curved fingers in a

> straight line to the keyboard. As this occurs, the fingers, being of unequal length, will propel the hand knuckles (the fulcrum for finger movement) up for the second and third fingers and down for the fourth and fifth fingers, forcing the fingers to employ different muscular coordinations for each note.

The hand and fingers have no need to preset in any position any more than we need to pre-form the muscles of our feet and ankles before walking on them. Such presetting of muscles can create a state of chronic tension in the hand. It also derails the natural tendency of the fingers, which move most quickly when they are relaxed before a specific action. The hand and fingers, which are brought to the keys by extensors of the forearm, with the upper arm supported at the shoulder, also benefit from remaining relaxed until the actual moment of key depression. Provided the movements of the arm, hand and finger are coordinated, the necessary muscles will immediately contract to support whatever activity is desired.[1]

FORMING THE HABIT OF GOOD COORDINATION

Finding a good coordination of movement is a tricky, and not so obvious, process. As Dr. William Westney has brought to our attention through his "Perils of Perfectionism" workshops,[2] we learn all bodily movements by means of trial and error. Knowing that 'practice makes perfect' bad habits as well as good, we tend to conscientiously focus our students' attention on playing the right notes from the start. While our intentions are good, the results of this strategy can leave the fingers and arms with a large amount of residual tension. Instead, when beginning a new piece, the focus should be on learning the right *movements*, not the right notes. If the appropriate movement is fluid, smooth, and coordinated, the right notes can, and will, be filled in later as the body learns from and adjusts to each movement, refining it until it becomes completely coordinated. Whenever there is tension present in an unrhythmic performance, I ask the student to begin at the start of the piece, playing all the wrong notes with the right rhythm and the right movement. When these two elements are free and correct, it becomes easy to 'fill in' the right notes. (Naturally, I do not allow the student to practice wrong notes in a piece. The above exercise is simply a quick technique for freeing the playing mechanism from the excessive tension that results from trying to play the right notes before coordinated arm and finger movements have been learned.)

LEARNING TENSION-FREE MOVEMENT THROUGH RHYTHM

To see and hear a pianist play who has had the benefit of a Dalcroze Eurthymics education, Kodály or Orff classes, or any listening/moving experiences prior to beginning piano lessons, is to (most typically) see natural, tension-free movement at the piano. I strongly urge all piano teachers to recommend these classes as complements to the beginning piano lessons for those students who have not already taken them. Piano lessons will be more enjoyable, productive and time-efficient, for both you and the student, if learning includes musical, coordinated movement *outside* of the piano lesson.

---

[1]Otto Ortmann, *The Physiological Mechanics of Piano Technique* (New York: E.P. Dutton & Co., inc., 1962) 158. For more information on this subject, also see the chapter, "A Fundamental of Movement."

[2]William Westney, Texas Tech University, Lubbock, Texas.

If the sequence of music study is correct, good technique should be a natural offshoot of the learning process. Beautiful music is much more difficult to create in a body filled with tension, and much of the tension with which pianists play today can be directly traced to their beginning piano lessons and the sequence in which they were taught their pianistic skills.

Unfortunately, the vast majority of methods books we use today direct the child's attention to the learning of notation first (the visual), before the ear has had a chance to develop (the aural). In later years, the pianist must then spend incalculable wasted hours attempting to reverse, repair, and retrain his or her nervous system to the more musical, natural process of hearing first, and then playing. George Kochevitsky suggests that the learning process in traditional piano pedagogy – seeing first → searching for a key → movement → look for next note sign – allows no time for the most crucial part: listening. He suggests that, from the beginning, the piano teacher should try to establish and develop the following:

Hearing first → **Anticipation of action** → **Movement creating sound** → **Auditory perception and evaluation of the actual sound**[3]

Before piano lessons begin, a child can have acquired an extensive music vocabulary by becoming immersed in music in appropriate ways from birth.[4] The child is then able to vocally execute patterns, sing songs, and chant rhythm chants in different tonalities and meters. After music lessons begin, audiation skills become the foundation for the teaching approach.[5] "Audiation is the hearing and comprehending in one's mind the sound of music that is not or may never have been physically present. It is neither imitation nor memorization. There are six stages of audiation and eight types of audiation."[6] Dr. Gordon stresses the need for development of audiation skills and the acquisition of a musical vocabulary before learning to read and write notation. The fact that pianists can actually play, without hearing the music first, is only too apparent in many performances.

> Pattern familiarity, in both the aural (hearing) and oral (speaking or reproducing) sense, is necessary for students to understand music. When music patterns are familiar, there is less tension in performing and more joy and interest in the learning process. Functional tonal patterns are taught within the context of a tonality, and functional rhythm patterns are taught within the context of a meter.
>
> In addition to learning audiation skills through pattern instruction, audiation skills are taught through movement activities, creating and improvising, and singing. Movement activities are important for developing rhythm and beat competency, while

---

[3]George Kochevitsky, *The Art of Piano Playing* (Evanston, Illinois: Summy-Birchard Co., 1967) 30.

[4]Edwin E. Gordon, *A Music Learning Theory for Newborn and Young Children* (Chicago: GIA Publications, Inc., 1997).

[5]Marilyn White Lowe, music teacher, Springfield, Missouri.

[6]Edwin E. Gordon, *Learning Sequences in Music* (Chicago: GIA Publications, Inc., 1997).

> singing develops tonal audiation. Teaching all of this through a large variety of games and activities makes a fun-filled lesson, and the keyboard becomes a friend. Physical tension is released through musical understanding and creative activities.[7]

Why do teachers have problems getting students, who would readily go to sports practice every day, to practice the piano? Is playing the piano not as much fun as playing a sport? And if that is so, why is it perceived by the student as less fun? Piano playing should have no problem competing with sports; after all, both are considered 'playing' and both require a similar honing of physical skills, which, for a young child, is inherently enjoyable. I believe the problem stems from the sequencing of the skills.

For most of the twentieth century, we have all used the same method books, which present the young child with a mountain of material – reading, counting, rhythm, technique, theory, music writing, history, etc. – that will surely overwhelm all but the most persistent and gifted students. In the process, we have managed to take all of the 'play' out of playing the piano.

We have managed to take all of the 'play' out of playing the piano.

> Why should beginners have to count out loud first, if they can more easily be taught to feel the beat internally?
>
> Why do we insist on having them read first when they can play so much more easily and freely by ear?

We have all heard the tragic stories of adults, who after years of piano lessons cannot play a note. They are our mistakes and our responsibilities. If they had been taught to hear first, and to play what they heard, they would have learned a pianistic skill that would have lasted a lifetime.

PRELIMINARY MOVEMENT

Before sitting down to the piano, it is a good idea to warm up the large muscles of the body in preparation for the coming activity. This is particularly important for students, who will have typically spent much of the day prior to their piano lessons sitting and writing, and accumulating a great deal of tension. The teacher can benefit also from getting up at the beginning of each lesson, stretching and moving to release accumulated tension. If the teacher's customary teaching position is to one side of the student's piano, his or her body will have been twisted in that direction, and will welcome the opportunity to move in a different direction. Maintaining that same, twisted position for most of the teaching day will cause muscles to retain uneven muscular tension that can easily be released by standing up and stretching in the opposite direction.

Exercise

- Stand with plenty of room around you, feet slightly apart.
- Gently rotate your torso to left and right, allowing the arms to swing from the shoulders.

  (While warming up is important to the body's muscles to function smoothly, stretching *after* any activity is equally (if not more) necessary.[8])

[7]Marilyn White Lowe has developed piano materials, based on Dr. Gordon's work, which easily take the student from hearing, to playing, to reading.

THE LEARNING PROCESS

"Practicing is, first and foremost, a psychic process, the working over of accumulated bodily experiences and the adjustment to a definite purpose."[9] It is the constant adjusting in the central nervous system to the proprioceptive stimulus received from the periphery that allows our movements to become coordinated. When a new movement is being learned, excitation of cells in the brain tends to spread, or irradiate, and involve cells not necessary to the motor process. With repetition, the excited area in the brain becomes more and more narrow, resulting in fewer and fewer muscle cells that are also being activated to accomplish the task. A coordinated movement, therefore, is a learned act that becomes easier and easier as we repeat and allow the body to make the necessary muscular and skeletal adjustments to refine a given motion.[10]

Repetition, therefore, is crucial to the learning of the movements and gestures the body and arms use in piano playing. Just as tennis students practice the forehand and backhand strokes before trying them with the ball, the young pianist can become comfortable first with the arm movements to be used in a piece. While a large arm movement can be learned and used very quickly, these movements usually require time and repetition to become truly coordinated muscularly.[11]

HEIGHT OF THE BENCH

As the student approaches the keyboard, the height of the bench becomes critical, particularly for the young child. Many teachers allow all of their students to sit on the same unadjustable bench, regardless of the child's age or size. This has the effect of forcing piano students into make new adjustments every time they move to a different piano, a situation that adversely affects accuracy and muscular efficiency. Imagine the inaccuracy of the playing of young violinists if they had to hold their instrument in a different position every time they played! Changing the center of balance and movement every time one plays a different piano interferes with the successful training of the central nervous system in the intricate and complex movements necessary for piano playing. Another concern is that the feet of most children do not reach the floor while sitting on the bench, leaving them without support for the body. Footrests greatly aid balance and movement around the keyboard.

Piano benches tend to be too high for all but the youngest and smallest of students. Looking for a lifted arm that is level and parallel to the keybed, check each student and adjust the bench accordingly.[12] For those teachers without an adjustable concert bench, try a collection of telephone books of various sizes in tandem with a low bench. As a student grows, a chair, with the telephone books added, may be substituted for the exact height. It is also important to make parents aware of the need to provide a bench of the appropriate height for the student at home.

---

[8]See the chapter, "Pushing the Physiological Envelope" for more information on this indispensable pianistic activity.

[9]Kochevitsky, *The Art of Piano Playing,* 13.

[10]Ibid., 26.

[11]For a catalogue of movements used in keyboard performance, see Seymour Fink, *Mastering Piano Technique* (Portland, Oregon: Amadeus Press, 1994).

[12]Many pedagogues suggest that the arm should be supported at the shoulder so that the forearm is level with the top of the keys. The position suggested above, with the arm level to the keybed, is discussed later.

SUPPORTING AT THE SHOULDER

There is some controversy over whether the pianist should let his or her arms hang from the shoulders, elbows by the side of the body, or whether there should be some lift of the arms involved. The main drawback to the relaxed, hanging arm is that, in this position, the hands cannot begin to approach a horizontal position in relation to the keyboard. Instead, the knuckles slope away toward the outside of the hand, leaving the fingers at a 45-degree angle to key descent. Even with maximum forearm pronation, which causes extreme tension in the wrist and arm, the hand cannot place the fingers in a vertical line to key descent.

To attempt to play the piano with the fingers in this position can do damage to the shape and functioning of the fingers; it is the anatomical equivalent of walking on the sides of your ankles. This position makes the playing of the fourth and fifth fingers difficult, as the tendency is not to move the fifth finger off the hand knuckle, but to move the whole outer side of the hand, including the knuckle, down for key depression. By allowing this poor coordination to persist, the student will continue to struggle with the fifth finger, as practice will not change the basic incoordination.[13] In a worst-case scenario, the pianist may suffer serious, physical damage and difficult retraining at some point in his or her career.[14]

The arms can be lifted to bring the fingers into a more vertical position to key descent. Also, the inertia of the hanging weight of the arm can be difficult to overcome without excessive muscular work. By supporting the weight at the shoulder, the arm is poised to move in any direction, quickly, with any amount of force.

Exercise

- Sit up straight with the shoulders relaxed downwards.
- Keeping the top of the shoulders from moving upward, slowly swing the elbows out to the side and bring them back.
- Move the elbows only so far as is necessary, approximately 20 degrees, to bring the fingers into a more vertical playing position.

TWO ROLES OF THE FINGER

The finger can be used for two purposes in piano playing:

1. In a supporting role as the end of a larger playing unit such as the arm.
2. As an active lever moving off a base supplied by the hand and forearm.

Since we all know that a small child has more control over the larger muscles of the body than they do over the smaller muscles, it would seem logical to start the child at the piano with the larger movements of the arm. In spite of this, many methods books begin the first lessons with adjacent and alternating finger move-

---

[13]I use the word incoordination from a lifetime of familiarity with Otto Ortmann's work. I refer you to his chapter on Coordination and Incoordination in *The Physiological Mechanics of Piano Technique*.

[14]For an expanded discussion of this issue, see the section Problems Resulting from Inefficient Alignment in "The Pianist's Physiology."

ments. These finger movements are the most muscularly complex actions that an adult pianist will ever be called upon to perform. To begin a child's first lessons with these difficult coordinations can tension in the fingers that will remain for the rest of the student's life.

The coordination of an individual finger supporting a movement of the arm is easier to teach and to learn, and, if presented in this manner, the finger understands how to support the larger playing unit *before* it is asked to actually move independently into the resistance of the key. Start by arranging the bench height so that the forearm, when lifted slightly outwards, is level with the keybed. I have found that students usually have more difficulty learning this coordination when the arm is parallel to the top of the key, as they are more likely to push the higher arm into the keys rather than allowing it to move downward in a relaxed way. As the keybed is the goal or distance of the arm movement, the student will find the movement easier if the arm has already experienced this level and the distance to which it needs to return.

This becomes even more important when the student is learning to set the base for finger movement. A slightly lower arm will not be as likely to be displaced upwards during finger movement, thereby making the coordination of finger muscles and the muscular exertion of the arm supplying the base an easier accomplishment. Once the coordination of finger and arm has been learned, the pianist can change the arm level to suit individual style.[15]

ARM MOVEMENT

Exercise

- Lift the arm slightly as described in the previous exercise. Place hands on the keyboard. With the weight of the arm supported at the shoulder and the weight of the forearm supported by the upper arm, the joints of the wrist, hand knuckles and fingers can be loose and relaxed.

- Decide which finger will be supporting the movement, and allow the arm to move downward into the keys. If the arm is already at the level of the keybed, a slight movement up to the top of the keys is necessary before making the downward movement.

- As the small finger muscles and the flexor tendons will automatically contract to support the arm movement, the pianist does not need to consciously think of contracting muscles. The pianist's intention is enough, because, if he or she does not properly contract, key depression will not take place. The pianist's attention should be on doing the *least amount* possible to accomplish the given task. Move the arm upward out of the keys. Be aware of an immediate relaxation in the muscles of the fingers and forearm.

[15]For a more in-depth discussion of the need to supply a base for finger movement, please see, "A Fundamental of Movement."

This coordination involves only a very small movement of the arm from the level of the top of the keys to the level of the keybed, and, if done properly, it will feel as if no muscles are contracting at all. Do *not* think of releasing weight from the shoulder. Continue supporting the weight of the arm at the shoulder. This is only an arm *movement,* not weight release.

Keep in mind:

- The finger needs to become familiar with the feeling of the *least amount* of muscular contraction that can support a movement of the arm and that does *not* release weight into the keys.
- The supporting muscles, the small finger muscles, and the hand and finger flexors must contract at the moment of key resistance, not before, and release immediately when the arm lifts the finger out of the key. The timing of these contractions and releases is critical.[16]

Checklist:

- ❑ The wrist joint and the hand knuckles must be as relaxed as possible during key descent and while the key is held down.
- ❑ If no weight has been released from the shoulder, the arm will feel as if it is floating in the air.
- ❑ If the finger is holding the key down with the least amount of effort, the arm should be able to be easily moved around by both the teacher and the student.

The muscular contractions necessary to hold down a key are minimal, yet, even these contractions may not release quickly enough when the key is released. The student must learn how to release these muscles immediately upon letting the key go.[17] I usually have the student lift the arm away from the keyboard and place it in the lap in one fluid motion. This encourages any residual tension to release. Stay with this phase of the learning process until all the parts of the movement have had the necessary time to be completely coordinated by the body. I would suggest repeating the down-and-up movement with a single finger until the student is comfortable with that finger. Then proceed to another finger.

LATERAL ADJUSTMENT FOR EACH FINGER

When another finger is attempting the down-up exercise previously described, it will be necessary to adjust the alignment of the skeleton behind the new finger. This can be done very simply by asking the student to move the arm slightly sideways until it feels as if the arm is in a straight line with the finger.

Exercise

- Press the finger into a hard surface, such as the fallboard. If all muscles are relaxed except those supporting the pressure, the bones will straighten automatically along the path of least

[16]Ortmann, *The Physiological Mechanics of Piano Technique*, 156.
[17]Ibid., 120.

resistance, the straight line of muscle pull. The finger bones and the bones of the hand should create a straight line with the forearm.[18]

- As you release one finger and press down on another finger, notice the sideways adjustments the arm makes to realign itself. (Pressure is used here only to demonstrate optimal skeletal alignment; pressure, at this stage, is not to be used at the keyboard.)
- When applying this principle of alignment to the keyboard, notice that the width of the piano key will cause a much larger sideways movement for the arm.

Have the student move the arm in its down-up movement, using one finger at a time, at different speeds (from slow, smooth movements to quick, short movements) until he or she is comfortable with the lateral adjustments necessary to support each finger. Remember to look for the instantaneous release of muscular tension. The student should try different dynamic ranges until the various movements and the sounds they create are firmly coordinated in the body and the ear for each individual finger.

LATERAL ARM MOVEMENT

Many of the students who were taught using a traditional five-finger position and the use of consecutive fingers during their first lessons usually have some difficulty moving the arm sideways when the reach of a sixth or larger is demanded. The tendency, invariably, is to keep the arm still and try to reach out for the interval with the fifth finger. By starting lessons with movements of the arm sideways using a single finger, we can circumvent this problem entirely.

Exercise

- Using the same finger, such as the third, play adjacent notes in a scale pattern. Move the arm down, then up, then sideways in three distinct movements, watching for any extraneous tension.

There are several advantages to starting with stepwise patterns played with the arm and using one finger only:

1. The body learns to move the arm first to place the hand and fingers where they need to play on the keyboard, instead of fingers learning to reach for the keys while dragging the arm along.
2. The arm learns to make the necessary sideways adjustments to supply a base for finger movement.
3. The stepwise patterns are learned by the mind, the ear, and the whole arm. A necessary process for later playing of scales in octaves.

---

[18]See the chapter, "The Pianist's Physiology" for more information on skeletal alignment.

4. When the fingers finally get an opportunity to move consecutively, it will be in the habit of moving with the least amount of effort, as the arm makes lateral adjustments for each finger. By keeping the tension out of the finger movement from the beginning, the student is more likely to be able to attain virtuoso speeds.

When the movement is comfortable and there is no tension prior to, during, or after it, try moving from the bottom of one key to the bottom of the next in one continuous, smooth motion. Freedom of arm movements is the key to freedom of finger movements. During this exercise, change fingers until each finger is comfortable supporting the arm immediately when called upon to play.

Naturally, this arm movement using a single finger should proceed through many intervalic patterns all over the keyboard. This will produce great confidence in the student as the arm learns the lateral distances needed to support the hand and finger properly. By working with students whose eyes are closed, their arms can better learn these spatial distances kinesthetically. Strangely enough, you will find that the students tend to be much less tense and move in a more coordinated manner when they are not looking at their hands and fingers!

Knowing in the body – knowing where the notes are and how to produce them – creates not only a tension-free movement, but forms the basis for reliability and security in performance.

Direct the students' attention to the kinesthetic *feel* of the movement. The importance of repetition here cannot be overstated. The arm will feel very uncomfortable when it first begins to move in larger intervals. I tell the students that this feeling of 'uncomfortableness' is simply the body telling them that it does not yet know *where* it is going. They must repeat the movement until, suddenly, they *know,* by a feeling in the body, exactly what the distance is, where the notes are, and that they have confidence in their ability to repeat the movement on demand. This type of *knowing* in the body – knowing where the notes are and how to produce them – creates not only a tension-free movement, but forms the basis for reliability and security in performance.

This coordination of a finger supporting a larger movement of the arm can be applied to any method book whose beginning pieces start with a stepwise progression using adjacent fingers. Simply play the pieces using the whole arm and one finger. When the student is comfortable with a single finger supporting the movement of the arm, you may have them try an individual finger movement.

FINGER MOVEMENT

Finger movement is one of the least understood aspects of piano technique.[19] If one starts a finger movement with a gentle *pianissimo* (where the least amount of muscular energy expended) the finger will learn a smooth, coordinated and tension-free movement. After this is perfected, louder and stronger movements can be added without excessive tension, as the student will continually strive for a coordinated movement, even at the loudest dynamic ranges.

Exercise

- Using the arm movement learned above, move the arm, supported by the finger, into the key several times.

[19]See the chapter, "A Fundamental of Movement," for the physiological necessity of supplying a stable base for finger movement.

- Now, stop the arm at the bottom of the keybed and, after allowing the finger to rise up to the top of the key, gently move it back down to the bottom of the keybed. This should not be a strenuous movement either up or down.
- Move the finger, as quietly as possible, up and down several times with the arm at the level of the keybed, making sure the hand knuckle and the wrist are as loose as possible.

Since the previous exercises have accustomed the arm to taking the finger down to the level that it must reach to sound a note, it will be support for the finger to move with the least amount of effort against the resistance of the key. Bring the student's attention to the slight flexion in the finger as the arm descends. There must be movement in the finger off the hand knuckle; otherwise, it is no longer a finger movement, but an arm movement. This movement downward in the finger should occur simultaneously with the downward movement in the arm.

CONSECUTIVE FINGER MOVEMENT

Finger movements using adjacent fingers are complicated muscular coordinations. As one finger is moving down into a key, the adjacent finger will be lifting out of a key, involving both flexors and extensors simultaneously.[20] The great amount of tension usually associated with this movement in young children will be diminished if the above steps have first been followed. Small children beginning piano lessons will be using the long finger tendons to play the piano, as the small finger muscles will not yet be fully developed. If the arm has first been taught to be a base for the finger work, the long flexors will not be overworked. Even though the speed with which these tendons can alternately contract and relax efficiently is limited because of their lengths, this speed is usually acceptable for most young children's repertoire.

A non-*legato* approach to the learning of this coordination works well, as it helps the arm to make the adjustments needed for each individual finger.

Exercise

- Use the same arm movement for each note. But instead of using the same finger for a series of notes, substitute different fingers, such as 1 2 3 4 5 4 3 2 1.
- Move the arm down, then up, releasing the key, then sideways in three distinct movements, making sure the arm is aligned behind each finger. Do not connect the notes.

These large up-and-down movements of the arm, combined with the use of the long finger tendons supporting these movements for each note, are the easiest way for young children to depress the keys of a piano. It is the natural coordination their bodies will choose if left to their own devices. At this stage, do not be too eager to interfere with this natural up-and-down coordination in the interests of attaining a smooth *legato* line. A young child can actually control and make a more beautiful sound using their whole arm, as long as they are not 'thumping'

---

[20]These opposing forces are described in more detail in Muscle Activity in Piano Playing in the chapter, "The Pianist's Physiology."

with the arm (dropping the weight into the keys). By not insisting on a *legato* at this stage, the student can be made more aware of the need for an immediate muscular release after a key has been played. He or she can also more easily experience the individual aspects of the total coordination.

During this process, teachers should always:

- Check for tension in the wrist and the hand knuckles
- Ask for the least amount of energy possible for a given dynamic level

When the feeling of a perfectly balanced and simultaneous finger and arm movement is comfortable, the student can then connect the notes between the fingers, while still moving the arm up and down to keep tension from creeping into the bridge and wrist.

It will take much more time and experience for the student to learn how to make a beautiful sound with the finger while the arm remains still. I believe in allowing the student's arm to move up and down for every key depression, until there appears to be no tension in the movement at all. When the student has experienced the freedom and looseness of the hand knuckles and wrist for every finger movement, including the thumb, he or she may make smaller and smaller movements with the arm until no 'down' motion is visible except for the first note of a group. The student will already have the crucial and indispensable feeling that the arm is behind every finger movement. And, whenever tension creeps into the playing from a more 'quiet' hand and arm, the teacher can have the student revert to the down movement with the arm until the tension leaves. It is the arm support that gives the finger its freedom to move easily, and it requires time and repetition to refine these movements until the least amount of energy is expended.

USE OF THE SMALL FINGER MUSCLES

For the very young child, the use of the small finger muscles to depress piano keys is not an option; he or she will naturally use the long flexors and extensors for key movement. After the early years, when the child is ready to play his or her first sonatina or attempt any rapid finger work, it is time to move to a different muscle coordination using the small finger muscles, assisted by the long tendons and supported by the base of the arm.[21] If the student fails to learn this new coordination, he or she will continue to use the long flexors and extensors for rapid finger passages, overworking these muscles and guaranteeing that the higher virtuoso speeds will never be attained. In addition to not being able to play fast with ease and comfort, the inability on the student's part to make this transition from one coordination to another can result in eventual disablement through tendinitis, chronic tension/spasm, nerve entrapments, including carpal tunnel syndrome, and a host of other debilitating ailments.

ROTATION OF THE FINGERS

There are other aspects of the hand and fingers of which pianists and teachers should be aware. For example, when the *opponens pollicis* in the thumb and the *opponens digiti minimi* in the fifth finger contract, they pull the fifth-finger hand knuckle toward the thumb. This muscular coordination is wonderful when trying

---

[21]See The Pedagogy of Stabilizing the Base in "A Fundamental of Movement."

to grip an object. It is not, however, very helpful at the piano.[22]

Because of the constant, everyday use in opposing the thumb, the fingers develop a normal muscle tone that naturally tends to rotate them outward, creating a 45-degree angle to vertical key descent. If the fourth and fifth fingers are allowed to stay in this outward rotation when attempting to depress a key, one of two incoordinations may result:

1. The student will depress the key through an *increase* in the rotation of the finger rather than a flexion off the hand knuckle.
2. The student will force the hand knuckle itself up and down for key descent.

The first can eventually cause pain, dysfunction and deformity in the fourth and fifth fingers. The second will most definitely limit the speed at which the student can play.

The following exercise is helpful in straightening the skeletal alignment and muscular rotation of the finger:

Exercise

- Press the second finger of the right hand into a hard surface.
- Keeping the fingertip in the same place, rotate the finger to the right (allow it to fall over in a 45-degree angle to the surface). Notice the angle and curvature that are formed. Notice how the arm and shoulder slide sideways toward the body because the finger can no longer easily support the pressure.
- Rotate the finger back to the left. Notice how the bones line up from the fingertip all the way to the shoulder.

This skeletal position of the finger is stronger and will more easily support any movement of the arm, loud or soft. The muscles will be pulling in a straight line, allowing the fingers to move more quickly and easily off the hand knuckles and automatically increasing the speed and endurance of the fingers. As the small finger muscles (which naturally pull in this alignment) are developed, the fingers will hold a more vertical shape through muscle tone, and a naturally developed hand, that has both strength and agility, will result.

IN SUMMARY

A child's first encounter with piano lessons will determine his or her lifelong relationship with the instrument; whether it will be one of ease, freedom, and joy, or one of tension, pain and struggle. The piano teacher has a major role in the results and, therefore, an enormous responsibility to help the student develop in a way that does no physical harm. Thankfully, the steps necessary to insure the young child's success at the piano are fairly straightforward:

- The sequencing of musical and pianistic skills is vital to the success of the student. Just as we learn to read our native lan-

[22]For a complete discussion of this subject, see "The Pianist's Physiology," Problems Resulting from Inefficient Alignment.

guage only after we have learned to speak it, we should teach our students to read the musical language only after they have learned to hear, sing, and play it.

- The joy of music, and making music at the piano, takes precedence over everything. A practice session at the piano should be at least as fun as a football practice.
- Teach the student how to care for his or her body by warming up with exercises and warming down with stretching.
- Care about the height of their bench and the students will too.
- Teach the larger arm movements first which form the foundation for the smaller, finger movements and your students will be more likely to develop a proficient and skillful technique for playing the piano.

Bibliography

THE MECHANICAL

Breithaupht, Rudolph. *Die Natürliche Klaviertechnik.* Leipzig: Kahnt, 1906.

Couperin, François. *L'art toucher le Clavecin.* Wiesbaden: Breitkopf and Hartel, 1961.

Deppe, Ludwig. *Arm Ailments of the Pianist. n.p.*, 1885.

Gát, József. *The Technique of Piano Playing.* London: Collet's, 1965.

Hess, Myra. Preface to *The Visible and the Invisible in Pianoforte Technique,* by Tobias Matthay. New York: Oxford University Press, 1947.

Kochevitsky, George. *The Art of Piano Playing: A Scientific Approach.* Evanston: Summy-Birchard, Co., 1967.

Le Guerrier, Claire. *The Physical Aspects of Piano Playing.* New York: Vantage Press, 1987.

Matthay, Tobias. *The Visible and the Invisible in Pianoforte Technique.* New York: Oxford University Press, 1947.

Merrick, Frank. *Practicing the Piano.* New York: Denman and Farrell, 1953.

Murray, A. "The Alexander Technique." *Medical Problems of Performing Artists* 1 (1991): 131.

Newman, William S. *The Pianist's Problems.* New York: Da Capo Press, 1984.

Ortmann, Otto. *The Physiological Mechanics of Piano Technique.* New York: E.P. Dutton & Co., Inc., 1962.

Pichier, Paul. *The Pianist's Touch.* Marshall, California: Perelen Publishers, 1972.

Schultz, Arnold. Preface to *The Physiological Mechanics of Piano Technique,* by Otto Ortmann. New York: E.P. Dutton and Co., Inc., 1929.

—. *The Riddle of the Pianist's Finger.* Boston: Carl Fischer, 1936.

Tatz, Shmuel. *The Piano Quarterly* 152 (1990-91): 62.

Whiteside, Abby. *The Pianist's Mechanism.* New York: G. Schirmer, Inc., 1929.

THE HEALTHFUL MIND

Arrien, Angeles. *The Fourfold Way: Walking the Paths of the Warrior, Teacher, Healer, and Visionary*. San Francisco: Harper, 1993.

Beck, Aaron and Steven Emery. *Anxiety Disorders and Phobias: A Cognitive Perspective*. New York: Basic Books, 1985.

Bruckner, Susan. *The Whole Musician: A Multi-Sensory Guide to Practice, Performance and Pedagogy*. Santa Cruz, California: Effey Street Press, 1997.

Buzan, Tony. *Use Both Sides of Your Brain*. New York: E.P. Dutton, 1977.

Csikszentmihalyi, Mihaly. *Finding Flow: The Psychology of Engagement with Everyday Life*. New York: Basic Books, 1997.

Davis, Ph.D., Martha, Elizabeth Robbins Eshelman, M.S.W., and Matthew McKay, Ph.D. *The Relaxation and Stress Reduction Workbook*. Oakland, California: New Harbinger Publications, Inc., 1995.

De Franceso, Charmaine and Kevin L. Burke. "Performance enhancement strategies used in a professional tennis tournament." *International Journal of Sport Psychology* 28, no. 2 (1997): 185-195.

Freymuth, Malva. *Mental Practice and Imagery for Musicians*. Boulder, Colorado: Integrated Musician's Press, 1999.

Gallwey, W. Timothy. *The Inner Game of Tennis*. New York: Random House, 1974.

Gawain, Shakti. *Creative Visualization*. San Rafael, California: New World Library, 1978.

Green, Barry with W. Timothy Gallwey. *The Inner Game of Music*. New York: Doubleday/Anchor Press, 1986.

Green, Barry with Phyllis Alpert Lehrer. *The Inner Game of Music Solo Workbook for Piano*. Chicago: GIA Publications, Inc., 1995.

Greene, Ph.D., Don. *Audition Success: An Olympic Sports Psychologist Teaches Performing Artists How to Win*. New York: ProMind Music, 1998.

Gordon, Edwin E. *Learning Sequences In Music, Skill, Content, And Patterns: A Music Learning Theory*. Chicago: GIA, 1988.

Hamann, Donald L. "An Assessment of Anxiety in Instrumental and Vocal Performances." *Journal of Research in Music Education* 30, no. 2 (1982): 77-90.

Hamann, Donald L. and Martha Sobaje. "Anxiety and the College Musician: A Study of Performance Conditions and Subject Variables." *Psychology of Music* 11 (1983): 37-50.

Hanley, Mary Ann. "Creative Visualization: Antidote to Performance Anxiety?" *The American Music Teacher* (June/July 1982).

Lehrer, Ph.D., Paul M., Nina S. Goldman, Ph.D., and Erik F. Strommen, Ph.D. "A Principal Components Assessment of Performance Anxiety Among Musicians." *Medical Problems of Performing Artists* (1990): 5, 12-18.

O'Conner, Joseph. *Not Pulling Strings.* London: Lambent Books, 1987.

Ostrander, Sheila and Lynn Schroeder, with Nancy Ostrander. *Superlearning.* New York: Delta /The Confucian Press, 1981.

Perl, Fritz. *Gestalt Therapy Verbatim.* Utah: Real People Press, 1969.

Chase, Mildred Portney. *Just Being at the Piano.* Berkeley, California: Creative Arts Book Company, 1985.

Ravizza, Kenneth. "Qualities of the Peak Experience in Sport." *Foundations of Sport Psychology*, ed. John M. Silva and Robert S. Weinberg. Champaign, IL: Human kinetics, 1984) 452-461.

Ristad, Eloise. *The Soprano On Her Head.* Moab, Utah: Real People Press, 1982.

Rosen, Charles. "On Playing the Piano." *The New York Review of Books* XL VI (October 21, 1999): 16.

Salmon, Paul G. and Robert G. Meyer. *Notes from the Green Room: Coping with Stress and Anxiety in Musical Performance.* New York: Lexington Books, 1992.

Shelley, Percy Bysshe, *The Sensitive Plant.* New York: Haskell House, 1972.

Shockley, Rebecca Payne. *Mapping Music: For Faster Learning and Secure Memory, A Guide for Piano Teachers and Students.* Madison, Wisconsin: A-R Editions, 1997.

Sloboda, John A. *The Musical Mind: The Cognitive Psychology of Music.* New York: Oxford University Press, 1985.

BODY

Bennett, Robert M. "Fibrositis/Fibromyalgia Syndrome: Current Issues and Perspectives." *American Journal of Medicine* 81 (1986): 3A.

Gowers, William R. "Lumbago: Its Lessons in Analogues." *British Medical Journal* I (1904): 117-121.

Rosen, Norman B. "Myofascial Pain: The Great Mimicker and Potentiator of Other Diseases in the Performing Artist." *Maryland Medical Journal* 42/3 (March 1993): 261-266.

—. "The Myofascial Pain Syndromes." *Physical Medicine and Rehabilitation Clinics of North America* 4 (1993): 41-63.

—. "Physical Medicine and Rehabilitation Approaches to the Myofascial Pain and Fibromyalgia Syndromes." *Bailliere-Tindall Clinical Rheumatology Series: The Management of the Fibromyalgia and Myofascial Pain Syndromes* 8 (1994): 881-911.

Selye, Hans. *Stress Without Distress.* Philadelphia: Lippincott, 1974.

Simons, David G. and Janet G. Travell. "Myofascial Origins of Low Back Pain." *Postgraduate Medicine* 73 (1983): 66-77.

Travell, Janet G. and Stuart H. Rinzler. "The Myofascial Genesis of Pain." *Postgraduate Medicine* 11 (1952): 425-34.

Travell, Janet G. and David G. Simons. *Myofascial Pain and Dysfunction: The Trigger Point Manual*, 2 vols. Baltimore: Williams & Wilkins, 1983.

Ward, Robert C., John A. Jerome, and John M. Jones, III, eds. *Foundations of Osteopathic Medicines*. Baltimore, Maryland: Williams & Wilkins, 1997.

Yunus, Mohammed, et al. "Primary Fibromyalgia." *American Family Physician* 25 (1982): 115-21.

Yunus, Mohammed, Alphonse T. Masi, et al. "Primary Fibromyalgia (Fibrositis): Clinical Study of 50 Patients with Matched Normal Controls." *Seminars in Arthritis and Rheumatism* 11 (1981): 151-71.

THE PEDAGOGICAL

Abrahams, Frank. "A Learning-Styles Approach for At-Risk Students." *General Music Today* (Fall, 1992): 22.

Briggs, Isabel Myers and Katherine C. Briggs. *MTBI Manual: A guide to the development and use of the Myers-Briggs type indicator*, 3rd ed. Palo Alto, California: Consulting Psychologists Press, Inc., 1998.

Bruckner, Susan. *The Whole Musician: A Multi-Sensory Guide to Practice, Performance, and Pedagogy*. Santa Cruz, California: Effey Street Press, 1997.

Fink, Seymour. *Mastering Piano Technique: A Guide for Students, Teachers, and Performers*. Portland, Oregon: Amadeus Press, 1994.

Freymuth, Malva. *Mental Practice and Imagery for Musicians*. Boulder, Colorado: Integrated Musician's Press, 1999.

Fry, H. J. H. "Overuse syndrome of the upper limb in musicians." *The Medical Journal of Australia* 144 (1986): 182-185.

Gardner, Howard. *Frames of Mind – The Theory of Multiple Intelligences*. Cambridge: BasicBooks, 1993.

Golay, Keith. "Four Types of Learners." *Keyboard Arts* (Spring, 1988): 3-7.

Gordon, Edwin E. *Learning Sequences in Music*. Chicago: GIA Publications, Inc., 1997.

——. *A Music Learning Theory for Newborn and Young Children*. Chicago: GIA Publications, Inc., 1997.

Hanna, Thomas. *Somatics - Reawakening the Mind's Control of Movement, Flexibility, and Health*. Cambridge: Perseus Books, 1988.

Hanson, J. Robert, Harvey F. Silver, and Richard W. Strong. "Learning Styles of At-Risk Students." *Music Educators' Journal* (November, 1991): 84.

Kochevitsky, George. *The Art of Piano Playing*. Evanston, Illinois: Summy-Birchard Co., 1967.

Lister-Sink, Barbara. "Piano Technique, Plain and Simple." *Piano & Keyboard* (March/April 1999): 18.

McCarthy, Bernice. *4MAT Coursebook I: Fundamental Training*. Barrington, Illinois: Excel, Inc., 1999.

Millman, Dan. *Body Mind Mastery*. Novato, California: New World Library, 1999.

Nicklaus, Jack. *The Best Way to Better Golf*. Greenwich: CT Fawcett Publications, 1967.

Tanner, Donald and Ann B. Stutes. "Teaching With a Practical Focus: Developing Learning Styles Awareness." *American Music Teacher* (August/September, 1997) 20.

Wilson, Frank R. *The Hand*. New York: Vintage Books, 1998.

—. *Tone Deaf & All Thumbs? – An Invitation to Music Making*. New York: Vintage Books, 1986.

—. "The Full Development of the Individual Through Music." *Update* 5. This article is adapted from an address presented by Dr. Wilson in the Ergonomic Council of the Music Industry VI in Washington D.C., November 12, 1982.

Contributors

GAIL BERENSON

Gail Berenson is Professor of Piano and Chair of the Keyboard Division at Ohio University, Athens, where she was awarded the "Distinguished Teacher of the Year" award for 2000. Prior to her arrival at Ohio University in 1975, she taught at the University of Illinois, Urbana. She maintains an active performing career, presenting solo, two-piano and a wide range of chamber music recitals. As a result of her distinguished work as a piano pedagogue, along with her reputation as an expert on musician wellness issues, she is much in demand as a performer, clinician, master class artist, adjudicator, author, reviewer and pedagogy consultant. She has performed and lectured in over twenty-five states, as well as Great Britain, Belgium, Switzerland, Israel and Canada.

Ms. Berenson has been a contributing editor to *Piano & Keyboard* and has authored a chapter entitled "Music Medicine and Today's Piano Teachers," for the third edition of James Lyke's book, *Creative Piano Teaching*. A frequent author for *Keyboard Companion*, she has also written for the on-line journal, *Piano Pedagogy Forum*. She serves on the Advisory Board for Heritage Music Press' new piano method, *Piano Discoveries*.

She has served on the Music Teachers National Association's Convention Steering Committee as Piano Chair and as a member of the MTNA Pedagogy Committee. She currently serves as Chair of the Convention Program Committee for the 2002 and 2003 conventions. She has held several national posts with the National Conference on Piano Pedagogy and the World Piano Pedagogy Conference, and is now chair of one of the National Conference on Keyboard Pedagogy's committees – Wellness for Pianists. A past president of the Ohio Music Teachers Association, she holds MTNA's Master Certificate in piano and piano pedagogy and was the 1999 recipient of OMTA's "Certified Teacher of the Year" award.

A Wisconsin native, Ms. Berenson's degrees are in piano performance from Northwestern University, where she studied piano with Louis Crowder and Guy Duckworth. Her students are performing and teaching throughout the United States in private studios and on college faculties.

JACQUELINE CSURGAI-SCHMITT

Jacqueline Csurgai-Schmitt a native of Dearborn, Michigan, began playing the piano at age three. Studying with Gerre Wood Bowers, she won many competitions resulting in radio and television performances and a scholarship to Interlochen National Music Camp. A graduate of the Honors College at Michigan State University, she studied piano performance with Joseph Evans & Henry Harris. She received a Masters of Music degree from Indiana University studying under Menahem Pressler, with further study included work with Jeaneane Dowis in New York City. While at Aspen Music Festival, she served as pianist with the Aspen Festival Orchestra, the Aspen Chamber Orchestra, and the Contemporary Music Festival Orchestra working under Richard Dufallo and coaching with George Crumb and Elliott Carter. Ms. Csurgai-Schmitt was on the piano faculty of George Mason University while continuing a performance career in Washington, D.C. She was a founding member of the *Cosmos Camerata*, which performed at the Cosmos Club for four years; other appearances included the Phillips Gallery and the Corcoran Gallery of Art.

During preparation for several European concert tours, Ms. Csurgai-Schmitt developed a repetitive stress injury in her right hand. After undergoing intensive physical therapy and retraining for twelve years, she began coaching with Mischa Kottler, Detroit's premiere pianist and pedagogue who assisted in the rehabilitative process. Ms. Csurgai-Schmitt now lectures on pain and dysfunction and presents seminars at universities and national, state and local music teachers' organizations. She is also the co-chair of The Pianists' Committee on Technique, Movement & Wellness.

Ms. Csurgai-Schmitt is an active performer in the metropolitan Detroit area. She holds the position of keyboardist with the Dearborn Symphony and has performed the Brahm's Piano Concerto No. 2 with Dr. Leslie Dunner conducting this orchestra. She held the position of President of The Tuesday Musicale of Detroit from 1998-2001 and was honored by the Dearborn Council of the Arts and Mayor's Office with the Artist/Performers Award. Recent performances include the Rachmaninoff *Rhapsody on a Theme of Paganini* with the Dearborn Summer Festival Orchestra, dedication of the Steinway Concert Grand Piano at the new Ford Community and Performing Arts Center in Dearborn, the 'Brunch with Bach' series at the Detroit Institute of Arts, 'Chamber Music at the Scarab Club', a 'Viva Verdi!' concert with members of the Verdi Opera Theatre and Liszt's Concerto No. 2 in A Major with the Dearborn Symphony.

WILLIAM DEVAN

William Devan received his B.M. and M.M. degrees from The Juilliard School, where he studied with Ania Dorfmann. He continued his studies with Hans Leygraf at the *Staatliche Hochschule für Musik und Theater* in Hannover, Germany, and he received the *Konzertexamen* Diploma in 1979. He was also a student of Jeaneane Dowis in New York and Aspen, Colorado.

Mr. DeVan won first prize in the international piano competition "Vianna da Motta" in Lisbon, Portugal in 1975. He subsequently gave two tours of Portugal, the second one under the sponsorship of the American Embassy in Lisbon. He has appeared in numerous concerts in Germany and the United States.

In 1985, Mr. DeVan was invited to play a recital and give a series of master classes in Taiwan. In 1991, he played two concerts in the Golden Music Festival held in Lisbon, Portugal. He was soloist with the Zagreb Philharmonic in a performance of the Prokofiev Piano Concerto No. 2 in G minor, and in a second recital he performed the twenty-four etudes of Chopin. He was re-engaged to play with the Zagreb Philharmonic in Zagreb, Croatia in January of 1993. In May of 1993 he performed two recitals in Australia. Thereafter he was re-engaged for recitals and a master class in 1995; he returned to Australia for a third time in May 1998. He has also performed in Paris, France in 1999. In January and February 2000, Mr. DeVan (a Steinway Artist) began a series of concerts titled "Classics for Children" in Birmingham, Alabama. The concert series was continued in January 2001, and again in 2002, at the Forbes Music Company in Birmingham.

Since 1980, Mr. DeVan has been head of the piano faculty at Birmingham-Southern College. For four summers he was the assistant to Jeaneane Dowis at the Aspen Music Festival in Aspen, Colorado. During the 1992 and 1993 concert seasons Mr. DeVan performed the thirty-two piano sonatas of Beethoven in a series of eight recitals held at Birmingham-Southern College. During the 1995-1996 season he performed the twenty-four preludes and fugues of J.S. Bach's *Well-Tempered Clavier*, Book One, in a series of eight lecture-recitals in Birmingham. In October 1999 he appeared as soloist with the Alabama Symphony, performing the Beethoven Choral Fantasy. A winner of two Mellon Foundation grants, he is co-author of *Schumann: Solo Piano Literature*, a comprehensive guide to the piano works of Robert Schumann. He is a member of the National Committee on Technique, Wellness and Movement, a committee whose presentations have been a part of the 1996, 1997 and 1999 World Piano Pedagogy Conferences. In August 2000, he was named Artist-in-Residence at Birmingham-Southern College.

DR. MITCHELL ELKISS, D.O.

Dr. Mitchell Elkiss, D.O. is a 1978 graduate of the Michigan State University – College of Osteopathic Medicine (MSU-COM). Board certified and currently in the private practice of neurology, osteopathic manipulative medicine, and medical acupuncture, Dr. Elkiss holds numerous positions throughout the medical community.

He has completed a Fellowship in Biomechanics at MSU-COM, and is a clinical assistant professor there in the Department of Internal Medicine. He is their chairman of the Post-graduate Program in Myofascial Release Technique. A Fellow of the American College of Neuropsychiatry, he is the president of Associates in Neurology, P.C. and is the director of its Center for Integrative Medicine. Dr. Elkiss is also chairman of the medical acupuncture board exam review program.

Blessed with a lovely wife, Sally Rosenberg, D.O., and two children, Liz and Isaac, Dr. Elkiss enjoys the pursuit of wellness, yoga, tai chi, cross country skiing, gardening and music, especially playing the bass.

SEYMOUR FINK

Seymour Fink, Professor Emeritus from Binghamton University, lives in Columbus, Ohio where he continues to teach piano as an Adjunct Professor at Capital University and part-time lecturer in the School of Music of The Ohio State University. He holds the Artist Diploma from Peabody Conservatory, and B.A. and M.M. degrees from Yale University. He has studied additionally with Ralph Kirkpatrick, Eduard Steuermann, Nadia Boulanger, Arthur Craxton, Paul Baumgartner, and Menahem Pressler. His long teaching career includes as well positions at Greensboro College, SUMY-Buffalo, Vassar College, and the Yale School of Music. He has performed numerous solo and chamber concerns in the United States and in Europe, with appearances in Germany, England, France, and Switzerland. He has toured extensively as part of the Brady-Fink violin-piano Duo, and recorded on the CRI label.

Mr. Fink has written numerous articles that have appeared in such journals as *Piano Quarterly, Piano & Keyboard, American Music Teacher*, and *Piano Life*. He is the author of the highly acclaimed book and video *Mastering Piano Technique*, published by Amadeus Press. He is co-chair of The Pianists' Committee on Technique, Movement, and Wellness. A recognized expert on piano technique and its pedagogy, he is a regular presenter at national meetings, offering lectures, master classes and workshops on topics relating to piano movement, pedagogy, and musicality. He brings to his presentations a wealth of European and American educational experience, worldwide observation of the pianistic scene, and over 45 years of college and university teaching experience.

PHYLLIS ALPERT LEHRER

Phyllis Alpert Lehrer holds a B.A. degree from the University of Rochester and an M.S. degree from the Juilliard School of Music. She is Professor of Piano at Westminster Choir College of Rider University where she directs the graduate program in piano pedagogy.

Ms. Lehrer has enjoyed an active concert career as a soloist and collaborative artist throughout the United States, Canada, the United Kingdom, Japan, Sweden, and Russia. She has also given lectures, master classes, and adjudicated internationally. At her New York and London debut recitals in Merkin and Wigmore Halls, she premiered works of American composers Dianne Goolkasian Rahbee, Jerome Jolles and Harold Zabrack.

With Barry Green, Ms. Lehrer wrote *The Inner Game of Music Solo Workbook for Piano* published by GIA. She has also written the practice suggestions for four books of *Etudes for the Development of Musical Fingers,* edited by Frances Clark, Louise Goss and Sam Holland and published by Warner Bros. She has recently edited *Chopin: An Album* and co-edited, with Paul Sheftel, several piano anthologies including *More Beginning Piano Solos, Classic Piano Solos,* and six volumes of *Mastering Classic Favorites,* which include performances and master class lessons on CD and MIDI files.

Her articles on performance anxiety and pedagogical topics have been published in *Clavier, Keyboard Companion, American Music Teacher, Early Childhood Connections,* and *The European Piano Teachers Journal.* A founding member of the International Society from the Study of Tension in Performance (ISSTIP), Ms. Lehrer has chaired committees and made presentations for the Nation Conference on Piano Pedagogy, World Piano Pedagogy Conferences, the European Piano Teachers Conference, and the Music Teachers National Association Conferences. She is the national and New Jersey Chair of the College Faculty Forum for the Music Teacher National Association.

Ms. Lehrer has recorded duo piano works with Ena Bronstein Barton and solo and duo works of Dianne Goolkasian Rahbee for Seda Productions.

BARBARA LISTER-SINK

Barbara Lister-Sink, 2002 recipient of the Music Teachers National Association Frances Clark Keyboard Pedagogy Award, is internationally recognized as a pioneer and leader in the field of injury-preventative keyboard technique. She produced the critically acclaimed video, *Freeing the Caged Bird – Developing Well-Coordinated, Injury-Preventative Piano Technique*, and has appeared extensively as performer, clinician, and adjudicator at state and national music conventions. She has given numerous workshops throughout the United States and is widely known for her revolutionary holistic training in injury-preventative technique. A member of the Editorial Committee of *The American Music Teacher*, her articles on piano technique have appeared in national and international music journals. She was a performer and presenter for the 1992 World Congress of Arts and Medicine in New York City, and has also presented workshops for the Canadian Professional Piano Teachers Association, the International Klavar Foundation and the European Piano Teachers Association.

A graduate of Smith College, she holds the *Prix d'Excellence* from the Utrecht Conservatory. Her teachers include John Duke, Edith Lateiner-Grosz and Guido Agosti. She has performed widely as a soloist and chamber musician throughout North America and Europe, and has recorded for National Public Radio, the Canadian Broadcasting Company, and Radio Netherlands, as well as for the Well-Tempered, Emergo, and Music & Arts labels. Formerly keyboardist with the Royal Concertgebouw Orchestra of Amsterdam, she was finalist in the 1975 Allesandro Casegrande International Piano Competition in Italy, and has performed at the New Hampshire, Skaneateles, Brevard, and Chautauqua summer music festivals. She has taught on the piano faculties of Duke University, the Amsterdam Muziek Lyceum, the Brevard Music Center, and she was a member of the artist faculty of the Eastman School of Music. Ms. Lister-Sink is currently Artist-in-Residence at Salem College in her native North Carolina.

ROBERT MAYEROVITCH

Robert Mayerovitch is a native of Montreal, Canada. He is a graduate of McGill University, where he was a student of Dorothy Morton, and Indiana University, where he studied with and assisted Menahem Pressler of the Beaux Arts Trio. He is Professor of Piano and a member of the Elysian Trio in residence at Baldwin-Wallace College, where he currently serves both as Chair of the Department of Keyboard Instruments and Chair of the Faculty. He performs extensively as a recitalist, chamber musician, collaborative artist, and soloist with orchestra.

Dr. Mayerovitch has received numerous performing awards, including first prizes in the Bartók-Kabalevsky International Piano Competition, the national competition of the Canadian Broadcasting Corporation, the Montreal Symphony Competition, the Indiana University Doctoral Concerto Competition, and the Quebec Music Festivals.

In addition to his professorship at Baldwin-Wallace, he has substituted for Menahem Pressler at Indiana University and with his trio has been a visiting professor at Middlebury College, Vermont. He is an active lecturer on pedagogical topics, including a continually expanding set of musical, pianistic, and psychological aphorisms entitled *Rules of Pianists' (and Other Animals') Thumbs.* He regularly makes presentations and moderates at state and national musical organizations, including the Music Teachers National Association, the World Piano Pedagogy Conferences, and the National Conference on Keyboard Pedagogy.

Dr. Mayerovitch has been a member of the editorial board of the *American Music Teacher*, a contributor to *Piano & Keyboard Magazine,* and a founding member of The Pianists' Committee on Technique, Movement, and Wellness. He is also an avid runner and marathoner, and writes sonnets with both musical and extra-musical themes.

DR. NORMAN B. ROSEN, M.D

Dr. Norman B. Rosen, M.D., is a graduate of Johns Hopkins University (1959) and the University of Maryland School of Medicine (1963), and was the first physiatrist (Specialist in Physical Medicine and Rehabilitation) in private practice in the Baltimore area. He is the founder and Medical Director of one of the first multi-disciplinary pain clinics in the Baltimore area - The Rosen-Hoffberg Rehabilitation and Pain Management Associates. This clinic has been certified by the Commission on Accreditation of Rehablitiation Facilities (CARF) for both Comprehensive Acute and Comprehensive Chronic Pain Management, the highest accreditations that a Rehabilitation Clinic can achieve. His staff of professionals includes physical therapists, mental health counselors, physicians, and physician extenders, and features a wellness philosophy.

An expert in pain management, arts medicine, sports medicine, fibromyalgia and myofascial pain, Dr Rosen is a pianist and competitive athlete who has dealt with a variety of pain conditions for the past 30 years on both a professional and personal level.

He has lectured and written extensively on such diverse topics as pain, musculoskeletal disability, piano wellness, fibromyalgia, myofascial pain and dysfunction, stress and wellness, multi-disciplinary management, sports medicine, pelvic pain, physical disabilities in visual artists, dance medicine, geriatric medicine, headaches, strokes, and low back pain. He also has lectured on the history of art and the role of physical and emotional disabilities on the creative process. He was Chairman of the Special Interest Group on Myofascial Pain for The American Academy of Physical Medicine and Rehabilitation and was a committee member on the Governors Commission (State of Maryland) Dealing with Low Back Pain and Neck Pain Costs.

Dr. Rosen was a featured speaker at the National Piano Pedagogy conference in 1999 and was a committee member of The Pianists' Committee on Technique, Movement, and Wellness of this organization.

DYLAN SAVAGE

Dylan Savage holds a D.M. and M.M. from the Indiana University School of Music and a B.M. from the Oberlin Conservatory of Music. He made his European solo debut in Rome, Italy, as the piano winner of the Rome Festival Orchestra Competition. His teachers include Sedmara Rutstein and Michel Block.

In his doctoral document, "The Application of Sports Training Techniques to Piano Practice and Performance," Dr. Savage pioneered the application of slow-motion video analysis, interval training, and cross training to improve piano playing. This groundbreaking research, featured on televised programs on NBC and PBS affiliates, has led to numerous master classes at leading music schools in the United States. His articles on this subject have appeared in national and international publications such as *Clavier* and *Pianoforte.*

Dr. Savage was a featured speaker and faculty member at the Performing Arts Medicine Association's Medical Problems of Musicians and Dancers conferences at Aspen, and a featured presenter at the National Piano Pedagogy Conference. In several World Piano Pedagogy Conferences, he presented and served as a long-term member of The Pianists' Committee on Technique, Movement, and Wellness. A former Artist-in-Residence at Bluefield College, he is currently Assistant Professor of Piano at Henderson State University.